WITHDRAWN

FATHERS AND CHILDREN

ALSO BY C. L. SULZBERGER

FATHERS AND CHILDREN

C. L. Sulzberger

ARBOR HOUSE New York

Manufactured in the United States of America

10 9 8 7 6 5 4 3 2 1

Library of Congress Cataloging in Publication Data
Sulzberger, C. L. (Cyrus Leo), 1912–
Father and children.

Bibliography: p.
1. World history.   2. Fathers and sons.   3. Fathers
and daughters.   I. Title.
D21.1.S85   1987   909   87–11406
ISBN: 0-87795-925-0

Extracts from the story of Sir Winston Churchill's interview with
his father's ghost published with permission of the Master, Fellows,
and Scholars of Churchill College, University of Cambridge.

IN MEMORY OF

David K. E. Bruce and Charles E. Bohlen,
two of this century's finest Americans
and most remarkable diplomats:
men of quality and noble character.

Acknowledgments

The author would like to thank the following individuals and institutions who, in one way or another, helped in the preparation of this book: American Library of Paris, Professor Manolis Andronikos, Debbie Balchin, Ambassador Etienne Burin des Roziers, Gail Dannahy, Dr. Stevan Dedijer, General Jean Delmas, Marcel Leroy, Nikolaos Martis, Paul McAdam, Metropolitan Museum of Art, Cheryl Mott, Helena Mulkerns, Eda Pallicr, The Lady Soames, Fiona Terris, Gino Tomajuoli, Marion Underhill, Stevee de Vargas.

Contents

Preface

Voltaire maintained that "History is but a pack of tricks we play upon the dead." Others have contended that the greatest prize obtained by victory in a war is the privilege of writing the history of it. (Imagine, had Hitler won World War II, what versions we would now be reading!)

History is neither tricks, prejudice, nor for that matter unchanging. It records mankind's deeds. But it also records other things such as natural disasters that occurred long before *homo sapiens* walked upright on the Earth. Man is not essential to history except in writing it, interpreting it from fossil relics, or making it. Perhaps when no form of humanity has survived here or escaped to another planet, some other form of intellectual creature will manage to recount how this particular experiment ended.

The various Ice Ages and prehistoric explosions that produced igneous rock antedated man by millennia. They did not require his presence to confirm their occurrence. One is reminded of Dr. Johnson's remark about the loneliness of a man "obscurely hanged."

To most of contemporary mankind—whose presence on this planet is momentary as measured against the world's existence—it is the human race's own history that matters. This was learned from the past by delving scientists or garnered after men mastered memory (like Homer) and then the art of writing. Eventually humanity's past became an almost obsessive topic.

In this analysis I have sought to study one aspect: Fathers with strong personalities, good or evil, and their outstanding children, each or both of whom had significance while they lived and left an impression behind them when they died. Of the fourteen family groupings observed, only two include daughters as "children." Else, I would have stolen more directly from Turgenev, whose famous novel was of course entitled *Fathers and Sons*.

But where, under such a listing, would there have been room for Queen Elizabeth I, Prime Minister Indira Gandhi, or, for that matter, Lucrezia Borgia, whose role was less dominating but more successfully insinuating as she seductively obeyed the orders of her father who happened to be Pope.

Why not Plato, Aristotle, Saint Francis, Mohammed (his daughter and son-in-law); the families of Shakespeare, Francis Bacon, Albert Einstein; those magnificent musicians the Bachs and Strausses? This is a book and not an encyclopedia. I chose my generational pairs to suit my interests and tastes.

One might also—and with even more regret—argue that it is otherwise biased. It should rather have dealt with mothers, not fathers, shall we say Olympias and her son Alexander the Great; or Abigail and John Quincy Adams. But in most of the long period covered by history's odd couples, the theory that men and women are "equal," with the same rights and powers, did not apply.

The influence of Olympias and Abigail was powerful on their sons if relatively indirect. For centuries, women were wise enough to acknowledge their subtle advantages and deal as queens, mistresses, or simple mothers and wives through men they could twist around without resort to dominance, like Russia's Catherine the Great. This avoided acquiring the reputation of being "bossy" or "mannish."

Of course, in any objective and complete approach to history the female role must be balanced against that of the male. The influence of acquired characteristics should be weighed against those inherited. (And the latter should be measured in terms of paternal versus maternal influence, if such can be assessed.) I fear my approach has been deliberately artificial: Mendelian in a paternal sense; Lamarckian only to a limited and perhaps more maternal degree.

It is astounding, when rummaging through history, to discover such blazing fathers and children as Philip of Macedon and Alexander the Great; Henry VIII and Queen Elizabeth I; the dreadful Borgias, Pope Alexander VI and Cesare; the two remarkable American presidents named Adams; Nehru and his daughter; the promising (but blighted) Lord Randolph Churchill and his glorious son Winston.

Of the fourteen families selected for discussion, undoubtedly the most normal (although magnificently talented) were the Bellinis and the Adamses. I think one might say they were also exceptionally "nice," a little-used word today.

The most cultivated were Henry VIII and Queen Elizabeth. Easily the most horrible were the sixteenth-century Borgias; or, if one drags in the ratty little Georgian shoemaker Vissarion Djugashvili because of his pockmarked, pock-souled son, Iosif, the "Stalins." The most pretentious were the Dumas, the bravest the two MacArthurs, the most intelligent Philip and Alexander. I have sought to interject contemporary approaches into these conjectures on human cause and mundane effect. Did Alexander the Great have what Sigmund Freud dubbed an Oedipus complex? If so, with what result? Evidence overwhelmingly indicates the world conqueror was Oedipal.

And Douglas MacArthur? A far less clear-cut case, despite recent testimony available. As for Iosif Stalin, there is no evidence to garner. There was little, if any, left in his modest parental cottage. He seems to have conjured up a genuine affection for his mother, and she for him. And when he was six, a very Oedipean age as far as Freud would have it, she protected the child whose ghastly, drunken papa was chasing him around with a knife.

Another extraordinary and unanticipated intrusion on history's normal course (if such a thing can be imagined) was that of syphilis. The disease was brought to Europe in 1494 by the sailors of Christopher Columbus, destroying its lustful victims ever since with dire results.

Cesare Borgia seems to have caught it. Possibly because of his magnificently strong constitution, he escaped its destruction; perhaps he even recovered from the malady, although such a cure seems unlikely before the discoveries of twentieth-century Paul Ehrlich.

Henry VIII almost certainly suffered from and probably died of syphilis and its consequences, fatally infecting his son the unfortunate King Edward VI. Had this medical "accident" not occurred, it is conceivable that Elizabeth, Henry's daughter by Anne Boleyn, would never have become the great Virgin Queen. There might then have been no ultimate British Empire. Dynamic British influence during the Renaissance might well have been minimal.

And how serious a consideration should be given to the possibility that nevertheless, as things turned out, Elizabeth was in fact tainted by congenital syphilis? Would this explain her unusual medical and sexual history?

Finally, we know of one modern, confirmed, especially tragic syphilitic case in Britain's highest circles. During the late nineteenth century, Lord Randolph Churchill, a gifted Tory politician, already a cabinet minister, had been infected. The malady galloped through his unresisting constitution. Within a few years he had died of its fatal mental consequence, paresis.

Considering how badly he got on with his son, Winston, before his own premature death, what kind of human and historical consequence might have been foreseeable had a healthy Lord Randolph Churchill dominated British Conservative politics and governments for the generation before his son moved in—as political observers were predicting?

The warp and woof of history are woven with accidents. Had World War II not broken out, Charles de Gaulle would probably have died as a little known military theorist who wrote remarkably well. Winston Churchill could have been regarded as a talented, bumptious fellow who produced excellent histories and biographies and who painted well enough to gain access to the Royal Academy.

It was history's accident, by fostering a well-timed war, that made of these two subdued talents great leaders who helped change fate. Yet, had they not already existed with all their latent qualities, to whom could history have turned?

Go further: the question on which no one can ever reasonably speculate—what would have happened if the seed of Lord Randolph Churchill and Henri de Gaulle had not entered the wombs of Jeanette Jerome and Jeanne Maillot?

History's fiber is thus designed by accident. Stalin's idea of "human engineering"—biological control, through state supervision, of breeding mankind from Marxist blood and Soviet experience—isn't yet remotely workable. History is simply made of coincidental spasms.

In 1588, had there not been a turbulent storm that wrecked King Philip's armada, today's British might be Spanish-speaking. In America, John F. Kennedy, who entered the White House buoyed by more popular hopes than any man since Roosevelt, was cut down before he had registered more than optimistic ideas. What might have happened had Lincoln been murdered four years earlier? Or if Marx had been spawned in a remote igloo by an illiterate Eskimo hunter?

How important to life in this world has been the political influence of religion which, on the whole, was an inherited characteristic? How different might today's world be had not Henry VIII, in a frantic search for male heirs, severed British allegiance to the Pope? And had Elizabeth subsequently come to the throne as a loyal adherent of Rome, how would Europe's power balance have changed? Even the Holy Father saw this clearly. "What a woman!" said Sixtus V. "What a princess. . . . If she were only a Catholic!"

And what conceivable historical difference might there have been had Winston Churchill's mother loved him as a little boy and not abandoned his affections to a strong, warm British nanny? After all, Jenny Churchill was not even twenty years older than her elder son (less difference in age than Alexander and his beautiful, wild mother, Olympias). Jenny, too, was beautiful and, in her more restrained way, wild enough. Had she accepted from her little boy the love he so wished to give her, might we have seen a different "Winston," not only gifted in defensive war but hell-bent on aggressive conquest, a trait Freud saw in true Oedipeans?

As it was, Churchill proved a better example of what Freud's pupil, Carl Gustav Jung, called the "extroverted intuitive." Of this type, Jung wrote: "He has a keen nose for things in the bud pregnant with future promise"; and also a "capacity to inspire his fellow men with courage." Surely the adult Churchill (like the adult de Gaulle) displayed such characteristics.

Was Douglas MacArthur, with his ubiquitous mother, more representative of the pure Oedipean type uncovered by Freud? I have sought in the portraits drawn in these chapters to recount not only the principal achievements of those dissected, but also to discuss the relationship of each particular father with a particular offspring. Where possible, I try to demonstrate how well or how badly each child followed in parental footsteps.

This is often tendentious as an exercise; especially so when the child leaves its own specific analyses of the father and these analyses differ markedly from each other, depending on when written. Thus, Svetlana Stalin indicates in her first book of recollections a distinct fondness for her terrifying parent. In her second book, however, she depicts his harshness and cruelty. She coldly unveils her dislike for her half-brother Vasily Stalin, the drunken air force general, and also her sympathy for Iakov, another half-brother, abandoned to die in a Nazi prisoner-of-war camp. Was this because her father hated him (which was the case) or because he wished to use him as an example to prove Stalin would not favor his own family over other Russians?

The most extraordinarily similar pair I think I have described is the Adams couple: father-and-son presidents, unique in America. It is proof enough that the son learned brilliantly at his father's knee. The lesson was democracy; popularity was not the prize to be courted, but service to the national cause. Neither was generally beloved; neither was reelected; both served their fellow citizens incomparably well.

One sees John Quincy had wholly digested these teachings when one remembers his career. Following splendid diplomatic positions abroad; having been a U.S. senator, the greatest secretary of state his country ever had, and then president, John Quincy was content to end his days humbly as his home district's congressman in the House of Representatives, on the floor of which he died.

It was John Quincy Adams who summoned the Czar's minister to the State Department and told him the United States "would contest the right of Russia to any territorial establishment on the American continent."

And yet, it was after that extraordinary moment, when Russians and British in the Pacific, and British, French, and Spaniards in the Atlantic were looking above the fury of their own battles at the naked continents of America, that John Quincy outlined the basis for future U.S. policy, named for his boss, President James Monroe. It has fortunately long been forgotten, above all in Washington, that a corollary principle of the "Monroe Doctrine" was nonintervention by the United States in Europe.

The Adamses, despite gigantic services to the nation, were astonishingly normal in behavior if compared with more flamboyant American chiefs of state like Jackson and the two Roosevelts.

A similar normality was that of the Bellinis whose painting dominated that of northern Italy at the height of the Renaissance when the air reeked of melodrama. Not only were all three Bellinis men of genius, but they schooled men of even greater genius: Titian and Giorgione.

From Alexander the Great to Douglas MacArthur and Iosif Stalin one can find dynamic energy among the characters herein described as having grandiloquent influence, talent for war, for politics, or in the realm of culture. Both among those who were good and whose influence was benevolent and among those who were wicked and whose influence was malevolent, they all proved, in their way, that much of history's tapestry is patterned by individuals.

This human design is less predictable than the geological or biological. It is easier to forecast the route of a descending torrent of molten lava or the area through which famine or smallpox are likely to spread than to predict decisions of conquerors or statesmen. Humans are not in themselves as large as events. However, they tend to stimulate the latter more often than the reverse. And men move more rapidly and dramatically than glaciers, even if on a smaller scale.

I hope I have given adequate thought in these selections to accidental impacts that play such a vital role in history. What would Alexander the Great have been without his father's prior establishment of an overpowering military force, without Aristotle as a teacher, and without his father's limitless ambition? How would Churchill or de Gaulle have been remembered, save as mediocre talents in the creative arts, had there been no World War II at the proper moment in their lives?

Had Henry VIII not condemned his feeble son, Edward VI, to death by syphilis, would Elizabeth Tudor have been but a barren, aristocratic old maid with a brilliant mind and bad health in Renaissance England? And how accurate is our perception of these historic characters today?

I suspect Alexander was the first well-known victim of Freud's discov-

ery, the Oedipus complex; but be this true or not (in either case unprovab
would that have changed our views of the great conqueror?

Another and far lesser military man, General Thomas-Alexand
Dumas, was almost certainly endowed by his novelist son with a personali
and physique he did not really possess. But Dumas *Père* ascribed to his fathe
all kinds of phenomenal abilities and ill-merited bad luck. The romanti
author wished to create a parent suitable to his own filial tastes.

Certainly, the general, Dumas *Grandpère*, was not a notable strategist.
However, he did father a remarkable son and grandson, which, in history's
roster, is by no means a common feat. Few genuinely great figures have
produced truly outstanding children; take de Gaulle, Churchill, Abraham
Lincoln, or Iosif Stalin.

Great individuals should not only be judged by their actions while alive
but by the monuments or scars they leave behind. Alexander's empire
bequeathed traces of Hellenic culture to peoples as far south as Egypt and as
far East as India's Punjab. Douglas MacArthur completely altered the
content of Japan's society and political methods while shrewdly leaving the
shell apparently undisturbed.

Sordid as were his reasoning and ways of applying his ideas, Henry
VIII sponsored a new religion and a more independent England. Elizabeth I
sowed the seeds of a vast empire which, in turn, passed on useful Western
ideas of life and government to millions of people. Elizabeth also devised a
whole new system of intelligence procedures and started the wicked history
of modern race prejudice.

What the Borgias produced as a legacy is ignoble, although Macchiavelli
thought Cesare's realpolitik, cynical as it was, could guide a worthy patriotic
Italian "Prince." The Bellinis helped shape a Titian and a Giorgione, in
addition to their own lovely pictorial testament.

John and John Quincy Adams worked nobly to purify and strengthen
the world's most powerful democracy. The latter foresaw, as shrewdly as
Toqueville, the coming competition between America and Russia. As for
Stalin, horrible as he was, he came to power in an inherently weak, chaotic
land and ruthlessly made it a frightening superpower.

Others inspired visions that have not been forgotten. Kennedy left
nothing as tangible as Franklin Roosevelt's New Deal which made democracy
safe for the world. But his dream of reinvigorating the American people
perseveres. De Gaulle established a Fifth Republic in ravaged France which
may endure as a concept as long as Bonaparte's *Code Napoléon*. And Churchill
led the British people to the peak of their historical glory even if forced to
witness the dissolution of an imperial system he hoped to renew.

These testaments are more important in judging the position of individual figures in history than the contemporary heights they climbed. And it is interesting that while Alexander made war and his own glory, thereby achieving greatness, it was war that made de Gaulle and Churchill, hoisting them from the well of obscurity.

What men leave to history is also contained in the legends they create by their manner of life. Philip and Alexander were surely the greatest father-and-son team ever known. Both Philip and Henry VIII were wise enough to choose outstanding teachers for their children, Aristotle and Roger Ascham. Alexander had himself proclaimed a god. Henry made himself head of a new church. Stalin turned an ideological doctrine into a terrifying personalized weapon of conquest.

Many of the individuals described in the ensuing chapters were dreamers who managed to live their dreams: from Philip and Alexander to de Gaulle and Churchill. In contemplating them, one is reminded of Arthur O'Shaughnessy's poem: "We are the music-makers, And we are the dreamers of dreams." But for dreamers who became great leaders, it was necessary to master the arts of action—the Bergsonian concept.

In pondering this, one is struck by a theme common to both Stalin and de Gaulle: fear. De Gaulle wrote that a leader must deliberately distance himself from others and quoted Lucretius: "First it is fear that created gods in the world." The General added: "The Chief must inspire prestige, of which one part is fear." Clearly Stalin practiced the same theorem: Churchill did *not!* Nor, for that matter, did MacArthur.

In assessing achievements, one must balance the positive with the negative. Napoleon left his *Code*—but also a wreckage. Churchill bequeathed the glory of victory; but also the reality of defeat for an England no longer capable of sustaining triumph.

De Gaulle's testament was a shapeless Fifth Republic—and a brief and evanescent dream of grandeur. The General once mused to me: "How do you define success or failure? Only history itself can define these terms. In reality, life and action are always made up of a series of successes and checks."

It is impossible to make generalized statements about the relationships of talented children to great fathers. I do not know of any impressive morphological approach in the field of historical genetics.

Certainly it is a rare phenomenon in creative art that an outstanding father should produce an outstanding son. Only in the field of music (the Bachs, the Strausses) does it seem less uncommon than in other artistic

realms. The Bellinis and the Dumas (reaching rather low on the shelf) are clear exceptions.

If you add the talent of the three Bellinis together you don't get Michelangelo. Dumas *Père* plus Dumas *Fils* don't amount to Shakespeare. Art is not arithmetic.

It is hard to reckon how much role genetics may play in the inheritance of military genius. Or is this simply acquired as a habit in children when a professional officer commends certain virtues and denounces vices such as cowardice in rearing his descendants.

For centuries there have been martial families in which a son was always expected to follow his father's footsteps and become a soldier. Whether the MacArthur genius showed by Douglas was inherited from his father or from his doughty Scottish ancestors, we cannot know; it might simply have been the atmosphere around the Wild West forts where his father served and stories of war were the controversial theme and where young Douglas played.

One cannot assess the relative capabilities of these rare family teams of soldiers. Certainly it might seem unjust to mention the MacArthurs and not the Lees; notwithstanding, both of the former earned the Medal of Honor. And surely Philip and Alexander of Macedon had far greater impact on history than Carthage's strategic geniuses Hannibal and Hasdrubal.

Normally it seems to be the case that dominating fathers cannot help but submerge their children. Winston Churchill's son Randolph used to say: "You don't know how difficult it is to grow up in the shadow of a great oak." And look at the unsuccessful offspring of Stalin, Franklin Roosevelt, and Abe Lincoln.

Genetics is a tricky and unpredictable science. Stalin wanted to develop "human engineering" in the belief, inspired by his experts Michurin and Lysenko (who themselves disagreed), that a new breed of super-Communists could be raised from a genealogical line that had acquired Marxist characteristics. Lovely, vapid Ellen Terry once suggested to Bernard Shaw that they marry and produce astounding children with his brain and her body. He scoffed: "What if they have your brain and my body?"

What a parent tells his child has profound effect. It could not have helped unfortunate Edward VIII, eventually King of England, to be told by his father (George V) that his newborn brother, Henry of Gloucester, had flown in through the window. When he asked where the wings were, Edward was told they had been cut off.

Nowadays history is mostly made by natural disasters, such as floods, or by outstanding humans. It is hard to identify genetic traits in the latter. Nevertheless, in those cases where there may be an exception, it is interesting to speculate. Such is the purpose of this book.

Karl Marx wrote that: "Men make their own history, but they do not make it just as they please; they do not make it under circumstances chosen by themselves directly encountered, given and transmitted from the past." Apart—I may add—from extraordinary congenital heritage.

The unexpected can intrude on even the most promising of the latter. Infection by disease whose form and cause cannot be ascertained is one such case. Syphilis, the Renaissance malady, came whining through fifteenth century Europe. It soon numbered among its victims famous leaders.

The three giants of World War II—Roosevelt, Churchill, and Stalin— were all to a considerable degree influenced by their mothers; at least, in each case the maternal personality was the foremost household spirit.

The modest cottage-shack where Stalin was reared in Gori and where his shoemaker father got drunk daily until he died was only one example of a home where a dominating woman prevailed.

Stalin's mother ruled the roost. She sent him to the theological seminary, and years later, after her icy, inscrutable son had already ruled a long time in the Kremlin, when she visited him she confessed a regret that he had not stayed on in Gori to finish his priestly education.

Henri Bergson was a philosopher and not a psychiatrist, although some of his work seems to have paralleled some of Jung's. He wrote: "By what signs are we to recognize the man . . . who leaves his mark on the events which destiny places in his path? Is it not that he encompasses a more or less long succession in an instantaneous vision? The greater the portion of the past he holds in his present, the heavier the mass he propels into the future, to press against eventualities still unformed. . . ."

All of the men and women I have described influenced the course of events. They changed the destinies of many thousands who lived during or just after their respective eras. It is interesting to examine them in terms of their genetic heritage and also in terms of later physical and psychological analysis.

We cannot be sure which of them suffered from what bodily or mental diseases, with some exceptions; nor what were the consequences in world affairs. Alexander the Great (almost certainly), Douglas MacArthur (perhaps), Churchill (possibly), and even Stalin could have been influenced by an Oedipus complex.

Yet who could imagine any of them stretched upon an analyst's couch? Least of all Stalin. Nevertheless the dictator seems to have loved his mother, as much as he may have been capable of loving. He certainly detested his father. Churchill came to love his mother only after he became adult and gained her help—too late for any Freudian games. Even Franklin Roosevelt's mother was a far more formidable figure and more influential in his life than his father.

The weirdest and most appalling instance of Freudian behavior may have been the incestuous affairs reportedly carried on between Pope Alexander VI and his daughter, and among Cesare Borgia, his son, and Cesare's sister, the lovely but poisonous Lucrezia.

History is not a science in the sense that geology, astronomy, physics, and biology are sciences. Neither is theology nor philosophy; yet their importance cannot be denied. The sciences are to their intellectual children somewhat as fire and the wheel are to later, not quite so elemental inventions: electricity and nucleonics.

But history is the teacher of prophets. They learn from it how the future may be shaped. As Max Weber, echoing Nietzsche, wrote years ago:

> No one knows who will live in this building. No one knows whether at the end of this formidable transformation, entirely new prophets will arise, whether old ideas and ideals of yesterday will assume a new vigor, or whether, on the contrary, a mechanical rigidity embellished by a kind of fossilized self-importance will gain the day.
>
> In the latter event it would be true of the "final men" of this evolution of culture that they would be mindless specialists, heartless men of pleasure. These nullities would boast of having climbed to a never previously reached peak of humanity.

The influences that combine to produce and affect the dominating human type—perhaps correctly called a "hero" (good or evil)—are a source of endless and fascinating discussion. I have sought merely to ascertain a few predominant characteristics that in some outstanding cases have clearly been handed on by the paternal bloodstream.

For, as Churchill wrote: "We are all variants. . . ."

FATHERS AND CHILDREN

Part One

MEN OF WAR

I

The Macedonians:
Philip and Alexander

My first direct acquaintance with the dynamic civilization of ancient Macedonia during the fourth century B.C., dominated by King Philip II and his son Alexander the Great, came on August 19, 1978. On that day, accompanied by Nikolaos Martis, minister for northern Greece, and by my beagle dog, Christopher, I successively visited the Salonika Museum's magnificent collection of Macedonian gold objects, the excavations at Vergina (in olden days, Philip's royal capital of Aigai), and finally its successor, Pella, where Alexander was born and where, as a little boy, the great world conqueror played on the marvelous mosaic floors.

As we approached Vergina-Aigai, seat of the Argead dynasty which ended with Alexander, where Philip was buried (Alexander's corpse was lost in the Middle East), a great flight of geese glided in V-shaped echelon overhead, their wings beating a mere shadow of sound, as they swung from Mount Olympus.

We were greeted by Professor Manolis Andronikos, Greece's most renowned contemporary archeologist, who had been painstakingly investigating the immense tumulus mounds beneath which it was for long suspected the Argeads had entombed their chiefs. In late 1977 the professor uncovered one small and one large mausoleum, the latter almost certainly that of Philip II. And on the very day prior to our visit he had managed to open up a third.

All of us were excited. Andronikos was confident from past digging into Aigai's barrow cemetery that new discoveries lay before him: iron and bronze armor; statuary; paintings; jewelry of gold, precious and semiprecious stones; pendants, gilt wreaths, ornate diadems, carved earrings; coins, ivories, helmets, weapons; kraters and other funerary vases decorated with carven Dionysiac figures; greaves, arrow sheaths; jugs bearing the jovial head of

3

Silenus, silver rhytons; and even perhaps another square solid gold larnax with the Macedonian star upon its heavy lid and cremated bones from a royal funeral pyre inside.

Martis and I were the first nonarcheologists to penetrate this haven of silent refuge after more than two millennia. It was one of the few tombs to escape robbers. As for little Christopher: what other beagle in all history has ever had the chance to lean across the threshold of twenty-four centuries inhaling eternity with quivering nostrils and scenting its dank, cool, odor, the odor of time—and death? He sniffed with unrestrained emotion before he was led off by an aide, and the three among us who were human entered.

Whose tomb it was we knew not; but that it belonged to a ranking prince, the professor had no doubt. He pointed above our heads at a stone lintel barely cleared of earth and dust, exposing a painted fresco of extreme beauty in design and in color from vegetable dyes, and he said: "This is one of a very few old frescoes found in Greece. We don't know the name of the artist who produced it, but we can now recognize his style from other works we have found in this northern region. He was clearly a great painter who wandered from city to city and court to court accepting commissions from those in power, and for which he was richly paid, much like Leonardo during the Renaissance."

Thus, passing beneath his lintel embellishments whose outlines were so fragile that they had been extensively photographed within moments of being dusted off, as swift disintegration was more probable than any restoration, came my personal introduction to the court of the last two Argead sovereigns.

We wandered over to Philip's tomb, already well tended and restored in the year since its discovery. This was a fortunate trouvaille. Many graves in the region had been sacked by ghoulish thieves throughout the ages. Quite apart from precious metals, hardly any paintings had been found intact, crumbling when the intruders burst in followed by eddying air.

After inspecting the powerful king's resting-place—bare of its luxurious ornaments, which had been taken to archeological workshops and museums—the professor led us into a room where his experts were putting together into their original form tiny fragments that had been discovered, most notably a large round shield of wood, leather, and cloth, with gold and ivory decorations, used for ceremonials only.

The gold work is at least equal to that of the Scythians and Thracians, Andronikos said. He showed us marvelous small gorgons' heads through a jeweler's glass, commenting that it is evident the Macedonians were a true Greek people; their common soldiers as well as dozens of generals had Greek names. The word "Macedonia" means "a place of *big* people" (the prefix *mac* in "macrocosm" has the same derivation). They were small compared to us, however, as evident from their leg greaves.

Martis, Christopher, and I finally drove off in the dark to Pella. Pella, where Alexander was born, is renowned for its large, beautiful mosaics (fourth century B.C.) of which I saw, by lamplight, a lion hunt, Dionysos on a leopard's back, a griffin attacking a deer, the rape of Helen. In the small museum there is a handsome marble statue of a hound, carved for a tomb, and hounds appear in hunting scenes, much admired by Christopher as well as his predecessors Philip and Alexander.

Finally I left Martis and drove to Edessa, where Philip II was assassinated at a feast in 336 B.C. This city was made into the protocapital in the seventh century B.C. by Perdikkas, first Macedonian king. It is beautiful: low mountains with streams and waterfalls, cliffs covered with luxuriant vegetation, nuts, wines, pomegranates, figs. There is a cave with stalactites and crayfish in the water, and an old bridge that bore the Via Egnatia, constructed by the Romans.

Philip of Macedon and Alexander the Great surely must be the outstanding father-son team of temporal leadership so far produced by mankind. In that realm they compare with such theoretical combinations as Homer fathering Shakespeare, Phidias fathering Michelangelo, or Plato fathering Marx. Philip was the first Hellenic ruler to implement the ideal of a united Greece based on the nation-state; possibly, indeed, the first true nationalist (perhaps excluding the leaders of far more ancient Egypt and China).

And, although he did not live to attempt it, he dreamed of and made initial preparations for an invasion of Persia, then the global superpower. The project was carried out by Alexander, who, before his death at the astonishingly youthful age of thirty-three, had thrust an army deep into India and up past Samarkand in the modern Soviet Union, after first conquering northeast Africa. He briefly assumed control of the entire civilized world as then known (except for China).

Like most statesmen and above all conquerors, they left little tangible to survive their triumphs for long. Greece itself, always infected by the habit of internal rivalry, fell apart once again as it had after Athenian and Spartan domination. It crumbled when Macedonia became a Roman province in 168 B.C. by the treaty signed at Amphipolis.

But Alexander, although his enormous empire dissolved inexorably, bequeathed the impact of Hellenic civilization, all the way from Italy to India. Even many Pathan tribesmen of contemporary Afghanistan and Pakistan are featured by gray or blue eyes beneath their turbans and boast of descent from the Hellenic legions of Skander, or Iskander as he is called in Asia. The most glorious portrait I have seen of history's most famous conqueror is the Hellenistic likeness carved on a large silver coin in the modest little museum at Peshawar, Pakistan, nestling below the Khyber Pass. This shows, in pristine state, Alexander's profile.

Philip was rather dour and ferocious looking. His grim, lined expression was emphasized by one blind eye, lost in battle. He was short—according to modern terms—stocky, and visibly muscular. Alexander, on the contrary, was a skinny little fellow, although taller than his father. He could not have been more than five feet five inches; he was lithe, quick, with striated tendons like a runner (which, indeed, he was), and exceedingly handsome, with curly hair, a firm chin, and high forehead. One imagines that tempestuous, hard-driving Philip had the deeper voice.

Both father and son had cities named for them, cities that still exist; but the difference between these places signifies the relative difference of their historical measure. When Philip's troops captured the Thracian town of Eumolpia, he named it Philippopolis. Today it still exists as Plovdiv, a sizable Bulgarian city on the edge of a vast rose-growing area whose attar once comprised Bulgaria's main cash export.

Alexander, more flamboyant, glamorous, and audacious than his father, built many towns including his own great metropolis at Alexandria, Egypt, naming it for himself. Alexandria was Egypt's capital for a thousand years and remains its largest seaport. Until the 1950s it contained one of the world's most sizable agglomerations of Greeks. They dominated the famous center's commerce, finance, and culture until they were squeezed out by Gamal Abdel Nasser.

Philip was a vigorous, strong ruler with much common sense and wisdom, except when he was inflamed by drink or women—which was often. During his reign the Macedonian state doubled its area and population. He increased its income (although not fast enough to finance his military campaigns). Above all, he laid the foundation for the expansive and aggressive foreign policy launched by his son, the only greater ruler of his people than himself. However, Alexander was so much greater that his name is still familiar to most people on the earth's six inhabited continents.

The two men successively dominated first Macedonia, then Greece, and finally the known world. All this within only thirty-six years. Philip ruled from 359 to 336 B.C. and Alexander ruled from 336 to 323 B.C.

*   *   *

Communication between north and south, the Aegean islands, and the west Asian Greek settlements had greatly increased by the fourth century B.C., and the more culturally advanced south's intellectual and artistic outlook attracted powerful Macedonia.

Although that state's society was simple, based on shepherds and peasants clustered around the landholdings of nobles, its Argead dynasty had provided a continuing source of competent leadership. These kings were traditionally surrounded by a council of elders and by the equivalent of a royal horse bodyguard, called the *hetairoi*, drawn from the sons of leading families.

The Argeads boasted of descent from Heracles and Zeus, and Alexander, never tainted by modesty, had himself proclaimed divine. They were an increasingly egotistical family and, when not campaigning, loved luxury, women (and often boys), and wine. They encouraged and appreciated art. Philip employed, among others, Nikomachos, the most famous painter of the mid-fourth century B.C. Writers and sculptors were attracted to his court. The iron and bronze armor worn by Philip's generals, as well as some of their weapons, were decorated with gold. When a prince was slain, horses were sacrificed on the pyre that consumed his body.

The Macedonians, who had settled in northern Greece half a millennium before Argead rule, spoke a bastardized dialect which eventually was absorbed by the Doric Greek of the south. This became the language of the Macedonian kings beginning with Perdikkas. As they strengthened their ties with the more civilized southern city-states, they also opened new political and intellectual horizons. Their Hellenic bonds were further fortified by the Persian invasion of the peninsula, which drew all Greeks closer together.

As Macedonian culture consequently benefited, local craftsmen imitated the artistic triumphs of the famous southern city-states and also benefited by acquiring new wisdom abroad. Philip's troops marauded from the Caucasus in the east all the way to the Pillars of Hercules in the west. Macedonian artists and artisans learned the secrets of Scythian and Thracian jewelers and gold, silver, bronze, and iron workers, especially after Philip defeated old King Ateas of Scythia and brought masses of booty back to Macedonia.

It was thus Philip who rescued his hitherto backward kingdom from relative obscurity. Alexander's father acquired much soldierly skill during the four years he spent in Thebes as a young political hosatage. The Thebans had established their eminence by defeating Sparta and were even taken seriously by mighty Persia. The youthful Macedonian came to know

Epaminondas, the Theban statesman-general who invented the heavy, deep-thrusting infantry phalanx and profoundly altered contemporary military tactics, becoming the most famous warrior of his day.

On returning north at a moment of confusion and civil strife, Philip seized the throne, to which his claim was valid, and began the great task of forming a Macedonian national army. In his *hetairoi* he already had a cavalry force. However, from his Theban experience, he also realized that a fully trained infantry was essential. He created this in his new *hupaspistai* spearmen and an adaptation of the phalanx formation. Unlike other Greek (save Theban) troops, the *hupaspistai* were armed with exceptionally long pikes.

Little more than a year after becoming sovereign and commander, Philip married the fiercely beautiful Epirote princess Olympias, who became Alexander's mother. The daughter of King Neoptolemos of the Molossians, a rugged, passionate people from the mountain region of what is now Albania, she was but one of Philip's wives and concubines and often quarreled with him. Yet, even after the royal couple separated, she retained a magic grip on her son, and Alexander was emotionally overwhelmed by her.

Philip successively, and with initially varying results, fought the Thessalians plus Athenian, Phocian, and Persian units. He gradually extended the boundaries and power of Macedonia but was never successful in taking firm hold of Athens, where he was fervently opposed by the magnificent orator Demosthenes. Demosthenes directed against the ambitious northern ruler a famous series of speeches known as the "Philippics."

Nevertheless, the Macedonian king captured Delphi and presided over its Pythian games in 346 B.C. More and more Panhellenic advocates, typified by Isocrates, another Athenian orator, began to regard Philip as the obvious leader for a crusade of all Greek states against Persia, the great power to the east. Philip himself relished the idea. He sent propaganda agents throughout Greece to promote the concept, failing only to convince Sparta.

It is likely that, had Philip not fathered one of the world's most famous men, he would still be regarded as an outstanding historical figure of ancient Greece. Before his murder at the age of forty-six, he had essentially unified the quarrelsome, jealous Hellenic peoples, raised the cultural level of his native Macedonia above that of most of its rivals, and created a mighty armed force behind whose implicit threat he managed to exercise skillful diplomacy.

Few military leaders, indeed, did more to alter the political balance of their times. With his army, the first great Macedonian force, he overran his Balkan neighbors, mainland Greece, the Aegean, and much of the Middle East. He came to the throne of a weak kingdom and, at a young age, left it powerful enough to dominate the known world. And no mere brutal warrior, with his personal gifts of diplomacy (aided by bribery of key envoys and the menace of military force), he managed to persuade other states to accept his leadership and goals.

As a commander of armies there is little doubt that the only contemporary Greek who ever surpassed him was his son. Philip improved on the concepts and weapons of Epaminondas, and learned from that intellectual Theban general the principle of striking with great superiority at the key, decisive point. He favored economy of force, speed, deception, surprise. He improved existing cavalry tactics as much as Hitler's Nazi generals improved the current use of armor in the twentieth century. And, with the long Theban spear, extended to the eighteen-foot *sarissa*, he produced the finest hoplite infantry yet seen, the *pezetairoi* (or "foot companions"). Finally, he developed the first complex and technically qualified military siege train with engineers and powerful catapults.

The historian Diodoros wrote that Philip owed his success as much to diplomacy and personal popularity among his soldiers as to courage and command talents. He often displayed generosity to those he had crushed on the battlefield, such as the coalition of Greek city-states defeated at Chaeronea; in another case, he took the initiative to end the war with defeated Athens, which subsequently became his ally. His eye focused only on a drive into Persia. He sent back his Athenian prisoners and the ashes of the famous city's dead, accompanied by a military guard including his son Alexander (the great conqueror's sole visit to Greece's cultural capital).

Philip's own genius—and he was the Hellenes' greatest national king as contrasted with their international conqueror, Alexander—was that he recognized the assets of the people he led and what lay at hand as a potential. Macedonia was the richest Greek state, with silver, gold, and iron mines and extensive bronze foundries.

Apart from his own military talent he relied on exceptional commanders such as Parmenion. And he had the advantage of total personal control of military, political, and economic policy. He could make decisions immediately; those who failed to carry out his orders swiftly knew they would be executed.

He was obsessed by two imaginative long-range dreams: to unite all Greeks in a Panhellenic program and to smash the threatening superpower, Persia. Although he was unable to conduct it himself, the war against Persia led by his son was Philip's greatest military achievement. For he built the machine that carried it out, dreamed the dream it brought to fruition, and also fathered its guiding genius.

Once he had subjected the non-Greek lands that lay north and east of Macedonia, he allied himself to the rest of Hellas, where he recognized his strength lay more in being benefactor than despot. Then in 336 B.C., he began his eastward drive by dispatching a vanguard of ten thousand men to Asia Minor, liberating Hellenic cities from the Hellespont to the Meander River, and preparing the outposts for the main body of his army as it got ready to strike.

Philip indoctrinated Alexander into the arts of war and governance at an early age. He assigned him to complete the control already won of a Balkan Europe up to the Sea of Marmora. He left him as his deputy in Macedonia at only sixteen. As lieutenant of the realm, Alexander was sent on an independent campaign against the northern Maidoi tribe and honored his victory by creating the first of many cities in his name, Alexandropolis. Philip entrusted him with the post of honor and glory in a tough battle against a Theban coalition and shattered its "Sacred Band," the cream of its army.

Philip never realized his Asian dream. At his daughter's wedding feast, that year, he was murdered by Pausanias, one of the seven royal bodyguards in attendance. The sovereign was struck down suddenly in his capital during a moment of solitude, and Pausanias rushed out through open gates toward the horses he and fellow plotters had made ready for escape.

The king and his train had approached the marital celebration at dawn, preceded by the images of twelve gods, in full raiment, and followed by Philip, dressed plainly in white. As they entered, he chose to walk alone and bade his guards to follow at a distance. It was then that young Pausanias ran up (unchallenged, as a guardsman) and stabbed his sovereign with a broad-bladed knife. The king died instantly. Pausanias tripped while mounting his tethered steed at the gate and was stabbed to death by a spear.

The report had it that the assassin smote down his sovereign because the latter gave him no redress in a quarrel among courtiers. However, Alexander's mother, Queen Olympias, was chiefly blamed for the crime because she was believed to have encouraged Pausanias.

Philip, like most kings of his time, was polygamous in order to insure an adequate number of heirs who could contest the succession. It appears more than likely that Olympias, by far the most outstanding of his wives, resented her rivals for the royal bed. She had an enormous influence over Alexander, her own son, and for those who see in their relationship a true Oedipus complex, it is noteworthy that Alexander, only married twice, was almost totally uninterested in sex.

Olympias married Philip when he was twenty-two and she no more than a girl. Indeed, she was barely twenty when Alexander was born in 356 B.C. She was by nature wild, often reputed to be a sorceress, lovely, jealous, and proud of her ancient family, which boasted descent from Achilles. She was furious to discover that, although used to sexual inferiority in a male-dominated world, she was of no importance except as a baby-making machine for the Macedonian court.

Philip, indeed, was vastly uninhibited. He had seven or eight royal wives including a Molossian, two Thessalians, a Getic, an Illyrian, and a Scythian. In addition he had countless mistresses and a genuine passion for Cleopatra, the niece of his general, Attalos, designated as one of two leaders for his planned Asian expedition.

Philip had agreed to go through a marital ceremony with Cleopatra, partly to please Attalos, and Olympias staged a furious tantrum. It was her jealous and vindictive personality that deliberately incited Alexander to oppose Philip, yet although the son lost little love for his father, he habitually respected, and admired him.

Theirs was a rough, violent society. As the carousing and drinking that honored Cleopatra persisted, Alexander imbibed more than was his custom, and, feeling the king's new bride to be a personal affront to his own beloved mother, provoked a drunken brawl with Philip. He had been seated in grim silence among his friends across the hall from the bridal couple when he suddenly staggered to his feet and shouted: "What of me, villain? Do you take me for a bastard?" He hurled his wine cup at one of the king's attendants.

The king sprang at his son, sword in hand, but tripped over a low table bearing food and fell flat.

"Look, here is the man preparing to cross from Europe to Asia," roared Alexander. "Yet he cannot even get from one couch to another without falling." Alexander was shoved from the room by friends before more trouble ensued.

According to Plutarch (who lived and wrote four centuries later), Alexander followed up the drunken brawl by taking the weird and lovely Olympias back to her native Epirus. From there she journeyed to self-exile in that country's northern neighbor, Illyria (in the north of what is now Albania).

This move enhanced Olympias's doting love for him and increased her already powerful emotional influence on the boy. It is not unlikely that his mother-fixation was encouraged by the fact that he was Olympias's junior by barely twenty years and she was still a fine-looking woman. There is nothing even remotely rumored concerning incestuous sex. Indeed, Alexander showed throughout his short life a certain disgust with sex. He used to say sex and fatigue were the only reminders that he was just another man. He had but one known love affair and died before his sole heir's birth. That posthumous son was slain as a baby during quarrels among court factions.

Olympias faded from history after Philip's death. There are no accounts of messages between her and her magnificent son. Philip is remembered by his contemporaries as a tired, brave, restless, haggard, hard-drinking, one-eyed man (he lost the other storming an Athenian fortress), but he left a stupendous legacy.

To start with, he bequeathed the dream of conquering Asia and the means to accomplish this. He left a magnificent military machine with new strategies, new tactics, and new weapons. He left a compact Greek nation, made up of autocratically-run slave-states to the north and largely allied Hellenic communities to the south. He left a diplomatic methodology of craft, bribery, flattery, and idealism that gained even the admiration of the anti-Macedonian Demosthenes. And he left a son to complete his vast dreams successfully because he had had him educated by Aristotle, the greatest teacher and scholar of his age.

When Alexander claimed his heritage, he is said to have called upon his people to remain calm. All things would be administered exactly as under his father. "Nothing," he assured them, "has changed except the name of the king."

Philip was buried with ceremonial pomp in Aigai, where his ancestors and relatives had been interred. His weather-beaten corpse was encased in a cuirass of hinged sheets of iron, edged and banded in gold, the breast decorated with six lions' heads; also a golden plate showing Athena in full armor. Above his head was the royal diadem that represented a crown.

Theopompos, a contemporary who wrote a *History of Philip*, thought him the greatest leader of the era. He was popular with his own armies because he fought in their front ranks, enduring hardships and terrible wounds. But despite the loot of his many victories and the increased production of his many mines—especially gold—he died leaving a large deficit in the state treasury, mainly because of the huge cost of his armies.

It is difficult to contemplate what might have happened to Greece and to the world had not death handed over to the brilliant but incautious Alexander his father's dream of eastern conquest. Alexander had one immense weakness: he did not know where to stop.

Despite occasional flaming quarrels with his violent father, the son owed him many debts, above all one beyond comparison: the finest education of his era. Philip chose the philosopher Aristotle, a Macedonian from the village of

Stageira to supervise the boy's learning. The great pupil of Plato, seeing in the youngster his "chosen vessel" for the fate of the Greek spirit, determined to make of him a true philosopher-king. In this he succeeded, whereas Plato himself, who invented that concept, had failed when he attempted a similar undertaking with Dionysios, tyrant of Syracuse. Aristotle had a broad view of Greek thought and achievement and, politically, was a Panhellene.

In 348 B.C., soon after Plato died, Aristotle had left Athens and its academy, going first to Asia Minor, then to the island of Mytilene, and finally to Stageira, the home of his father on the Chalkidike peninsula. His father had been a friend and physician of Philip's father, King Amyntas III, and Stageira had become part of Philip's domain.

The philosopher created a special school for Alexander in a rural retreat at Mieza (near the present Naoussa, center of Greece's best red wine). In a place called the Nymphaion, on the cool slopes of Mount Vermion, he taught the crown prince and some of his famous "Companions," a select group, walking and talking with the youngsters in the manner of Plato's peripatetic school.

The young heir studied there until he was sixteen, learning Greek history, geography, flora, fauna, mathematics, astronomy, and the military arts. He became an avid reader and from then on always carried with him his personal copy of the *Iliad*. This became known as "the casket copy." He later kept it under his pillow beside his dagger. He regarded Homer's tale of Troy as a handbook of warfare.

From boyhood Alexander showed himself an athlete. He could outrun his playmates and thought of himself as an Achilles, hero of his mother's family. He developed into a strong, handsome, intelligent lad who was at first deeply attached to his teacher, Aristotle, who "had shown him how to live well." But in later years, long after he had left his tutelage, their friendship diminished.

While he was still under Aristotle's influence—at the age of fourteen— he was home, at Pella, when Philoneicos, a Thessalian, brought Philip a horse named Bucephalas.

The king and several friends watched the animal go through some trials. They came to the conclusion that he was savage and unmanageable, for he allowed nobody to mount him and even reared if anyone approached. The ruler was furious at being offered such a vicious, unbroken beast. He commanded that it be led away and sold for a very high price.

Alexander watched in silence. Finally he said: "What a horse is being lost. All because they don't how to handle him and haven't the courage to try." Philip was angry, but remained silent. Finally, when his son repeated his observation, the king shouted: "Do you find fault with your elders because you think you know more or because you can manage a horse better?"

"At least I could handle this one better," said the boy.

"And if you fail, what penalty will you pay for your impertinence?"

"I'll pay the horse's price, thirteen talents."

"Done," said the father as the watchers burst into laughter.

Alexander approached Bucephalas, took his bridle, and turned his face into the sun, having noticed that the horse shied at the sight of his own shadow. Then he ran alongside the animal a short distance, stroking him. With no advance indication, he cast aside his cloak and vaulted onto his back. Bucephalas galloped madly a few hundred yards before realizing he had met his match, slowed down, and answered willingly to the rein. When the boy brought the magnificent steed back and dismounted, Philip embraced him and said (according to Plutarch): "My son, you must find a kingdom large enough for your ambitions. Macedonia is too small for you."

It is probable these words were not exactly as quoted. Plutarch writing about Alexander was comparable to Chaucer writing about Charlemagne in terms of intervening time.

But already Philip was dreaming of his grand conquest of Persia, in which his heir would play a role and finally benefit from the triumph the king himself expected to achieve. Also the story accords with the passionate and stormy relationship between father and son which could swiftly shift from love to hatred, admiration to contempt.

In Philip's mind it had always been an auspicious augury that he had received in the same year three fine pieces of news: Queen Olympias had borne him a son; his army had routed the mountain tribes of Illyria; and his horse had won its race at the 106th Olympic Games.

Alexander had grown into a splendid youth whose portraits were subsequently executed by fine artists: Lysippus in sculpture, Apelles in painting, and Pyrgoteles in graven gems. The followers of Lysippus and Apelles sought to reproduce the slight leftward tilt of the handsome subject's neck, the melting look in his eyes, his fair, ruddy skin. Father and son were both prone to moodiness and outbursts of choleric rage—partly perhaps because of their complex subconscious relationships with Olympias; and also because they were increasingly excited by the feasting and hard-drinking habits of the Macedonians.

It is to Philip's credit that, despite Alexander's obvious passion for and prejudice in favor of his mother, he succeeded in attracting his son's admiration. Yet this also appears to have been mixed with a strange jealousy.

As Philip extended Macedonian power from the Caucasus to the Gulf of Corinth, Alexander is reported to have said many times to Ptolemy and others: "Father will do everything. At this rate he'll leave no conquests for you and me."

The boy heard much about the planned long march eastward whenever he was at court and again at school under Aristotle who was strongly anti-Persian. Indeed, it is probable that he first heard from the latter an outline of Philip's dream and a vision of his own short life: the conquest of Persia, the superpower, and the establishment of Greek cities at strategically or commercially useful points amid the ashes of his Eastern empire.

Macedonian generals and aristocratic landowners were opposed to the idea of such a huge war, and both Philip and Alexander were threatened again and again by plots led by noblemen.

The lesson of his father's end for Alexander must surely have been that disagreement with the king's policies inevitably led to conspiracies against the king's life. Feuds burned long and dangerously in that warlike society where there was usually more than one claimant to the throne.

Thus, although only twenty at the time, this brilliant, cultivated, brave, and experienced young statesman-warrior was well chosen to face the formidable jealousies and feuds besetting his kingdom and to carry on with his father's great dream that even Aristotle had commended.

Philip's assassination and the consequent confusion delayed an inevitable blow in Macedonia, which was the base for the assault. But, after Alexander had demonstrated his martial qualities against restive Greek states, he was chosen captain-general of the Hellenes against the barbarians in Corinth.

According to one of many legends about Alexander started in Corinth, Alexander had paid a call upon the renowned philosopher Diogenes of Sinope, then living in the wealthy Corinthian trading center. Diogenes was lying on the earth, head propped on an elbow. When asked by the Macedonian ruler if there was anything he could do for him he replied: "Yes. You can stand a bit to the side out of the sunlight." When some of his retinue sneered at the philosopher, the sovereign replied: "You may say what you wish, but if I were not Alexander I would wish to be Diogenes."

In 335 B.C. Alexander started his earth-shattering march with a drive across the Balkans and over the Danube. The following year he headed into Asia with a force of 6,000 cavalry and almost 45,000 infantry, enormous for those days. With this formidable weapon, forged by his father, he set out to fulfill Philip's great dream of crossing the Hellespont and occupying immense areas to the east.

Those who speculated on the reasons for Alexander attacking the oriental superpower received the same answer: "It never occurred to him not to." At the start of the invasion he signed away estates and crown property to his officers until nothing was left and Perdikkas asked him: "Your majesty, what are you leaving for yourself?" "My hopes," he replied. "Very well," Perdikkas answered: "Those who serve with you will share them too."

Undoubtedly spurred on by the teachings of Aristotle and his own pillow companion, the *Iliad*, Alexander began his enterprise by visiting Troy and sacrificing to the Ilian Athena and the Homeric dead. Then he poured oil on the column that marked the grave of his mother's ancestor, Achilles, and ran a race by it naked with his companions, crowning the funerary stele with a wreath. He remarked that Achilles was fortunate in having discovered a faithful friend while he lived and a great poet to sing of him after his death.

Asia had not heard the heavy tramp of Greek infantry or the clatter of Greek horses since the northward march of Xenophon's ten thousand mercenaries to the Black Sea sixty-seven years earlier. Alexander's army of Illyrians, Macedonians, Thracians, and contingents from most Hellenic states (excepting Sparta) burst inland from the Hellespont at Arisbe.

It was at Granicus that the invading force found the satraps' legions lined up against them. There, according to a code of chivalry shared by both Macedonians and Persians, a cavalry clash began with opposing chieftains honor-bound to fight in hand-to-hand single combat.

Alexander, with a noticeable shield he believed to have been that of Achilles and with tall white plumes attached to his helmet, hurled himself from one corner of the battlefield to another, exhorting his men. When he had shattered the troops of Darius III, he boasted of his achievement by sending to Athens, which he carefully courted, 300 captured suits of armor with the following inscribed message: "Alexander, the son of Philip, and all the Greeks with the exception of the Spartans, won these spoils of war from the barbarians who dwell in Asia."

Powerful Sardis fell to him without a blow, followed by the strongholds of Aeolis and Ionia. Alexander gained control of the harbors to prepare an immense logistical operation which aimed to establish him as ruler of the entire empire.

After overcoming Halicarnassus in a stubborn fight, he veered inland to Gordium on the high Phrygian plain where King Midas once ruled. There the latter's chariot had been tied up by a complex bark-knot to a cornel tree and local legend said that the man who could untie this knot would rule the world. Alexander hacked it open with his sword.

In 333 B.C. he headed southward to liberate the Greek cities of the Asian coast, a dream long entertained by leading Hellenes, not least among them Aristotle.

On the Issus, where he regretted his inability to swim, he achieved a brilliant victory causing such slaughter among the Persians that the tall, handsome Darius and his remarkably beautiful wife fled eastward. He then captured the exposed Phoenician cities of Tyre and Sidon, selling their inhabitants as slaves, and marched southward through Palestine to Gaza.

The gates of Egypt were open, and the Greek conqueror was seen by most of that ancient land's population as a deliverer from Persian tyranny. Capitalizing on this mood, he sacrificed to the gods of Memphis and formally became pharaoh. During that winter of 332–331 B.C. he rested his troops and took two significant personal actions.

The first was an expedition to the Oracle of Zeus Ammon on the Oasis of Siwa, whose priest hailed him as the god Ammon's son, a role Alexander was delighted to assume. Lysimachos the Bodyguard, when he became King of Thrace, was the first to put Alexander's head on his coins wearing the ram's horns of Ammon, who had once been a ram-god. The type became classic: in Eastern legend Alexander became Alexander the Two-Horned.

The second was to gather his engineers and architects and lay the foundation of Alexandria, thus creating a new commercial center for the eastern Mediterranean world he had seized. Alexandria was the greatest of several cities similarly named that the Macedonian conqueror built as far away as Turkestan.

After resting and regaling his troops in Egypt during 332–331 B.C., Alexander at last turned back to his principal military goal—that inherited from his father—the conquest of the mighty Darius, whom he hoped to humiliate by capturing him alive. In 331 at Gaugamela, he conquered the Persian, who, gravely wounded, expired in the carriage of noble friends. They had stabbed their ruler and fled with a cavalry guard when they learned the Greeks were closing in.

Alexander passed the winter merrymaking in the imperial palaces at Persepolis. Meanwhile he drafted 30,000 young Persians into his army and had them trained as spearmen and javelin throwers. He respected the royal women-folk, calling the captive queen "Mother" and standing in her presence until invited to sit. He also paid particular attention to one of her daughters, Stateira, whom he was to marry long afterward for reasons of state.

In 330 B.C. he ordered his rested army, which he had enlarged by forced recruiting, to take Ecbatana. Then he marched eastward into Parthia with his treasury enriched by the gold and spoils of Susa and Ecbatana. From there, exceeding the limits known to Greek geographers, he crossed the Oxus and the Jaxartes and penetrated deeply into the modern Soviet Union before deciding to switch southward into the Hindu Kush range towering over Afghanistan and then deep into India.

The invaders were confused and fascinated by their new enemies. Arrian wrote: "The Indians are the darkest of mankind except the Ethiopians." The Greeks called the fakirs they encountered "naked philosophers." At first they were fear-smitten by the ponderous elephant charges of King Poros. On seeing crocodiles in the Indus River, Alexander himself initially thought he had come to the headwaters of the Nile, thousands of miles away.

When he captured Poros, Alexander said: "Ask him what he would like."

"To be treated like a king," was the answer.

"Certainly," said Alexander. "But what would you like personally?"

" 'Like a king' covers everything," came the reply.

Alexander restored his kingdom, with additional territory, and founded Nikaia, the "City of Victory," at the scene where he had defeated the Indian ruler of the Punjab.

Alexander then descended the Indus River and ultimately swung westward and homeward supported by a navy under Nearchus which sailed close to shore from one Alexandria in Baluchistan in the east to another in Babylonia toward the west. His Macedonian troops were beginning to grumble with fatigue, and he, the young monarch, had at last seriously fallen in love for the first time—with Roxane, the beautiful daughter of a frontier lord. He married her in a Persian ceremony whose central rite was the eating together of a wheaten cake. Alexander impulsively cut it with his own sword.

His conquests had taken him from Siwa and Thebes in Egypt to the headwaters of the Aral Sea, the mouth of the Indus, and the length of the Persian Gulf. He had learned new military arts, including the way to counter the massive charges of Poros's elephants. He had married two brides: Roxane, and Darius's daughter Stateira. And he had lost many of his best friends and closest companions. None was more mourned than his thirty-year-old warhorse, Bucephalas, who died of wounds inflicted by the archers of Poros.

In his faithful steed's memory, Alexander sadly founded the city of Bucephalia on the banks of the Hydrespes. It was there that he learned the philosophy of empire by coming upon the tomb of the greatest Persian ruler: "Oh man," he read, "whoever you are and wherever you come from, for I know you will come, I am Cyrus who won the Persians their empire. Do not therefore grudge me this little earth that covers my body."

Not much later he had occasion to ponder these poignant words. On rejoining Nearchus and his ships in Babylonia, he celebrated with a two-day carousal that ended in an inexplicable fever. A few days later he lost the power of speech. Word was given permitting all Macedonians in his army to file through his chamber man by man and bid him farewell. On June 28, 323 B.C., he died.

Alexander had never named an heir. The Argead monarchy was not hereditary by primogeniture but managed to supply its rulers on an improvised system of survival of the fittest. The violent contest for power began in the women's apartments. A few weeks after his death, the lovely Roxane had produced a boy, Alexander "Aegus." Leading Macedonian officers wished him to succeed Alexander, but most of the infantrymen objected to the prospect of a long regency. They proposed instead that the dead conqueror should be replaced by his half-brother Philip "Arrhidaios."

Bloodshed settled the argument. Roxane lured her rival, Queen Stateira, with a fake letter, had her murdered together with her sister, and hid the bodies in a well. In this crime Perdikkas served as Roxane's accomplice. "Philip Arrhidaios" was chosen as a figure-head under a regency council of Perdikkas, Leonnatos, Antipatros, and Krateros. This system foundered.

Olympias subsequently spread reports that Alexander had been murdered, putting many men to death including those coming to the fore as successors. Roxane and her son were executed while he was still a boy, after a vain attempt at flight. His half-uncle was also slain. "Philip Arrhidaios" simply vanished as a historical nonentity.

Those of the great king's lieutenants who came to the fore as Hellenistic rulers of the disintegrating Asian-Egyptian empire were Perdikkas, Ptolemy, Lysimachos, and Seleukos, commander of the footguards and known as "the Conqueror."

But none of the commanders even aspired to the talents or dominating personality of Alexander. The latter's arrogance was equaled only by his famous courage. When Darius, after a lost battle, offered a huge ransom for imprisoned noble ladies and proposed peace negotiations, Alexander simply advised the Persian ruler that further communications should not be sent as equal to equal but humbly, as to the Lord of Asia from one of his subjects.

When the Persians offered a still greater ransom and a large cession of territory, one of Alexander's "Companions," Parmenion, suggested: "I would accept that offer if I were Alexander."

"So would I," said Alexander, "if I were Parmenion."

He scorned to take Darius's striking wife as his concubine and dismissed the beautiful Persian ladies as "an irritation to the eyes." (That was before he met Roxane.) When friends brought to him from the booty of a battle an exquisite jeweled casket "suitable for the keeping of a king's greatest treasure," he placed within his copy of the *Iliad*.

Confronted with the high, fortified mound of Gaza he was about to attack, Alexander announced: "The more 'impossible' it is, the more I will take it. For the dead will disgrace the enemy, and not to have taken it would disgrace me."

From the moment he became King of Macedonia, his financial position was shaky because of the vast cost of his armed forces; but he was confident he would conquer enormous Persia and thus raise the necessary working capital. (From Persepolis alone, it required 4,000 mules and 500 camels to carry away the gold and treasures of his army's loot.)

Much is known of the appearance, habits, and personality of Alexander from the writings of Arrian, Onesicratus, Callisthenes, Nearchus, Aristobulus, and Clitarchus. He was of modest height but of lean, sinewy build. His hair rose abruptly from his brow giving a leonine suggestion. He carried his head slightly to one side. His cheeks were lean and he always shaved clean, setting this fashion for five centuries in the Greco-Roman world. His gaze was clear; his face short-chinned and dominated by a bony square jaw.

During his youth he was abstemious in the raucous Macedonian court, but the more he campaigned the more heavily he drank. His diet was relatively simple. He tended to eschew vulgar luxury and ostentation in costume, later adopting the comfortable Iranian native dress of embroidered jacket and trousers. He was not cruel for his day but employed barbaric savagery. For example, when he captured Bessus, the murderer of Darius, he had his limbs bound to two bent trees which tore him apart when released.

As a warrior he was unusually brave and had a talent for inspiring his troops and commanders. His vision was limitless. He acted as his own chief of staff and generally left to Parmenion charge of the defensive left wing while he attacked on the right. His technical services were efficient, and he had a thorough knowledge of logistics and the importance of using naval transport whenever possible. His wounded were cared for promptly. After a battle, Alexander sought always to visit his field hospitals.

He was master of the mechanical military complexities of his time, bringing up siege trains swiftly, putting catapults into action as fast as possible, battering down walls or spanning them with drawbridges on wheeled towers or mining their foundations.

He had masses of pontoon boats for river crossings. On suitable occasions, he sought to enliven the morale of his soldiers with musical and dramatic entertainments. He took the precaution of sacrificing to the Moon, Sun, and Earth in the hope of producing eclipses before battles, to enhance his enemy's fear.

Just as he was usually temperate with food and drink, but given to sudden outburts of excess, he courted popularity with his troops but could also be coldly ruthless. When Parmenion sent him a message that he was heavily engaged and needed help to save what baggage he had left, the king replied: "Tell Parmenion that if we win we shall have the enemy's baggage; and if we do not, every brave man will be dead."

As he prepared to launch his invasion of India (327 B.C.) he realized his forces were overladen with booty and had lost their needed mobility. One morning, when his baggage trains had been loaded, he ordered that his own be burned, then those of the "Companions," and finally of all Macedonian officers and troops. A great cheer went up, followed by the customary battle cry. Those who subsequently ran short on campaign necessities were aided. The lightened army first struck and successively outflanked and outmaneuvered the formidable battle-wagons with their scythed wheels and the thunderous elephants first encountered in the armies of Darius, then Poros.

During his brief life, Alexander conquered huge areas: Turkish Anatolia, Syria, Palestine, Egypt, Armenia, Babylonia and the vast Persian empire, much of India. He went from the Black Sea to the Caspian and Aral and traversed the length of the Persian Gulf and the Baluchi coast of the Arabian Sea.

He ravaged Turkestan, crossed the Oxus, Jaxartes, and Indus rivers, and scaled the jagged peaks of the Hindu Kush, emerging in the lovely flowerland of Swat. He slaughtered several kings and conquered cities, renaming many of them after himself. From Taxila in the northern Punjab all the way back to recalcitrant Sparta, everything was his.

It is perhaps a blessing that Alexander's embalmed corpse vanished in ways not yet confirmed (there is even a "sarcophagus of Alexander" in Istanbul that is not authentic). It is known that after his death in Babylon it was intended to inter his body at Siwa Oasis in the Shrine of Zeus Ammon, the god with whom he had deliberately identified himself. However, Ptolemy I, first Hellenistic ruler of Egypt, intercepted the cortege at Memphis, burying it there temporarily until a magnificent tomb could be elevated in the conqueror's own city, Alexandria.

Later a new resting place was built by Ptolemy IV, who erected a mausoleum where Alexander's remains could be surrounded by the loyally Greek Ptolemies. The original golden coffin was replaced by one of crystal. This disappeared amid riots during the late third century.

Alexander's empire swiftly disintegrated just as did the remnants of his person. But his lightning thrusts across three continents paved the way for new forms of culture in the areas trampled by his hard-bitten soldiers. Greek thoughts, habits, literature, music arose in new or revived cities: Pergamon, Ephesos, Magnesia, Delos, Rhodes, Kos, Cyprus, Antioch, Seleucia, and the numerous Alexandrias from eastern India to Afghanistan, and Baluchistan, all the way to the Nile delta. There by far the greatest of them all endures today, even if it is no longer faintly Grecian.

And Alexander took with him a brand new culture and brought mixed increments of others back when he started his return march westward accompanied by Greek scientists, scholars, geographers, botanists, and other fascinated students of the people, lands, flowers, and animals with which they became acquainted.

Cultures have never been so swiftly and so successfully intermingled before or since. Greek art stamped the Gandhara and Matura sculpture of India. Indian sages adopted Greek astronomy. Ashoka, India's first great reformist-ruler and of partially Macedonian descent, ordered his laws written in two languages: Aramaic and Greek.

When Alexander was on the verge of taking off for Asia, he asked Aristotle what present he should like from there. "Bring me an Indian philosopher," the old sage said.

He did better: he gave more than he received. The Greek tongue became the ancient world's international language. Hellenic rulers, sculptors, museums, mints, libraries, and academies of science began to proliferate in the orient.

Can something so vague as glory be a testament? Look at Homer. We know little of him save that he was blind. We are not even positive that he alone composed the *Iliad* and the *Odyssey*. But we do know he was great.

Lesser men have bequeathed to the world fantastic works of art and literature, political theories, and scientific discoveries. But none has transcended Homer's name as tantamount to greatness in poetry. Philip and Alexander were history's greatest family team. The one dreamed a dream and built up the machinery to bring it to reality. The other realized the dream.

II

Martinet and Genius: Frederick William and Frederick the Great

Ever since the first Teutonic tribes migrated into Europe, Germans have been renowned for their military prowess. In 9 A.D. their general, Herman (known as Arminius by the Romans), defeated an army of the emperor Augustus in the dark Teutoburg Forest. When he received news of the disastrous battle Augustus is reported to have said, referring to the general who commanded his lost forces, P. Quinctilius Varus: "Varus, Varus, give me back my legions." From that time on Germans were the most solicited mercenary soldiers in Europe, and history has been studded with the names of famous German warriors: Moltke, Schlieffen, Clausewitz, Ludendorff, Hindenburg, Rommel. Most renowned of all was Frederick II, King of Prussia, the eighteenth-century genius of the battlefield.

Frederick, who lived from 1712 to 1786, was the third son (his elder brothers died) of an eccentric but methodical Prussian ruler, Frederick William I, who carefully prepared his country and his frail heir for the arduous experience of battle. During the conflict known as the War of the Spanish Succession the young Prussian served at the Duke of Marlborough's headquarters and became entranced by his army experiences at the victory of Malplaquet (1709), which he often referred to as "the greatest day of my life." After that triumph, he resolved to build a powerful Prussian army so that he could conduct for his small East European state a fully independent foreign policy. Almost coincidental with this early resolve, when he was only twenty-three years old, two years after he ascended to his throne, Frederick William embraced the practical Christianity of Pietism, a religious movement that suited his strict Protestantism and energetic disposition.

The young ruler proved to be a stern disciplinarian and a rigorously thrift-minded sovereign who was determined to be his own minister of finance and field marshal. His greatest passion was his army. He built this into a disciplined force of 80,000 out of a total population of fewer than three million, and he paid for its proficiency with a war chest of eight million thalers, an immense sum for his day. He elaborated a rigidly mercantilist commercial and industrial policy whose revenues, based on agriculture and forestry, were almost doubled during his reign.

Frederick William was eminently dislikable: coarse, brutal, a pertinacious, hard-working man who created a military bureaucracy that has often since been seen as a typical expression of German political method. Even the civil service was subjected to military discipline. A fractious nobility was retrained into a loyal officer class that easily accepted the concepts of efficient organization.

This workable system brought with it much human unhappiness and a neglect of intellectual and cultural development. Frederick William paid no heed to ideas that could not be harnessed to his Spartan concepts of statecraft. His passion for his soldiers was shown by his refusal to appear in public save in military uniform. His special delight was a so-called regiment of Potsdam Grenadiers, known as the "giants' guard," which was made up of extremely tall men whom he bought or attracted from various corners of Europe.

Foreign sovereigns seeking his favor would often present him with one or more huge soldiers as a gift. Sometimes the king's agents seized seven-foot peasants and smuggled them from their native heath. An Irish giant named Kirkman was kidnapped from the streets of London in an operation costing a thousand pounds. A tall Austrian diplomat was grabbed when he descended from a hansom cab in Hanover. The tallest of all the king's men was a towering Prussian whose head could not even be reached by a man of ordinary stature. When the Grenadiers marched beside the royal carriage they joined hands above it. The king even tried unsuccessfully to breed a race of giants by forcing tall men and girls to marry (as Hitler was later to breed his S.S.).

Frederick William was determinedly unattractive. He suffered from manifold illnesses including painful gout, piles, headaches, and abscesses. His personal prejudices became uncontrollable, and his hatred for France, which had become Europe's great power under Louis XIV, was revered. If he heard that country mentioned, he would hit the person who spoke its name with his cane, often breaking noses and jaws. In one of his violent rages he smashed an entire dinner service of priceless Meissen china. Miscreants condemned to hang were sometimes dressed for the gallows in French clothes.

As his diseases progressed, Frederick William became vastly fat, with protruding eyes and splotched complexion. His family life was harshly unpleasant. Queen Sophia Dorothea showed him no sympathy or friendship and told courtiers their sovereign was mad. His heir, young Frederick, treated him almost like an enemy, mocked his religiosity, adored things French, and disliked hunting, his father's favorite pastime. The son pretended to hate military uniforms and affairs and called his own uniform his "shroud." As a result of his blatant indiscretions, abetted by his mother's, he was often beaten, starved, and humiliated by the king.

The one consistent joy in Frederick William's life was his collection of Grenadiers. Sometimes, when he was in a sour mood, he would improve his humor by parading several dozen of these giants through his bed chamber. During convalescence from one of his illnesses, the Prussian tyrant had learned to paint with some skill, if no notable talent, and he liked to depict himself with groups of his favorite soldiers. He signed the paintings "F. W. in tormentis pinxit."

He had very few intimates and only two genuine friends among them: the Prince of Anhalt-Dessau, a field marshal; and Count von Grumbkow, one of his generals, who had considerable influence on young Frederick's early life. Anhalt is credited with inventing the modern military drill of soldiers marching together in step as well as several words of command still used. He also introduced iron ramrods for infantrymen to use in their muskets, thus considerably increasing fire power. It was he, above all, who showed Frederick William how to make the Prussian army the most efficient and skillful military force in Europe. Grumbkow, on the other hand, was a civilized minister with a shrewd sense of humor. The king knew that he was in the pay of Austria, but with a rare cynical humor said this relationship in no way changed his own policy and brought in foreign currency to Prussia.

When young Frederick was a little child his father had some affection for him and took him to army maneuvers. As a toy, he presented the boy with a formation of 181 small boys constituted into a regiment called the Crown Prince Cadets. This strange unit was reviewed both by the Russian czar, Peter the Great, and by King George I of England.

As young Frederick grew older his father elaborated a set of rules for his education. He was to be instructed in history, but only starting with the sixteenth century—not long after the family's ancestral house of Hohenzollern first assumed the title Elector of Brandenburg. Frederick William wished to instill in his heir a contempt for Classical civilization which, he held, had demeaned the Germanic race, and he ordered that the boy be instructed only in the cultural and religious traditions of German sources. Everything French was dismissed as effeminate.

The complex rules of etiquette common to most other eighteenth-century courts were to be ignored, and Frederick was taught to rise early with no aid from attendants and to retire when he felt fatigued. He was to be particularly taught about German lands, especially Prussia and the nearby territories it coveted. Above all, the son must eschew Catholicism—and laziness. And he should avoid the temptations of a soft, woman's life.

Two men were charged by the king with supervising the heir's education: Jacques Duhan, as tutor (despite his French ancestry); and General Count Finck von Finckenstein, as governor. The Frenchman won his job because he had come to the king's attention in a siege where he displayed extraordinary bravery in the days when a soldier could fight in any army, regardless of his nationality, so long as he did not engage against his own sovereign's forces. Finckenstein was a well-known warrior who had survived many conflicts, above all several engagements against the French.

Under this doughty pair, young Frederick led an austere life. He rose at 6 A.M., knelt by his bed to thank God for permitting him to survive the night, washed without soap, and had his hair combed but not with the fashionable powder of his day. At 6:30 he read prayers with Duhan and the royal servants. His lessons lasted from seven to eleven, when he washed with soap and was at last powdered before going to his father, the king, with whom he remained until two. His instruction only ended at five o'clock when he was released from schedule to do what he wished until bedtime at 10:30. The king adjured that the boy "must try to be clean and tidy and not so dirty."

The consequence of this rigid upbringing was that Frederick was always slovenly, adored things French, and quietly disliked his stern parent. However, later he came to realize that Frederick William had prepared Prussia well for the dominant role it would play under Frederick himself, bequeathing him a well-ordered state with a frugal financial structure, a sound economy, a disciplined population, and a magnificent army that was far superior to those of its neighbors. When the great Prussian came to write his memoirs as an old man, he said of his father with an appreciation he never displayed while Frederick William was alive: "His spirit was transcendent, he penetrated and understood great objectives and knew the best interests of his country better than any minister and general."

Although young Frederick grew up detesting what he considered the Gothic past of the Germans and proclaiming that in all of Prussia there were few if any thinking persons, he was forced by his own impressions to acknowledge that there was a striking difference between the Prussian state ruled by his father and the savage, disorderly lands of Poland, which largely surrounded it. Prussia struck him as prosperous, contented, and efficient while Poland seemed a relative desert, fiercely chaotic. But despite the systematic and martial tenor of his upbringing, he cherished a cultural hunger which expressed itself early. He began to collect a library in secret and learned how to play the flute. He also began to develop a relatively free-thinking philosophy of his own. All this enraged his father, who frequently struck him as punishment. Therefore, when he was eighteen and on a tour of western Germany with the king, Frederick saw the opportunity to escape to England, which was ruled by the Hanoverian family of his mother. But the youth was betrayed and caught. He was degraded and brought before a court-martial as a deserter.

The court declared itself incompetent, and Frederick was consequently imprisoned in the fortress of Küstrin. There he was made to watch from his cell the execution of Lieutenant Hans Hermann von Katte, who had taken part in planning the flight. He fainted as Katte's head was struck off by a saber outside his window. Subsequently, he placed himself at his father's mercy and after a formal reconciliation was released at the age of twenty and given command of an infantry regiment. Also, to please Frederick William, he reluctantly married Princess Elizabeth, a niece of the Holy Roman Emperor, but it was an unhappy marriage without offspring. He hated his bride even before he saw her. Shortly after the wedding he was sent as an observer to the army of Prince Eugene of Savoy, who was the most renowned commander of the day.

Although his life became increasingly devoted to military activities, Frederick spent much time in two small houses designed for him by a friendly architect, and conversed there with friends or his sister Wilhelmine, whom he loved all his life. From Duhan he had already learned that most of the literate people he knew had no time for German writers but sent to Paris for their books and spoke French to each other. French architects were the fashion for wealthy German princes, and Versailles the unattainable model for their most splendid efforts. When German aristocrats sought a better way of life than that of a robber baron, many turned to Paris even in preference to the Teutonic capital of Vienna.

Wilhelmine, his loyal and steadfast sister, encouraged Frederick to read and study at every opportunity. Duhan, although censured on occasion by the bigoted king, helped Frederick to master a good French prose style and encouraged his passion for French literature and history. Frederick always preferred to express himself in French; his German was incorrect if colorful when he spoke, and he was almost unable to write in it.

By the time he was twelve, Frederick, who had had a miserable childhood until then, had made it clear that he hated the rough ways of his father and his court. He was frequently beaten—for leaping from a runaway horse or wearing gloves in cold weather. Yet by the time he was fourteen he had been named a major in the Potsdam Grenadiers, a small (five foot seven) officer among giants, thin, delicate with immense, protruding blue eyes. It was during this period that he became close to Johann Joachim Quantz, the musician, brought to Berlin by Queen Sophia Dorothea, who had developed a new and improved flute and who taught Frederick how to play it. He began to attend secret musical evenings, wearing an embroidered robe, with his hair fluffed, feeling entirely French. To be French was his great desire. He said in later life that he was happy to have spent his first three years on earth during the reign of Louis XIV, the Sun King, and to have been Voltaire's contemporary. France was Europe's preponderant power at that time.

Although Paris pursued a policy of keeping the German states divided, its influence in Protestant Germany was strong, helped along by the thousands of Huguenots who had settled there during the seventeenth-century persecutions. Numerous members of the Prussian bourgeoisie had been born in France. French was the lingua franca of Frederick's household, and at least half of his staff, including the cook, were French. Some evenings the household took part in plays, often by Racine or Voltaire.

Frederick's secretary, Charles Etienne Jordan, was a French refugee, a prosperous Huguenot pastor of whom the prince often said, "Wise, discreet Jordan, more lovable than Erasmus." When he succeeded to the throne, Frederick wrote him: "I am your friend and brother more than your king." Jordan was the only person to whom Frederick used the familiar pronoun *tu*. Another Latin, the handsome Venetian Francesco Algarotti, who was exactly Frederick's age, joined the prince's court and attracted his affection.

It has long been thought that Frederick was a latent homosexual, a preference less rare among distinguished generals than is often realized. When Frederick was at last crowned king, he rode without escort to the ceremony in a small carriage with Count von Keyserling, his last governor, appointed by Frederick William, and with Algarotti. He dozed with his head on Algarotti's shoulder, and the two called each other affectionately "Auguste" and "Mécène."

That he lacked heterosexual tendencies is amply indicated. The only woman he ever seemed to care for was his sister Wilhelmine. Sir Charles Hanbury Williams, the English Minister in Berlin, wrote about the queen: "It is impossible to hate her and although his (Frederick's) unnatural tastes won't allow him to live with her, common humanity ought to teach him to permit her to enjoy her separate state in comfort." He also said with undisguised venom: "The thing his Prussian Majesty has in the greatest abhorrence is matrimony. No man, however great a favorite, must think of it—if he does he is certain not to be preferred." Nancy Mitford, who wrote a splendid book on Frederick, concludes: "The general impression one gets after reading his works and letters is of somebody less interested in sex than in friendship." He especially delighted in letters he received from friends and generally answered them personally, particularly correspondence from Voltaire. The great Frenchman, whose name is so closely associated with that of the Prussian king, regarded Frederick alternately as a friend, enemy, and hero during their long association. When Frederick wrote to him, he generally signed his name as Fédéric, which seemed to him especially French and therefore to be employed as a particular signature to his most eminent correspondent.

The epistolary exchange began with a letter to Voltaire that seemed as painstaking and eager to impress as if written by a child seeking to convince his teacher. It was only much later that he felt at ease with the French philosopher-satirist and showed his relaxed view of Voltaire's nation ("if God made the world for me, he put France there for my entertainment.")

Voltaire's interest was excited as he learned of comparatively liberal reforms instituted by the king. Torture as a usual prelude to execution had been banned. The Prussian militarist declined to wear spurs in order not to pain his horse. He decreed religious freedom and ended press and literary censorship. He endorsed free speech, observing, "I do what I like, and the people say what they like." Voltaire began to address him as "Your Humanity."

After the two first met, Frederick wrote his secretary, Jordan: "I have seen that Voltaire whom I was so curious to know, but I had my fever upon me and my brain was as confused as my body was weak—his table talk is so dazzling that you could write a brilliant book simply by recording it." Voltaire himself recalled: "He had wit and charm, and besides he was a king." However, after their first get-together, which lasted three days, there was often a persistent uneasiness between the two. Nevertheless, Frederick wrote his new-found idol: "Be sure of the tender esteem with which I am your very faithful friend."

During the initial period of their association, Frederick put himself out to please Voltaire. He gave him a pleasant house near his new palace of Sans Souci, where the Frenchman finished his fine history, Le Siècle de Louis XIV. Voltaire corrected the manuscript of Frederick's enormous Art de la Guerre. He said of his loyal host that he was Spartan in the morning, Athenian in the afternoon; that he built barracks and fortresses but also palaces and academies of learning and opera houses; that he encouraged literature and art. He described Frederick in a letter: "There may be greater kings, but there are few more amiable men. What a miracle that the son of a crowned ogre, brought up with the beasts of the field, should understand the graces and subtleties of Paris. He is made for society."

Frederick chatted interminably with his French friend and happily played his flute. Nevertheless, as time rolled on, the two men became increasingly aware of each other's weaknesses, and the relationship cooled as Voltaire started to get on the king's nerves. The Frenchman's observations on warfare grated on Frederick as stupid and presumptuous, spiced by silly remarks such as: "The bullet speeds, the powder flames." When Voltaire journeyed to Frankfurt on his way back to France, the king's representative, a pompous fool called Baron von Freytag, refused to permit him to move on without written royal permission. The Frenchman tried to escape. He was caught and thereby made a public spectacle of himself.

Voltaire maintained that he who has a pen has a war and opened hostilities with Frederick with his quilled weapon. He confided in a manuscript, withheld from publication at the time, that the king was a miserly homosexual who considered himself "a literary genius."

The Duc de Nivernais, a special emissary of King Louis XV of France, has left an interesting pen portrait of Frederick during his latter years: "Impetuous, vain, presumptuous, scornful, restless, but also attentive, kind, and easy to get on with. A friend of truth and reason. He prefers great ideas to others—likes glory and reputation but cares not a rap what his people think of him. . . . He knows himself very well but the funny thing is that he is modest about what is good in him and boastful about his shortcomings."

His normal routine at his favored new residence of Sans Souci was highly regular. He rose early, though reluctantly. After giving the day's orders to his aide de camp, a general, he started his own daily schedule. At ten o'clock, he wrote letters or, in good weather, took a book to the garden, followed by a couple of his beloved Italian greyhounds. At noon he dined, frequently with writers and wits as well as military men. He whiled away a good meal until three o'clock, drank much coffee and watered champagne, and consumed fruit from his own greenhouses. After lunch he walked or did administrative work. Supper was at ten, generally followed by a concert of chamber music accompanied by Frederick and Quantz on their flutes. The king, who played with great talent, practiced religiously. When he retired, his favorite dog, Madame de Pompadour, slept in his bed beside him.

Frederick was usually unable to sleep while campaigning but passed the night reading and writing poetry. He was an avid admirer of Racine. He was also an eager and copious author, starting with his essay on the condition of Europe in 1736. He saw the diverse German states as waiting to be organized. He wrote two long studies of warfare in which he expressed great sympathy for the condition of the "unhappy" peasant soldiery. His *Histoire de la Guerre de Sept Ans,* which appeared posthumously, was acclaimed as the work of a great French author and hailed as comparable to the *Commentaries* of Julius Caesar.

For me the most interesting observations on Frederick's character are those of British diplomats. Lord Malmesbury, England's Envoy Extraordinary in Berlin during Frederick's last years, wrote in March 1776:

> I have seen him weep at Tragedy; known him pay as much care to a sick Grey Hound as a fond mother could give to a favorite Child; and yet the next day, He has given orders for the devastation of a Province: or by a wanton increase of Taxes, make a whole district miserable; and what will perhaps appear still more contradictory contribute to his own Brother's Death (August-Wilhelm), by continuing to him Marks of His displeasure the Whole Time of his last illness. Again, He is so far from being sanguinary, that He scarce ever suffers a Criminal to be punished capitally, unless for a most notorious Offence: Yet, in the last War, He gave secret orders to several of His Army Surgeons, rather to run the risk of a wounded Soldier's dying, than by the Amputation of a limb, increase the Number and Expense of His Invalids. Thus never losing sight of His Object, He lays aside all Feelings, the moment that is concerned: And although as an Individual, He often appears and really is Humane, Benevolent, and Friendly; yet, the Instant He acts in his Royal Capacity, these Attributes forsake Him, and He carryes with Him, desolation, Misery and Persecutions, where ever He goes.

In May 1780 Sir Hugh Elliot, minister of London to Bavaria, dispatched from Berlin this opinion:

> His Majesty still finds opportunities to cultivate letters and the Conversation of men of genius. Ever attentive to attach to His service those whose talents may be profitable or ornamental to his Court, He admits to private interviews the Strangers who frequent it, and has, in several instances during the course of His

reign, selected those of the greatest celebrity for the Companions of His leisure hours.

Historically speaking, Frederick made his particular mark on the map of Europe by war. He had developed a strong bias against Austria's Habsburg dynasty and was dissatisfied with Prussia's weak political and diplomatic position despite the strong and efficient army bequeathed to him by his father. He began his reign in 1740 by expounding as a political program many enlightened ideas that ran counter to the famous Florentine political philosopher and enunciated in his own *Antimacchiavell*.

His first military act was to dissolve Frederick William's ridiculous "giants' guard." The roads of Europe were soon cluttered up by massive, clumsy dolts stumbling homeward while the Potsdam Grenadiers were reorganized into an efficient fighting force. He also raised seven new regiments to increase the finely drilled army that had been his legacy.

As he embellished his military position, he developed an alliance with Russia at the expense of Poland, in between, and to the dismay of Austria, with which state Frederick had decided collaboration was not possible. He conquered West Prussia, joined Vienna and St. Petersburg in the Polish partition and fought the Austrians in Bohemia during the War of the Bavarian Succession, forcing Maria Theresa's son, Joseph von Habsburg, to abandon his claims. He made Prussia into an astonishing military state which at the same time was comparatively enlightened by new reforms.

He broke up the prevailing political system in Europe by seizing Silesia from Maria Theresa, accumulating an immense war chest and boosting the size of his army. In doing all this, he became surprisingly popular with his soldiers, who invented a whole repertoire of affectionate tales about "old Fritz" in his threadbare uniform and silver walking stick. But despite his preference for strong Prussian peasants as trusted cannon fodder, he chose to command them with aristocratic officers, often foreign. His *Instructions Militaires du Roi de Prusse pour ses Généraux* was written in French, the language he frequently used for his orders.

In fact Frederick held a rather cynical view of the private soldiers whom he disciplined and led so well. He claimed they would probably starve if not serving the state and that the nobility would go to pieces without doing battle. He argued that people fall too easily into decadence in peacetime and cited the Roman empire as a great example of this.

Like his father, he decreed strict discipline as essential, but ordered that his troops be better fed than the enemy's. He took several measures against desertion, including never letting his troops know in which direction he intended to march. He saw marauding as a great source of trouble.

He recognized speed of movement and the need for suitable terrain as vital factors in arranging a battle. His officers were enjoined to learn as much as possible about the country in which they were preparing to fight. He said that one could send others to find the answers to these problems, but that it was better to do it oneself. In a speech to his commanders at Berlin, he enjoined "humanity to unarmed enemies," but he was ruthless about seizing conquered property.

Frederick was quite fearless. He once remarked to a principal general: "Don't you think it astonishing that you and I should be quite safe among sixty thousand men who all hate us, all larger and stronger than we are, and armed? Yet they tremble before us." He was horrified at the thought that he might be captured on the battlefield, and throughout the Seven Years' War he carried a "little box" of poison to insure against being taken alive. He regarded it as foolish that his men often sang hymns before a battle, saying in his wholly irreligious way: "I don't like that; my buggers are frightened."

Frederick was not given to subtle concealment of his objectives. Although Austria's Maria Theresa at first regarded him as a loyal imperial vassal, she was soon disabused. Frederick acknowledged he went to war to acquire a reputation and to increase the power of Prussia. He selected Silesia, the Viennese empress's possession, because the French, English, and Dutch had no reason to interfere with him there and because it would augment his domains with agricultural and industrial wealth plus a largely Protestant population. He instructed his first minister, Count Heinrich von Podewils, to draw up a legal claim to the territory as "the work of a good charlatan" and then proclaimed: "Having, as is well known, interests in Silesia, I propose to take charge of it and keep it for the rightful owner."

Frederick was accustomed to winning battles and was astonished to find himself losing that of Mollwitz. He had not been on speaking terms with his field marshal, the able Count von Schwerin, who ultimately saved the day. Frederick fled the field, giving rise to Voltaire's quip that he felt no gratitude to any living creature save the horse that bore him to safety from Mollwitz.

On June 11, 1742, Frederick and Maria Theresa signed the Treaty of Breslau, which awarded both Upper and Lower Silesia to the Prussian while the empress wept for her lost province. Austria had been gravely weakened. Moreover, Frederick had proven the worth of his army, the only one in Europe not composed of mercenaries, and his own talent as a field commander.

In September 1744 he mobilized with amazing speed and launched an attack on the Bohemian capital of Prague, which he captured from its Austrian owners, leaving Maria Theresa with a burning hatred that sought only to humble Frederick and deprive him of his conquests. Nevertheless, on Christmas day 1745 the peace of Dresden was signed, confirming Prussia's possession of Upper and Lower Silesia as well as the county of Glatz, terminating the conflict. All of Frederick's aims had been realized while most of Europe outside of Prussia remained at war. "When one has the advantage," Frederick was to say, "is he to use it or not?" He added later: "The jurisprudence of sovereigns is commonly the right of the stronger." Professor Harold Temperley assessed the situation accordingly:

> One great advantage Frederick had over almost every other state: his economy was so great, his stewardship so careful that even in the strain of war he had never resorted to loans. England's subsidies and his own parsimony had enabled him to pay for everything as it fell due. Hence though the Seven Years War imposed gigantic suffering on Prussia, it did not tax or mortage her resources in the future. At the moment when Austria was laboring under mountains of debt, Prussia, owing to Frederick's system of making income balance expenditure, was encumbered by no tax on posterity.

Apart from his own genius for warfare and ability as a sovereign Frederick from the start possessed the best drilled infantry in the world, inherited from his father, which enabled his field commanders to accomplish brilliant maneuvers. Yet discipline sometimes lagged, and in a subsequent campaign known as the Potato War because of the stealing of crops by deserters, his opponent, the Holy Roman Emperor, Joseph, remarked: "The King of Prussia stays here to forage and I to recruit."

The Seven Years War (1756–1763) was Europe's greatest and bloodiest eighteenth-century conflict and represented Frederick's most sustained military performance. It sprang from the continuing dispute over Silesia between Prussia and Austria, but its most significant results were the permanent introduction of Russia into central European affairs and the British victory over France in distant Canada, thus having ultimately profound effects on the global power balance. After 1763 European states no longer ranged against each other in relatively isolated or simple dynastic and religious patterns. The horizon broadened immensely; diplomatic history became more complicated.

On May 17, 1756, the French King Louis XV signed a pact at Versailles with Maria Theresa under which France would help Austria recapture Silesia and would receive in return important cities and positions in the Low Countries and the Rhineland. The war commenced with several French victories over the British, but William Pitt became prime minister and consoled his sovereign with the prescient words: "We shall win America on the continent of Europe."

To achieve this aim, London helped to keep the Europeans, and above all the French, fighting as long as possible among themselves. Russia's Empress Elizabeth, who hated Frederick, joined a coalition against him and was promised East Prussia as an ultimate reward. She and her partner, Maria Theresa, made open military preparations and, with their joint populations of 100 million, prepared to squash the five million Prussians. The Elector of Saxony also participated, hoping to occupy Berlin which was but thirty miles from his frontier. But Frederick, who was encouraged by British financial aid and diplomatic support, decided on a swift preventive attack. He started operations with an assault on Dresden, the lovely Saxon metropolis.

The Austrian empress sent an army to aid the elector, but Frederick defeated it at Lobositz. Saxony surrendered and was placed under Prussian administration for the duration of the conflict. Voltaire quipped caustically: "If Frederick continues to be lucky and glorious, my old liking for him will be justified. If he is beaten I shall be avenged."

In 1757 Frederick resolved to hit and smash the Austrians before their slow-moving French and Russian allies could attack. He drove into Bohemia and Prague. Nevertheless, he paid dearly for his victory, and the Austrians joined with large French and Russian armies to force him to abandon east Prussia. Frederick recovered his confidence and pulverized a French force at Rossbach, near Leipzig, causing Voltaire to comment shrewdly that Teutonic nationalism had been born on that battlefield, changing the German destiny. The conflict ended with a crushing Prussian triumph at Leuthen with enormously heavy casualties. Maria Theresa piously expressed the hope: "In the end God will have pity on us and crush this monster."

Russia's Empress Elizabeth died in 1762, thus saving the situation for Frederick, whose forces, despite the brilliant generalship of their commanders, had been sadly depleted by the overwhelming manpower superiority of the enemy alliance. The new czar, Peter III, admired the Prussian ruler and enabled him to make his claim to Silesia permanent, a fact formally recognized in the Treaty of Hubertusburg of February 15, 1763.

Both Austria and Prussia found themselves in a difficult situation when the conflict ended. Russia had deserted Austria and Peter had entered into full partnership with Frederick, but Peter's widow and successor, the Empress Catherine, soon withdrew to a neutral stance. The former warring powers were persuaded by the King of Poland's death to band together and partition his disorganized country, cynically obliterating the independence of the gallant Poles in contravention of all diplomatic law. Frederick, who gained less than Russia or Austria from this surgery, sneered at Maria Theresa, "She took though she wept," while the French ambassador in Vienna quipped, "She carved territory from Poland with one hand and used her handkerchief with the other."

The Polish surgery was completed in 1772. Frederick gained only 644 square miles and 600,000 inhabitants but reinforced the strength of his small nation. Austria gained the most in wealth and Russia the most in quantity of land. Yet the greatest result of the war and this partition was the introduction of Russia to the border of Germanic lands in central Europe.

Frederick was a military genius whose talent for leadership greatly impressed the soldiers who fought for him. When he spoke emotionally to his troops before battle, they often wept, and they hailed him as "Fritz" when he exchanged coarse jokes with them. He showed much concern about their morale, fed them well, and issued wine to all ranks. He sought to employ them on advantageous ground and to support them with decisive artillery. In his military instructions to his generals, he recalled that the big guns are decisive; Marshal Turenne had seventy, but what would he say to the 200 Frederick had assembled? Lord Acton, in his *Lectures on Modern History*, said Frederick was the first great soldier to reject the doctrine that a tactically inferior force could be strategically superior; he proved that "nothing can destroy the enemy except a pitched battle."

John Burgoyne, the British general who became unhappily famous in America for his 1777 defeat at Saratoga, had commented with inaccurate bias on the military state of Prussia in 1766–1767:

> The excellence of the Prussian troops appears the more extraor-
> dinary when we consider the disadvantages attending them
> unknown to other states. The ranks are filled up perhaps more
> than a third part with strangers, deserters, prisoners, and enemies
> of various countries, languages, and religions. They cannot
> therefore be actuated by any of the great moving principles which
> usually cause extraordinary superiority in armies; they have

neither national spirit not attachment to their prince, nor enthusiasm nor hopes of fortune, not even prospect of comfortable old age to inspire them.

In an army thus composed, it is wisdom and sound policy to sink and degrade all intellectual faculties, and to reduce the man as nearly as possible to mere machinery, and indeed as nature has formed the bulk of the King of Prussia's subjects that is not very difficult. . . . many of his disciples suppose his necessity to be his choice. . . . the vigor of the army is in the subalterns and noncommissioned officers who undoubtedly are the best in the world.

These observations are interesting as coming from an experienced British officer but do not coincide with the great majority of contemporary opinions which stress that the bulk of Frederick's forces were made up of his Prussian subjects and that they had extraordinary "attachment to their prince."

Ever since his accession to the throne in 1740, Frederick had been Germany's disturbing genius, and he swiftly displayed his ability to teach his age lessons in both war and policy. He defeated successive coalitions during coming years, and even diplomatic setbacks could not persuade him to relinquish key possessions he had gained like Silesia. With little tangible aid except financial grants from England, he managed to defeat alliances that included Austria, Russia, Sweden, France, Saxony, and a collection of German states from the Holy Roman Empire.

As a philosopher-despot he demonstrated several reform achievements in his administration. For his time he was an enlightened ruler, banishing whores and luxury from his court and living for the most part in Spartan simplicity. He sought to insure equal justice for rich and poor and scorned the customary degradation of torture. The administrative machine he established was both economic and efficient. And on the battlefield he was superb. The Marquis de Belle-Isle, a French general and diplomat, wrote of Frederick: "He was born with a first-class intelligence, which pushes him toward great designs; he is full of fire; has a keen and penetrating sense of what men are like, quick to pounce on and take advantage of their foibles; never asks advice and indeed could not do so safely since he is surrounded by people in the pay of Austria. He has no heart whatsoever."

The philosopher Hegel thought Frederick's Prussia an ideal state in which the king took an eager interest in such small things as the raising of chickens, the price of coffee, the manufacture of porcelain, as well as boosting national revenues, maneuvering armies, and acquiring new territories.

During his later years Frederick was a semi-invalid. He had to be carried about like a sacred object because of his painful gout and hemorrhoids. His legs were often covered with rugs and his swollen hands hidden in a muff. He was tormented by abscesses in his ear. He lost so many teeth that he could no longer play his beloved flute.

His final illness began in August 1786. For two days he suffered, spending much time in a chair listening to a courtier reading from Voltaire's *Précis du Siècle de Louis XV*. On his last evening, he lay in bed awake as his dog shivered, and ordered his servants to cover the hound with a quilt. On August 17 he died and was buried on the terrace of Sans Souci beside his horse and his dogs. Twenty years later Napoleon stood with his officers beside the coffin, which later had been transferred to Berlin's Garrison Church, and said: "Hats off, gentlemen. If he were still alive, we should not be here."

III

The Progeny of Napoleon's Black General: Alexander Dumas, Père et Fils

I have always been fascinated by the legend that the father of Alexander Dumas was the strongest, stupidest general in the armies of Napoleon. In the hopes of casting some light on this report, I drove one day to the old fortified seat of Vincennes, accompanied by my faithful companion Christopher Beagle. Vincennes, once a royal castle, has held among its military memoranda the *Service Historique de l'Armée de Terre* of France since those impressive documents began to be classified in orderly fashion during the eighteenth century.

An appointment had been arranged some days earlier with the chief archivist Le Général Jean Delmas, who had compiled for me all available material on Dumas. Christopher, who was not allowed in these august and austere quarters, was guided through the old forest by a kindly sergeant driver.

Before we commenced our serious research, Delmas explained that it had not been an easy task since, during the Napoleonic era, there had been no less than four generals surnamed Dumas. However, his aides and scholars had come up with all available material, he said, pointing to a thick folder on his desk beside which nestled a book called *The Dictionary of Georges Jix: A Dictionary of Generals and Admirals of the Revolution and the Empire* (as translated from the French). Delmas said the archives were complete save for the period of the 1920s. When the Nazi army occupied Paris during World War II, its historical experts had carefully carted off to the Reich the entire collection for that decade.

"Why?" I inquired, puzzled.

"They were looking for all information on German citizens who collaborated with the French during the period when we occupied the Rhineland."

"You mean like Konrad Adenauer?" I asked.

"Precisely. But the Germans are very orderly. So far as we can determine, there is nothing from our other dossiers missing."

A prim, erect, sharp-featured man, Delmas first interrogated me politely on the reasons for my research, and I told him they were partly to satisfy intrigued curiosity and partly because I was considering writing an essay dealing with the three principal Dumases: the general; the great novelist famed the world around as author of *The Three Musketeers;* and his son, who wrote the well-known work—first as a play, then as a novel— entitled *The Lady of the Camellias.* The latter two, both bearing the Christian name Alexander, generally referred to themselves and each other (and so did the entire literary world) as *"Dumas Père"* and *"Dumas Fils."*

"Well," said Delmas. "Let us begin. It is going to be a long task."

The general was quickly and definitively located as Thomas-Alexandre Davy de La Pailleterie, called Alexandre (or Alexander, in English), and born in Jérémie, Saint Domingue in the Antilles, March 25, 1762, and died at Villers-Cotterêts, Aisne, February 26, 1806. He was the bastard son of Marquis Alexandre-Antoine Davy de La Pailleterie and a black slave, Cessie Dumas.

The young mulatto's desire for a military career is easily understandable if he was as huge and powerful as generally described. Jix refers to "his tall stature and his Herculean strength." But was this indeed the case? An original leave permit from his regiment shows the dragoon was granted such permission in 1792 and specifically describes him as "five feet eight inches" tall. Certainly even in that era of somewhat smaller humans, five feet eight was not "tall stature" and did not forcefully imply "Herculean strength," unless he was built like a Bulgarian weight-lifter.

Whatever his intellectual and physical capacities, Dumas had a remarkably swift series of promotions. In July 1793 he was named *général de brigade;* barely two months later, *général en chef* (commander in chief) of the Army of the Western Pyrenees; three months after that, *général en chef* of the Army of the Alps, fielded by the government of the Revolutionary Committee of Public Safety. The next year he was made commander of the Brest Coast, and then *général de division* on the Sambre-et-Meuse. Later he commanded all cavalry in the Italian campaign, then was appointed head of a cavalry division at Mantua. The confusion in ranks, according to Delmas, results from the fact that in those days there were only two ranks of generals: brigadier general and major general (*général de brigade*); above came the Marshals.

His succession of commands implies that Dumas was considered a courageous officer. A Bonapartist general, Thibault, recalled of him:

> There was another *général de division* under Masséna's command, named Dumas. He was a mulatto, not without ability, and quite the bravest, strongest and most active man whom I have ever known.
>
> His reputation in the army was extraordinary. His many deeds of chivalrous daring and athletic skill were quoted far and wide. Nevertheless, in spite of his great personal courage, and no matter how important the duties laid upon him, and even of his being known as one of the foremost soldiers of his day, destiny never seemingly intended Dumas to be a general.

All this adds to the mystery; why should he receive one command after another if he was considered incompetent in high quarters? Even if Bonaparte truly told Desgenettes, senior medical officer of the French army in Egypt, that "intelligence was not his strong point" (which remains to be proven), there have been many successful generals in the past—some in Napoleon's armies—who were far from bright. Bonaparte, it is known of course, preferred lucky commanders to skillful ones. No one can say Dumas was lucky. Delmas ruefully agreed, when I observed as much.

On the Egyptian expedition, it is evident—although the reasons are not entirely clear—that he did not get on with Napoleon. He was surely more republican-minded than the future emperor. On the way back to France, Dumas was aboard a ship captured by the Kingdom of the Two Sicilies (then commanded by France's enemies) and held a prisoner by the Neapolitans. When he was finally released, he asked for a new post as soon as his health would permit but complained of a painful growth on the eye (called a *loupe*). He also requested pay due to him for his months as a prisoner of war, but neither this nor his wife's appeal for a pension—after Dumas's death—was granted. The refusal for the latter was made on the ground that he had not died on the field of battle. A few of Dumas's old comrades made mention of the late general's exploits, and Napoleon barked curt refusal. It even proved impossible to obtain a scholarship for his son Alexander, the famous author-to-be, at a *lycée* or a military school.

One might assume that this would be the succinct, final record of

General Thomas-Alexandre Dumas had it been left to the chroniclers of that confused, disorderly moment in French history. But fortunately for the literary edification of future generations, if not for the cool bones of accurate history, the general's son, Alexander Dumas *Père*, one of the world's greatest storytellers, took it upon himself to write in much detail about his parent in his memoirs.

The tales the son tells about his military father are exuberant, if surely often untrue. Dumas *Père* was a great storyteller and writer of fiction, and I venture to say his picture of the general ranks high among his delightful fictional creations. It is virtually positive that young Alexander's assertion that he had "often" seen his father ride into a stable and chin himself on the crossbeam while raising his heavy cavalry charger between his knees, is impossible. Likewise the account of Papa thrusting four fingers into heavy musket barrels and lifting them parallel to the ground is highly improbable; especially since young Dumas, as well as many others, asserts the general had delicate, small, ladylike hands and feet. It all seems derived from sixteenth-century legends young Alexander heard while working in the Royal Orléans household. But anyone capable of inventing d'Artagnan and the Count of Monte Cristo was capable of embellishing that already unusual character of Napoleon's mulatto general, the "Horatius of the Tyrol."

The real head of the family, Alexander-Antoine Davy de La Pailleterie, a French marquis of aristocratic Norman lineage, went off to the Antilles in search of a sugar fortune. He ended up living on a modest estate on the southwestern peninsula of Saint Domingue with a young black slave known as Marie-Cessette Dumas, who soon produced Thomas-Alexandre. After her death when the boy was thirteen, Pailleterie decided to return to France, where he disembarked under the alias he had employed in the Caribbean, Antoine Delisle. Two years later, in 1775, he sold his property. It is probable that his boy, the future general, was brought back to France in 1776 by a Lieutenant Roussel, who listed him for the authorities as his "slave Alexandre." For some years thereafter, the marquis and his son lived together at St. German-en-Laye, outside Paris.

Dumas *Père* wrote that, when he was twenty-two, he went to the well-known Nicolet theater, which specialized in ballet. One evening he picked up an attractive girl, asking if she "liked Americans," as the French then referred to their Antilles colonials. He had a slight altercation with a nearby Frenchman, who sniffed at him as at a "servant." That was apparently the end of the affair. Dumas *Père*, however, embellished the same event in his memoirs, saying the lady was a lovely Creole with a loose reputation, and when she and Thomas-Alexandre were approached by an "impertinent musketeer," the youth chucked him over the rail into the orchestra below, then fought him in a duel. Thomas-Alexandre was summoned before a magistrate, the Duc de Richelieu, to whom he appeared as "Count de La Pailleterie," and was merrily released by the duke, for whom his father, the marquis, had acted in the role of second at another and fatal duel. So says Dumas *Père*.

Young Thomas-Alexandre decided two years after that incident to enlist in the army and intended to do so under his paternal family name of Pailleterie. For lack of great influence at a court already shaken by political tremors and with no training as an officer, he sought to enroll in the Queen's Dragoons as a common trooper.

His father, the marquis, was snob enough to rebuke him accordingly: "Son, I don't intend that you should drag my name among the last ranks of the army." In 1786 he signed up as Dumas, a simple horse soldier, and joined a garrison at Laon.

So agitated were the times and so uncertain the future, with embattled France ringed by enemies and torn by mounting internal dissent, that the courageous young mulatto within four years found himself promoted to the rank of lieutenant-colonel under the name Thomas-Alexandre Dumas. He had been billeted at Villers-Cotterêts, a former hunting seat outside Paris of King François 1, in the home of a charming girl named Marie-Louise Elizabeth Labouret. He married her, under the name "Lt. Col. Dumas, son of Alexandre-Antoine Davy de La Pailleterie," on November 28, 1792. Shortly after the marriage, he was dispatched to the volunteer "American Legion."

Alexander Dumas *Père* takes special pains when referring to his father to correctly call him "the (republican) general Thomas-Alexandre," etc. For there is no doubt that his republicanism did not exactly please his parent whose family had received its marquisate from King Louis XIV only in 1707. There is also much reason to believe that it played an important role in his dispute with the great genius first listed on the rolls as General "Buonaparte," then "Bonaparte," then "Napoleon," first consul, and finally "Emperor Napoleon I." When Thomas-Alexandre first entered military service he renounced both his title (to oblige the marquis) and his coat of arms, substituting the slogan *Deus dedit, Deus dabit* (God gave, God will give). But this modest switch clearly did not disturb his son, the author, despite Alexander's known penchant for snobbery and social climbing. Of course these events long antedate the novelist's sentient personality, as he was but four years old when the unhappy mulatto general died.

According to Dumas *Père*, as soon as his father was promoted from the ranks and rose rapidly up the ladder of generalship, he became a close associate of many of the aristocrats who managed to float atop the turgid foam of the revolution, including the La Fayettes, Lameths, Dillons, Lauxuns, and the great fencing master, Laboissière. And, on at least one occasion, as already described, he had to do with the Duc de Richelieu, a great marshal whom, after he captured Spain's Porto Mahon, gave mayonnaise its name.

The novelist describes the new recruit as "one of the handsomest young men it was possible to see," which statement is not borne out by any paintings or drawings of the young trooper in the museum of his hometown, Villers-Cotterêts. By this time Dumas *Père* is calling his parent "gigantic," at five feet nine inches tall, by no means yet huge but a one-inch gain. He describes him as "a true American cavalier, a gaucho," of whom famous and redoubtable warriors were jealous.

The cavalry trooper's first commission as general was given at Bayonne (and this is known fact, not Dumas fiction). From there he zigzagged across western France from the western Pyrenees to the Vendée. He earned a reputation for energy and courage and reestablished a semblance of order and discipline in the ferment of brigandage and sacking that was an inevitable harbinger of revolution. In 1793, at the age of thirty-one, he was named *général en chef* of the Alpine command, succeeding the famous heavy cavalryman Kellermann, who was to become one of Napoleon's more redoubtable commanders.

General Dumas made a name for himself, his son says, as a great rock-scrambler and hunter of chamois, and distributed several thousand crampons to his troops to enable them to mount jagged peaks. According to his son, the general achieved notable successes thanks to his courage and strength. For his efforts he was ordered back to Paris and threatened with that increasingly popular instrument, the guillotine, charged with an offense of which he was ultimately acquitted.

It was at this stage of his career that he was bothered for the first time by a painful growth on his eye which became constantly worse and from which he may well in the end have died. Alexander *Père* claimed the growth resulted from one of three duels in which the general maintained the precedence of the queen over the king, neither of whom had yet been executed by the mob.

At this point Napoleon entered into his life, signing an order to him as "chief of the army of the interior." Dumas was swiftly shifted to the army of Sambre-et-Meuse, then to the Army of the Rhine, and finally back to the Alps, but one example of the confusion and contradictory orders that gripped

France at that moment of internal revolution and external wars against a shifting panorama of enemies. It was only then that Bonaparte decided, in concert with Barras—who was to be the last surviving member of the revolution's executive directorate before Napoleon swept it away with a coup—that a massive victory over Italy and its Austrian allies was required. General Dumas, commanding a veteran Alpine division, swept down to Milan in 1796 at Bonaparte's orders and, according to his son Alexander, was especially admired by the conqueror's consort, Josephine, herself a Creole.

According to his novelist son, a Venetian spy was brought before the cavalry commander and was caught swallowing a morsel of paper. He was dosed with an emetic, after some rough pleasantries about having his guts ripped open, and a secret dispatch from Francis II, the Holy Roman Emperor and chief of the anti-French coalition, was extracted from a small ball of wax. This included tiny script ordering a new plan of action in the Po valley, and also disclosed that Venice and Tuscany were secretly aiding Vienna. As a result of his coup, Dumas received from his commander in chief's headquarters at Milan (dated December 28), the following:

ARMÉE D'ITALIE
RÉPUBLIQUE FRANCAISE
Liberté—Égalité
Bonaparte, général en chef de l'armée d'Italie,
au général Dumas

I have received the letter brought to me by your aide de camp; it was impossible to have more apt information on the essentials. . . . I beg you to send the spy you have arrested under good escort to Milan.

I congratulate you on your good success and foresee a better one.   *Bonaparte*

Nevertheless, it was not long before hints appeared that Bonaparte was far from enamored of Dumas. At an interrogation he asked how he had replied to the withdrawal orders he received from his superior general, Serrurier.

Dumas answered: "Retreat to the devil if you wish; I won't bat an eye; as for me, I'll kill but I won't retreat."

"Do you know," asked Bonaparte, "if you were to write me a letter like that I would have you shot?"

"That's possible; but you would probably never write me a letter like the one General Serrurier wrote me."

According to Dumas *Père:* "That's true, said Bonaparte simply."

Soon afterward General Dumas, who was surely not short on courage, fought a heroic battle against great odds in front of Mantua, capturing six enemy standards, which he was ordered to turn over to Serrurier, whom he detested. He wrote Bonaparte: "General: I learn that the prick charged with making a report to you on the battle I fought remained in an observation post throughout the affray. I wish him no more similar observations made while he is shitting in his pants. Salutations and brotherhood. Alex. Dumas."

To no one's astonishment Dumas was coldly demoted and transferred to another front.

Within six months Bonaparte had taken 100,000 prisoners, 400 cannon, and destroyed five Austro-Italian armies in Italy. The frightened pope ceded to France Avignon, Ancona, and the Romagna. But Dumas never regained Bonaparte's good graces, although General Joubert reported to the emperor that the mulatto horseman had become "the terror of the Austrian cavalry." This encomium was confirmed shortly thereafter in the Tyrol, where, near Brixen, Dumas held a bridge alone against a series of charging Austrian dragoons, was sabered three times, and had a steed killed under him. Subsequently, he was widely called "Horatius of the Tyrol" by his admiring horsemen. His cape was scarred by seven bullet holes, none of which grazed him.

That was no doubt a flamboyant, romantic, and devil-may-care period of warfare. Dumas *Père* recounts in his memoirs that one day his father was seated at a table with Generals Hoche and Marceau; all three were ranked as *généraux en chefs* of armies. One was twenty-four, one was twenty-six, and Dumas, the eldest, was thirty-one.

Joubert, who was the victorious general of the Tyrol, owed much of his success to Dumas's exploits as a cavalryman and repaid this debt by using his own good relations with Bonaparte to praise his black general to the irascible Corsican. Indeed, it was thanks to Joubert that Bonaparte grumpily relented and suggested to their mutual friend: "Send me Dumas." The sensitive, hot-blooded mulatto sulked but finally agreed to go and see his fiery little boss.

Bonaparte, according to Dumas *Père*, started the interview tactfully by saluting the "Horatius of the Tyrol" and flattering the last vestige of bitterness out of the sullen dragoon. Then the supreme commander requested him to organize a complete army of cavalry divisions, something like the panzer armies Adolf Hitler was to create almost a century and a half later. While the initial bureaucratic phases were being taken care of, Dumas was appointed governor of the province of Trevisan in Venetia.

The astoundingly victorious north Italian campaign in which both the Italian city-states plus those forces rallied to the Pope and also the immense, well-commanded armies of the Austrian empire were shattered, ended with the Treaty of Campo-Formio in 1797. Vienna yielded its control of Belgium, Mainz, Mannheim, and Austrian Lombardy, and Bonaparte was henceforth established without rival as the military genius of his day.

Promptly, with more than a slight memory of the achievements of an earlier conqueror, Alexander the Great, he mounted an expedition against Egypt and by the sheerest accidental luck missed the British Admiral Nelson's warfleet, which was hoping to intercept him. The French transports, inadequately protected by gunboats, landed at Alexandria, where the great Jean Baptiste Kléber attacked the walls largely manned by ardent, tough Turks. General Dumas was one of the first French commanders to land, and, according to his admiring if not always accurate son, "his great height and brown color" somewhat resembling the Arabs, strongly impressed the garrison. Once again, according to Dumas *Père* Bonaparte sent for the mulatto general and ordered him to head the small vanguard intruding inland, so its members could see the skin of the very first general they had to deal with was not of an unfamiliar hue.

Dumas *Père* claims with much justice that the morale of the expeditionary force left much to be desired. Nelson had at last found the French and destroyed their fleet at Aboukir, pretty well cutting them off from home. Aboukir was one of the great naval victories of history. Not only did the French lose ten times as much as the British; Napoleon's army suddenly found itself isolated in Egypt; the recapture of Malta (briefly seized by the French) was assured to Nelson; Britain's Mediterranean prestige was restored; and all Europe was heartened in its resistance to the French juggernaut.

Alexander Dumas stresses his father's "spirit of republicanism" at this time and also says he was bored by lack of an adequate command, having been made city commandant in Cairo, which was not a fighting job. His tendency toward bad humor was greatly enhanced by the growing depression of the entire invading army, cut off as it was by Nelson's victorious fleet. Bonaparte was fully aware of this bleak mood and bawled out a group of generals, selecting Dumas as the principal target because he was one of the tallest and allegedly saying: "Your five feet six inches wouldn't prevent you from being shot in two hours." He later bawled out the dragoon for "behaving badly toward me and seeking to demoralize the army" (at least, so says Alexander the fiction writer).

According to the novelist, his father told Bonaparte he opposed all dictatorships from that of Sulla to that of Julius Caesar, and he requested permission to return to France at the first possible opportunity. Bonaparte said he would place no hindrance in his way. Shortly before his departure from Egypt, General Dumas discovered a rich treasure in the house of a wealthy bey where he was quartered and turned it over to Bonaparte with a note saying "an honest man doesn't change his conscience."

The dragoon was able to find space aboard a small ship bound for Europe called *La Belle-Maltaise* and embarked with General Manscourt and other discontented French officers and civilians who had been granted permission to leave. He was captured at Brindisi by vessels of the Neapolitan Kingdom of the Two Sicilies, which had meantime aligned itself with Austria against France.

As a prisoner the general was warned that attempts would be made to poison him, his son contends, and, he claims, his death was caused by some form of stomach cancer resulting from such efforts; other versions, though, have it that the growth in his eye turned malignant in the end. Despite all his requests for amnesty or exchange, Dumas was kept a prisoner of war for twenty months until he escaped via Ancona through a friendly mediary. The general wrote a long, somewhat sad account of the drawn-out incident when he got to Florence, then in French hands.

He claimed to have left Egypt only because of bad health (which wasn't true) and even acknowledged his friends regarded him as complaining of "an imaginary illness." But he said he suffered from paralysis in the left cheek, intestinal pains, and vomiting, leading him to the belief that he had been poisoned in the course of medical treatments he had sought. In fact, although he was later treated on return to France by the best known physician of the times, Dr. Jean Corvisart, he never improved.

It was finally arranged through the Austrians, Neapolitans, and French that Dumas would be formally freed and exchanged for the renowned Austrian General Karl Mack, captured at Ulm. Bonaparte, disheartened by military failures both in the Levant and Italy, set sail from Egypt for the French harbor of Fréjus, where he arrived in 1799. Promptly thereafter he staged his famous coup of the 18th Brumaire and made himself first consul.

When Bonaparte was back in France, General Dumas wrote him somewhat pitiably requesting the back pay due him for his long incarceration as a prisoner of war. He never received recompense, although in 1793 he held the rank of *général en chef* of the armies of the Republic and although he was at the time of writing the senior general officer of his grade who had served Bonaparte faithfully in Italy and Egypt. His pleas were never acknowledged. After his return to his modest home in the austere town of Villers-Cotterêts, warned that he would soon be dead, General Dumas sought to see Napoleon, who refused to receive him. Shortly thereafter he died, a poor man living with his wife's family. He was never even awarded the very lowest grade of the Legion of Honor. Napoleon knew how to hate. When Dumas's widow implored a group of Dumas's friends, all generals or marshals, to beg the emperor to grant her a pension, Napoleon said curtly: "I forbid you ever to speak to me of that man." Marshal Jourdan, one of the group, wrote Madame Dumas that only the widows of those slain in battle were eligible for assistance.

By far the most famous of the remarkable trio of Dumases was Alexander Dumas *Père*, who is still almost as widely read around the world as during his lifetime and was endowed both with incredible energy and a limitless imagination, each of which served him well.

Alexander was born July 24, 1802 to the dragoon and his wife, Marie-Louise Labouret. The boy proved to be intelligent, if mentally lazy. A hulking, muscular youth, he was fond of physical exercise and always dreaming of soldierly weapons.

The confused politics of France following the Battle of Waterloo were a handicap for such a self-assured young man as Alexander. He tried studying for the priesthood but was ultimately fortunate in obtaining, through his father's friends, employment in the office of the Duc d'Orléans, later enthroned as King Louis-Philippe. He found lodging at 1, Place des Italiens and a desk in the Palais-Royal, headquarters of the Orléans political faction.

On the same landing as his room was a small dressmaking workshop run by a woman named Catherine Labais, a native of Rouen. She became his mistress and later presented Alexander with a son, the Dumas *Fils* who became almost as famous in the nineteenth-century *beau monde* of Paris as his father. While the little dressmaker supported the latter, he collaborated on unsuccessful plays with a Swedish nobleman. His first triumph was *Henri III et sa Cour* produced by the *Comédie Francqise*, which earned him the friendship of the renowned Victor Hugo. The Duke d'Orleans, his patron, made him librarian of the Palais Royal.

Dumas *Père*'s initial striking dramatic success was *Antony*, produced at the Porte Saint-Martin before a hysterically clapping audience. Young women fell passionately for the role of Antony and fashionable youths vowed themselves prepared to blow out their brains for the female lead, Adèle d'Hervey. Suddenly, at twenty-eight, the already obese young man with a tinge of Negroid ancestry in his features, found himself the day's most celebrated dramatist, ranked with his great friend Hugo. Indeed the two were often fêted together as the "two rivals."

After both political and literary ups-and-downs, the dizzying success of *Antony* inflated Dumas's inherent self-confidence. He had charming manners, was well-set up, very much a dandy, and by no means as gross in appearance as he was to become. He had a thick head of hair and non-African blue eyes which twinkled above his cocky mustache. He triumphed with countless women after he abandoned his mistress Mélanie Waldor. In 1840 he married the actress Ida Ferrier, from whom he soon separated.

After King Louis-Philippe had entertained at a lavish fancy-dress ball, Dumas's friends urged him to do the same because "Yours will be better in two ways. You won't have the people who go to royal parties and you won't have the *Académie*." He managed to gather in his modest apartments Paris's greatest painters: Delacroix, Nanteuil, and the Boulanger cousins, who were all among his personal friends.

Dumas *Père* was a famous collaborator and depended heavily on his assistants. His play *La Tour de Nesle* was received with raves as a fashionable melodrama, but drama, as a form, was leaving the forefront of French literature for the novel: de Vigny's, Hugo's *Notre Dame de Paris;* Balzac; Merimée; Zola.

Recognizing this trend, Dumas made a thorough study of the craft of Walter Scott and concluded correctly that there was a fortune to be exploited in the realm of fictionalized French history. Since his experience with the little-known Swede, Leuven, he had found it convenient to work in tandem with other writers and started his new endeavors with the collaboration of Fréderic Gaillardet, Jules Janin, and Auguste Maguet (with whom he wrote *The Three Musketeers* and who was by far his most successful partner).

He even worked in tandem with the eccentric poet Gérard de Nerval, who sometimes strode the boulevards dragging a lobster on a leash, other times pulling a piglet with the pope's face painted on its pink behind.

The Musketeers series was as well known in Britain as in France and was a favorite of Andrew Lang, William Thackeray, and Robert Louis Stevenson. At the height of his glory, in one year (1844) Dumas completed a second great romance twelve volumes long *The Count of Monte-Cristo*. Of all his novels there is no doubt that those he accomplished with Maguet were the best. Maguet, however, was never alone able to approach his collaborator's talent.

Evidently to satisfy his vanity while at the same time developing an assembly-line method of producing books, Dumas meticulously copied out in his own handwriting all those portions of his manuscripts written by collaborators. In this way he hoped to persuade literary critics and historians of the future that he had written every word himself.

Dumas *Père* as a personality was perhaps most renowned for the astonishing vitality he had inherited from his father. He knew everyone of importance from the king of France to George Sand to Garibaldi, the unifier of modern Italy. His triumphs with distinguished (and other) women were prodigious. At twenty-eight he was already considered the greatest dramatist of his time, and he was as highly esteemed as the far more talented Victor Hugo.

This boundlessly zestful man had no scholastic pretensions, despite the fact that most of what he dealt with pretended to relate fact. "What is history?" he inquired boastfully. "Oh, it is the nail on which I hang my novels."

In all French literature there is nothing comparable to his quantitative production (with or without helpers) during the decade starting with 1845. And most of his works were prodigiously long; many were continuations of each other; and some were occasionally repetitious, spanning an intensely active period from the sixteenth century to the termination of the French monarchy. Like so many other French authors, past and present, he did everything to gain admission to the *Académie*—and failed. He even abased himself and wrote to the editor of *La Revue des Deux Mondes*, a prestigious intellectual journal: "Do mention me in the *Revue*, in connection with the *Académie*, and express wonder that I am not up for election." And again, two years later: "Put a piece about me in your periodical with the *Académie* in view. I am not on the next list of candidates, but feel pretty sure that people are surprised that I am not."

He never was accepted; but neither was that more finely honed talent Zola. Nor, this century, were Proust, Gide, Sartre, Malraux.

During the 1840s, when Dumas's career was at its zenith, he made countless enemies among jealous rivals, with his bragging, his flaming waistcoats, his penchant for blazing decorations. People sneered at his book "factory," which could financially seduce such gifted writers as Nerval. He was attacked in a widely read pamphlet, *Fabrique de Romans: Maison Alexandre Dumas & Cie*.

Today Dumas's most widely known novel is *The Three Musketeers*, but close behind nudges *The Count of Monte-Cristo*. Like so many of the fires that continually ignited in Dumas's brain, this struck by accident when he learned that an islet of that name not far from Elba was renowned for its shooting. After composing at feverish speed his book based on that name, he decided to celebrate his triumph by building his own "Château de Monte-Cristo" on a property he had already leased at Saint-Germain-en-Laye to which he had transferred the famous *Comédie Française* theatrical troupe. Subsequently, he changed his mind and constructed an identically named "Renaissance château" in an "English park" near Bougival.

There he lived like a grand duke. Six hundred friends were invited to his housewarming, catered by an expensive restaurant. And proudly he strutted among his guests, resplendent in his decorations. These splendiferous tastes (which also included an apartment in the capital) proved excessive even for his pocketbook. He was declared bankrupt and Monte-Cristo was sold for a pitiful sum.

Dumas's personality was as colorful as his books, and he could transfix an audience with his conversation. There is one report that he described the Battle of Waterloo to a group of generals who had taken part in the affray, moving about imagined divisions with impeccable skill. One listener allegedly said: "But, my dear sir, it wasn't like that at all. We were there." Dumas replied cheerfully: "All I can say, General, is that you didn't pay attention to what was going on."

As both novelist and short story writer Dumas *Père* continued his extraordinarily popular "cloak and épée" romances right through the middle of the nineteenth century, piling new intrigue on old intrigue and adventure on adventure, so that his originally youthful daredevil characters gradually aged in print. Even the young gallant d'Artagnan became a mature musketeer officer, and Porthos, one of the famed three musketeers, died heroically. At the same time he founded a *Théâtre Historique* primarily to feature his own dramas.

Despite his rather snobbish personal attachment to the royal French house of Orléans, his political opinions were republican, and he always bore a grudge against Napoleon for the way he had treated his father. He was enthusiastic over the 1848 revolution and unsuccessfuly sought an electoral post in the department of the Yonne. In 1853 he established a daily, *Le Mousquetaire*, devoted primarily to literary and artistic criticism. This was succeeded four years later by *Monte-Cristo*, another journal.

The Goncourts wrote of him:

Dined yesterday with the Princess—a company of literary men, among them Dumas. A kind of giant with a negro's hair now turning "pepper and salt," the small eye of a hippopotamus, bright, shrewd and forever on the watch even when the lids are half closed, and all this in an enormous face, the features of which are vaguely hemispherical, like those the caricaturists give when they portray the moon with human characteristics. There is something about him very hard to define in verbal color. What he talks about is facts, curious facts, *staggering* facts which he drags up in a hoarse voice from the recesses of a tremendous memory. And always, always, always he talks about himself, with the vanity of a great child which never gets on one's nerves.

Old Dumas was still lively enough to conquer a young American actress, Adah Isaacs Mencken. She had been married three times already before she wedded him, contending it was "love at first sight." Two days later she sailed away and, after a serious illness, died in 1868.

Dumas *Père* lingered on three more years. His output had been so prodigious that he was wholly or partially responsible for ninety-one works. He wrote plenty of trash and forgotten, picayune trifles, but his vivid, dashing tales are still devoured by the youth of innumerable lands. It is hard to see how this obese bundle of brash energy had time to tumble from dinner to dinner and bed to bed in perhaps the most brilliant, liveliest Paris of all time. Duelist, bankrupt, lover, coxscomb, roué, loyal friend, and father, when he left the scene, he left a huge gap.

He was buried in December 1871 at Neuville-lès-Pollet, shortly after the Franco-Prussian War. Subsequently, Dumas *Fils* had the body exhumed and taken to the family property at Villers-Cotterêts, where he was lain beside his father, the unlucky general whom Bonaparte detested.

How different was Alexander Dumas III. I had a great-uncle who lived many years in Paris: a mediocre landscapist and miniature painter who inhabited the *Ville Lumière* during the epoch of Dumas *Fils* and George du Maurier, authors of those respective hits *The Lady of the Camellias* and *Trilby*, only the first of which manifested gleams of talent.

My relative became a respected gourmet and amateur chef, and he found the dizzily intellectual wit of the *Grands Boulevards* quite overwhelming. It is possible that he, like others, exaggerated the brilliance if not the gusto of the era. All these years later, most of it seems like tinseled boredom. But how will our own braggart Jet Age sound two generations hence?

Although *Trilby* is associated with Paris during the gay, wastral, scandal-ridden Third Republic period, the French-born Englishman, du Maurier, had less talent and less personality than the bumptious, witty younger Dumas.

Dumas *Fils* recalls of his mother: "Happily my mother was a good woman, and worked hard to bring me up." He also acknowledged his father's true quality, writing: "By a most lucky chance he happened to be well-natured and as soon as his first successes as a dramatist [enabled him to do so] recognized me and gave me my name."

Later, when the generous Marie endorsed this act to help him along the path of fame, she had also to confess she was unmarried in order to make the inheritance deed legally valid under a complex law. Many, many years later, long after the father had deserted his former mistress, who was currently living a model life, Dumas *Fils* suggested the two old people formally marry. She wisely and modestly refused, writing a friend: "I am over seventy. I am always ailing and live very simply with one servant. Monsieur Dumas would blow my little flat to pieces. It is forty years too late."

For decades these famous roués, known to each other as well as the entire beau monde of Paris as Dumas *Père* and Dumas *Fils*, shared similar lives and affections despite the age gap between them. The father wrote his offspring: "When you, too, have a son, love him as I love you, but do not rear him as I have brought you up." The younger said: "My father is a great big child whom I had when I was a small boy."

There were striking similarities between the two writing Alexanders. Both were burly, bloated men with slightly Negroid features. Both bustled with energy and had successes with many of the leading beauties of their time. Both suffered from prejudices: *Père* more from the Negritude of his features; *Fils* from the broadly advertised stigma of his illegitimate birth. Physically as well as mentally they were unusually close and had inherited a large genetic strain from the unlucky general who founded their literary dynasty and was both so muscular and so unfortunate, yet bore up against unwarranted injustice.

Dumas *Fils*, despite an acid wit, had none of the exuberant literary talent of his father. Indeed, had he never met an exceptional beauty of modest upbringing, an actress who called herself Marie Duplessis, one evening when he was seated in a front-row box overlooking the stage, his entire career could well have been otherwise and the world might never have known his talent.

The two were precisely the same age; both born in 1824. She had worked at a dressmaker's (clearly a Dumas family hunting ground) and swiftly struck that section of the Parisian audience marked by Parisian rakes: the Contades and Delesserts; the rich aristrocracy and gentry. She possessed graceful, natural manners and had carefully educated herself, reading the fashionable classics and mastering uncomplicated piano compositions. And her beauty was outstanding. Dumas *Fils* wrote: "She was tall, very slender, with black hair and a pink and white complexion. She had a small head and elongated eyes which had the enameled look to be found in the women of Japan. But there was in them something that indicated a proud and lively nature. Her lips were cherry-pink, her teeth the loveliest you could have hoped to see anywhere."

Dumas *Père* later described how his son introduced him to this ravishing conquest. One evening while attending a routine performance of the Théâtre Française, he felt a hand reach out of the door of a box, catching his coattails. It was Dumas *Fils*. "Come in here for a moment, Father," his son said.

"I opened my eyes. An adorable young woman of twenty, or twenty-two, was alone there with Alexander and had just bestowed upon me a far from daughterly greeting. I recognized her from having seen her more than once, 'in front' [on stage]. She was Marie Duplessis, the lady of the camellias."

The father instantly saw that this ravishing girl was in fact much more than that. He later recalled: "She was one of the last of those rare courtesans who had a heart." But it was evident to his experienced eye that the cost of keeping her in style would ruin his boy, who had little income.

Maurois, the excellent French biographer, who commendably leafed through truckloads of dossiers at Villers-Cotterêts, assembled many amusing facets of her character. When a friend asked why she had such a passion for lies, she said, "They keep the teeth white." She was forced by the inescapable law of the courtesan to shift from one wealthy lover to another in order to maintain her wardrobe and her reputation.

Dumas *Fils* wrote her in 1845: "My Dear Marie—I am neither rich enough to love you as I would wish, nor poor enough to be loved by you as you would. Let us both, therefore, forget—you, a name that cannot mean very much to you, I, a happiness that is no longer possible for me."

Marie surely never wished to break with him, but, it has been said, "she had become so indifferent that she gave no more thought to the day's love than she did to the morrow's passion."

She came to know *tout Paris*, from Franz Liszt to the Comte de Perregaux, whom she married in England. Finally, afflicted with tuberculosis, she died at the age of twenty-three, amid the frenzy of carnival in 1847.

Two months later the only one among her lovers who had made the name Marie Duplessis famous rented a tiny room outside Paris and reread her letters. Ignoring French literary fashion, which favored recounting love in poetry, Dumas *Fils* used prose and produced an autobiographical novel. *The Lady of the Camellias* was a success but only achieved its full acclaim when he rewrote it five years later.

Dumas *Fils* accepted his splendid triumph in a different spirit than his father. Writing came hard for him. Having lost his taste for courtesans, he had an unhappy love affair with Nadejda Knorring, widow of a Russian prince, whom he married after fathering her baby.

Gossip-prone Paris was delighted. The *Goncourt Journals* recount:

> This evening, at the Princess's, we were treated, for the first time, to a taste of young Dumas's wit. There is zest in it, somewhat on the coarse side, which nevertheless, always strikes home: ripostes which cut everybody to ribbons without any consideration for good manners: self-assurance which amounts to insolence and gives to all he says a sort of success: most noticeable of all a cruel bitterness . . . but, beyond any doubt, a humor stamped with his own personal mark, mordant, cutting, with plenty of "zip"—a great deal better to my mind than what he puts into his plays, because of its economy and its improvised sharpness.

There was passion but rarely companionship in his sexual relations. He once confessed: "All that adultery amounts to is, for the woman, hatred, and for the man contempt. So what's the point. . . . The novel of *The Lady of the Camillias* was the first fruit of those impressions."

These bitter thoughts do not accord with the general impression of champagne bubbles and elegance usually associated with Dumas *Fils*. Indeed, he held disastrously pessimistic world views. He foresaw an incomparably vast war between West and East. In many respects his visions transcended those of Jules Verne: huge explosions shattering cities; mines hurling whole landscapes into the sky.

Young Dumas was much more profoundly thoughtful than his father. Yet the two remained close, affectionate, and proud of each other. The offspring admired his parent: "He is what he is without realizing it. That is the sign by which one recognizes men of real, natural genius. Even if a lecher who misused his energies was an undoubted aspect of the man, he was a good man and a generous writer."

There was a congeniality in their opposite personalities. "I find my subjects in my dreams; my son takes his from real life," said Dumas *Père*. "I work with my eyes shut, he with his open. I draw, he photographs."

To my mind there is no comparison between the best works of Dumas *Père* and *Fils*. Invention, imagination, has to most literary ages (not our own) an advantage over acerbity. Although the son had a more acute intelligence than the father, it was unable to compensate for the lack of the ungloried invention possessed by the father.

Early in 1870 Dumas *Père*, an aged and almost forgotten figure, left Paris for the Midi. When he reached Marseille, he first heard of the declaration of the Franco-Prussian War. Maybe because so much of his life had depended on illusion, the news of initial French disasters crushed his soul.

Weakened by a stroke, the lovable old man arrived in the Puys de Dome and rang his son's doorbell. "I have come to you to die," he said. Dumas *Fils*, greeting him warmly, reported: "My father was brought to me completely paralyzed. It was a painful sight. Beware of women. That is the lesson to be drawn." (A different credo from that upon which he himself had risen to fame.)

There is little doubt that the stronger personality of the pair, Dumas *Fils*, handled the sad denouement with dignity. On December 6, 1870, he wrote George Sand: "My father died yesterday, December 5th, at ten o'clock in the evening, without pain. You would not be to me what you are if I did not send this news, first of all, to you. He loved and admired you more than any other woman."

That great mistress of distinguished men answered from Nohant, April 16, 1871, the moment postwar communications began to resume on a normal basis: "You are reported to have said about your father: '*He died, as he had lived, without noticing.*' I don't know whether you did actually use those words, or whether they have merely been attributed to you: but here is what I wrote in the *Revue des Deux Mondes*: '*His was the genius of life, and he was not aware of the coming of death*'—which means the same."

It is fascinating to speculate about the three generations of this family. Dumas *Grandpère* might easily have entered history as a great hero, a second Bonapartist Marshal Ney. But misfortune and bad luck twisted him into a mediocrity, something abhorred by Napoleon. Dumas *Père* loomed as a brilliant storyteller, but not a literary giant to be compared with Hugo, Balzac, or Stendhal. Dumas *Fils* was a one-work author—of the mawkish play and novel *The Lady of the Camellias*. But he was a charming companion, and the most profound and original thinker of the family.

IV

The Only U.S. Field Marshal: Arthur and Douglas MacArthur

Throughout history there have been various kinds of hereditary professions. These have generally been royal and known by the last name or titular seat of the original great chief who founded the lineage: thus, the Habsburg, Hohenzollern, Valois, Ottoman, Orleans, Tudor, and Romanov "dynasties." But the term has been expanded into other usage, for example it is applied to extremely wealthy titans: the Rockefeller, Ford, and Mellon dynasties in the United States. On and off for centuries, there have also been military families whose scions were trained to command. Among them have been Prussian Kleists, French Condés, and American Lees and MacArthurs.

Of this last category the most famous in the United States (if but briefly) was the MacArthur dynasty. Although it included only two members, both generals, father and son, each was renowned for his prowess and his personal valor.

The younger MacArthur, Douglas, was certainly one of the most contentious professional soldiers who ever fought. Although sneeringly referred to as "Dugout Doug" by many of his troops, his fearlessness, dash, and sangfroid were remarkable, and he was well known for personally seeking out risk and danger while quite unarmed. He is never reported to have flinched, save at sea (an element with which he had an inherent physical disagreement). It is well to remember that Nelson invariably suffered from *mal de mer*.

Douglas MacArthur, having escaped to Australia from the Japanese-occupied Philippines on the specific orders of Washington, halted the enemy advance in Papua and then started his gradual but accelerating sweep back northward to Tokyo as commander of all Allied forces in the southwest Pacific. It was an immense theater.

58

During this wartime period Churchill invited a young British friend of mine to dine at Chequers, the prime minister's official country residence. My friend was fascinated by an immense globe of the world, painstakingly marked out and embraced by an intricate glass device that could calculate in miles and fractions thereof all terrestrial measurements.

Puffing the glow of his customary postprandial cigar, Churchill showed by the gleam in his eye how pleased he was to glimpse his guest's puzzled attention. "Remarkable device," the P.M. said "We couldn't get it into Number 10 [Downing Street, where he officially resided in London], so we brought it here."

With little effort for an elderly man, slightly lubricated by brandy, he then pointed his cigar at an obscure East Asian dot marked by a tiny Union Jack. "There," he announced with a satisfied resonance, "we have the headquarters of Admiral the Lord Mountbatten, in charge of Allied forces in Southeast Asia.

"Now have another look," he said walking carefully around the bulging, rotund map, following the complicated plexiglass circumference machine with its neatly marked-off distances and smoothly moving adjustable gadgetry: "Way down here on the right you can see another little marker. This one is the Stars and Stripes. The flag of the United States of America. Command post of General Douglas MacArthur, Allied chief in the vast arc of the southwest Pacific."

He stared through his spectacles at the magnifier on which emerged the numerals 6,600. "Sixty-six hundred miles apart," he announced with satisfaction. "Tell me, do you think that's far enough?"

There was awed silence at this huge testimonial to Allied might—and problems between prima donna chieftains—at the peripheries of what so many thought of as the main struggle, in Europe. Within a year the young guest had been parachuted behind German lines and been killed by a sniper's bullet.

Not only Churchill but many others matched this remarkable pair of rival heroes who barely knew each other, came from different nations and contrasting circumstances, but had about them a genteel and romantic sense of battle, an ability to exploit fate and handle men.

Mountbatten—tall, lithe, and exceptionally handsome, with an enchanting wife and, as far as can be known, few adversaries except the Enemy—had the inherited advantage of royal blood, close connections with what was then still the world's greatest empire, and a splendid tradition in Britain's finest service, the Royal Navy, one of whose destroyers was sunk under his feet.

MacArthur had few tangible assets but the personality he was born with. His were the relatively modest ties with the distinguished upper strata of a far-from-jingoistic and socially democratic society. Yet he too was physically well-endowed, a bit shorter than the admiral but lean, fit, and hawkishly good-looking.

With only a modest diet and a regular calisthenics regime, he managed to retain almost until death the figure of an athlete—which he was not.

Mountbatten was a dynast by advantage, inheritance, and wealth. MacArthur was a military dynast in a country and era that had largely discarded the old-fashioned "service families," used to contributing at least one of their sons each generation to fight on because it was the tradition of their upbringing. Yet, outside of Britain, Germany, and Japan the species had largely ceased to exist.

The first MacArthur in the United States who distinguished himself as a warrior was Arthur, who earned the Medal of Honor as a lad during the Civil War battle of Lookout Mountain. He was subsequently commissioned in the postwar Union Army in 1900 until discharged as Philippines Commander by Secretary of War Elihu Root. It is odd indeed that both father and son should receive the greatest symbol of glory our nation can give and also eventually be assigned to command the Philippines; even odder, without doubt, is the fact that the father was removed from those islands by his immediate superior in Washington and, but a half century later, the son was bluntly eliminated from all and any commands he held, above all in Japan and Korea, by tough little President Harry Truman, who worshiped no dynasts of any variety.

Both Arthur and Douglas MacArthur demonstrated during their terms of Filipino office that they understood the Asians they administered and were admired and loved by them in a striking paradoxical way when contrasted with the disputes and debates that ensued among the Americans who had originally posted them there. Both had a rare un-Caucasian lack of racism and were revered by Orientals who were irksomely accustomed to the boorish arrogance of high-ranking whites with their exclusive clubs and assumed air of superiority.

Douglas MacArthur was brilliant and versatile: probably the best American general since Robert E. Lee, although the worst presidential aspirant with a military background since Lee's battlefield adversary, U.S. Grant. He was the only American who ever served as dictator of an entire nation—the Philippines—where he was also the only American ever to hold the rank of field marshal anywhere. He was brilliant, persuasive, and endowed with magnetic powers to charm. From West Point plebe to five-star general, his record was outstanding. His appearance was dashing, his mind clear and quick.

He became absolute ruler of Japan, effective superior to the emperor, and a curious twentieth-century version of the former political system of the shogunate. The reality of his true power was shown when the emperor, Hirohito, claiming divine descent, first called upon the victorious U.S. commander after the war—not vice versa. But he proved to be a highly benevolent and popular despot.

MacArthur understood the Japanese in a strikingly intuitive way, as he also did the Filipinos and the Koreans. Perhaps Douglas had learned something psychological about Orientals when his father, dismissed from Manila, was assigned as an observer in the Far East and wangled a job for him as a traveling aide. But why should the son later dream of becoming president of the United States with three equal powers: executive, legislative, and judicial? MacArthur knew the American political system well but misjudged it, more than once. He imposed democracy on Japan, a defeated power; yet undefeated America, which was inherently democratic, never took to him politically.

An additional paradox is that he, the top enemy, proved himself to be the most popular man in Japan. The very aspirations of his character that won him esteem and affection there were abhorrent to most Americans. In fact, at no moment did he ever stand a true chance of being freely chosen head of the U.S. government. His Asia First policy earned him far less votes than Roosevelt's Europe First, of which Dwight ("Ike") Eisenhower became the symbol and Marshall the architect.

It is unseemly to imagine this of a fine and honorable man; nevertheless, he was probably at least partially prodded into his lamentable efforts to seek the White House in order to put his thumb in the eye of Truman, who had dismissed him during the Korean War, and in that of his former aide, Eisenhower, whom he jealously disliked despite occasional professions to the contrary. I knew Eisenhower well and can vouch that the dislike was reciprocated.

The American people in the mass preferred Eisenhower to MacArthur, just as they preferred Eisenhower's war theater, Europe, to MacArthur's Pacific. Moreover, there is reason to believe that despite his successful career, Eisenhower was a man wholly untainted by ambition even if this very fact may have jaundiced MacArthur's view of him.

The concept that Ike regarded himself as a civilian in uniform—both as an army officer and during his eight years in the White House—won him the love of his countrymen more than the theatrical MacArthur's ostentation and handsome fearlessness. General Ike used to say of the man whom he served as an aide in Manila: "I studied dramatics under him for five years in Washington and four in the Philippines."

If Eisenhower was a grown-up version of Tom Sawyer, MacArthur sought successfully to be his country's *beau idéal* as a soldier. A handome, lean youth from the start, he grew increasingly handsome almost until the very end of his career. He indulged a taste for élan from those days in World War I when he was America's youngest general officer, and donned a uniform costume suitable to his aquiline features: muffler flung about his neck, bent wire framework shaping his cap, like that of a World War II fighter pilot. Later he took to stressing the informality of his simple shirts and trousers and to clamping a homely corncob pipe in his firm, clean-cut jaw.

Arthur MacArthur, whom Douglas greatly admired, was not bred to be a soldier, although he was descended from a hardy Scottish clan with bellicose traditions. His own father was named a federal judge by President Grant, in 1870, and he served the cause of civilian justice until his death in 1896.

Young Arthur's call to the colors came through the circumstance of fratricidal war. His northern upbringing placed him in the Twenty-fourth Wisconsin Infantry Division. With this unit, in Tennessee, he was commissioned a first lieutenant when he was only seventeen, and he won his family's first Congressional Medal of Honor a year later. From then on, like his more famous son, he was renowned in the army for dauntlessness and superb egotism.

In fact, Arthur became so outrageous in his behavior that Secretary of War Root relieved him of all Filipino commands in 1901. Although Root has vanished into anonymity and never had a chance to be president, the circumstances of the dismissals of father and son are indeed striking. Douglas and President Truman were even more different personalities than Arthur and Secretary Root. The theater of the second dismissal, during the Korean War, was on a far vaster stage; yet both events were tense drama.

Douglas MacArthur was a blatantly intelligent man, melodramatic, patriotic, immensely attached to his family. He always said of the night his dad died: "Never have I been able to heal the wound in my heart."

Yet, in fact, his mother probably had more influence on him than did Arthur, and did all in her power to flagrantly advance his career. She even insisted on moving to West Point when he was at the military academy. Here there is a strange, if limited, resemblance between young MacArthur admiring his ambitious father and at the same time asking his lovely mother to further his promotions through influential friends, and the early relations of Winston Churchill with his parents. The general's maternal plantation forebears and snobbery infected the son, for whom the mother cherished such ambition.

She summoned all her social connections to push for his promotion. In 1917 she wrote Secretary of War Baker: "I am deeply anxious to have Colonel MacArthur considered for the rank of Brigadier General. . . . Cordially yours, Mrs. Arthur MacArthur." When he failed to reply she wrote again: "I believe the entire Army, with few exceptions, would applaud your selecting him as one of your Generals."

She also wrote General Pershing, not an enthusiast for her boy: "emboldened by the thought of old friendship for you and yours and with the knowledge of my late husband's admiration for you [and knowing that 100 appointments as general would soon be made] I am most anxious that my son should be fortunate enough to receive one of these appointments." Quite clearly Douglas approved of his mother's servile attempts to advance him by appealing to high authority.

Following graduation from West Point and after touring the Far East with his father (incidentally earning the unhelpful dislike of the subsequent general, George C. Marshall), he led a dashing raid on Vera Cruz during the 1914 Mexican-border troubles. He was consequently recommended for his Medal of Honor, which he didn't receive for three decades.

During World War I Douglas MacArthur performed with distinction, ability, and inventive audacity, earning more decorations for gallantry than any other U.S. officer. MacArthur proved his cool courage—and was not simply a competitive, inspiring leader who felt he could get the most out of his men by being seen in front of them. He was wise, without fear, and blessed with great intuitive instinct. But in his younger days, he also displayed a damaging capacity to make powerful enemies, including Marshall and Eisenhower.

Despite his natural assets, he undoubtedly suffered from three blazing weaknesses: vanity (which as Virgil tells us is the root of evil); overweaning confidence in his own judgment at the expense of wisdom proffered by others; and—a blemish not uncommonly found in great men—the tendency to misjudge the value of those he selected to surround him and to advise him. Many of his immediate counselors were a poor lot.

Few among MacArthur's entourage had enough self-confidence to venture to display grade "A" qualities. His staff was larded with odd characters who favored a dictatorial government in Washington, and, against this background, one wonders if one should not read deeply into the observation of Ambassador Clare Boothe Luce, no shrinking violet herself: "MacArthur's temperament was flawed by an egotism that demanded obedience not only to his orders, but to his ideas and his person as well. He plainly relished idolatry."

Indeed few doubted his military genius. Winston Churchill called him "the glorious commander"; Lord Alanbrooke said he was "the greatest general and strategist the war produced," Viscount Montgomery described him as "America's best soldier" of World War II.

After MacArthur's Korean crisis, Churchill called the American "a fearless military leader whose daring was feared by those who profited by it." He suggested that his critics should instead "pay deserved tribute to the legendary service of a great soldier."

Field Marshal Lord Alanbrooke, chief of Britain's General Staff and probably its most brilliant, if acerbic, soldier, confided to his diary that MacArthur "outshone Marshall, Eisenhower and all other American and British generals including Montgomery."

Emperor Hirohito's staff considered MacArthur's maneuver into Bataan from beleaguered Manila and Corregidor a "classic, a great strategic move." General Pershing, whose voice had never been friendly, dubbed it "a masterpiece, one of the greatest moves in all military history."

Pershing added later: "It is not often given to a commander to achieve the ideal of every general—the surrounding and annihilating of his enemy. But MacArthur, with greatly inferior forces, has achieved this three times in the last eighteen months." Pershing referred to the Kokoda-Milne Bay campaigns, the Bismarck Sea operation, and the operations around Lae and Salamaua as the Americans struck back at the Japanese with deadly venom.

Nevertheless, the admiration for MacArthur among Asian leaders and the adulation for him among the Oriental masses tended to exceed that tendered to him by most American leaders and, in political terms, ordinary people. In part this was probably derived from the general U.S. impulse to look toward Germany and Europe as the great threat, even though west of the Rockies, the popular slant perceived greater danger in the Pacific.

MacArthur's achievements in the Orient, considering what he received in the form of limited material and manpower, is miraculous, despite mishandling of his air force when the surprising assault was launched at Pearl Harbor. The latter error was perhaps abetted by the confusion and incompetent communications between Washington and its system of intelligence interpretation and dissemination.

MacArthur's broad range of knowledge and tactical genius more than made up for Japan's swift and well-prepared strategic advantage as well as its ability to select key base positions and seize them before America or its allies were ready for any kind of counterattack. The general's Southwest Pacific theater was at no time allotted so much as a fifth of the national war effort. Eisenhower's troops landing in North Africa were provided with fifteen tons of supplies per man, thrice that granted in the Pacific. MacArthur led only twelve percent of all Americans sent overseas to fight.

Of course, at the start Allied strategists wholly misled themselves. They considered a Pearl Harbor unimaginable. By June 1942 the Japanese, at war just six months, had wiped out all resistance in the Philippines except a cluster of lesser guerrillas and had actually reached across the Pacific to seize two important islands from American Alaska.

Yet, from his new short-lived headquarters in Brisbane, Australia, the unflappable MacArthur had mapped out the course and method of his reactions. In August the First U.S. Marine Division hit the fringe of New Guinea, the southern continent's last barrier, and the general had already calculated the formula for his reaction: In Papua (South New Guinea) he decreed: "We must attack, attack, attack."

This was to be a war of airborne logistics with planes carrying fighting men, ammunition, and guns. These troops served him immutably to move forward the bombardment line. Through dripping, dank, sweaty jungle, his forces fought their way northwestward, bypassing key points (like Rabaul) and thus sealing off the Japanese.

During the more than two years that elapsed between MacArthur's arrival in Australia from his Filipino island fortress of Corregidor and the time of his return to the Philippines, he lost fewer casualties than Eisenhower did in the Normandy invasion. Within two years the Southwest Pacific commander's soldiers had fought back almost two thousand miles against a tough enemy aided by a jungle-covered, sea-girted, craggy terrain.

In Adelaide, Australia, MacArthur had told the press: "The President of the United States ordered me to break through the Japanese lines for the purpose, as I understand it, of organizing the American offensive against Japan, a primary object of which is the relief of the Philippines. I came through and shall return."

He did.

He began this triumph by troubled thoughts in the 1930s as field marshal of the Philippine forces responsible to the Manila government. He was already predicting that within a short time "total war" based on "maneuver and movement" and "command of the air" would face the world.

Marshall, who was himself a remarkable, strong, stern, and prescient officer with, on occasion, a rough edge to his tongue, although he had no illusions about MacArthur's genius, foresaw plenty of difficulties with him. He warned Secretary of War Stimson there would be trouble between this glamorous warrior and the U.S. Navy. Nevertheless, he considered the general's loss would be an unthinkable blow. When MacArthur, by Roosevelt's and Churchill's agreement, was assigned to the Southwest Pacific, the adjoining theater of the South Pacific was placed under U.S. Admiral Nimitz.

Without the swiftly reconstituted U.S. Navy it would surely have been impossible for MacArthur to stage his famous "return" to Manila and drive onward to Tokyo. The general himself acknowledged this and cooperated well with his neighboring Pacific armada. But he so flattened the Japanese, cruelly mauled in sea battles, that he was able to advance virtually at will as the war approached its end.

With the Philippines totally free, twenty-three Japanese divisions had been exterminated. The U.S. Air Force, still under army command, had crippled Japanese communications. And the steady pounding of Nimitz's naval planes, carriers, and guns moved past the stepping-stone islands of the Pacific, leaving Japanese garrisons bound by themselves to trees which they swore to defend against the last American.

MacArthur never acknowledged the generous support he and his strategy received from Washington thanks to the granitic persuasive powers of his old opponent, Marshall. The two men met only once during the war, at luncheon off the Papuan coast. MacArthur had started an elegant, egocentric tirade: "My staff—" "You don't have a staff, General," Marshall said. "You have a court." His sarcasm clearly referred to the group of admiring officers MacArthur had assembled about him, many of them more noted for adulation than ability.

MacArthur had always shown talent for attracting support from key political figures. In December 1937 he had been recalled from service abroad and had promptly resigned. This was just a year after he had accepted a field marshal's gold baton from the Filipino government, something no other American would have dared to do. Yet none of this damaged the general's subsequent career.

Thanks partially to the demands of his well-connected mother he had been an *American* general since the age of thirty-eight, when World War I was drawing to its end. He then became West Point's superintendent, was involved in the famous Billy Mitchell battleship-bombing case, married, divorced, took a Eurasian mistress (racially shocking to army circles), and tarnished his public reputation in 1932 by his personally publicized role in dispersing the penniless Depression Bonus Marchers.

In 1934 he bought off his mistress for cash. Three years later he married the loyal, courageous Jean Marie Faircloth, who gave birth to his only child, Arthur MacArthur IV, in Manila and who warned commanders of ships on which he traveled to place eight pillows on the general's bed under head, knees and elbows.

Jean, his second wife, was clearly *the* woman in the general's life (if one excepts his unusually influential mother). The first Mrs. Douglas MacArthur seems to have been a rather dull snob and plainly didn't care for the army atmosphere.

Although his mother worshiped him and looked after him to an apparently excessive degree, there is no reason to assume Douglas was influenced by an Oedipus complex. He certainly held his father in great esteem, and they seem to have mutually admired each other. Yet before World War II, he lunched daily with his widowed mother in Washington and telegraphed her when he traveled by plane, confirming his safe arrival.

Jean was quite evidently a true and adoring wife. There is no evidence MacArthur had any other mistress save the commercial Eurasian who allowed her passions to be bought off without a fuss. Indeed, it would seem that although he was enormously coveted and admired by women, sex played a rather small role in his life—as in that of Alexander the Great.

I have never come across any gossip or malicious rumors concerning his sex life, apart from old tales from retired officers or their wives about the Eurasian mistress. And it may be pointed out that generals and military heroes are romantic subjects among American gossips, especially such outstandingly handsome men as MacArthur. It was pretty well known by almost any G.I. of World War II who their commanders were "shacked up" (or living) with in areas as far apart as England, North Africa, Italy, Austria, and Japan. I heard many malicious or unkind yarns about MacArthur, but none of them which I can recall as licentious.

Nor was his career ever marred by such incidents; despite the initial Philippines defeat, his star shot upward; the long-delayed Medal of Honor was awarded, and in 1944 he was named a U.S. five-star general (the field marshal of the Philippines vanished).

This is a bizarre record for a once-contemned (Bonus March) hero, unconventional sponsor of genetic mixtures (refreshing in the conventional, racist United States of that era), and frank careerist who allowed his proud mother to help push him to the top. But when his term as U.S. chief of staff neared its end he advised Manuel Quezon, the Filipino leader, and resumed his field marshal's post. This almost doubled in pay and allowances the yearly sum he would henceforth receive from Washington.

On May 18, 1950, in Tokyo, MacArthur expressed the following views. He obviously did not foresee the Korean War, which came the next month and got near to being global when the Chinese intervened. He told me:

> The basic reason I have for concluding that there will not be a war soon is because of the changed nature of war. The scientists of the world have developed in such an extraordinary degree the processes and ways of accomplishing mass killing that war is no longer rationally a means of settling international problems.
>
> Its destructiveness has become so great that there can be no winner. Both sides lose. It is almost a form of mutual suicide. Therefore it is not an acceptable rationalization as a means of settling international quarrels.
>
> In this respect you have to remember that war at the beginning was a sort of gladiatorial contest. You might start with the basis of the fight between David and Goliath. From such an individual contest it became a struggle of professional units fighting gradually in more obscure corners of the world. But the results of these military engagements were accepted in peace treaties by the governments represented by these armies, and therefore at least some results were accomplished.
>
> However, as the world became more closely integrated, war became a more total concept involving every man, woman, and child and for settling of quarrels. The opinion of the masses of the world is against it. That is a relatively recent development, and it is true of all the masses in all countries of the world.
>
> During the last 150 years, if you look back, you find that international wars were invariably preceded by a period during which one or the other side—and sometimes both sides— became prepared and believed that if they were successful in war they would triumph thereby. They looked upon war as a short cut to power. Thus, always one side or both sides were relatively prepared not only in the sense of military force but in a psychological sense; public opinion approved, and that was of great importance.
>
> At the present time that is not the case. The public realizes all too well in terms of the last war that there can be no real

victory in a future war. Therefore, on neither side is there psychological preparation. The Russian masses are probably just as opposed to a shooting war as the Anglo-Saxon masses. Therefore, many incidents have taken place during the last few years which in the past would have led to war but which have been passed over.

I don't believe that war is imminent because the people of the world neither desire it nor would they be willing to permit it. That goes for both sides. That is the basic reason for my belief that war is not upon the doorstep. [A dubious confidence on the verge of the Korean conflict, which became almost global.]

We know that we do not intend to start an aggressive war. We have no such thought in our national mind, and we are only preparing defensively in case of a tragic emergency. It is quite possible that the Russians are preparing in exactly the same way. Russian propaganda indicates their belief that we are preparing an aggressive action. Therefore the Russian is also arming defensively. But there is no indication on either side of preparations for an aggressive, offensive war.

Furthermore, I think it is foolish to assume that the Russian would start an aggressive war now. He is doing so well under the present no-shooting war that he would probably and logically wish to continue the present successful system. It is a rare thing, in sports or anything else, when a man changes a winning combination.

He argued:

The Soviet is patient. He thinks in terms of decades or centuries. He is not an Occidental but an Oriental. He is white, he is partially located in Europe; he has our gregarious instincts. But at heart he is a tatar. He is like Genghis Khan. It is an Oriental trait to be patient. They deal in decades or centuries. This is against our nature. When we want a thing done, we want it done right away or tomorrow. But the Russian will lay down a railway that he wants to use in twenty-five or fifty years.

We must never forget that Asia includes perhaps 1,250 million people and maybe sixty percent of the assets of the world. Yet it has the lowest standards of living perhaps in the whole

world. It is manifest destiny that the effort of future civilization
will largely be an Asiatic problem devoted to raising the standards
of that huge area.

I wish there was more effort to face the fundamental problem
of doing away with war. For example, the United Nations should
look squarely at the problem of abolishing war. Yet the United
Nations continually asks for its own armed forces. It talks of
fighting to maintain the peace. That is a ridiculous anachronism.
I am a hundred percent disbeliever in war.

As is the case with many military leaders, MacArthur carefully
cultivated an appearance and personality that would inculcate his ideas of
leadership in those he encountered. Of exceptional intelligence, with a mind
that showed its finely honed qualities from West Point days onward, he was
not only an impressively attractive if, on occasion, autocratic figure but his
presence and manner showed an extraordinary and magnetic quality.

He always seemed at ease and relaxed—but in a feline manner, ready to
spring. He cultivated an easy informality symbolized by his corncob pipe
and clothes that would have been rumpled if less well pressed. He had a
sympathetic smile—although not outgoing or toothy—and a gentle, thoughtful way of talking in a well-modulated voice. He was always under full
control of himself without appearing even remotely tense. What really lay
inside his handsome mask is extremely difficult to assess. Some have said he
was a "Mama's boy," referring to the dominant mother.

MacArthur seemed to make rather few mistakes in individual human
relations, but those he did make were costly—as, for example, the two I have
mentioned: in the instances of Marshall and Eisenhower. His relationships
with the public at large were remarkably effective, although some of his own
press officers privately disliked him. He successfully cultivated a chosen
personality with which to present himself to his armies and to the world—as
did the earlier and more imperious Napoleon and Wellington.

Indeed, General Douglas MacArthur made remarkably few mistakes in
the immensely grave issues of war and peace itself, and, despite blots, his
record was dazzlingly positive.

The first vital episode in a negative sense was permitting his air force to
be destroyed on the ground by Japanese planes—nine hours after word had
reached his headquarters of the Pearl Harbor disaster in Hawaii. Especially
because of his admired talents, his delay and failure in that incident remains
a mystery.

His second blazing mistake was the total inability to foresee a North

Korean attack in the spring of 1950. Secretary of the Interior Harold Ickes charged that MacArthur had been caught wholly unprepared by that event, a theme later echoed by President Truman.

And his final basic miscalculation was that the drive northward to the Yalu River and China's frontier, after his dazzling Inchon landing in Korea, would not provoke an armed Chinese reaction.

Before pursuing the consequences of the last error, it would be wise to recall and to stress again these days the social and economic effects of the revolution he personally imposed on Japan, after he had flown into Yokohama totally unarmed, following the world's first nuclear bombardments and the total surrender to him and the Allied powers. One year later, in 1946, a constitution he had devised became the governing law of more than 80 million militant Japanese.

MacArthur, regardless of flaws, was a great man, and great men change the structure of the world by the way they use their power.

By the Japanese constitution, drafted and enacted under MacArthur's supervision, class and hereditary privileges were abolished and the militant Shinto religious discipline rejected. Agricultural reforms placed more than ninety percent of the land in the hands of those actually farming it. A formidable new structure of civil liberties, trade unions, and equal rights for women was written into the code of governance. And he did his best to outlaw war effectively by demilitarizing belligerent Japan, a policy later reversed by Washington.

Obviously, these good intentions have been modified by ensuing fact, especially in the realm of militarism. As long ago as 1950, W. J. Sebald, MacArthur's chief State Department adviser, sniffed that it was unrealistic to think of Japan as an unarmed "Switzerland" of the East and that MacArthur's was a foolish dream. But, although Japan has started back along the road of newer, better, and more forces and weapons in recent years, as the result of unanticipated American prodding, it has stuck to its antinuclear position.

MacArthur became the first U.N. commander over a mixed (but predominantly American) international force. The experiment underscored the difficulties of such commands. President Truman said the objective of the United Nations in Korea was "to restore peace there and to restore the border." However, a U.N. resolution subsequently called for "the complete independence and unity of Korea"—quite a different thing, considering that the country was geographically, politically, and ideologically bisected in a de facto sense.

Even Secretary of State Dean Acheson, hardly a MacArthur enthusiast, acknowledged that the free world and South Korean forces couldn't just advance "to a surveyer's line and stop." MacArthur himself was inclined to caution. He played the follow-through on his Inchon landings with delicate skill. He well recalled from his young days as his father's aide that in 1904 Russia had made a Japanese attack across the thirty-eighth parallel (now dividing the two Koreas) the *casus belli.*

In fact, he was never given precise orders on what to do. The confusion is brutally reflected when comparing U.S. Secretary of Defense Marshall's secret cable to MacArthur—"feel unhampered tactically and strategically to proceed north of the 38th parallel"—with the U.N. commander's equally secret reply—"Unless and until the enemy capitulates, I regard all Korea (North as well as South) as open for our military operations."

He was still sticking to the limitations fixed by Washington as interpreted by the secretaries of defense and state. He even proposed that South Korean soldiers should remain southeast of the Yalu's delta, despite the impetus of his remarkable Inchon flanking operation. Yet the General Assembly ordered him to conquer North Korea.

To be fair to the general, despite the adulation he had justifiably received for military genius on the road to Tokyo and political vision when charged with governing Japan, he was brought down by confusion. Marshall cabled saying Truman wished to confer with MacArthur in the Pacific that October (1950).

On modest Wake Island, the general discounted the chances of intervention from China or the Soviet Union, which he thought was militarily weak in eastern Siberia. Truman firmly forbade an attack on Chinese bases in Manchuria and rejected MacArthur's project to widen the war in any way. However, he endorsed the general's denial of a sanctuary to the enemy across the Yalu.

After the Wake conference, MacArthur prepared an air bombardment to sever the Yalu bridges. On November 6, 1950, he was directed by the Joint Chiefs of Staff in Washington to defer bombing targets within five miles of China's border. When MacArthur pointed out the military illogic of this instruction and demanded the right of hot pursuit as Chinese troops drove across the Yalu, George C. Marshall, Dean Acheson, and Truman himself approved. But our U.N. allies objected. American policy was reversed, and MacArthur's career was doomed.

He fell back cleverly, minimizing potential losses. The public stormed— not against the international and national confusion that simultaneously condemned and protected his reputation, but against him. Ambassador Charles E. Bohlen told me MacArthur had "made a terrible mistake" in launching the final stage of the offensive that provoked Chinese entry into the war. The brilliant diplomat David Bruce felt the general should have worked for "a fixed line in Korea and a neutral zone."

The argument has lapsed. Many—including myself—have shifted from one opinion to another. But Truman really didn't help things, except for proving the authority of civilian rule in America, when he fired MacArthur from all his commands, barking: "The son of a bitch isn't going to resign on me." And the general foolishly, unsuccessfully sought to challenge the president.

In March 1955 I spent an evening in a large circular wooden bathtub in the southern port of Pusan with South Korea's defense minister, Admiral Sohn Won Il; Foreign Minister Young Tai Pyun; and General Chung Il Kwon, chief of staff. They all agreed MacArthur had made two crucial mistakes. He split his command so that chaos resulted when the Chinese punched a hole between the halves; and, refusing to contemplate possible Chinese intervention, he had no prepared alternative position on which to fall back.

Matthew Ridgway, MacArthur's successor, said the general had misinterpreted intelligence about China and showed bad judgment by predicting the U.N. forces couldn't hang on—as, under Ridgway, they did. Truman complained that any armistice hopes had been wrecked when MacArthur "openly defied the policy of his commander in chief, the president." But Field Marshal Montgomery observed from the sidelines that generals are never given adequate directives, which had been the case with MacArthur.

Shortly before yielding his NATO command to run for the White House, MacArthur's private bête noire, Eisenhower, told me in Paris: "MacArthur's recall has served one very useful purpose: it has certainly proved to the Russians that we are not arming with aggressive intentions. They can have no illusions on that score now." Despite sour remarks among intimates concerning his former boss's vanity and ambition, Eisenhower always publicly praised MacArthur's military talents.

It was an odd and somewhat pitiful sight to witness the last contest between the two great American generals. I sincerely think Eisenhower had no political aspirations, but, as the symbol of victory in a "Europe First" and pro-NATO policy thoroughly endorsed by the Democrats and proven victorious in the field, he and his infectious grin plus his natural diplomatic tact made him an obvious candidate for the Republicans, eighteen years out of the White House. MacArthur, carried away by his own glory, was already making less and less of a secret of his final, if supreme, postwar ambition. As early as 1943, Roosevelt's personal chief of staff, Admiral William D. Leahy, had noted: "If General MacArthur should get the nomination he would be a very dangerous antagonist for anybody, including Roosevelt."

But, despite his enormous appeal abroad, MacArthur never developed a political following at home. Roosevelt once told him: "I think you are our best general, but I believe you would be our worst politician." This was confirmed in 1952.

Before the Chicago Republican convention, MacArthur boasted to the American Legion that he had wrecked a secret Democratic plan to give both Formosa and a U.N. seat to Mao Tse-tung. Yet he never got anywhere except with the far-out right. In the Wisconsin primary, MacArthur won only eight delegates against Harold Stassen's nineteen.

When he finally showed up at the convention, he looked tragically old, fumbling, surrounded by little known has-beens who never, in fact, were. He was given the honor of making the keynote speech. I wrote at the time: "He said nothing but sheer baloney. One could feel the electricity gradually running out of the room. I think he cooked his own goose and didn't do much to help Taft" (Eisenhower's chief party rival). Eisenhower, of course, won both the nomination and the election.

Four years later, in 1956, two Democratic leaders worked hard to get MacArthur's public backing for Adlai Stevenson against Eisenhower. All he did was say in private: "If Eisenhower is reelected president, it will be the greatest disaster in American history. I know just what will happen. He will go off to the golf courses and the trout streams of the country, and then he will just disappear. There won't be any American government at all."

Later, after Jack Kennedy's election restored the White House to the Democrats in 1960, he called on MacArthur, who said: "All the chickens are coming home to roost, and you are living in the coop."

In the spring of 1964, he developed severe kidney and liver failure. His last known act was a plea to President Lyndon Johnson to stay out of Vietnam. Then, on April 3, 1964, after having reversed a formula he made famous from an old army song, he first faded away and then, in a peaceful coma, died. The end was sad, bitter, and meaningless for a man who had seen so much triumph and served his nation so brilliantly.

But he took great glory to the grave with him and added much luster to the splendid name of his renowned father. Together the two men led in creating, protecting, and handing freedom to a short-lived American empire in Asia. They were excellent soldiers, but only one, the son, ventured into the unknown field of politics—disastrously.

Both were splendid generals who were dismissed by civilian officials with whom they had disagreed. Each was admired for his courage and personal independence. Both were involved (as observer and as enemy) in the last two major wars of Asia, with Japan against this century's superpowers: first Russia, then America.

Part Two

RENAISSANCE AND AFTER

V

Two Tudors: Henry VIII and Elizabeth I

Henry VIII, most brutal, most flamboyant and most intelligent of the Tudor kings of England, bequeathed his three heirs an extraordinary legacy: the finest education available at a time when the full Renaissance was starting to flourish in the British Isles; a burgeoning navy; a nationalistic and divisive religious policy; and sadly unhealthy constitutions, which may very well have been tainted by hereditary syphilis. Henry was certainly afflicted with that disease. There seems little doubt that his sickly son and heir, King Edward VI, who died at the age of sixteen in 1553 (some alleged it was of consumption), had many symptoms not related to tuberculosis, including eruptions on his skin, loss of hair, then of nails, and finally a disintegration of his toes and fingers.

There was surely something wrong with Henry's health, something that could be passed on by heredity, and his children, legitimate and illegitimate, displayed symptoms of an odd and unpleasant sort. Each of them, including the immortal "Virgin Queen" Elizabeth, suffered particular maladies at the normal age of puberty. Mary experienced a false pregnancy after marrying King Philip II of Spain.

But, although Henry VIII was an extraordinary, cold, callous, and infinitely licentious man, he was also a monarch of great brilliance who began life with immense hopes. His father, Henry VII, who ended the War of the Roses with his victory at Bosworth Field in 1485, did his best to heal the wounds and desolation that had riven England, and was far-sighted enough to recognize the need for intellectually qualified rulers. One may therefore say with justice that, having established his own reign by force, he could well foresee that an improved system of governance over the long term was essential for the health, wealth, and stability of his kingdom.

79

Henry VIII was the first English monarch to be educated under Renaissance influence, which in itself was an important factor in the development of his own curiously complex and by no means benign character. His tutors included the leading English poet of the time, John Skelton, whose blunt verse displayed unabashed prejudice against the Scots, who were eventually to inherit the United Kingdom when the Stuarts took over in 1603 from the childless Elizabeth.

Apart from the brutality and cold wickedness of Henry VIII, one must give him credit (thanks to his father) for perhaps the best regal education bestowed by a king upon his heir since Philip of Macedon hired Aristotle to teach Alexander the Great. His was really in some ways a personality closer to Macchiavelli's realpolitik portrait of a "Prince" than the insidious Cesare Borgia, the Florentine's actual model.

Although later renowned in history for his numerous courtships, six wives, and heartless brutality, it should never be forgotten that Henry VIII, when he came to the throne in 1509, aged eighteen, was already an omnivorous reader, a linguist fluent in four modern and two classical tongues, a musician and composer, a keen historical scholar, and a determined promoter of institutionalized learning. It is certainly arguable that without this cultural tradition given by his father to Henry VIII, a cruel but versatile and far-seeing monarch, Renaissance England might not have benefited from the works of Hans Holbein (Henry's German-born court painter) and—under his highly educated daughter Elizabeth—from John Donne, Francis Bacon, or William Shakespeare.

For better or worse—and there are those who speak for each side of the argument—Henry allowed his lusty sex life and quest for a legitimate son, added to the concept of Reformation (which was then an increasingly powerful ideological factor in Europe), to incite him to break from the pope and the Roman Catholic religion, to create the Church of England, and in the end to discard the Catholic Catherine of Aragon, daughter of the Spanish king. He then took on successively an astonishing series of official wives (who were therefore titular queens) in search of legal male heirs.

This maternal marathon, with its contrapuntal theme of beheaded queens who had been discarded, is one of history's more unpleasant episodes. But the Church of England (with its overseas branches whose methodology and doctrine differ little from Rome's even if the sovereign of the United Kingdom is not acknowledged as a *religious* symbol) is a vigorous and far-from-stagnant theological force today. Henry was in fact cool to Protestant dogma but was anti-Rome and insistent that state should dominate church.

The Tudor dynasty was both brief and melodramatic, yet, despite its short duration and its often bestial brutality, its 118 years—especially those dominated by Henry VIII and Elizabeth I—are studded with factionalism, violence, gore, theology, naval strategy, and creative artistic genius, above all literary genius. Taken together, this ferment added greatly to the permanent heritage of Britain and the English-speaking world.

It is an interesting phenomenon that faction or partisan groupings and opinions should have played an especially powerful role during the short, dynamic Tudor regimes. Lady Margaret Beaufort, mother of Henry VII who won his throne on the battlefield, had strong views on this as described in a great sermon given about her by the Bishop of Rochester, John Fisher. He recalled: "If any factions or bands were made secretly among her head officers, she with great policy did bolt it out, and likewise if any strife or controversy, she would with great discretion study the reformation thereof."

As David Starkey, the British historian, points out: "This, according to the *Oxford English Dictionary*, is the first use of the word 'faction' in English." And yet Henry VII gained his crown only by employing the strongest factional force to obtain it after royal rule had virtually dissolved under Henry VI, Edward IV, and the bloody usurper Richard III.

Henry VII, when he took over, sought to destroy factionalism as a political factor and asserted his central financial influence to weaken the great lords while at the same time maintaining as much distance as possible from individual government and court functionaries. He stood apart as a rather remote spectator from entertainments staged in the royal name.

Having seen the dangers of exaggerated factionalism and the example selected by Bishop Fisher, he divided the medley of court servants and then created a powerful Privy Chamber headed by the Groom of the Stool, whose main personal duty was to attend to and watch the sovereign's performance of excretory needs. This proved to be an effective way of generally insuring royal privacy and keeping the monarch's distance.

Henry VIII roughly terminated this discretion and hauteur. His very first action was to have two of his father's most trusted ministers beheaded. He then broke up the subtle division of powers his father had arranged to strengthen the sovereign's position against any scheming rivals and did away with the recently reconstructed past. He had no taste for the normal business of governing and left this in the hands of a single, small executive council which almost immediately split into factional disputes between the eager advisers of Henry VII, led by the Bishop of Winchester, and the Earl of Surrey's bellicose war party.

His next break with the past came the year after his accession when he personally took part in a tournament at Richmond, wounding his opponent. He thus swept away the ban on royal participation in court entertainment. He stuffed his Privy Chamber with personal friends and made the Groom of the Stool a boon companion instead of a semianonymous, menial servant. The upshot of these rapidly accomplished changes was that the king himself became the target and cynosure of factional attention.

Henry VIII thus, before he was twenty, accomplished what was simultaneously a political revolution in governance and a social revolution in aristocratic behavior. However, an anxious group, which felt that the king was playing an increasingly unseemly role, too personal and bumptious, successfully aided the quiet rise in influence of Thomas Wolsey, cardinal, chancellor, and often referred to as "the second king."

Wolsey succeeded in restraining Henry and restoring some of Henry VII's more subtle methods of management, both for the sake of order in England and, to some degree, for Wolsey's own purposes; he was not a man wholly lacking in ambition. The cardinal soon showed increasing skill in managing his erratic sovereign while, at the same time, muting pretensions to an executive role of the Chief Council of which he himself was head. This ended the potential danger of factionalism becoming a menace from within the council and, using his position as the monarch's principal favorite, he tolerated no new rivals within the Privy Chamber.

By the time Henry reached his early thirties, the king who had been a strong, bluff, hearty young man, athlete of the Field of the Cloth of Gold, sadly discovered that he was entering middle age (as was normal in those days). He became increasingly obese, more greedy for food and drink, and subject to the jovial influence of a really youthful group of carousing companions, some as young as fifteen, who were known with a touch of a sneer as his "minions" or "pretty boys."

The voracious king continued to exceed in virtually all forms of pleasure and vice. For many years before his death, he was listed medically as suffering from a "sorre legge," which could have been syphilis rather than gout. By the age of fifty-five, it was evident that his life, despite the exuberant vitality with which it had begun, was drawing to its close.

Once a handsome, powerful sportsman, he had become a mass of disgustingly loathsome infirmities: his features bloated, and (eventually, according to a study by the *British Medical Journal*): "so unwieldy in body that he could not pass through an ordinary door and could be moved from one room to another only with the help of machinery and a number of attendants. His legs were swollen and ulcerated and festering sores caused an unbearable stench. Toward the end he could neither walk nor stand."

That a father in such distorted condition should pass on physical malignancies to his children would not be surprising had they all been born of one mother and during one brief span. But this was in no sense the case. His first legitimate child, the daughter of Queen Catherine, was born in 1516, when her father was twenty-five, and lived to rule after her younger brother's death, earning the unfortunate sobriquet "Bloody Mary" because of her devout loyalty to her mother's Roman Catholic ties and her persecution of the new Protestant Church of England created by Henry. And physicians today differ on whether a syphilitic father must necessarily infect all offspring after he himself sickens.

Following Catherine's official discard, Henry made Anne Boleyn—the mistress whom he had flaunted openly before Catherine—his queen. Henry had had what he wanted of Anne as a bedmate, but he wished a legal wife who could produce a male heir to the throne. Cardinal Wolsey urged him along this course, promising that Pope Clement VII would agree to his divorcing Catherine.

But as French armies moved into Italy, Clement realized his papacy might fare better if it were linked to the Spanish protection of Emperor Charles V. He reneged on all ideas of seeing a Spanish queen offended in England. Henry thought the pope not worth conciliating; he brusquely divorced Catherine and married Anne. She produced no male heir but the immortal Queen Elizabeth instead, and then was beheaded for adultery in 1536. Wolsey was forced out of all his offices and died.

The king thus broke with the Roman Church. All monasteries were dissolved, and an English Bible was authorized that moved English religious dogma nearer to the Reformation doctrine of the Ten Articles.

Meanwhile, the king again married, this time to Jane Seymour, who presented Henry with the boy baby who became the short-lived Edward VI. Jane died after the effort. Henry then married Anne of Cleves, who had been sponsored by the dubious Thomas Cromwell, successor to Wolsey. Anne proved herself both personally distasteful and politically unnecessary to Henry, who divorced her and had Cromwell beheaded. He then wedded Catherine Howard, candidate of the reactionaries' faction, and beheaded her in 1542. She was succeeded by Catherine Parr.

Henry was an extraordinary and in many respects atrocious personality with his bevies of queens and mistresses, his addiction for the headsman's axe, his regard for religion as a purely political tool, and his essentially despotic, egotistical character. Yet, especially in his youth when he was handsome, quick, and vigorous, he could prove a most attractive personality. His religious reformation was in fact desirable from the viewpoint of most

Englishmen, and it was thus a fortunate coincidence that his sex life and passion for a male heir (but feebly satisfied) coincided with political and ecclesiastical conditions that favored a breach with Rome even though it was stimulated for private and dynastic reasons. His tyrannical supremacy over the Church saved England from the kind of civil war that had been touched off by religion in much of Europe.

In a material sense, the immense care Henry took to build up England's naval power was of signal importance. Its first great consequence was to enable the establishment of a British empire. He also helped cement the unity of England, Wales, Scotland, and Ireland and, strangely enough considering his autocratic temperament, to develop and extend the parliamentary system. Moreover, Erasmus, the great polymath, wrote to Sir Henry Guilford: "The English court contains at present more persons of real knowledge, and ability than any university in Europe."

The one thing none of the Tudors was really able to stamp out for England's benefit was the continuing tendency toward "faction" first identified by Lady Margaret Beaufort. Her son, Henry VII, was the most successful of his line in opposing this trend, but that is possibly only because the weakness in the prevailing monarchical system was probably at its worst and most permanently rooted when he attained power. He recognized he couldn't hold on long if the throne rocked too much.

Yet vendettas began to arise again between high personages. They were notable under Henry VIII among the champions of different rivals for the continually shifting role of queen; and between influential families like the Boleyns and the Carews, the Somersets and the Northumberlands. There was even a spat between rival high Protestant factions under the ailing Edward VI, which lasted into the early part of Queen Elizabeth's reign.

Individual participants shifted: Walsingham versus Sussex; Leicester versus Cecil. To a degree, depending upon the factionalists, the sovereigns, and the issues of the moment, it was as John Foxe, author of the *Book of Martyrs*, wrote of Henry VIII, who was at times far less dynamic than he himself imagined: "King Henry, according as his counsel was about him, so was he led." And in this critical issue, he showed himself far less discerning and weaker than his father who, with his self-contained strength, had suppressed the worst features of factionalism and distanced himself from the individuals involved.

Henry VII appears in the light of history as the most resolute of the Tudor sovereigns. Henry VIII was the gaudiest, vainest, brightest, and a strange mixture of health and illness, culture and bestiality, good sense and insanity, cruelty and wisdom, political myopia and long-range planning. Edward VI was merely a meaningless (although obstinate and even sometimes fanatical) semicolon in history because of his increasingly feeble health. Since there was no other legitimate male heir, he was succeeded as sovereign by Queen Mary, who ruled for five years. Yet, although as a girl she was removed by Henry VIII from his court and treated as a bastard, she was later, with the aid of Parliament, re-established in rank after accepting bitterly humiliating conditions and succeeded Edward as sovereign when he died in 1553. Despite her historical nickname of "Bloody Mary" because of her brutal treatment of unrepentant Protestant leaders, she was, in fact, from the start clement toward those who had taken up arms against her. But she was inexperienced in the art of government and basically innocent in international political affairs. She married King Philip of Spain, restored the Roman religion, and obtained papal absolution for England's past disobedience to the Holy See.

When the old heresy laws were revived, an era of persecution and public executions started. She began to suffer from the delusion of false pregnancy at forty-two and was perhaps fortunate to have died before things got worse, as, during her five-year rule, the kingdom appeared headed into a chasm.

Among historians, those who have sought to defend her point out that she was in no way cruel by nature and certainly kind to the poor of her realm. Her intentions were good, but the majority of her subjects were undoubtedly heretical toward her beliefs and stirred up enmity against her, an enmity that has managed to persist through time.

The two outstanding Tudor rulers, as history will have it, do not include the calm, stern Henry VII, who established the dynasty, but that astonishing effigy of personal disintegration, Henry VIII, and his extraordinary daughter, Queen Elizabeth, who may well be the greatest sovereign modern Britain ever had but was certainly peculiar. For the latter quality, one cannot fairly blame her. A sensitive, cultivated girl, she was reared in surroundings of blood, thunder, licentiousness, and horror and was never in a position to be sure of her own life or liberty until she herself came to the throne. By then she had been so toughened by experience—since girlhood—that she could lead her country successfully through dangerous battlefields to grandeur.

Henry VIII's children suffered the weirdest and most distorted upbringings imaginable. Catherine of Aragon (who must have passed on at least some of her observations to her daughter, "Bloody Mary") had been compelled to watch her husband courting Anne Boleyn for six or seven years, a good deal of the time under the single roof that sheltered all of them. Before he got rid of Anne, Elizabeth's mother, Henry had fallen in love with Jane Seymour and moved her into the palace.

Then he decapitated Anne and married Jane next morning. When she died, he married Catherine Howard; later, after cutting off her head, he had two more wives. How could any child remain normal with such a background? Elizabeth's father, who had six wives in all, murdered her mother. Then Lord Seymour paid feverish suit—unsuccessfully—to the young girl, who didn't know where her real home was or would be or even what faith to practice. For some four years after Seymour was beheaded for his impertinent ambitions, Elizabeth was clearly in bad psychological condition. She had at least two physical and mental breakdowns.

All Henry VIII's children—and with clear reason—had their moments of imbalance. The king's bastard, the Duke of Richmond, died at seventeen after a long period of ill health. Mary, who suffered so much along with her mother, Catherine, was forced to commit perjury as a Catholic when she swore her father was supreme head of the Church and also that she was illegitimate. She consequently became a chronic invalid long before she was twenty: warped, embittered, infirm, and immutably headed for an early death. And I have already mentioned the syphilitic probabilities of King Edward VI's morbid symptoms.

It is no surprise, therefore, that Elizabeth inherited anemia, rotten teeth, a weak heart, and a flaccid constitution with a consequent series of illnesses. What is surprising, however, and here I find disagreement among medical men, is that Edward alone seems surely to have been tainted by venereal heritage while the other children perhaps simply broke down or failed during the approximate period of puberty. Moreover, the sores on Henry VIII's legs are argued by some to refer simply to bad gout or varicose veins and by others to ordinary and syphilitic boils.

There can be little doubt that the once-splendid constitution of young Henry had been wrecked by his middle-age troubles; apart from the sick children produced by his wives and mistresses, several were simply stillborn. Bloody Mary, the eldest daughter, may have had various miscarriages and what was called ovarian dropsy. Both Anne Boleyn and Jane Seymour had grave obstetrical difficulties.

That Elizabeth, after such a hellish and abnormal childhood in such warped surroundings and with such precarious health, should have survived to become one of history's most romantic and competent queens is a virtual miracle. She was a pawn in the game of Catholic and Protestant factions (the sport, on whatever terrain, being the Tudor curse), and was preceded to the throne by a sick man and a religious fanatic. Yet she triumphed over incredible adversity with her astute bravery and intuitive feeling for survival.

Indeed, it was the miserable girl Elizabeth who conceived of the very idea and phrase of "Great Britain," which became the immense British Empire. It was Elizabeth who demonstrated a remarkable instinct for choosing the best among her courtiers, men like Burghley and Leicester (the latter having often been dubbed her lover), Raleigh, Drake, etc. There is an enduring argument about her sex life. Being descended from the lusty Henry and the lascivious Anne Boleyn, Elizabeth may well have had yearnings, but that hardness of her childhood and the probable malformation of her genes may well have restrained her. Nor do physician-historians all agree on whether she escaped all consequences of her father's venereal malady.

Thomas Seymour had himself made a baron and lord high admiral under Edward VI and is believed to have proposed to Elizabeth a month after her father's death. But she eluded his power grab, and he turned to Henry VIII's widow, Catherine Parr, who married him—and later found her husband in Elizabeth's arms. The lord high admiral was declared guilty under a bill of attainder and, without trial, met that Tudor familiar, the headsman.

Elizabeth had been opposed to marriage as a career since her childhood, and the Seymour experience heightened this prejudice. There is little doubt that she had great distaste for the marital institution after the fate of her mother and of Lady Jane Grey, Henry VII's daughter, the consequences of her sister Mary's marriage to King Philip II of Spain, and the extraordinary activity of the executioner throughout the sixteenth century for political, religious, and sexual reasons.

Despite the strains, terrors, and uncertainties surrounding her, she displayed genius and a certain egotistical, bold literary ability presented in lovely penmanship. She also spent much of her private time confirming the value of the education her father had ordered for her by doing quite a few useful translations into Latin, Italian, and French of prayers that had been composed in English by Catherine Parr. Moreover, she kept up this intellectual activity.

When she was sixty-four, an ill-advised Polish ambassador addressed a slighting discourse to her, and she astounded him with an angry torrent of Latin in reply. She was not only familiar with the classics but exceedingly fluent in French and Italian. Later she confided to a crone of her acquaintance that as a girl she knew six foreign languages better than her own.

Her favorite subject for study was history, although she found time to continue with architecture, astronomy, mathematics, music, and logic. Her education had been supervised during girlhood by John Cheke and Roger Ascham, the latter being then England's outstanding scholar.

During the first decade of her reign, foreign policy was her leading state preoccupation. One by one she managed to find her untutored way successfully through settlement of the religious argument (which was highly influential in terms of diplomatic affairs), separate interventions in Scotland and France, a bitter trade dispute with Holland, and a crisis over the seizure of Brill by the Sea Beggars in 1572, followed by France's Saint Bartholomew's Day Massacre, an affront to all Protestants.

The ultimate goal sought by Elizabeth and her advisers was to avoid a heightening of tension with Spain. It was clear, judging by hindsight, that an Anglo-Spanish collision was inevitable from 1576 on, but Philip II instructed his statesmen and military leaders to pacify the Netherlands first. England sent mercenary troops to aid the Sea Beggars on the Dutch coast (under Spanish suzerainty), and the French and Dutch churches in London raised funds among their congregations to arm and finance a company of volunteers to fight against the Spanish in Flushing. But despite delays in the sailing of the great naval armada being constructed by Philip's ship-builders for an invasion—delays caused by Admiral Drake's raid on Spanish ports and by Philip's own parsimonious efforts to cut down expenditures through personal royal checks, the Great Fleet sailed in 1588. It was thwarted by Aeolus, the god of winds, rather more than by Drake's bold and hardy seamanship.

It is a matter of great fortune for England that Elizabeth's worst illness was between 1548 and 1552, so that she had sufficiently recovered in time to face the terrible crises that racked her realm but eventually led it to its full Renaissance glory. During her bad period, she suffered from melancholia, weeping, headaches, shortness of breath, and difficulty in concentrating. She never became a strong, durable girl; nevertheless, her willpower and imagination were indomitable, and she regained considerable physical vigor.

One commentator wrote that in "1572 the Queene also herselfe, which hitherto had enjoyed very perfect health, (for shee never eate meate but when her appetite served her, nor dranke Wine without alaying) fell sick of the small pox at Hampton Court. But shee recovered again before it was heard abroad that she was sicke." The same writer added: "1603—the Queen, which hitherto enjoyed her sound health, by reason of her abstinence from wine, and most temperate diet [unlike her father] which she often said was the noblest part of physicke, being now in her Climatericall yeere, to wit, the seventyeth yeere of her age, began to be assayled with some weaknesse both of health and old age."

Some medical experts who have studied available records of the physical and mental conditions of the legitimate and illegitimate offspring of Henry VIII are of the opinion that Elizabeth's increasingly pronounced anemia, decaying teeth, and numerous other worsening symptoms of decline may very well be the direct sequels of the lack of a strong constitution, which in turn was the result of a diseased father. It was only by extraordinary intelligence and a formidable will that Elizabeth had managed as well as she did before the inevitable set in.

It is known that in late 1562, aged twenty-nine, four years after she ascended the throne, Queen Elizabeth had smallpox. She later suffered amenorrhea (absence of menstruation), but, at the time, diagnosticians mentioned no suspicion of inherited syphilis. It is conceivable that skin diseases from which she suffered resulted from bad diet, but it is also possible they were actually symptoms of congenital venereal taint. But then, some physicians have argued in recent years that there is not even absolute proof that Henry himself suffered from that dreaded disease. The debate is wholly inconclusive.

Another disability came over Elizabeth as she grew older: her exquisite talent for calligraphy degenerated into a scrawl. But this could indeed have resulted from bad vision, faulty glasses, or general debility. One simple conclusion by medical historians is that Elizabeth was not robust enough to shake off minor ailments and consequently was needlessly prone to more serious diseases. She was never in blooming good health at any time before 1588—year of the famous Armada—and then, eight years later, she failed badly. But at no point in her life, high or low, is there the faintest hint of anything that precluded active use of her brain and, indeed, remarkable mental ability.

And, although there are many doubts concerning her normal feminine sexual capacities and enjoyment, she was sufficiently athletic to take part in hunts and to dance sedately even at an advanced age.

At the time of Wyatt's unsuccessful rebellion against Catholic Queen Mary, many of Elizabeth's enemies—both political and religious—urged Mary to have her half-sister done away with, and the Habsburg Emperor Charles V sent Mary a special envoy to argue for such a solution. But Elizabeth used her poor health skillfully as a political weapon and persuaded Mary's physicians she hadn't the strength to leave Ashbridge, where she was quartered. She thus delayed her final incarceration in that ghastly fortress, the Tower of London, festooned with the heads and bodies of convicted traitors. And once again Elizabeth, by her combination of wits, luck, and astounding reserves of energy, escaped the headman's axe and the Tower itself, although when she was eventually taken there, she remarked mournfully, "This night I think to die."

In 1554 Philip II of Spain married Mary, although he had preferred the Protestant Elizabeth, hoping thus to thwart the French plot to place Mary Stuart on the English throne should the present incumbent die. When Philip's suit succeeded, most Englishmen feared the birth of a Catholic heir, and the Spanish Inquisition was installed in Britain, beginning its intolerance and executions. It was after this event that "Bloody" Mary earned her dreadful nickname. But Mary soon demonstrated her latter-day Tudor difficulties in producing a baby.

I have taken pains in this essay to stress the physical and sexual aspects of that remarkable father and daughter, Henry VIII and Elizabeth I, who dominated the short Tudor dynasty. Because these physical and sexual aspects were so vitally important to the inner cores of their strong characters, they had a very special influence on the course of European and world history.

In a well-known scientific "opinion," one expert concluded of Elizabeth: "In a medical sense her sexual system was blasted. She had neither the instinct of sweetheart or mother—for these instincts are impossible in such a frame as hers. I think her selfishness—for her crown and her kingdom as much as for herself—must be sought in her really sexless condition. Elizabeth toyed with young men but one cannot conceive more than that." This is a rather strong opinion in view of the fact that Elizabeth is so often described as an attractive woman (hard to believe, if one looks at most paintings and miniatures of her) and that her name was sexually linked by gossip with Seymour, Dudley, Raleigh, Oxford, Blount, Essex, and Anjou, among others and in varying degrees and ways. The Earl of Leicester, a tall, handsome scholar-athlete, was probably the closest friend Elizabeth ever had and, except for Burghley, remained in her intimate counsels the longest period.

But there is no doubt Elizabeth was the last true royal autocrat in western Europe. She insisted upon complete and absolute domination until the end of her days because she genuinely believed this was the best thing for her country, and her love for England was almost certainly the only passion that ever possessed her. She was the total boss. She told her Parliament: "I will have here but one Mistress and no Master." She sent word through her Lord Keeper, Bacon, that parliament should not "meddle with any matters of state." This made France's Louis XIV seem almost liberal.

Once when the speaker of the House appeared with the customary request that its members be free from arrest, have access to her royal person, and liberty of speech, she replied that liberty of speech existed in the House: "but they must know what liberty they were entitled to; not a liberty for every one to speak what he listeth or what cometh in his brain to utter: their privilege extended no farther than a liberty of Aye or No."

It was Elizabeth, by the way, who, in 1596, introduced a formal racial policy in England with a decree requesting the removal of "Diverse blackamores brought into this realm, of which kind of people there are already here too many." This policy, ordered in view of a surge of unemployment at the time, was not unusual in Europe of those days when racial prejudice was first starting to stir.

In fact, even prior to the white Anglo-Saxon immigration, there had been blacks in England among the soldiers serving in Caesar's legions and occupying army. Nevertheless, I believe the first document embodying British racism was Elizabeth's.

None of her greatest aides, such as Essex and Burghley, did anything except what they were told to do. They were really the queen's glorified clerks or secretaries. As the historian Frederick Chamberlin concluded: "The western world has never seen such another absolute monarchy; and no view that Elizabeth was not the real power, driving force, and brain of her government ever obtained among her contemporaries. Every monarch in Europe so considered her. The Pope said that he and she were the only rulers capable of their tasks."

The two greatest members of the Tudor dynasty, Henry VIII and his youngest legitimate child, Elizabeth, were certainly the most flamboyant, brilliant, and humanly interesting sovereigns of England, even though it may be contended with more than a little validity that Alfred the Great, a largely legendary individual, was the most important. Henry truly introduced to his country the violent, colorful, intellectual excitement of the Renaissance, furnished it with the naval weapon that ultimately gave it an empire "on which the sun never sets," and for wholly godless reasons sponsored a new religion that matured and endured.

All these new developments flourished under Elizabeth I. Hers was the intellectual and cultural Renaissance of Francis Bacon, Marlowe, and Shakespeare; the era of the great explorers and pirates like Drake and Cavendish, the circumnavigators who made England rich and strong. They stimulated the tough, imaginative, individualistic population to make of their country, hitherto a second-rate European power compared with France and

Spain, a mighty, aggressive, greedy, imperial agglomerate, exceedingly difficult to invade, and a dominant world factor until the mid-twentieth century.

There is no doubt that Elizabeth herself was the dynamic force behind these developments. She was widely respected and feared. Two popes, Pius V and Gregory XIII, excommunicated her. Almost each contemporary tenant of the Vatican throne sought to encourage murder plots against her. Sixtus V, who helped to finance the Spanish Armada's unsuccessful invasion in 1588, said of Elizabeth: "What a woman. What a princess. Ruler of half of one small island, she snaps her fingers at the two greatest kings in Christendom [Spain and France]."

One institution developed under (and probably by) the "Virgin Queen" was the magnificent British intelligence service, which is still an important factor in international calculations. There are art students and intelligencers who believe that a symbol of this highly secret but widespread and vital factor in Elizabethan power is allegorically represented in the famous "Rainbow" portrait of Queen Elizabeth painted around 1600, probably commissioned by Francis Bacon and Robert Cecil with the sovereign's own knowledge. The artist is not known, but it is believed to be an Anglo-Flemish painter, perhaps Marcus Gheeraerts II. The work now hangs in Hatfield House, the splendid seat of the Cecil family, marquesses of Salisbury.

Experts on various aspects of the Renaissance point out that Elizabeth was the most intellectual monarch of her time and was fascinated by the then fashionable language of symbols and ciphers. This encourages the belief (described by Dr. Stevan Dedijer of Sweden's Lund University) that the portrait was—as conceived by those who commissioned it—a deliberately mysterious statement of the policy that made Britain "Great" for so long: scientific, commercial, naval, intellectual, espionage, etc.—all as depicted in the contemporary language of symbolism.

By studying the elaborate patterns of human eyes and mouths woven into the silk of the dress Elizabeth is wearing, one comprehends the attention she personally devoted to intelligence—so much so that the papal nuncio in Flanders reported to Rome: "The Queen of England, I know not how, penetrated everything." Mary Queen of Scots wrote the pope that Elizabeth had agents close to him—and Francis Walsingham, her chief intelligencer, knew this because he secretly read Mary's letters himself. It was Walsingham who stressed that open eyes and ears (as depicted in the "Rainbow" picture) were vital to intelligence. One motto of the queen was *"Video, Taceo"* (I see, but say nothing).

In 1582 Britain first recorded an annual secret service budget (750 pounds a year). All the most important Elizabethan court figures were given instructions on what to observe before they took off for Europe on the customary Grand Tour. At a festival in 1595, Francis Bacon cautioned the queen and her chief ministers: "Have care that your intelligence, which is the light of your state, do not go out or burn dim or obscure."

An effort to understand the curious symbolism and intentions of this provocative portrait, which deliberately flatters its subject by depicting her as a lovely, youngish woman when she was already a hag of almost seventy, shows that it is a preconceived boast and not a simple work of art. Therefore it is more interesting, more significant, and more helpful than the artist could possibly have understood, in demonstrating to scholars the deliberate plan and methodology conceived by Elizabeth and her principal advisers to produce a huge global empire.

In a weird way, Henry VIII, the father, brutally and energetically pushed England's intellectual, political, and naval Renaissance into flower (the way Philip of Macedon had built the foundations for a land empire in Greece). Elizabeth I utilized and directed these initial efforts to full advantage, producing a situation from which an overseas empire burgeoned that was at least comparable to the far briefer imperial domain of Philip's son, Alexander.

VI

A Testament of Beauty: Jacopo, Gentile, and Giovanni Bellini

Perhaps the greatest family cluster of painters known to history was produced by the Renaissance family of Bellini in the Most Serene Republic of Venice, one of the richest, greatest maritime powers of all time.

It is customary to assume that great painters and great poets, like Athena, should spring suddenly from Zeus's head—as in legend—rather than from the thighs of parents properly mated according to the views and theories of modern genetics. There is no more reason to suppose that the harmonious and complimentary ideas of Shakespeare's or Pushkin's mother and father were responsible for the superb genius of their sons than to speculate along similar lines in the cases of Duccio, Velasquez, or Leonardo da Vinci.

The timing of the artist's birth and the circumstances of the milieu surrounding him, added to the taste and desires of his generation, the wealth and culture of his surroundings, and the teachings handed on to him are easily of far more importance than the accidental encounter of certain genes.

The arrival in the world of painting from the Zeus's brow of the Venetian republic could be said to coincide with the birth of Jacopo Bellini, believed, without certainty, to have been in 1396. He lived through almost three quarters of the great fifteenth century. He was the first early Renaissance painter of Venice, and, together with two of his sons, Gentile and Giovanni, fathered a school of art that included such Venetian giants as Giorgione and Titian.

Venice was a secular power long before Jacopo's birth. It maintained a fluctuating dominance in the eastern Mediterranean and the Adriatic against formidable combinations of Italian rivals such as Genoa; Barbary pirates; the Byzantine emperors and then their successors, the Ottoman Turkish sultans;

and even those feudal Norman and Frankish lords who set up temporary but fierce independent fiefdoms, primarily in Greece, after the sacking of Constantinople in 1204 and, above all, following that great city's fall to the Turks in 1453.

The balance of power in the vital strategic and commercial area connecting the Black and Marmora Seas with the eastern Aegean, the Nile delta, Crete, the Dodecanese islands, the Peloponnesus, and the Adriatic was of enormous importance to the economic and cultural exchanges of East and West. Indeed, the Old Port of the tiny island of Spetsais, off the Gulf of Argos, where I lived in Greece for many years, served as the central point of a fierce fight between the Venetian fleet and the galleys and galleons of allied Genoa and Constantinople bound from Monemvasia to the Bosphorus and Black Sea for gold (like the ancient Argonauts), wool, wheat, timber, furs.

Venice's success in destroying most of this armada en route to the northeast in the thirteenth-century battle of Sette Pozzi was one of several key encounters of the Middle Ages that helped Venice reaffirm its hardiness and renown. It was this and many other little-known confrontations that enabled the tough, greedy Venetians to become a European power for more than three centuries.

How extraordinary that so small a city, situated on an Adriatic isle and with a population of only 160,000 in the sixteenth century, should have shown itself so adept at empire-building. But its inhabitants were intelligent, strong, with the toughness and frequent red hair brought southward by invading Teutonic and Slavonic tribes who overran the earlier Wendish settlers. The Venetians, elated by the respect and homage shown them by other nations, some of which should have been greater and some of which were, developed an original system of government with *doges* elected from the aristocracy ruling a republic made up of an essentially trading and manufacturing community with a high standard of living, and producing a civil service and, above all, a professional diplomatic service that was the envy of contemporaries.

The steadily growing wealth of Venice, not seriously damaged by the cupidity of the Slavic Dalmatians across the Adriatic, financed a famous fleet acknowledged by the Golden Bull of the Byzantine Emperor Basil, which traded privileges to Venetian merchants in exchange for emergency availability of the republic's navy if the Greek ruler needed help when Genoa was disinclined. Despite the jealousy of their constant rivals, the Genoese, the Venetians are said to have numbered about 200,000 in the city on the Golden Horn—or more than there were in Venice itself. They were reputed to have held a large quarter of the Byzantine capital in terror with their lusty brawls.

The Italians were scarcely true to the spirit of their accord with the emperor on the Bosphorus. When the Fourth Crusade was proclaimed at Soissons, France, and its leaders applied to the Venetians for troop transportation to Constantinople, the doge, Dandolo, withheld the needed ships until the crusaders first conquered Zara and Dalmatia for the republic. Then, after this blackmail, the fleet sailed.

Constantinople was sacked, and Venice, for its double-dealing role, was awarded "a half and a quarter of the *Roman empire*," which is what the Byzantines called their domain. They were the eastern offspring of Rome's twin heirs. It was Venice, as a first-class European power, which dealt out the fiefdoms to Frankish mercenary chiefs more interested in personal gain in Balkan regions than in moving on to the Holy Land.

The Venetians knew the value of a quick ducat. They scandalized Christendom by entering into a treaty with the Ottoman Turks and, in seesaw wars with Genoa, the remnants of Byzance, and even the Turks, held onto the eastern Mediterranean and control of the Levant trade. The decline of the republic began at the end of the fifteenth century and the beginning of the sixteenth, which is the acme of the Bellini period in painting.

Venice had already acquired, on coastal battlefields, such artistic treasures as the famous four horses of St. Mark's Cathedral, brought westward from Constantinople, and the mosaic techniques with which the Turks had lavished the adornment of their magnificent mosques and palaces. The taste for artistic beauty had been deeply instilled. Local craftsmen learned even more from the stolen treasures, acquiring talents which they embellished with their own genius.

It is curious to compare the cultural mirrors of the Dutch republic and the Venetian republic, both small but mighty states which had great influence at the height of their political and military fame. When one visits the Mauritshuis in the Hague, perhaps the finest small museum in the world, one sees on its walls the greatest painting ever produced in the Netherlands—and it mirrors with incredible precision the finest century in Dutch history.

From around 1600 to around 1700 the array of genius is fascinating; Vermeer and Rembrandt coincide with a moment when Dutch arms were successfully combatting the great Spanish army and defeating British ships. There is no equivalent museum in Venice. But if one looks at the dates of the lifespan of the Bellini clan—those who ignited the gradual Venetian genius in painting—one finds that its sunburst rises with empire. And one sees no hint of a strategic decline (like Holland's), only a rising sunburst on the global scene.

The Minerva from whose body (a figurative forehead) Jacopo Bellini emerged at the end of the fourteenth century was Franceschina, the wife of a tinsmith named Niccolo. Since painting was still behind the times in Venice, as compared with Tuscany and other flourishing Italian centers of the immediate pre-Renaissance period, Jacopo's artistic inclinations evolved early.

He studied in his home city under the accomplished Umbrian master Gentile da Fabriano, who had come to Venice in search of work and pupils, of whom he found several. When Fabriano went to Florence, Jacopo followed him and learned still more about classic style and natural grace from Donatello, Ghiberti, Masaccio, and Uccello than his original Umbrian master could ever teach him.

By 1429 Jacopo had returned to Venice as an accomplished painter in his own right and established his talented family by marrying a girl from Pesaro named Anna. She bore him at least one son, Gentile; there is argument about whether Jacopo's second son, Giovanni, was the child of Anna or another woman. A daughter named Nicolosia was also produced.

The atmosphere in which this creative clan lived in the earlier half of the fifteenth century was vigorous. Looking backward, it hinted strongly of the coming full glory of the Renaissance splendor that followed Constantinople's fall in 1453, when so many scholars and artists fled to western cities from the Turks, spreading their emigré knowledge and talent.

On its own, Venice, through its widespread trade, its fabricating knowledge, and its newly developing painters like Jacopo Bellini, Gentile da Fabriano, and nearby Verona's Pisanello, was embellishing the republic's reputation as a cultural center. A large *companile* or bell tower towered above St. Mark's Cathedral in the city's main square.

Quaintly-prowed gondolas glided through the canals past stone filigree palaces. And every Ascension Day the doge rode in his "bucentaur" (*buzino d'oro*, or "golden bark") to perform the ceremony of "wedding the sea," which sumptuously commemorated the republic's maritime dominion and specifically recalled Doge Orseolo II's conquest of Dalmatia. Such splendor could not but dazzle the impressionable minds of young painters.

In 1436 Jacopo journeyed to Verona and then southward to Ferrara, where he established connections with the ruling family of Este and the Malatestas of nearby Rimini. In that city the artistic household dominated by Jacopo was extended when his daughter, Nicolosia, married the famous painter Andrea Mantegna of Padua, later a great master of Mantua. Had the theory of transmission of artistic genes prevailed, there could have been little better possibility for its proof than the children of a Mantegna and a Bellini;

but alas, there is no such indication. I believe firmly in my Athena theory of creative genetics.

It would seem that Jacopo died around 1470. (There is no reliable record, but, in documents now available, Anna began to call herself a widow in that year.) By the time of his death, Jacopo, together with Fabriano and Pisanello, had brought the artistic potential of Venice to full maturity. An abundance of his paintings and drawings still exists in museums and album collections of Western Europe. Jacopo's new achievements in depicting perspective were highly original, and a now-lost book on perspective was dedicated to him by a Paduan scientist.

Jacopo was the first of the Bellinis to establish a contemporary and enduring reputation, and he attracted a small group of followers and helpers, although nothing like those who later flocked to his sons, Gentile and Giovanni, who themselves began their careers as their father's pupils and assistants. From 1466 on, Gentile (1429–1507) became renowned for his independent ability rather than as a talented member of a family "school" or "collective." He began to receive important personal commissions, such as his portrait of Cardinal Bessarione, and was also knighted by the German Emperor Frederick III during the latter's visit to Venice. He was a versatile craftsman who restored frescoes, became a famous portraitist, and was made official painter for the Most Serene Republic.

When Sultan Mohammed II asked Venice to provide him with an outstanding painter, Gentile was sent to Constantinople, where he remained two years, leaving his brother Giovanni to attend to commitments he had already made in Venice. Gentile was dispatched in the galleys of the Most Serene Republic, whose commissioner in Constantinople presented him to Mohammed. Giorgio Vasari reports that:

> [He was] treated with much favor as something new, above all after he had given that Prince a most lovely picture, which he greatly admired, being well nigh unable to believe that a mortal man had within himself so much divinity, so to speak, as to be able to represent the objects of nature so vividly.
>
> Gentile had been there no long time when he portrayed the Emperor Mohammed from life so well that it was held a miracle. That Emperor, after having seen many specimens of his art, asked Gentile whether he had the courage to paint his own portrait; and Gentile, having answered "Yes," did not allow many days to pass before he had made his own portrait with a mirror, with such resemblance that it appeared alive.

The Sultan's portrait is now unfortunately ruined. But many specimens of Gentile's Turkish voyage remain, including a small watercolor of a scribe and drawings of other types on the Ottoman scene.

When Gentile returned home to a warm welcome from his brother, Giovanni, he was awarded a provision of 200 crowns a year for the rest of his life. He then took up his earlier pledged commitments.

These included canvases commissioned by the signoria of the republic from several artists: both Gentile and Giovanni Bellini; Alvise Vivarini; Carpaccio; and eventually Titian, Veronese, and Tintoretto. The idea was to glorify Venice, but much of the work was later ruined by salt spray sheeted in by the famous Adriatic bora storms.

All the Bellinis seem to have worked feverishly so long as they were alive and well. Gentile, who lived until 1507, was at work on a painting of Saint Mark at the time of his death, so his brother, Giovanni, took up the brush and finished the project. Happily, it has been preserved in the Brera Museum of Milan.

As the eldest child, Gentile virtually grew up in his father's shop. Well attuned to the fairy-talelike narrative sensitivity of the late Gothic period, he was attracted by what he heard of his brother-in-law, Mantegna. Nicolosia's husband was then painting in nearby Padua, whence the fame of his novelties and new approaches had begun to spread.

It was surely as a result of this period that Gentile learned to design the doors of the organ in Venice's St. Mark's Cathedral, the case for the Byzantine crucifix of Cardinal Bessarione, and the "Annunciation" now in the Lugano collection of the Thyssen family. He developed a dramatic but heavy and unsubtle technique that was later rendered more delicate by painters of the High Renaissance. But his portraiture was superb. He was much sought after: Mohammed II, Queen Catherine Cornaro of Cyprus, and the doges now figuring in London's National Gallery and Venice's Correr Museum.

Giovanni Bellini, who was four years younger than Gentile and lived until 1516, also started with his father, but at the age of twenty-four he opened his own studio in San Lio. He continued to collaborate often with his father and brother, as exemplified in the chapel in the Church of St. Anthony in Padua, where all three joined in designing and decorating the chapel for the heroic mercenary leader Gattamelata. This was completed and signed by the two brothers in 1460, but subsequently lost.

After Gentile's Turkish sojourn, a place had been kept open for him by the republic to resume working beside his brother on a great series of historical pictures illustrating the role of Venice in the wars between the

Papal States and the Emperor Barbarossa. These were on canvas and in oil, to avoid the destruction to frescoes caused by the city's stormy climate. Unfortunately, they were destroyed by fire in 1577. The series depicted the pope standing in St. Mark's Square; the Emperor Barbarossa receiving the Venetian envoys, and then preparing for war; the pontiff urging the doge and signoria to equip thirty galleys for battle against the Germans, and then blessing the doge and Venetian senators.

Gentile followed the example of his father, Jacopo, in proving that his best talent was in individual portraiture. The severity of the manner he had learned during his time in Padua contrasted strikingly with the increasing luxuriousness of the blossoming Renaissance.

Giovanni (1430–1516) is probably the most renowned of the Bellinis. He also, from an early age, came under the influence of the dry Paduan school of his brother-in-law, Mantegna. This manner seems, on close scrutiny, to have remained a dominant factor until Mantegna transferred to Mantua and the court of the Gonzagas, acclaimed as the most cultured court in Italy.

From then on Giovanni produced a considerable series of religious paintings which display an original combination of Paduan severity in drawing, a complex rigidity of drapery, and a particular human pathos specifically attributed to Giovanni himself. He was also called upon by the republic to act as conservator of art in the great ducal palace, but neither his own nor his restored works in that lovely building survived the terrible fire of 1577.

Practically all of his original works are in tempera. In those days Venetian painters made panels rarely, and when they excepted their rule, they only used fir wood brought down by ship from the Teutonic and Scandinavian lands, primarily along the river Adige. Frescoes were risky because of the salty damp from the sirocco and bora winds, and canvas, a strong, easily handled material whose surface could readily accept oil paints, eventually became popular among the artists.

It was Giovanni who shifted increasingly from working with tempera to oils, a new medium first introduced to Venice by Antonello da Messina. This brought a more worldly charm and softness to some of his work and encouraged him to introduce groups of singing and viol-playing angels to attend upon his saints.

The last dozen years of his life saw him become so popular an artist that he was overwhelmed with commissions he could not accept. In 1506, when Albrecht Dürer, the greatest German painter of the Renaissance, visited Venice for a second time, he described Giovanni as "still the best in painting" and marked by courtesy and generosity to foreign visitors.

Both artistically and in a worldly sense Giovanni's career has been called: "upon the whole the most serenely and unbrokenly prosperous, from youth to extreme old age, which fell to any artist of the early Renaissance." His influence was indeed greatly magnified by many remarkable pupils, of whom the most famous were Giorgione and Titian. He has been dubbed "the greatest painter of his age and the father of the age of Titian."

His own independent view of art and the painter's role was made plain when the Duchess of Ferrara asked him for a detailed symbolic painting whose concept she outlined. He replied that he was used to suiting himself and to giving pleasure without restrictions.

Vasari, a sixteenth-century painter and architect of indifferent talent but a famous art historian and critic, was said to be "a great copyist, a painstaking writer, and never did critic wield a milder pen if he chanced to be writing of Florentine art, or a more prejudiced one if he dealt with things of Venice." Yet he, who wrote more than four hundred years ago, has become a prime sourcebook and influence of current opinions.

George Hay's book on Bellini both cites and balances Vasari, writing: "Giovanni, or Gian Bellini as he is generally called [except in Venetian argot], is one of the most fascinating painters of the fifteenth century. He has left many a lovely picture to the world, but alas he was no diarist, he had no Boswell, and there are gaps in the history of his life that will never be filled up."

Hay points out that Vasari dealt but briefly with Jacopo Bellini, founder of the dynasty and, according to Vasari, "It is said that the new paganism held more attractions for him than the old faith, and that the majority of his commissions were from the great and flourishing secular institutions of the Republic."

Vasari wrote that Jacopo Bellini, Giovanni's father, painted on canvas, not wood, and in the comparatively rare latter case, it was on fir floated down from Austria and Germany.

Vasari apparently felt that Jacopo's hints of paganism left Giovanni virtually untouched, and it is known the younger son rejected many commissions offered by wealthy patrons with no desire for sacred subjects and did not fulfill others.

Hay noted that when Giovanni was born, in 1430, Venice was "on the road to her ultimate decline . . . and, although Venice had annexed nearly a dozen provinces in half a century, the outlay had been out of proportion to the results. At the same time, the Venetians did not know that their splendid state was on the downward road."

Gian Bellini was a hard worker and serene spirit despite the historically critical moment when he lived; he died sixty-three years after Constantino-ple's fall—the acme of the Renaissance. His pupil Titian found it easy to depict pagan goddesses and the Christian God and saints with equal ease; but Gian Bellini made no concessions to the neopagan age, save a single bacchanalia painted for the Duke of Ferrara.

It is an interesting aspect that the family association of the two generations of painters could so benefit the swift artistic changes and techniques that were occurring in the early and mid-Renaissance. Jacopo, having traveled extensively in Italy's cultural centers, knew Florence at the time of Brunelleschi, Padua where Giotto's tradition was then still very strong, and brought back to Venice new ideas together with the hint of the revolutionary pagan sentiment introduced.

Gian Bellini developed these new ideas to such a degree that they made possible the beauty of his outstanding pupils, Titian and Giorgione. The new learning proceeded hand in hand with the emphasis on personal loveliness which had all too often been relegated to the background by the Church in earlier periods. This can be seen in Giovanni's pictures, which bring sensuous beauty and emotion to canvas in a degree perhaps previously unknown.

The Venice of Gian Bellini's most active period must have been particularly fascinating and stimulating. The envoy of the French King Charles VIII, Philippe de Commynes, arrived in 1494 and recalled a memoir:

> I was taken along the High Street. They call it the Grand Canal and it is very broad. Galleys cross it and it is the fairest street, I believe, that may be in the whole world, and fitted with the best houses. The ancient onces are painted, and most have a great piece of porphyry and serpentine in front.
>
> It is the most triumphant city I have ever seen and doth most honor to ambassadors and strangers. It doth most wisely govern itself, and the service of God is most solemnly performed.

George Hay accepts this French diplomat's emphasis on beauty and triumph, and for him it helps to explain why "Gian Bellini became a lover of the world in its most picturesque aspect, accepting without hesitation the traditional explanation of its creation. . . ." Hay continues:

> His appeal to the layman is direct and spontaneous.
>
> A countryman who has never seen a studio can respond to the exquisite beauty of Bellini's Virgins and Children, can feel the charm of the sunshine that fills the air and lights sea and land, can

recognize the infinite glamor of the roads that wind away into the mysterious distance of the background, can enjoy the rich, almost sensuous, coloring.

Although few personal tales of Gian Bellini's life exist, there is one interesting report that as a young swain he dressed up like a nobleman of Venice seeking a portrait and visited the studio of the popular Antonello da Messina, who undertood the commission. Bellini is said to have studied the entire procedure closely and to have learned many technical details.

Giovanni's continued fidelity to the Church despite pagan influences that had been introduced to him through his father is shown in his almost obsessive fascination with altar painting. John Ruskin called his altarpiece in the Church of St. Zaccaria one of the "two finest pictures in the world." This is no mean tribute even though Ruskin's opinions are now regarded as frequently flawed.

Unfortunately, none of his large works remain, although they were much admired in his time. These included a representation of Pope Alexander III receiving Frederick Barbarossa after the end of the Schism of 1177, and three others of the same pontiff on ceremonial occasions. They were frescoes and guaranteed by Giovanni to outlast the sirocco and bora winds for at least two centuries, but in less than half that time they were destroyed by fire.

Although Gentile had been selected by the republic to visit Constantinople when Mohammed II asked for a Venetian artist, Giovanni had been named official painter to the state and did a portrait of Doge Loredano when he succeeded to that esteemed office in 1501. This is especially noteworthy because it is known that Titian was already working in Gian Bellini's studio at the time.

Also in 1501, Isabella, Marchioness of Mantua, sent a representative to Venice to ask Giovanni to paint a secular subject. He was by then an old man, as things were then generally measured, and simply accepted an advance payment and turned to other work. Only three years later, after the marchioness and her agent had persistently badgered him (she proposed to take legal action), was the painting accomplished. She asked for a second secular picture, and after much tergiversation he refused.

Isabella d'Este, of whom a poet wrote: "At the sound of her name all the Muses rise and do reverence," was a highly intelligent and also persistent, obstinate woman. She had seen and admired Gian Bellini's work in Venice before asking a friend named Vianello to obtain for her a pledge from Gian to do a picture.

The old artist brusquely told Vianello he was busy working for the signory in the Doge's Palace and was taken up every day from early morning until nightfall. Vianello seems to have been an experienced bazaar trader. When the painter said that nevertheless he might consider altering his schedule should he be paid 150 ducats for a painting, Isabella's agent haggled him down to 100 ducats, of which an advance of 25 ducats was accepted by Bellini as a pledge.

Only after that, according to the extraordinarily rich and voluminous correspondence that has been preserved from the marchioness's papers, did Bellini ask precisely what she wished. Isabella replied with words that would not today be considered to have much precision: she wanted anything antique and, in effect, moralistic in its purport. But the painter kept dodging specifics, went to his estate inland, and showed he could not be located.

The marchioness finally lost her temper and told Vianello: "We can no longer endure the villainy of Giovanni Bellini." She instructed her agent to apply to the doge for Gian Bellini's imprisonment for fraud. It appears that this stimulated the painter to react.

Despite the fact that he held the respect of the doge, Leonardo Loredano, whose portrait he had made, Giovanni was clearly alarmed and hastened to show Vianello a "Nativity," three-fourths finished. He also sent Isabella an almost ignominious letter of excuses. She graciously replied: "Your 'Nativity' is as dear to us as any picture we possess."

It was shortly after this incident that Dürer came again, in 1506, to the city-in-the-sea and remarked that the Venetians were agreeable companions and "some" of them could paint. But he praised Gian Bellini highly and even offered to purchase one of his pictures.

From that point on, the available records have little to report on Giovanni until 1513. Then, well over eighty years old, his status as official painter to the signory was challenged by his own magnificent pupil, Titian. The latter informed the Council of Ten that he was more interested in fame than profit (as he had demonstrated by refusing to serve the pope) and desired the first available vacancy in the German Foundation then existing on the same terms as Zuan Bellini (the Venetian way of spelling Gian Bellini).

Bellini, his pupils and his friends were irked, despite the acknowledged and increasing reputation of Titian. (The same thing happened years later when Tintoretto tried to take over an official position from the older Titian.) Titian was eventually told by the council that the job could not be his until Bellini's commission had come to an end. But the council started an investigation of the project and what had already been accomplished by old

Giovanni and decided that not enough had been produced for its investment.

It was decided there had been too much laxity in supervising expenditures of the Most Serene Republic during the years since the treaty between France, Austria, Spain, and the Papal States had been concluded at Cambrai. Although Venice had been induced to seek aid from the sultans of Turkey and Egypt, earlier losses had been followed by the vanishing of Venetian influence in Lombardy, Verona, Vicenza, and Padua. The republic had not yet regained its force and vigor.

In this atmosphere Gian Bellini died in his ninetieth year, November 29, 1516. Some years later Vasari commented: "There were not wanting in Venice those who by sonnets and epigrams sought to do him honor after his death as he had done honor to himself and his country during his life."

The last grand Italian master of purely religious subjects had expired. The way had become clear for the advance of Giorgione and Tintoretto, after whom a rapid decline would ensue. Moreover, admiration for Gian Bellini's work shrank continually because of the number of pictures from his studio bearing forged signatures. It was only after the rise in the nineteenth century of studious critics like Crowe, Morelli, and Bernard Berenson that a revival ensued.

Giorgio Vasari, whose anti-Venetian bias has already been mentioned, relegated Giovanni Bellini to the group of acknowledged "masters" whom he criticized for having "sought with great efforts to do the impossible in art by means of labor, particularly in foreshortening and in things unpleasant to the eye which were as painful to see as they were difficult for them to execute." However, since that early and pro-Florentine critic included in the same group Piero della Francesca, Ghirlandajo, Botticelli, Mantegna, and Luca Signorelli, it is easy to mitigate or even ignore such negative views.

When Gian Bellini's death was described by the sixteenth-century critic-historian (who lived only less than three generations later than his subject), Vasari wrote: "Finally, having lived ninety years, Giovanni passed from his life, overcome by old age, leaving an eternal memorial of his name in the works that he had made both in his native city of Venice and abroad, and he was honorably buried in the same church and in the same tomb in which he had laid his brother Gentile to rest." Whatever may be said of Vasari's prejudice in favor of Florence (where he, a native of Arezzo, studied and worked) and against Venice, he surely had a soft spot for Gian Bellini.

The most reasonable intellectual explanation I have read of the flowering of Venetian Renaissance painting in general and the Bellinis in particular is that of Bernard Berenson, the great American connoisseur, expert, and critic who amassed the collection of Mrs. Henry Gardner in Boston and who spent the last decades of his long life in his lovely villa, I Tatti, outside Florence. He wrote:

> The Church from the first took account of the influences of color as well as music upon the emotions. From the earliest times it employed mosaic and painting to enforce its dogmas and relate its legends. . . . At about the time when [Gian] Bellini and his contemporaries were attaining maturity, the Renaissance had ceased to be a movement carried on by scholars and poets alone. It had become sufficiently widespread to seek popular as well as literary utterance and thus, toward the end of the fifteenth century it naturally turned to painting. . . .
>
> We find the Venetian painters . . . more and more intent upon giving the space they paint its real depth. . . . As early as the beginning of the sixteenth century a few of the greater Venetian painters had succeeded also in giving some appearance of reality to atmosphere. The painters of the end of the fifteenth century who met with the greatest success in solving these problems were Giovanni and Gentile Bellini, Cima da Conegliano and Carpaccio, and we find each of them enjoyable. . . .
>
> It is significant that Venice was the first state which made a business of preserving the portraits of its chief rulers. Those which Gentile and Giovanni Bellini executed for this end must have had no less influence on portraiture than their mural paintings . . . had on other branches of the art.

Berenson referred to Giovanni as "that great but unconscious revolutionary" who developed the method by which color became "the chief if not sole instrument with which his effects were to be produced," although he had "passed through an initial phase of intense precision of outline."

It was with Giovanni that the genius of the family flickered out. There had existed, indeed, one other painter, almost certainly connected with the family, but not gifted: Leonardo Bellini, who was born around 1425 and apparently remained active well into the second half of the fifteenth century. Some say that he was a nephew and some say that he was a grandson of Jacopo, great original chief of the artist clan. But he was never seen as notable; indeed, his miniatures appear to be his most considerable contribution to the gaudy burst of Renaissance painting. There is no evidence that he was ever an intimate member of the Bellini family nor a close collaborator with any of them. The great trio of father and sons—Jacopo, Gentile, and Giovanni, on the other hand, represented the sperm, the body and the soul of the luminous, long-lasting school of Venetian art.

Apart from the enduring greatness of the Bellini clan, its mere existence demonstrates that on rare occasions splendid painters can hand on the torch of their talents by normal genetic vigor as has been demonstrated among families in other fields, such as Philip and Alexander as strategists or the two Dumas as writers.

I know of no other cluster of intimately related painters who managed to achieve enduring fame. But there can be no doubt that it was advantageous, for Gentile and Giovanni Bellini, inheriting that flash of genius passed on by their parents' loins, were able to benefit from the teachings of their father, Jacopo, and perhaps their brother-in-law, Mantegna, to polish their natural genius, and to achieve immortality themselves and through their own pupils, like Titian and Giorgione.

Yet, in its conception and form, this book is not couched as an analysis of familial artistic talent. My thought throughout has been the juxtaposition of any father with his children and how, if such proved to be the case, one generation's genius or malevolence—at any rate, an outstanding talent—manifested itself in its immediate descendents.

Sometimes, as in the case of Philip and Alexander, it has been a furious bonfire of genial explosion. In others, such as Alexander VI and Cesare Borgia, it has been a blazing malevolence. Surely there are many more paired occasions of sire and offspring less melodramatic and therefore less known, when a sturdy, talented, noble stream of goodness and ability has flowed from one bloodstream to its successor—like the flamboyant but magnificently virtuous Adams family of Massachusetts or the gifted, joy-giving Bellini family in Venice. Jacopo, the first artistic clan chief, bequeathed to his two brilliant sons, Gentile and Giovanni, through his own genes and his personal example, one of history's few family testaments of beauty.

VII

Mafia in the Vatican: Pope Alexander VI and Cesare Borgia

In contemporary argot, the famous Sicilian terrorist brotherhood, the Mafia, is known as "the Family" and generally associated with evil and racketeering, in both of which it has customarily displayed great skill and ardor. A considerable number of its members have graduated to positions of wealth, power, and social eminence after the ugliest, most immoral, and most sordid of beginnings.

But the taste for lawlessness, avarice, murder, bribery, kidnapping, rape, torture, and every vile aspect of crime had its greatest and (one must admit, most garish) familial success in the late fifteenth and early sixteenth centuries when the Hispano-Italo clan of Borgias took over the Holy See and the Papal States under the pope's secular administration, climbing to the highest degree of Renaissance prestige, holding vast temporal influence, immense wealth, and a political clout that redounded throughout Europe.

At the same time, the Borgia clan was undoubtedly the most wicked center of its era and certainly the most wicked that ever gained control of the well-organized pontificate of the Roman Catholic Church. Indeed, one might argue that it was morally even more wicked than that other Spanish organization, the Inquisition, which applied its widespread sadistic tortures in the name of God to press Catholic orthodoxy's cause. As Orville Prescott has written:

> The reasons for the moral decline of the Church in the Renaissance were many and dated back well into the Middle Ages. During the absence of the popes in Avignon and during the Great Schism much of Italy suffered a political state of near anarchy. The distant popes seemed far more intent on collecting funds

and on imposing their rule by military conquest than on exercising the spiritual leadership of their exalted office. The cardinals and legates they sent from France to Italy did much to debase the reputation of the Church.

When the popes returned to Rome from Avignon early in the fifteenth century, conditions in Italy were only a little better. It was plain to all the popes that the papacy as an institution and even their own lives were not safe unless the temporal power of the Church was secure. That meant not only that the popes must be absolute rulers of the city of Rome but that wherever possible they should rule the states of the Church directly and not just through nominal vicars. The larger the area the popes actually governed, the safer the Church would be. So all the popes waged wars and some of them—notably Sixtus, Innocent, Alexander and Leo—waged them to make their relatives princes under papal supremacy.

Everywhere, in all religions, more slaughter has been done in the name of God since the concept of divinity was invented by men in prehistoric times, than in any other name: war, storm, earthquake, greed, territory, gold, sex, or any abstract ideology. Sect has murdered sect—as in The Thirty Years' War—ever since humanity's dawn. Moslems have slain heathens; Hindus have slain Moslems, and Buddhists have been slain by Hindus; Jews have been slain by Christians, and Mohammedans by Jews— all in the various names of God, be he Allah, Baal, Zeus, Jesus, Bodhisatva, or Jehovah. Jews mowed down Philistines and, centuries later, were incinerated by Nazi neopagans. Among the worst examples I know of cruel death associated with theological creed is the assassination on a diabolical scale of Protestant sects by hired mercenaries in medieval France and the disgusting excesses of satanic murder committed by the family of the Borgia Pope Alexander VI in Rome—without even vague reference to holiness.

Indeed, had it not been for the surfeit of wicked excesses developed by the Roman Church during Alexander's papacy—the ostentatious lewdness, the publicly carnal orgies, encouraged by this most diabolical of any pontiff in a diabolical era, the mass sale of indulgences, the murder, torture, and cynical double-crossing in which Church leaders figured prominently—and if, at approximately the same time, King Henry VIII of England had not yearned to satisfy his pride and royal tradition by producing a legitimate male heir, quite conceivably the Protestant Reformation might never have assumed so violent and widespread a tenor. It could have simply petered out in gradual correction of abuses while encouraging both the pope and the king or the pope and Luther to live up to their sworn responsibilities: an imaginary version of Pope John XXIII in Rome, a neo-Erasmus among the Teutons, and a latter-day male Elizabeth in London after Henry's divorce received papal approval.

Without the almost simultaneous impacts of Alexander and Henry, there might have been no such dramatically extensive a rebellion in Christianity, sponsored by two political superpowers with an indignant inquisitorial reaction. But too vast a storm of outrage against what is today symbolized by the non- or anti-religious activities of a pope and a Christian king broke down the shards of any tradition of unity left in Christendom's major societies.

The collapse of a previously established society was overwhelming Europe on a piecemeal basis as the Turks destroyed Constantinople and eastern Christianity, Spain moved in the direction of unifying the Hispanic states, and France pulled itself together as a great power. But Italian energies were dissipated in fraternal quarrels among the various Italianate governments or external empires. Meanwhile, general morality vanished together with traditional feudal order.

Rodrigo Borgia displayed great craft and flamboyant style on his way up the ladder of command. He was known for his vigorous personality and untrammeled physique as well as for a dignified and noble presence—when desirable. No one questioned his perspicacity, astuteness, or ambition, his persuasive ability or his capacity in the management of difficult problems. Throughout his career he was prepared to join Iberian toughness to complete lack of principle, and he made a personal fortune out of his ecclesiastical career before he ever became pontiff.

The Borgia family's initial prominence in the international field came from a methodical jurist in southern Spain, Alfonso Borja (the Spanish spelling) who, even before he was a priest, was named a bishop and, in 1444, a cardinal in payment for his aid in dethroning the antipope. With the assistance of secular chiefs indebted to him, he raised himself to the Holy See in 1455, choosing the name Calixtus III when he tottered to the throne at the age of seventy-seven. He sought to crown his reign by achieving two objectives: increasing the political authority and realms of his family, and raising a great crusade to regain Constantinople from the Moslem Turks.

His first objective was soon traditional among Borgia chieftains. During the period of Borgia eminence, the tribe managed to produce two popes, five cardinals, and numerous bishops shoved to power in that most immoral of times. Later, one modest Borgia, Francesco, was canonized.* The spring-board of their distinction was Xativa, a small town near the port of Gandia in Valencia, southern Spain, where the dukes of Borgia (the Italian spelling) and their coat of arms, a bull in a golden field, were honored for helping the King of Aragon conquer the Valencians.

The second objective was always at auction for a price. The papal secretary of Calixtus—for a handsome fee—had the family relationship officially "distanced" between an illustrious French count, Jean d'Armagnac, and his sister so they could "legally" marry. The pope saw to it that one third of the 24 million ducats received by the pontiff for the favor was paid to his nephew Rodrigo—eventually himself pope as Alexander VI—for his role in arranging this dirty affair.

Calixtus managed to have two nephews, Rodrigo and Pedro Luis, sons of his sister, raised to the cardinalate once they had agreed to accept his surname, Borgia. He set the family pattern in the Holy See by naming Pedro Luis, captain-general of the papal citadel of Sant'Angelo, then governor of a handful of important cities, and finally prefect of Tuscany. Each of these posts went for a price in ducats. Only one single cardinal, the pious Capranica, objected—utterly in vain.

As Alexander VI he had a reputation as a shrewd politician and administrator. He was handsome, eloquent, and wielded an insidious charm; few influential people caviled at his lack of religious feeling and neglect of ecclesiastical obligations. He at once betrayed the inordinate Borgia passion for family advancement, and in all, five members of the Borgia clan received the red cardinal's hat during his tenure.

Rodrigo pretended to strict defense of Church dogma and made no secret of his particular preference for female saints. Already when in Valencia and not yet widely famed, he was renowned for his "gay features and happy air," which earned him enormous popularity with attractive women. And in the corrupt fifteenth century, when even the Church had been increasingly infected, nobody expected a handsome young cardinal to observe his vows of chastity with serious rigor.

Few people saw anything odd in the fact that the young prelate, barely thirty, danced publicly in "dissolute fashion" or amused himself in the same

---

* Francisco de Borja y Aragon, a sixteenth-century duke (of Gandia) who became a Jesuit after his wife's death, was canonized in 1671, in all probability because he was backed by the influential Jesuitical order and by Church figures who wished to show that there may have been *some* good in the Borgia mafia.

licentious way as his seventy-year-old uncle, the pope. Nevertheless, the Mantuan chronicler, Schivenoglia, was depressed at the fact that Rodrigo, since the age of twenty-five, had shown himself "capable of committing every evil."

Cardinal Rodrigo Borgia clung steadfastly to his hunger for richness and power. At the same time, he displayed intelligence and superb tact when required, as in negotiating the marriage of Ferdinand, King of Aragon, and Isabella, Queen of Castille. He was a pronounced favorite of Ferdinand and became famed for his sumptuous way of life.

The only restraint in his taste for excesses, even while pope, was limitation to a simple, restricted diet of food. Even his son Cesare and his nephew Cardinal Monreale subsequently regarded it as a penitence to dine with the Holy Father, Alexander VI.

Rodrigo had no taste for literature or poetry but adored music and above all the dance. He was an exceptionally mundane cardinal, even for that epoch, and enjoyed hunting, carnivals, the theater, and licentious public displays. Like most princes of the Church, he was also renowned as a heavy gambler.

Cardinal Borgia lived openly and luxuriously in Rome with Vanozza di Catanei, titular wife of Giorgio de Croce and then of Carlo Canale. Subsequently, he had the same relationship with Giulia Farnese, known as "La Bella," titular wife to Orsino Orsini. In both cases—above all after Rodrigo became "Holy" Father himself—these *ménages* were acknowledged by everyone.

"La Vanozza," as she was called, mothered his children and thereafter did all in her power to assist their advancement. Rodrigo first met her in Mantua in 1461 and was overwhelmed by her charm and beauty, while Vanozza responded to his handsome magnetism. Their daughter, Lucrezia, famed for her loveliness as well as for the evil spoken of her, was said to have her mother's straight nose and her father's strong chin.

It is probable as well that Lucrezia inherited her clear blue eyes and long silky golden hair from Vanozza, who also gave her clerical lover three other children: Cesare; Giovanni, the second Duke of Gandia (his father, Rodrigo, was the first to hold the title); and Gioffre, prince of Squillace (who married a Spanish princess, Sancha, who was simultaneously the mistress of his two brothers).

As was then the custom, Cardinal Rodrigo started moving Cesare up the road to glory at a precocious age. When only seven, he was named apostolic protonotary and canon of Valencia, rector and archdeacon. Later, Innocent VIII did Cesare's father a favor by making the son bishop of Pamplona.

Cardinal Rodrigo, the Spaniard, was elected Pope Alexander VI in 1492, Spain's *annus mirabili*, when Columbus discovered America, and Ferdinand captured Granada and, jointly with his wife, expelled all Moors and Jews. In order to celebrate, Cesare Borgia organized a bullfight before the Vatican.

Several other candidates for the papal throne had been backed with huge sums by rival lay potentates seeking political influence; holiness didn't weigh much in the fifteenth and sixteenth centuries. What the pope needed more was a strong character, largesse to buy votes, and strategically placed, well-armed friends around Europe.

When Rodrigo Borgia, possessing all these attributes, was elected by his fellow cardinals and, as Vicar of Christ, took the name of Alexander, he was sixty-two years old, yet still a strong, lusty figure of a man. As the gong of the Capitol resounded while his papacy was proclaimed, a huge mob gathered, surging slowly toward the Holy See, and the cardinals gravely formed up to render homage.

It was indeed hard for destiny to look ahead. The new pontiff was clever, experienced, a hard worker, a consummate man of the world, a fine diplomat, strong, possessor of unusual charm, dignified, and an eloquent orator. But a great many of those present also knew well the corrupt circumstances and outright purchase which had produced this scandalous choice.

Nevertheless, as suitable to Borgia tastes, the *prossessio* or procession from the Vatican to the Lateran and the papal coronation were unusually splendid and worthy of a handsome, noble Pontiff. A protonotary had written in large letters on an arch erected over his house: "Rome was great under Caesar, now she is greater; now Alexander VI reigns: Caesar was a man, he is a God." (A rather pretentious claim by a highly immodest pseudoclerk on behalf of a man who only called himself Christ's vicar.)

A witness described Alexander as "worthy of the occasion. He rode a horse white as snow, with a serene forehead and majestic dignity." A member of the snobbish Porzio family described him as tall, with a skin neither too ruddy nor too pale, black eyes and heavy lips. He was strikingly eloquent.

Even in this grand *prossessio* the public for the first time got a hint that the new, less-than-holy father was subject to occasional physical strokes of the type known as syncopes. Despite his vitality and vigor, he suddenly fainted with apparent fatigue at the entrance to the Lateran basilica and had to be supported to the altar by a pair of cardinals until he was brought back to consciousness by dashes of cold water in the face.

This seems to be the first Roman public display of an embarrassing weakness for an energetic man, but it is certain that those who knew Alexander well were aware of this strange fallibility during his days as a cardinal. In subsequent papal processions, he was stricken several times by the same peculiar illness. For that reason the pontiff did his utmost to discourage fatiguing ceremonials.

He began his pontificate with what appeared to many to be excellent intentions. Several diplomats reported his desire to reform the papal court, reestablish peace in Italy, and take up his uncle's expressed quest to march in a crusade against the Turks. But such promise was disappointed. Alexander proceeded to fill the important offices of the Vatican with rich personal clients including what was regarded as an excessive number of Spaniards.

During the procession, the young Cardinal Medici murmured into his neighbor's ear: "Let us flee. We're in the gullet of the wolf; he'll devour us all." Within days, pious Romans were confiding to each other that Borgia's elevation was a proof of the anger of God, as the Dominican Friar, Girolamo Savonarola, had foreseen—a prophecy strikingly fulfilled through the invasion of Italy by the ravaging troops of France's King Charles VIII. The Florentine envoy remarked sourly that there was no joy in Rome and added that yet another Spaniard had little chance of becoming popular.

No popes of the period were exactly renowned for conforming to the proprieties and behavior suited to that supreme religious post, but Alexander was by far the worst. He demonstrated that a Borgia in the Vatican was a far greater evil than would be the presence of an Al Capone or a Lucky Luciano in the modern American White House.

Alexander's tenure clearly had a malign effect on the position of the Church vis-à-vis the gathering forces of Reformation. Seventeen years after Alexander's death, Martin Luther wrote of the pontificate: "I do not admit that I owe any obedience to the Pope [by then Leo X]. . . . I hate that man of sin and son of perdition, with all his kingdom which is nothing but sin and hypocrisy." The German said of the Holy See: "It is more scandalous and shameful than any Sodom or Babylon. . . . Its wickedness is beyond all counsel and help." He might have been composing the first electric telegraph message, sent three centuries later: "What hath God wrought?" The Lutherans began to identify the papacy with the "great whore" and the pope with the Antichrist himself.

Alexander displayed an uninhibited taste for nepotism. Cesare was promoted from his modest see in Pamplona to the great bishopric of Valencia, despite the anger of King Ferdinand, who began to recognize dangers of his own dynastic position with the growing prestige of his former Borgia favorites. The new pope also named his nephew, Giovanni Borgia-Lançol, Bishop of Monreale.

Alexander decided to employ the beautiful Lucrezia to further family political advancement, although she was still only eleven years old. Despite her youth, she already knew a surprising amount about sex, having, it was said, witnessed at close hand many of the antics of her holy parent. But the original engagement desired for her by Alexander was deferred. While these proceedings occurred, Alexander's current mistress, Giulia Farnese, produced his baby, the only papal offspring ever born actually inside the Vatican itself.

Shortly thereafter, Alexander's agents arranged that Lucrezia should marry a Spanish nobleman, the son of the proud Count d'Aversa; but this proposition also fell through as a result of Alexander's shifting political ambitions. She was eventually wedded to Giovanni Sforza, Lord of Pesaro in the Romagna, a widower twice the age of his lovely golden-haired wife, by this time thirteen.

Because of her youth it was agreed (for a sum) that the ceremony would be delayed for one year. When the event finally took place, such were the celebrations which followed that one observer asserted that the pope, then sixty-three, behaved as actively as he had when but a twenty-eight-year-old cardinal.

This marriage was eventually annulled and the ravishing Lucrezia was handed on, for dynastic reasons, to Alfonso, Prince of Biseglia. He was subsequently strangled after his father lost his throne as king of Naples. The murderer was Cesare's most proficient and highly paid assassin.

Still lovely and personally as well as politically desirable, Lucrezia was married in 1502 to the crown prince of Ferrara and finally died in childbirth, leaving behind a legend compounded of lust, lechery, incest, beauty, and slavish devotion to her evil father. She was almost certainly less wicked than totally feeble and pliable, and it is unlikely that she was, in fact, much maligned by the most exaggerated rumors concerning her tainted morals and sometimes quietly devilish behavior.

Giovanni, said sometimes to be Cesare's son, sometimes the pope's own, was given the dukedoms of Camerino and Nephi. Alexander's grandson, by Lucrezia, became duke of Sermoneta.

On September 20, 1493, Cesare was made a cardinal, thus further strengthening his own and his family's position. Alexander used the occasion to make a curious gesture toward propriety, in honor of his own bastard son;

he published a bull proclaiming the legitimacy of Cesare as son of Vanozza and her then-husband, Domenico d'Arignano, this formality making him technically more eligible for the red hat.

One year later, jealous of Spain's rising power among the divided Italian states, the French king, Charles VIII, invaded Italy and stirred up a hornet's nest of trouble. The French invaders were the first army in Europe to haul a wagon-train of cannon on a long campaign. These frightened the Italians increasingly as they smashed down the strongest stone walls of their citadels. A few years later, the great poet Ariosto was to ask: "How did this infamous and ugly invention ever find a place in human hearts?"

It had been a dismal omen for the pope when his old rival in the Sacred College, the tough, fighting Cardinal Della Rovere, initiated a fruitless negotiation for an alliance with Sultan Bajezet of Turkey against the "most Christian" monarch, Della Rovere's host, the French king.

While still a cardinal, Alexander had employed the Spanish against the French and vice versa. Although mindful of his relative Calixtus III's hope to raise a new crusade against the Turks, he had continually made secret compacts with Sultan Bajezet while at the same time exerting pressure on him by keeping the Ottoman emperor's brother, Prince Djem, prisoner and charging the Supreme Porte 40,000 ducats a year to support him in customary style. Djem, indeed, was permitted to hold his own Islamic court at the same time as Alexander staged his luxuriously dictatorial orgies or formalities in the Vatican.

Bajezet became increasingly alarmed at the possibility Djem might lend himself to some scheme to seize the Ottoman throne, and eventually offered the Holy Father 300,000 ducats, together with what was said to be the tunic of Christ on which the Roman soldiers threw their dice before the cross, to have him murdered. But before Alexander could benefit from the offer, he was forced to dispatch the Turkish prisoner to the King of France, in the great game of treachery.

On the last day of 1494, Charles battered his way into Rome. While Alexander cowered behind the fortifications of Sant'Angelo, armored French knights, artillery, and terrifying regiments of Swiss and German mercenaries paraded unopposed.

They stayed for one month, during which Alexander was able to display his negotiating skill. Although Alexander's enemies among the cardinals were urging Charles to summon a council to depose the pope, what primarily interested the king was promise of papal backing for his planned projects of further conquest, and Alexander was frightened into agreeing that French forces could cross papal territory on their march southward to Naples.

For a cardinal's hat, Alexander suborned Briçonnet, Charles's confidential adviser. As a result, the king's interest in a council was dropped. However, when Charles marched on to Naples, he took with him Cesare Borgia as a "legate"—in reality a hostage for his father's behavior—and also Prince Djem. Djem died suspiciously soon at Charles's camp near Naples.

The French expedition was doomed to fail. It was not equipped for a continuing occupation and conquest. Charles's army was immobilized in Naples, a prey to fever; the Aragonese princes of that southern kingdom eluded him, and the people resorted to guerrilla warfare. Cesare escaped from supervision and went into hiding.

Meanwhile Alexander encouraged an anti-French alliance, the so-called Holy League, with Maximilian of Habsburg, Ferdinand of Spain, and Milan and Venice. Charles decided to retreat.

Alexander VI was no fool; he was simply a scabrous villain in what should have been the wrong profession. Unquestionably a talented man, he ended up as the most immoral, sexiest, most power-hungry, and vicious pope in the history of the Holy See, intelligent but not wise enough to understand that the antics he encouraged and himself practiced would split up the Church whose unity he so much desired. His antiprophet was Savonarola, burned in Florence in flames that might better have consumed the Borgia chief.

It is far from Alexander's sole fault that the Catholic Church was in such miserable shape in the late fifteenth century. As the brilliant historian, John Addington Symonds wrote:

> All the Cardinals, with the exception of Rodrigo Borgia, were the creatures of [Pope] Sixtus or of Innocent VIII. Having bought their hats with gold, they were now disposed to sell their votes to the highest bidder. The Borgia was the strongest, richest, wisest, and most worldly of them all. He ascertained exactly what the price of each suffrage would be and laid his plans accordingly.

Yet the gang installed by the ambitious, ruthless new pontiff and headed by his attractive but detestable son Cesare used its new positions and increasing immorality to establish in the name of the Church a hateful, tyrannical rule that exceeded anything hitherto practiced even in the worst-run temporal states of Italy. Cesare personally hunted down the important Varani family and murdered almost all its male members. After capturing Roenza, he publicly insulted and then drowned or strangled its leaders, who were brought to Rome.

His agents told him the Bishop of Cetta, in France, had repeated one of

Cesare's secrets; so he had him poisoned. On behalf of his father, he bribed Cardinal d'Amboise in order to maintain Borgia credit with Louis XII, who had succeeded Charles VIII as French king.

The combined policy devised by Alexander and executed by Cesare used the pope's theoretical spiritual prestige, the Church's wealth, the skills of murder and assassination, dictated diplomacy, and threats of the most menacing sort against potential personal opponents. Papal pressure sought to dismember nations to the profit of the house of Borgia—by fraud, blackmail, and sacrilege.

No such persistent and widespread evil could endure, even in the lax, immoral licentiousness of cynical Renaissance Italy, and the final knell was sounded, according to common report, when Alexander and Cesare invited themselves to dinner with Cardinal Adriano of Corneto in his vineyard. It was rumored that Adriano's butler had garnished the affair with goblets of poisoned wine. Either by mistake or with the deliberate connivance of Adriano, the wine was allegedly served to the self-invited guests—who choked in agony and died. This is the version believed by the well-informed gossip Cinthio. Francesco Guicciardini adds that "all Rome ran with indescribable gladness" to see the papal corpse.

There is no doubt that at least the portion of the tale referring to Cesare is untrue. He outlived Alexander by four years, expiring at the minor siege of Viana, in Navarre, in 1507. Guicciardini and others believe Alexander actually died a victim of some malevolent illness, a black and swollen mass.

The Marquis of Mantua wrote his wife: "In his sickness the Pope talked in such a way that those who did not know what was in his mind thought him wandering, though he spoke with great feeling, and his words were: 'I will come; wait yet a little while.' " This was alleged by gossip to be addressed to Satan.

Regardless of the cause of death, Guicciardini, the great sixteenth-century statesman-historian, summarized accordingly:

> So ended Pope Alexander, at the height of glory and prosperity about whom it must be known that he was a man of the utmost power and of great judgment and spirit, as his actions and behavior showed. But as his first accession to the Papacy was foul and shameful, seeing he had bought with gold so high a station, in like manner his government disagreed not with this base foundation.
>
> There were in him, and in full measure, all vices both of flesh and spirit; nor could there be imagined in the ordering of the

Church a rule so bad but that he put it into working. He was most sensual toward both sexes, keeping publicly women and boys, but more specially toward women; and so far did he exceed all measure that public opinion judged he knew sexually Madonna Lucrezia, his own daughter, toward whom he bore a most tender and boundless love.

He was exceedingly avaricious, not in keeping what he had acquired, but in getting new wealth; and where he saw a way toward drawing money, he had no respect whatever; in his days were sold at auction all benefices, dispensations, pardons, bishoprics, cardinalships, and all court dignities: unto which matters he had appointed two or three men privy to his thought, exceeding prudent, who let them out to the highest bidder. He caused the death by poison of many cardinals and prelates, even among his intimates, those namely whom he noted to be rich in benefices and understood to have hoarded much, with the view of seizing their wealth.

Guicciardini stressed his brutal cruelty and lust for violent murder:

There was in him no religion, no keeping of his troth: he promised all things liberally, but stood to nought but what was useful to himself: no care for justice, since in his days Rome was like a den of thieves and murderers: his ambition was boundless, and such that it grew in the same measure as his state increased: nevertheless, his sins meeting with no due punishment in this world, he was to the last of his days most prosperous.

He recounted his personal career:

While young and still almost a boy, having Calixtus for his uncle, he was made Cardinal and then Vice-Chancellor: in which high place he continued until his Papacy, with great revenue, good fame, and peace. Having become Pope, he made Cesare, his bastard son and bishop of Pamplona, a Cardinal, against the ordinances and decrees of the Church, which forbid the making of a bastard Cardinal even with the Pope's dispensation, wherefore he brought proof by false witnesses that he was born in wedlock.

Afterwards he made him a layman and took the Cardinal's

dignity from him [to qualify Cesare as duke of Valentinois] and turned his mind to making a realm; wherein he fared far better than he purposed, and beginning with Rome, after undoing the Orsini, Colonnesi, Savelli, and those barons who were wont to be held in fear by former Popes, he was more full master of Rome than ever had been any Pope before. With greatest ease he got the lordships of Romagna, the March, and the Duchy; and having made a most fair and powerful state, the Florentines held him in much fear, the Venetians in jealousy, and the King of France in esteem.

Then having got together a fine army, he showed how great was the might of a Pontiff when he had a valiant general [Cesare] and one in whom he can place faith. At last he grew to that point that he was counted the balance in the war of France and Spain. In one word he was more evil and more lucky than ever for many ages per-adventure had been any pope before."

Some Roman rumor-mongers asserted that Alexander had bargained with the devil at the time of the cardinals' conclave that elected him and had sold his soul on the basis that he would retain the Holy See twelve years, and that seven devils were seen in his death chamber as he expired.

The pope's son was an exceptional man, despite his extraordinary wickedness. His personal motto was *Aut Caesar aut nihil* ("Either Caesar or Nothing"). He was not only well-connected and trained by a master of unscrupulousness, his father, but he was highly intelligent, versatile, and ruled by limitless ambition. He had been born a bastard, illegally legitimized to become a cardinal, and then had his relationship with the Church formally severed to qualify him for a dukedom.

He was brave, strong, handsome, most attractive to women, and an extraordinarily fine athlete who could fell an ox with one blow of a fist. He kept his marksmanship well-honed by shooting down selected convicts in the Vatican courtyard. He would name his target, then choose a fatal point, and slaughter the cowering victim while his father, the pope, and his golden-haired sister, Lucrezia, looked on in admiration.

There is no doubt that even the wise, shrewd, broadminded Niccolo Macchiavelli was dazzled by this lusty prince of the Church, and the Florentine diplomat and scholar Guicciardini somehow managed to obscure to his own moral sensitivity some of the shrewd judgments he made on Cesare. Both writers, contemporaries of their subject, were overwhelmed by their own assumption that, after all, politics was but a means to an end.

Macchiavelli, the famous Florentine statesman, political analyst, thinker, and dramatist and writer chose Cesare as a model for his "Prince," because he foresaw (perhaps correctly) that he was the type of leader best suited to unify the eternally quarrelsome, violent and amoral Italian states, neither endowed with the remotest sense of nationhood on their long, sea-girt peninsula nor with any true pride in what their Roman ancestors had achieved in establishing a splendid empire.

Macchiavelli was dispatched on two occasions to seek to stave off the menaces Cesare was concocting against the magnificent city-state of Florence. On the first (1502–3), he was impressed if appalled by the ferocious manner in which Cesare dealt with a group of mutinous captains at Sinigaglia.

The second time he encountered Cesare was after the death of Pope Alexander VI, followed swiftly by that of his successor, Pope Paul III. Macchiavelli had been sent by Florence to observe events at the conclave which soon elected the dour, martial Julius II. During this last personal view of the historical drama, he witnessed with mounting scorn and deception the inglorious decline of his chosen "Prince." And when the latter was finally imprisoned by the new powers that were, Macchiavelli commented that this was a fate he "deserved as a rebel against Christ." His philosophy of history, while sound, had been too much influenced by the evil and corruption of his times, which he sometimes tended to consider irremediable.

Macchiavelli shrewdly observed in *The Prince* that Cesare's history showed both the weakness and strength of fate. He wrote: "He acquired his dominion by the aid derived from his father's position, and when he lost that he also lost his power, notwithstanding that he used every endeavor and did all that a prudent and able man ought to do in order to plant himself firmly in those states which the arms and fortune of others had placed at his disposal." The objective of Macchiavelli in stressing these points was to caution his employer-ruler, Lorenzo de' Medici, against the mistakes that eventually brought Cesare down.

Symonds, looking back from the mid-nineteenth century with its more acute appreciation of morality and less willingness to tolerate evil as a means to success, wrote in his *Renaissance in Italy:*

> The cruelty of Cesare Borgia was only equalled by his craft; and it was by a supreme exercise of his power of fascination that he lured the foes who had plotted against him at La Magione into his snare at Sinigaglia. Paolo Orsini, Francesco Orsini, duke of Gravina, Vitellozzo Vitelli, and Oliverotto da Fermo were all

men of arms, accustomed to intrigue and to bloodshed, and more than any one of them were stained with crimes of the most atrocious treachery. Yet such were the arts of Cesare Borgia that in 1502 he managed to assemble them, apart from their troops, in the castle of Sinigaglia, where he had them strangled.

Having now destroyed the chiefs of the opposition and enlisted their forces in his own service, Cesare, to use the phrase of Macchiavelli, "had laid good foundations for his future power." He commanded a sufficient territory; he wielded the temporal and spiritual power of his father; he was feared by the princes and respected by the people throughout Italy; his cruelty and perfidy and boldness caused him to be universally admired. But as yet he had only laid foundations. The empire of Italy was still to win; for he aspired to nothing else, and it is even probable that he entertained a notion of secularizing the Papacy.

France was the principal barrier to Cesare's design. Louis XII (successor to Charles VIII) was at last fearful of the danger, but since Louis had invited the Spaniards into Naples, Cesare possessed a way to rid himself of French control. He turned to Spain, and then played off one monarchy against the other to his own benefit.

Then he took four precautions to the great admiration of Macchiavelli:

In the first place, he systematically murdered the heirs of the ruling families of all the cities he acquired. By this process he left no scion of the ancient houses for a future Pope to restore. In the second place he attached to his person, by pensions, offices and emoluments, all the Roman gentry, so that he might be able to keep the new Pope a prisoner and unarmed in Rome.

Thirdly, he reduced the College of Cardinals, by bribery, terrorism, poisoning, and packed elections, to such a state that he could count on the creation of a Pope, if not his nominee, at least not hostile to his interests. Fourthly, he lost no time, but pushed his plans of conquest on with the utmost speed, so as, if possible, to command a large territory at the time of Alexander's death.

Cesare supplied Macchiavelli with a notable example of the uses of cruelty. Having found the cities of Romagna in disorder, he determined to quell them with a terrifying governor. And he chose Messr. Ramiro d'Orco, "a man cruel and quick of action, to whom he gave the fullest power." But it did not suit Cesare to incur personally the discredit of cruelty. Accordingly, he had him decapitated and exposed to public view to prove his death. Macchiavelli wholly approved this formula: that cruelty should be employed for positive aims, but that the prince should shun the hatred it inspired.

Macchiavelli's ethics were based upon a conviction that men are altogether bad. When discussing the question, he decided: "It is far safer to be feared than loved, if you must choose; seeing that you may say of men generally that they are ungrateful and changeable, dissemblers, apt to shun danger, eager for gain; as long as you serve them, they offer you everything, down to their very children, if you have no need; but when you want help, they fail you."

Two crimes supervised by Cesare that his ethically numb father could not forgive were the murder (by stabbing and drowning) of his brother, Alexander's eldest son, the Duke of Gandia, and the stabbing of Perotto, the pope's personal minion. The reason for Gandia's assassination seems to have been a combination of jealousy and assurance for Cesare himself of priority in the Borgia family. The pontiff, when he learned the news, broke into a torrent of screaming anger, keeping to his bedroom and howling like a dog.

As for Perotto: imagine the head of the Roman Church clasping his homosexual lover as his son, Cesare, sprang out and stabbed the boy so that blood splattered the papal robes as he died.

Alexander had initially intended to make his eldest son, Giovanni of Gandia, a powerful secular prince who might even aspire to the throne of Naples. But this hope vanished after Cesare's thugs took care of the pontiff's favorite, and the gossip marts of Rome filled with rumors that the two brothers had been rivals for the love of their beautiful sister, Lucrezia (which report shows the destitute condition of Borgia Rome's morality).

The pope himself demonstrated that he was so awed by the terrible Cesare that, once his first torrents of rage and frustration had dried up, he suspended the official inquiry into Gandia's assassination. From then on he labored to advance Cesare's cause even more feverishly and sought his promotion to a secular principality, thus causing his departure from clerical ranks.

In return for papal annulment of France's King Louis XII's first marriage and a dispensation for the second, plus tangible gifts, the king assured the pontiff he would no longer oppose papal dominance of Milan and Naples. Furthermore, as a supreme gesture, he invited Cesare to visit his court, vested him personally with his dukedom of Valentinois (Cesare became known to Italians as the "Duca Valentino") and married him off to the King of Navarre's sister.

Having thus completely reversed his policy toward France, Alexander resumed his quest for Borgia lands and power, using Cesare, the new duke, to overrun all Romagna with French weapons and strong mercenary support. The pope and his son pursued their basic strategy to insure possession of conquered areas: they captured the capitals and murdered the ruling princes: at Camerino, Sinigaglia, Bologna, Pesaro, Rimini, and Forli.

Alexander VI was the man who made the Borgia family powerful by using all the advantages of his religious and temporal authority in the Church and the Papal States, and benefiting from the astonishing flabbiness of moral standards that prevailed in Medieval-Renaissance Italy. He was a stronger, firmer man than his predecessors and, according to Guicciardini, displayed "craft and singular sagacity, a sound judgment with extraordinary powers of persuasion; and to all the grave affairs of life he applied ability and pains beyond belief." His consuming ambition was to remove leaders who could threaten him and to eliminate their power bases whether in the Papal States, Naples, or Venice.

A cynical sinner (and wholly conscious of the fact), he tolerated public perversions that few lay potentates would have allowed even in those extraordinary days. And always he used his Spanish heritage and his own children to further his aims, even placing Cesare in the chief role after the latter had had his favorite oldest scion, the Duke of Gandia, murdered.

For decades the entire moral scale of European society and its supposedly holy symbol, the papacy, had been rotting. It had become customary to buy bishoprics for youngsters who weren't even close to being priests, to designate cardinals with an eye to political support in distant parts, to raise huge sums by selling benefices and saintly relics. The saying was coined under Alexander: "He sells the keys, the altars, Christ. Well, he bought them, so he has a right to sell them."

And his allies in the rise to preeminence were nobles and hired thugs who used murder and poison as their tools. It is reckoned that Alexander's men poisoned five cardinals and that, for example, on one single day in 1500 twelve red hats were auctioned off to those willing to support the Borgia power game and to pay for the privilege.

Clearly, Guicciardini had Alexander VI in mind when he wrote: "In our corrupt times the goodness of a pontiff is commended when it does not surpass the wickedness of other men [as Alexander's did]. But the morality of the Church before, after and above all during the pontificate of Rodrigo Borgia smelled like a cesspool."

Membership in the College of Cardinals had long become a political purchase, and many cardinals behaved simply like ward-heelers. Prince Alfonso of Portugal was named cardinal at seven (with the limitation that he could not take office until fourteen) and Cesare Borgia at eighteen.

Macchiavelli—whose realpolitik occasionally resembled, in some respects, Hitler's—wrote: "Owing to the evil example of the papal court, Italy has lost all piety and all religion whence follows infinite troubles and disorders; for as religion implies all good, so its absence implies the contrary."

The primate of Christendom had come to be regarded as a secular potentate—and of the most vicious, immoral variety. The crimes known to have occurred under Alexander—the most famous of which were arranged or led by his son, Cesare, equaled only the cynical corruption of the Church itself. During Alexander's pontificate, eighteen Spanish cardinals were created—five of them from the house of Borgia. As for the pontiff's personal behavior: Guicciardini judges him "most sensual toward both sexes."

Rodrigo Borgia was as astute as he was immoral. His most generous bequest to Cesare and Lucrezia, the two children who survived him and whom he adored, was the family power, obtained in true mafia fashion, and a profound legacy of licentious immorality, which they aped with great skill, plus the knowledge that they could do no wrong since, inferentially, their sins were tolerated by the true faith and blessed by God's vicar on earth. Their father, the pope, set a gaudy personal example. No wonder they behaved as they did. Cesare was the incarnation of ruthless, sadistic immorality, and Lucrezia was a beautiful zombie prepared to sleep with or poison anyone if Alexander so desired.

It would be quite outrageous for any serious person—historian, statesman, theologian, or patriot—to even attempt to argue that Pope Alexander VI was a great churchman or even remotely useful or religious. He was a typically ambitious Renaissance noble, covetous, brave, greedy, licentious during an epoch when such was the accepted if not universally admired habit of that social breed. He was brilliant and he was wicked; a lecher and a liar, not even true to his beloved family as witness the speed with which he transferred his affections to Cesare Borgia after the latter murdered his elder brother.

To conclude, one may say of this two-generation mafia in the Holy City that it accomplished little of permanent value save the customary generosity shown by Renaissance Mycenases to the leading artists of their era. Alexander VI has surely earned himself a unique position as the wickedest pope of a lot that was far from benevolent or saintly in his time; and Cesare, his son, became a mistaken literary hero for a moment in the most famous work of the most famous political philosopher of his day, but not before the latter worthy had regretted the character of his choice. Here, in truth, one may say, "Like father, like son." Were these astounding characteristics acquired or inherited? Surely—and blazingly—both. What a pope! What a prince! One conceived by Satan; the other admired by "Old Nick" Macchiavelli.

VIII

A Magician and His Manager: Leopold and Wolfgang Amadeus Mozart

On January 27, 1756, shortly before the outbreak of the Seven Years' War, Joannes Chrysostomus Wolfgangus Theophilus Mozart was born in Salzburg. All his life he enjoyed being called Amadé, short for "Amadeus" (the Latin for Theophilus, or "God-love"), but in his family he was generally known as "Wolferl," little Wolfgang. He was the youngest of seven children of whom only one other survived, Maria Anna, known as "Nannerl." His father, Johann Georg Leopold Mozart, was a musician, composer, and teacher employed as a violinist in the establishment of Salzburg's prince-archbishop. Leopold's musical talent was considerably below his cultivated knowledge of the medium.

Leopold took a job as fourth violinist in the prelate's orchestra and wrote a manual on the violin and how it should be played. He spent most of his life in Salzburg playing and giving lessons. He never rose above the hierarchical rank of deputy Kapellmeister in the archbishop's establishment and consequently devoted himself to the passionate advancement of his brilliant son's career. He developed a self-righteous belief that he had sacrificed himself for Wolferl.

The little boy's astounding talents first became evident at the age of three. Leopold had already started giving Nannerl lessons on the clavier, and the tiny boy enjoyed sitting down at the keyboard to imitate her. When he was four his father began to teach him as well as his sister. The boy showed he could play various pieces correctly and also started to produce little compositions of his own. His first known attempt was a minuet in G. At four he composed a clavier concerto and also began playing the violin. At seven he asked if he could join a quartet at home as second violinist. His father found it difficult to teach the little boy because he already seemed to know everything by instinct.

Wolfgang made his initial public appearance at Salzburg University at the age of five, and the following year, along with Nannerl, was taken by Leopold to Munich, where the two children played the harpsichord before the Elector of Bavaria. Leopold, who had failed in his own dream of finding fame and fortune in Salzburg, soon recognized that his own career lay in furthering that of his own children. Nannerl had immense talent; but she was not a magical genius like Amadeus. Wolferl soon displayed a genius that was to mark him as an infant prodigy only even remotely rivaled by Felix Mendelssohn half a century later (but Mendelssohn's adult talent never equaled that of the other boy genius).

And Leopold had the discernment to recognize that his small son was more than a performing prodigy; he was, indeed, an amazing creative musician. He trained the small boy to write manuscripts of his compositions in beautiful, orderly patterns. Johann Adolf Hasse, the veteran composer, observed that Leopold, "as far as I can see, is equally disconcerted everywhere. . . . He idolizes his son a little too much." And the father failed to see the need for sufficient mental and physical rest for Wolferl and Nannerl. He confessed: "Every moment that I lose is lost forever, and if I formerly knew how valuable time is to youth, I know it more now. You are aware that my children are used to work; should they learn to make excuses . . . my whole building would fall to the ground. Custom is an iron path." Leopold admonished Wolferl that each moment of his learning time was priceless, equal to weeks in an ordinary life. Yet the boy seemed to know everything before it was taught to him because of his astonishing musical intuition.

Leopold was a good father and a thorough teacher. He was also a shrewd manager of the talent he was sponsoring and an excellent publicity man who busily circulated news about his remarkable children. He would surely have been happier if Wolfgang had achieved great renown in Salzburg, which would have brought fame and fortune to his father in encroaching old age. He was, indeed, a calculating opportunist. As he saw the need to extend his son's renown and horizons, he planned for his conquest of Europe with precision and thoroughness. By the time Wolfgang was twelve, he had been paraded through England, France, Switzerland, and the Low Countries, in addition to the Habsburg cities of Munich and Vienna.

In 1769, when Amadeus was only thirteen, Leopold began devoting an increasing proportion of his time to him at the expense of the public life of Nannerl, who had grown into a tall and beautiful young woman—unlike her small, unprepossessing brother. The boy had already, despite his youth, written half a dozen symphonies, three piano concerti, and two indifferent operas, apart from other works, and the father at last felt Amadeus was ready for an extended tour of music-loving Italy.

At the end of 1769, father and son journeyed to Italy and crossed from city to city along the extended peninsula. Leopold had obtained a leave of absence from his employer, the prince-archbishop, and set out to establish his boy as a youthful European genius. He steeped the youngster in all forms of Italian music and gave him a grounding enabling him to write operas in true Italian style, later joined in a new form of musical drama by combining it with the techniques of German Singspiel. Wolfgang learned new possibilities of song and the loveliness of varying types of church music.

An instance of Wolfgang's astonishing natural genius occurred when he and his father visited Rome during Holy Week 1770. They went to hear the *Miserere,* and the boy listened intently. Afterward, he took out a pen and ink and wrote the entire piece down from memory. Leopold wrote to his wife: "We have it! . . . We shall bring it home with us."

Years after the instructive Italian tour, Leopold was to advise his son, by then a youth in Paris:

> It now depends solely on your good sense and your way of life whether you die as an ordinary musician, utterly forgotten by the world, or as a famous Kapellmeister, of whom posterity will read—whether captured by some woman you die bedded on straw in an attic, full of starving children, or whether, after a Christian life spent in contentment, honor, and renown, you leave this world with your family well provided for and your name respected by all.

At fifteen, Wolfgang had found himself at a relatively loose end, with no brilliant invitation on the horizon, and his thoughts began to turn toward Paris. During a childhood visit to Paris, he had written a concerto at the behest of the Duc de Guines and his father had come to know the Bavarian Friedrich Melchior Grimm, intimate of Diderot and lover of Madame d'Epinay.

For this second trip to Paris, Leopold consigned his son to his mother's care and gave them a long list of introductions to important people including members of the court of Louis XV. The most helpful of these proved to be Grimm, who later was named a baron under the Empire. Wolfgang took care to stay as close as possible to Grimm, heeding Leopold's diplomatic counsel.

"Life in Paris," Wolfgang wrote, "is very different from life in Germany, and the French ways of expressing oneself politely, of introducing oneself, of craving patronage, etc. are quite peculiar; so much so that Baron von Grimm used always to instruct me as to what I should say."

The trip was arduous as was always the case in those days. Passengers crowded into a coach from dawn to dusk bumping along rutted, dangerous roads and sleeping in dirty inns, filled with vermin. When they reached Paris, they found the streets deep in filth, punctuated by carriages spattering slime and slops. Amadé and his mother occasionally traveled in the relative luxury of sedan chairs. Wolfgang unsuccessfully sought a job, but, disdaining his father's advice, declined one as organist at Versailles. His second visit to France wound up sadly: His mother died in lonely despair; and a romance he had had earlier with Aloysia Weber, the sister of his future wife, Constanze, had ended unhappily. Wolfgang returned to Salzburg and humbly accepted a modestly paid post as cathedral organist for Archbishop Colloredo.

Amadeus was indebted to Leopold for a respectable upbringing, an outstanding education, and a stimulating early development, but Mozart was not nearly so preoccupied as his parent in the prospects of posthumous fame. Unlike his father, he was not keenly aware of the concept of "posterity." Leopold was capable of communicating his plans and building up visions of the future that seemed to hold little particular meaning for the boy. The father served his family as its head, a major domo, impresario, and travel agent. He selected itineraries, whether he was to join in the journey or not. He arranged accommodation and letters of credit and useful, well-phrased introductions.

Some time after Wolfgang's wedding to Constanze, Leopold wrote his son: "I think you should consider me your best friend rather than your father; since I have proven a hundred times over that I was more concerned for your good fortune and pleasure than for my own." He also wrote him: "Consider whether I have not always treated you kindly, served you as a servant his master; even provided you with all possible entertainment and helped you to enjoy all honorable and seemly pleasures, often at great inconvenience to myself."

When Leopold's original employer, the old archbishop, died, he was succeeded by Hieronymus, Graf Colloredo. The new prelate was stingy, unpopular, and showed a preference for foreigners in his employ.

The father and manager of the prodigious son was a didactic and rather disagreeable man to his family and tended to marked servility toward those outside it whom he wished to impress. He was an educated, ambitious man who was intelligent enough to be deeply disappointed in himself. But he threw himself energetically into the promotion and management of his son whom he proclaimed a "Wonder of Nature." Out of a talented, sophisticated boy genius, he had created a perfect musician.

But even when the son was living far from restrictive Salzburg, Leopold sought to guide his behavior along unpleasant lines. Thus he wrote to him: "I recommend you to think when at work not only of the musical but also of the unmusical public. You know that for ten true connoisseurs there are a hundred ignoramuses! Do not neglect the so-called popular style which tickles long ears."

He added subsequently: "Do your best to keep the whole orchestra in good humor; flatter them, and by praising them, keep them all well-disposed toward you." Although a cultivated man, Leopold had suffered enough disappointment to consider bowing and scraping a useful habit worthy of his boy's adoption.

For all his personal pomposity and materialism, Leopold was a careful, even doting parent, who preached temperance and respect for virtue in a loose age and a sophisticated environment. He carefully warned Wolfgang against sexual promiscuity, which, he cautioned, almost invariably resulted in disease. Years later when, despite his father's disapproval, he was engaged to be married, Wolfgang wrote to his father of his intended married life:

> I simply cannot live as most young men do in these days. In the first place, I have too much religion; in the second place, I have too great a love of my neighbor and too high a feeling of honor to seduce an innocent girl; and, in the third place, I have too much horror and disgust, too much dread and fear of diseases and too much care for my health to fool around with whores. So I can swear that I have never had relations of that sort with any woman. . . .
>
> I assure you that I am often obliged to spend unnecessarily, simply because I do not pay attention to things. I am absolutely convinced that I should manage better with a wife (on the same income which I have now) than I do by myself. And how many useless expenses would be avoided! True, other expenses would have to be met, but—one knows what they are and can be prepared for them—in short, one leads a well-ordered existence. A bachelor, in my opinion, is only half alive.
>
> She is not ugly, but at the same time far from beautiful. Her

whole beauty consists in two little black eyes and a pretty figure. She has no wit, but she has enough common sense to enable her to fulfill her duties as a wife and mother.

Leopold's distaste for Constanze—he had even withheld permission for the marriage to occur—made for an uneasiness in family relationships. In the end he had given only angry and tardy consent to the marriage. Leopold apparently took grim satisfaction in announcing he washed his hands of all financial responsibility for or aid to the young couple. Wolfgang wrote of the wedding, "When we were joined together both my bride and I shed tears. All present, even the priest, were much moved, and all wept."

Wolfgang was understandably hurt that his father clearly disapproved of the marriage. He must also have been distressed by the frosty behavior of his father and sister when he visited Salzburg with his wife in 1783. Constanze was given no presents, no appropriate gift, no kindness. Understandably, she never forgave Leopold and Nannerl, just as Nannerl never forgave her for marrying her brother. As old ladies in Salzburg, they lived near each other without ever even seeing one another.

The one foreign capital Wolfgang yearned to revisit was London, where he had spent some time as a boy with his family. He had been attracted by the young king, George III, whose taste for plain living had suited his amiable wife, Queen Charlotte, before whom Wolfgang and Nannerl had performed. He had been enamored by the friendliness of the atmosphere, and later, during his wanderings on the continent, he had made friends with several English musicians and actors. The composer often thought of returning.

When the great Joseph Haydn departed for England in 1790, leaving his friend Wolfgang in Vienna, the latter had just declined an invitation from an opera promoter there. Although another was promised to him by Haydn's mentor, Wolfgang never received it. This was a particular disappointment.

In 1786 Mozart had suggested an English voyage to Constanze, but the two small children they now had posed a problem. So Wolfgang wrote his father proposing they leave the two babies with him in Salzburg while they were away. Leopold furiously refused. He wrote caustically to Nannerl: "Not at all a bad arrangement! They would go off and travel—might even die—or stay on in England—leaving me to run after them with the children." He was scarcely a nice grandfather when the children involved were not proven geniuses!

Old age, however, did soften several of Leopold's selfish bigotries. With his wife gone, he seemed increasingly prepared to allow his young Wolfgang to choose his own path. When he visited Wolfgang in Vienna he went with him several times, at first reluctantly, to meetings of the Freemasons with whose order his son was affiliated. Leopold finally joined himself, accepting the gentle pledge of brotherly love that was a sharp change from his previous acceptance of uncompromising dictation from the priesthood. On February 16, 1785, he wrote to Nannerl, with undisguised pride, that after an evening of chamber music in Wolfgang's home, Haydn had come up to him and said: "I tell you before God, as an honest man, that your son is the greatest composer I know, either personally or by name. He has taste and moreover the greatest science in composition."

Death came for the grouchy, syncophantic old manager of the vibrant musical magician in the spring of 1787, at a time when Amadé himself had been suffering from bouts of illness and despondency and increasingly fatalistic moods. When he first heard from Nannerl that their father had fallen seriously ill, Wolfgang wrote to him from Vienna:

> I am sure I need not tell you how greatly I long for reassuring news from yourself. Indeed I expect it, even though I have accustomed myself to expect the worst on all occasions. Since death, when we come to consider it, is seen to be the true goal of our life, I have made acquaintance during these last few years with this best and truest friend of mankind, so that his image not only no longer has any terrors for me, but suggests, on the contrary, much that is reassuring and consoling! And I thank my God for blessing me with the opportunity (you understand me) of coming to recognize Him as the key to our true blessedness.

Wolfgang was referring, of course, to the Masonic teachings that had replaced so many of his earlier unquestioning allegiances to church dogmas. The reflective son concluded: "But should you, against all expectation, be no better, I beg you will not . . . will not conceal it from me, but tell me, or have me told, the whole truth, so that I can come with all human speed to your arms!"

However, when Wolfgang received the news that his father had died on May 28, he was "neither astonished nor shocked." His loyalty to his paternal promoter had been notable, but it had suffered a severe blow when Leopold's selfishness made it impossible for him to go to England. Thus, the old man—a bitter, prejudice-ridden figure—died apart from his pride and joy, his breadwinner. He had been instrumental in developing an uninhibited creative genius, although his bigotry and material greed seemed often to wreck it.

Wolfgang had been a small child with weak limbs, a spindly body and an oversized head. He remained small and spindly all his life. But his accomplishments were such that, in an age that worshiped musical prodigies, his fame spread rapidly. At five, he wrote a minuet and a trio for the piano. At six, his father took him and Nannerl to Vienna, where he performed in the uniform of a tiny cavalier. When Empress Maria Theresa heard him, she took him on her lap and embraced him. He was seven, "a little man with his wig and sword," when the great Goethe saw him in Frankfurt. We know of no relations he had with other children save Nannerl, four and a half years older than Wolfgang. But the adult world was at his feet.

His childhood was never normal. What one might term his "public life" started when he was five and played the part of a chorister at the Salzburg Gymnasium. From ages six to ten, he traveled constantly with his father and sister and never set foot in a schoolroom or learned anything save from and through his father. He adored arithmetic and scribbled formulas on tablecloths and wallpaper. Starting at six, he produced several short keyboard compositions. He enjoyed playing the violin or the clavier in chamber music ensembles arranged by Leopold. Oddly enough, considering his abnormal life, he was noted for an equable disposition. It is medically mysterious that his delicate physique was able to survive twelve youthful years of arduous travel and public performance.

Leopold advertised his children's concerts abroad accordingly:

The little girl, who is in her twelfth year, will play the most difficult compositions of the great masters, the boy, who is not yet seven, will perform on the clavecin or harpsichord; he will also play a concerto for the violin, and will accompany symphonies on the clavier, the manual or keyboard being covered with a cloth, with as much facility as if he could see the keys; he will instantly name all notes played at a distance, whether singly or in chords, on the clavier, or any other instrument, glass, bell, or clock. He will finally, both on the harpsichord and the organ, improvise as long as may be desired and in any key, thus proving that he is as thoroughly acquainted with the one instrument as with the other, great as is the difference between them.

By his elders, he was respectfully treated as a gifted adult on musical matters. He was warmly welcomed by Johann Christian Bach, son of the great Johann Sebastian and music master to Queen Charlotte of England. He played before Louis XV of France, whose Versailles court welcomed him. He astounded distinguished audiences by playing perfectly on keyboards covered with a cloth. This was a trick first learned to please the Holy Roman Emperor Francis I. When he was eight and nine, while in London and the Hague, Mozart began the immensely complex job of writing symphonies.

Mozart kept on improving the magical abilities with which he was born. At first he developed the ability to imitate proficiently the prevailing musical styles in the capitals to which his father took him; but soon his creations became profoundly original and imaginative.

His gift for the violin, the harpsichord, and the piano was formidable; he could improvise in various styles, accompany at sight, add a bass to a given theme, and name any note that was sounded.

His ear was perfectly attuned. In Rome the pope awarded him the Order of the Golden Spur. He played a clavier sonata at sight in alternating duet with Johann Christian Bach when he was eight. At age eight, he also played for Madame de Pompadour in Paris and when she spurned his effort to embrace her, he piped up: "Who is this that does not want to kiss me? The empress kissed me."

The arduous upbringing his father had given him produced positive results. When Leopold fell ill in England while the three were on tour, the little boy took advantage of the quiet prescribed and sat down with Nannerl and wrote his first complete symphony—at age eight. This was followed by three more symphonies and several piano and violin sonatas.

The big gap in the young musician's life was friendships with peers. He rarely saw people his own age and had the habit of mixing with adults who flattered him enthusiastically. Not until he was thirteen, when he was in Florence, did he meet an English boy of his years, Thomas Linley, also a musical prodigy (if far inferior). They became close friends, gave a joint concert, and played violin duets. In his late teens, Wolfgang lost his heart to the half-English Nancy Storace, a fine singer. When he was twenty-one, he struck up a vivacious friendship in Munich with his cousin Maria Anna Thekla, whom he affectionately called by the diminutive for cousin, Bäsle.

Wolfgang had a modest share of romantic involvements, and for a time was deeply enamored of Aloysia Weber, the daughter of Mannheim friends, a lovely girl with a beautiful soprano voice. She was quite uninterested. Some time after she had spurned him, the eager young musician courted her younger sister, Constanze, a rather attractive girl with whom he shared the rest of his short life.

As he matured and became relatively less dependent on his father, Mozart loosened his ties with the straitened life of Salzburg. After a stormy interview, he was discharged by the archbishop, and spent an increasing amount of time in Vienna, despite Leopold's contempt for that capital as having "no love for anything serious or sensible" and catering to "utter trash, such as dances, burlesques, harlequinades." But it was a musical melting pot and had become an unparalleled home base for many great composers such as Haydn, Beethoven, Schubert, and, of course, Mozart himself. Of these, only Schubert was born there.

In Vienna, Amadé developed his famous friendship with Haydn, whom he later acknowledged as his equal and dubbed "Papa." He used to play viola in a chamber music quartet in which Haydn was first violin.

Soon after settling in Vienna, Mozart married Constanze, who bore him six children of whom only two survived infancy. But the composer's family made his life more restrained. Wolfgang was regarded as a sensational pianist for several seasons, but he was not a great popular success as a composer, despite the discerning view of connoisseurs like Haydn.

Although he had been brought up as a traveling man, a wanderer, once he settled in Vienna, Mozart's habits became relatively more fixed. He was given a post as a court Kammermusicus at the modest salary of 800 gulden (his predecessor, who had just died, Christoph Willibald Gluck, had been paid 2,000). The job meant little more than writing dance music for imperial balls, yet he at least had a status in the royal service.

He took occasional trips in search of employment or fame, especially to Berlin, where he had an affair with the beautiful soprano Henriette Baranius, and to Prague, which gave him more acclaim than any other metropolitan audience during his career. When Bondini, the manager of the Prague opera house asked Haydn, a few days after Wolfgang had left the Bohemian capital, if he would produce an opera buffa to succeed Mozart's, Haydn with customary generosity replied: "It would be a risk to put myself in competition with the great Mozart."

It was opera that seemed to fascinate Mozart most in the realms of musical creation. He did not truly come into his own in this field until he found the proper librettist, despite lovely successes in comic opera and Singspiel. That librettist, who managed to inspire the composer's universal creations, was Emanuel Conegliano, a converted Italian Jew known by his baptismal name, after the bishop who baptized him, Lorenzo Da Ponte. Lorenzo had actually been ordained a priest but scarcely ever performed that office. He was a literary adventurer who cut a swath in European society and hobnobbed with royalty. He wound up his varied career as professor of Italian at Columbia University in New York. Lorenzo was a friend of the scabrous Giacomo Casanova de Seingalt, and Casanova actually contributed some fragments of verse to the libretto prepared by Da Ponte for *Don Giovanni*.

Don Giovanni was created as a literary character for opera by Da Ponte from a series of Spanish legends deriving from Don Juan Tenorio, who killed his commander after seducing the man's daughter. The opera was written to order as a commercial product for Bondini in Prague. Both Da Ponte and his friend Casanova had earned scurrilous fame for their amatory exploits in various capitals. It was Da Ponte who also conceived for Mozart the operatic *Marriage of Figaro* based on the Beaumarchais play.

Lorenzo was a first-rate theater poet. He said of their collaboration: "As fast as I wrote the words, Mozart set them to music." Wolfgang had already demonstrated immense versatility by the time he settled in Vienna. He was certainly the Habsburg capital's finest pianist, despite small hands that remained plump and white regardless of all the use he made of them. He also demonstrated amazing scope as a composer. Before he had teamed up with Da Ponte on what were to be his most famous operas, he had developed what was thought a "Turkish" style with such productions as *The Abduction from the Seraglio*, the first German comic opera. He proved adept at the Italian opera buffa and also spoken recitatives in Singspiel. *Figaro* rapidly became immortal in the German repertoire. *Don Giovanni* was more Italianate, and *The Magic Flute* was a true and brilliant German Singspiel, or music drama. He produced many concert scores such as the exquisite "Eine Kleine Nachtmusik," a string serenade, and turned out prodigious numbers of waltzes, as that gay dance, at first in minuet time, took hold of Vienna. And he wrote several symphonies, a form that, like the quartet, he learned from Haydn whom he acknowledged as a master.

Yet Mozart never achieved in Vienna, which prided itself on its sophistication, the enormous popularity he knew in Prague, where he was an idol and earned good money.

Don Giovanni flopped in the Habsburg capital, and the Emperor Joseph said: "That opera is divine; I should even venture that it is more beautiful than Figaro. But such music is not meat for the teeth of my Viennese." The Emperor Joseph had at first greeted Wolfgang cordially, but he showed no inclination to financial generosity. Indeed, the disgruntled Salzburger wrote: "These Viennese gentry (by which I mean chiefly the emperor) must not imagine that I am in the world purely for the sake of Vienna! There is no monarch on the globe I would sooner serve than the emperor—but I will not be a mendicant for any post." The chief court composer, Antonio Salieri, a man of mediocre talent, saw to it that the royal princess was not taught by Amadeus. Joseph, an enlightened ruler, did not have the judgment to acknowledge Mozart's true genius.

As a consequence, Mozart's financial situation deteriorated badly, and, as he was no longer in great demand, because of the absence of royal favor, his concert appearances dropped off. He needed funds, and he began to borrow, repeatedly asking his friends for loans. While Salieri was paid a handsome salary for his court functions, Mozart was limited to a pittance. He made some money by teaching, which he did not enjoy (he even declined the honor of instructing the young Beethoven). His joys were limited, and he attended many tavern drinking bouts with chums like Da Ponte and the Storaces as well as enthusiastic Masonic rites with his brothers in the lodge. He had established the agreeable habit of Sunday morning open house where he harmonized with friends, but was so poorly off that he had to charge admission. Chamber music was his special joy at the Sunday get-togethers (although he was a master of every known form of composition).

Wolfgang, while still a young man, was not strong enough to success- fully resist the financial, emotional, and professional odds that were muster- ing against him. He grew thin, nervous and increasingly subject to the minor infections prevalent in an era that knew nothing about sanitation. He caught an illness that some believe was a kidney disease and others think was typhoid. At the end of November 1791, he was confined to his bed, nursed by Constanze and her youngest sister Sophie. Early December of that year he died. The cause was later diagnosed as rheumatic fever.

There has been much argument about the cause of his death. Some have claimed that the fatal disease was uremia, others that he was poisoned by the disagreeable Salieri, still others that he died of syphilis, for which he was being treated with mercury. Dr. Carl Vogel, his physician, reported that he suffered "searing pain" and had a "painful urge to urinate."

By any standard, his death was premature, as he was but entering into a period that normally would have been highly productive. According to his wife, Wolfgang had been possessed for months by the idea that he was being poisoned: "I know I must die; someone has been giving me aqua toffana [a form of arsenic]." Salieri is said to have proclaimed on his own deathbed: "I did not poison Mozart. It is a pity to lose so great a genius, but his death is just as well for us. If he had lived, not a soul would have given us a crust of bread for our work." Today the most common explanation is that the great composer expired of uremia, following kidney trouble.

The great Mozart was buried in a Viennese pauper's grave at a cost of eleven florins, twenty-six kreutzer, paid by his widow. Emperor Joseph authorized a benefit concert under his patronage and allowed Constanze a life pension of twenty-two gulden a month. With this, plus royalties from Mozart's manuscripts, she still needed to take in boarders to survive, for the musician had accumulated many debts and had been paid a mere pittance for *Figaro, Don Giovanni,* and *The Magic Flute.*

The portrait of Mozart handed down through time in the form of letters, diaries and recollections indicate that although he was an extraordinary magician from the moment of birth, he was not a pleasant man. He was jealous, petulant, ungracious, disloyal, irritable, and resentful. But perhaps most unpleasant are the indications that he suffered from coprophilia, which is defined in the *Concise Oxford Dictionary* as "undue interest in faeces and defecation." Stefan Zweig, to the dismay of Mozart's admirers, specifically calls coprophilia a part of Mozart's erotic nature.

It is adduced by those who insist on Mozart's purity that in the eighteenth century, which he inhabited, the bodily functions and their organs were not called by their Latin names but by their vulgar ones. This may indeed be the case, but the composer seemed to go out of his way to insist on coprophiliac tendencies even in his extensive correspondence. Thus (translating literally from the German) he signed a letter to Bäsle: "Believing and shitting are two very different things" and also, "W.A. Mozart, who shits without a fart." To Constanze he evoked her "lovable, kissable little ass." He told his mother, "Keep well my love. Into your mouth your ass you'll shove. I wish you good night, my dear, but first shit in your bed and make it burst." He dismissed Salzburg and the prince-archbishop with: "I shit on both of them."

Normal emotional cravings are infrequent in his correspondence such as this letter to Constanze written two years before his death, which describes an erection and adds: "Arrange your dear sweet nest very daintily, for my little fellow deserves it, indeed, he has really behaved himself quite well and is only longing to possess your sweetest. . . . Just picture to yourself that rascal; as I write he crawls onto the table and looks at me questioningly. I, however, box his ears properly—but the rogue is simple . . . and now the knave burns only more fiercely and can hardly be restrained."

Wolferl's love for Bäsle was probably genuine and durable although it was translated from boyish passion to adult warm friendship. His adoration for Aloysia vanished before her indifference, but he persisted in his admiration for her magnificent singing voice. Unlike his friends Da Ponte and Casanova, Mozart does not seem to have had many women in his life.

He certainly had abiding affection for Constanze, who displayed sympathy and understanding for his shifting musical moods. But she sometimes was tempted to stray from the path of virtue, and Wolferl wrote to her (August 1789):

> A woman must always make herself respected or else people will begin to talk about her. My love! Forgive me for being so frank, but my peace of mind demands it as well as our mutual happiness. Remember that you yourself once admitted to me that you were inclined to *comply too easily*. You know the consequences of that. Remember too the promise you gave to me. Oh, God, do try my love. Be merry and charming to me. Do not torment yourself and me with unnecessary jealousy. Believe in my love, for surely you have proof of it and you will see how happy we shall be. Rest assured that it is only by prudent behavior that a wife can enchain her husband. Adieu.

Probably only three of Mozart's feminine admirers may be conceived as having been his mistress. Apart from Henriette Baranius, there was Nancy Storace, the half-English girl with whom he maintained contact through the years despite the rarity of occasions when they met. She was perhaps the only woman who justified any jealousy on Constanze's part. She married an English violinist, but separated from him and urged Mozart to come to England. The third, Magdalena Hofdemel, was the attractive young wife of Wolfgang's Masonic lodge brother and his pupil on the piano. Beethoven once declined to play in her presence on the ground that "too great an intimacy had existed between her and Mozart."

It is hard to enumerate and classify his male friends, many of whom were wholly inconspicuous and their existence was not recorded in history's footnotes. Certainly the most loyal, most noble, and perhaps the most talented was Haydn, who was his faithful and uninhibited admirer for many years. An unknown Viennese named Michael Puchberg loaned him generous sums when he was hard up for money. Lorenzo Da Ponte was a true collaborator and operatic inspirer, and once Mozart had rid himself of the thought that the Italian librettist might be "in league" with the hated Salieri, the two partners were on good terms. Suspicion and disloyalty were facets of Mozart's character that were not agreeable.

Oddly enough for a central European, Wolfgang's only real circle of foreign friends was English-speaking: the Storaces; Thomas Attwood, a twenty-year-old organist to whom he gave lessons; and Michael Kelly, a Dublin-born tenor. Kelly wrote an interesting memoir of his Salzburg connection before he himself opened a shop inscribed: "Michael Kelly, Importer of Wines and Composer of Music." Mozart wrote to his father in 1782, after hearing of British naval victories off Gibraltar and off Trincomalee: "I have heard of England's victories and am greatly delighted for you to know that I am a dyed-in-the-wool Englishman."

In appearance Mozart was decidedly unprepossessing. He was sometimes identified as "the funny little man with the light hair." He was not more than five feet four inches tall, of slight build and habitually pale. His face had been lightly marked by smallpox. He had a mane of fine fair hair, of which he was proud, a heavy upper lip, and a large fleshy nose with pronounced nostrils. Altogether, he was not handsome.

Contemporaries report that when he was playing the piano his expression changed, becoming more serene. His eyes settled into a steady calm gaze, and his muscles conveyed the sentiment expressed by his music. He styled his hair to obscure a strange malformation of his ears. In his middle age (he was never old), he grew stout and developed a double chin.

He showed a tendency to frequent bad company, from which Constanze sought to isolate him. He was restless and given to nervous fiddling with his watch chain or his hat. Music was always on his mind. He composed at meals, while playing billiards, while talking to friends. Usually he didn't even bother to test his ideas on the piano. His wife said: "He wrote down music in the same way as he wrote letters." He composed the entire overture to *Don Giovanni* on paper the night before its opening performance, so that the orchestra had no chance to rehearse it.

One endearing aspect of Mozart's personality was his love of pets. He had a particular fox terrier bitch named Bimperl, whom he adored. At various times he boasted a pet grasshopper and several canaries. But his best known pet was a starling for which he paid thirty-four kreuzer, a paltry sum, entered in his account book. The bird could whistle themes from some of his piano concertos. When it died in its cage, Wolfgang buried it in the garden and composed an elegy for it:

A little fool lies here
Whom I hold dear—

> *A starling in the prime*
> *Of his brief time,*
> *Whose doom it was to drain*
> *Death's bitter pain.*
> *Thinking of this, my heart*
> *Is riven apart.*

He also owned a horse during his latter years and, on his doctor's recommendation, took a ride every morning.

The only other regular exercise he knew was a "favorite walk" every day. At the age of eleven he had been taught to fence, and it is known that he enjoyed dancing. He adored bowling and playing billiards, and had his own table.

Occasionally he smoked a pipe. He enjoyed playing cards (especially piquet) and airing Bimperl. But the family diversion was target-shooting using air guns firing darts, a regular Sunday afternoon activity enjoyed with friends. He ate with good appetite, and his favorite dish was liver dumplings with sauerkraut. He wrote of eating magnificent cutlets ("che gusto") and, another time, "a delicious slice of sturgeon." He liked to drink wine, beer, and punch.

He was not a voracious reader (although he knew the works of Beaumarchais), and had little interest in contemporary affairs, paying no heed to the French Revolution. His moods were unpredictable. Karoline Pichler, a Viennese author of historical novels, recalled:

> Once I was sitting at the piano, playing 'Non più andrai' from Figaro; Mozart, who happened to be present, came behind me, and my playing must have pleased him, for he hummed the melody with me, and beat time on my shoulders; suddenly, however, he pulled up a chair, sat down, told me to keep playing the bass and began to improvise variations so beautifully that everyone present held his breath, listening to the music of the German Orpheus. But all at once he had enough; he jumped up and, as he often did in his foolish moods, began to leap over table and chairs, miaowing like a cat, and turning somersaults like an unruly boy. . . .

He lived in Vienna during his final years, but he was not as enthusiastic as he might have been because the Viennese and their court paid insufficient respect to his talent.

Wolfgang had an ill-concealed distaste for France. He and Nannerl were introduced to Paris as children, but did not enjoy the visit, although the Bavarian author and diplomat Grimm had pronounced them "true prodigies" and did all he could to help their father arrange concerts. When Wolfgang returned to the French capital aged twenty-two, he complained: "Paris is greatly changed; the French are not nearly as polite as they were fifteen years ago. Their manners now border on rudeness and they are detestably self-conceited." After he gave twenty-four long lessons in musical composition to the daughter of the Duc de Guines, he was dismissed with a payment of three Louis d'or, which he refused. In 1778, on a subsequent Parisian trip, Wolfgang wrote his father of a humiliating experience at the residence of the Duchesse de Chabot:

> M. Grimm gave me a letter for her, so I drove there. . . . I kept my word and went. I had to wait for half an hour in a large ice-cold, unheated room, which hadn't even a fireplace. At last the Duchesse de Chabot appeared. She was very polite and asked me to make the best of the clavier in the room, as none of her own were in good condition. Would I perhaps try it? I said that I should be delighted to play something, but that it was impossible at the moment, as my fingers were numb with cold; and I asked her to have me taken at least to a room where there was a fire. "Oh oui, Monsieur, vous avez raison," was all the reply I got. She then sat down and began to draw. . . . I kept on thinking: "If it were not for M. Grimm, I would leave this house at once." At last, to cut my story short, I played on that miserable, wretched pianoforte. But what vexed me most of all was that Madame and all her gentlemen never interrupted their drawing for a moment, but went on intently, so that I had to play to the chairs, tables and walls.

Wolfgang was born a Catholic and remained one all his life, but there is no evidence that he was especially religious. His feelings toward his church seem to have been cool but conventional until he became a Freemason. After 1782 he never went to church except to attend performances of his own liturgical works. Even on his Italian journeys he expressed somewhat critical views of the priesthood. He thought of his Masonic brethren not as antireligious but as acceptable to all faiths. However, the priest who had been summoned to his deathbed stayed away because he considered Wolfgang an apostate.

* * *

Mozart was born with more natural talent, I venture to say, than any other artist in history. Many musicians would challenge this statement and claim that Felix Mendelssohn, in their metier, was Amadé's equal as a prodigy. I can only say that, from personal taste, I immensely prefer Mozart, both boy and man. One might claim that the infant painter Giotto matched his brilliance in another art. Such assertions are meaningless, but I venture the personal opinion that this is difficult to prove. To my own taste, Mozart and Johann Sebastian Bach are the most superb composers; and Mozart started out ahead early.

His own instrumental gift was striking in its versatility. He played all string instruments. He was a splendid virtuoso on the piano and the clavier, especially before an appreciative audience, a factor that was of particular importance to his sensitive soul. He played and composed for a variety of instruments even including the glass harmonica invented by Benjamin Franklin out of drinking glasses filled with varying amounts of water.

Perhaps his greatest achievement in instrumental music was his series of piano concertos. This form hardly existed before him. The combination of a solo instrument with a full orchestra was particularly congenial to him. Once he had found Da Ponte as a librettist, his operas assumed striking beauty. The two men collaborated in three astounding successes: *The Marriage of Figaro, Don Giovanni,* and *Cosi Fan Tutte.* Wolfgang loved his *Magic Flute* (libretto by Emanuel Schikaneder) as much as he was pleased by *Figaro.* Until his end, Mozart, was composing dance music, concertos, Singspiel, serious opera, and sacred music. All told, he produced 626 compositions.

After his death, the cities in which he had dwelled raced to capitalize on his former presence. Vienna, which he had disliked because it showed little appreciation for his talent, revived his works. He had detested his birthplace, Salzburg, which nevertheless erected a statue of him and holds an annual festival in his name.

Mozart, who was scarcely without vanity, would have been deeply pleased to see how Brahms, Wagner, Berlioz, and Strauss acknowledged their debt to him in their music and also in their words. Haydn and Beethoven had been the first to acknowledge that they had learned most from Mozart. In 1787, when Wolfgang was still living, the noble Haydn wrote to a Prague connoisseur:

> If I could impress upon the hearts of music lovers, especially the
> great ones, how inimitable are Mozart's works, how profound,

how musically intelligent, how sensitive (for this is how I understand and feel them), then nations would compete to possess such a jewel within their walls. Prague should hold onto the precious man—and reward him, too. Without that, the fate of great geniuses is sad indeed, and gives posterity but little encouragement to strive further; unfortunately, this is why so many promising talents succumb. I am angered that this unique man, Mozart, has still not been engaged at any royal or imperial court. Forgive me if I have gotten off the track; I love the man too much.

When his own English publisher expressed an interest in acquiring a collection of Mozart pieces, Haydn said: "Buy it by all means. He was truly a great musician. Friends flatter me by saying that I possess some genius, but he stood far above me."

Haydn died in 1809; at his funeral the music performed was Mozart's "Requiem." It was also performed following Beethoven's funeral in 1827. Thus did one great musician take his leave of another.

Søren Kierkegaard wanted to start a sect to revere Mozart. The theologian Karl Barth imagined that angels would play Mozart's music before the Lord. Napoleon praised his opera *Don Giovanni*. In a poem, Keats wrote: "But many days have passed since last my heart was warm'd luxuriously by divine Mozart." And George Bernard Shaw, that famous music critic, wrote in 1893: "It is as still true as it was before the Eroica Symphony existed that there is nothing better in art than Mozart's best."

Part Three

IDEOLOGUES

IX

The Dynasts of Democracy: John and John Quincy Adams

On October 4, 1961, I was received in the White House by President John F. Kennedy, and at the start of our lengthy chat he said: "I met your wife at lunch." We were staying in Washington with Phil and Kay Graham, owners and publishers of the *Washington Post*. I knew they had taken my wife, Marina, to a *Post* book luncheon honoring Harvard's publication of a volume of the Adams papers, and that Kennedy would attend a small special reception to which the Grahams and Marina would also go.

"Charming," the President said. "Is she French?"

"No, Greek."

"But then how can she be an Adams?" he inquired, leaning forward in his rocking chair.

"What do you mean?"

"Well, I thought most of the people at the party were Adamses."

Immediately I got the drift and explained we were staying with the Grahams who had sponsored the affair. From then on Marina was known to Kay and Phil and a few close friends as "the Greek Adams." She was mischievously delighted by the sobriquet and the complications of explaining whenever by chance someone not in on the story overheard the phrase. And she was flattered as well because, although they were by no means as well known a clan abroad as the Roosevelts, for example, the Adams family meant at least something distinguished to anyone with a good European education.

Family dynasties have been rare in modern politics. On the contemporary scene there is little doubt that India's Nehru-Indira Gandhi father-daughter team leads the list. The Churchill line in England has displayed, since the seventeenth century, a continuous energetic strain that retains in its blood stream a vast potential for genius: but only twice has this exploded into

149

full blossom; John Churchill, the great statesman-general, first duke of Marlborough and, in this century, that versatile Shakespearian genius Winston Spencer Churchill, who led his country to victory in its greatest war.

The United States is the only multiparty democracy that has touched several times on a form of political heredity. The Taft dynasty included one president and one who "nearly made it." The Kennedy dynasty, funded by the great and somewhat ill-gotten wealth of its founder, a New Deal official and ambassador, could boast one tragically short-lived chief of state of striking potential, one important cabinet member, and one senator with an eye long-fixed upon the White House. The two distantly related Roosevelt families each produced a great president whose descendants were political mediocrities.

By far the most successful as well as the most honorable of families whose sons were elected to office or appointed to positions of public service generation after generation was and is the Adams family of Massachusetts, which could boast the exceptional distinction of forgoing compromise with honor and principle for the sake of advancement, yet continuing to succeed. The two greatest dynasts of the Adamses were, of course, John, the second U.S. president, and John Quincy Adams, the sixth president, both of whom were singularly intelligent, upright, honorable men who never courted honor but were awarded top distinction by their country.

A superb account of this remarkable, talented, and patriotic dynasty has been compiled by the historian James Truslow Adams, himself not connected with "*The* Adams Family." He notably recalls their tale in a lucid book that tells of the achievements of the entire Adams tribe from the seventeenth through the twentieth centuries. This is not only acute, discerning, and well written, but so magnificently organized that the entire account is unraveled in less than four hundred pages. My own essay deals only with the two outstanding Adamses who became presidents.

There is no true civilian equivalent to the Congressional Medal of Honor, top award for battlefield bravery which was granted to one father-son pair, Arthur and Douglas MacArthur. Had such a decoration existed, it would certainly have been more than merited by John Adams and his brilliant son, both fine men and great presidents: scrupulous, honest, and unafraid. There were other remarkable leaders in our early days whose names are so well known they need no mention; but no such couple of dynasts. And the fact that ever since, generation after generation, their descendants continue to play leading parts in our society's role of honor is a commemorable celebration from which the nation benefits—and, one hopes, will long do so.

Many unusual aspects feature the origin of the American dynasts. They started as plain folk. When Henry Adams immigrated to Boston in 1636 with a wife and nine children, there was nothing notable about him. He was of undistinguished English stock and, by the colonial authorities, was granted land to establish a foothold near the Massachusetts town of Braintree.

They settled in quietly, the most simple English of what were to become the great American families, and it is a curious comment that during three generations of diplomatic successes in disputes with England, this most English of U.S. clans carried the burden. As the greatest of them all, the *pater familias*, John Adams confided to his son: "If I were to go over my life again, I would be a shoemaker rather than an American statesman."

English as the Adamses were by antecedence and multiple political convictions, from the moment that the American colonies began to feel the burden of dependence and the impulse toward freedom, they moved with unhesitating sturdiness to demand their rights, to stand on their own feet, and with a lack of chauvinism (a nineteenth-century concept), worked unyieldingly for total freedom.

Oddly enough, the great diplomatic successes of earlier generations of Adams statesmen—including two presidents, a secretary of state, and numerous diplomatic envoys were, as I have said, successes against the British. Yet the inherent honesty of the tribe's character, handed on from generation to generation, never conceived or admitted any version of distorted emotionalism and maintained on both sides of all international arguments a determined, patient, forthright, if discreet, approach. The sculptured strength of the family, as it moved from four generations of obscurity in the tiny seventeenth-century village of Braintree to a leading position within the international eighteenth- and nineteenth-century world, was based on intellect and strong character.

Neither John Adams nor John Quincy Adams proclaimed himself an ideologue. Theirs was not an era stuffed with definable "isms," such as communism, socialism, fascism, naziism, etc. Theirs was a simplified time of monarchy, ranging from absolute authority for the king, to incipient democracy, as already developed under the crown in England.

Even in revolutions such as Britain's (seventeenth century) and France's (eighteenth century) and in the American war of independence, the upheavals generally began in opposition to a person, a group, or to a situation and only later developed their own more precise rationale. The American revolutionary movement assumed a genuine ideological precision with the Continental Congress and the series of resolutions it passed, all of which led up to the U.S. constitution.

It was as a constitutional lawyer and supporter of the struggle between all forms of individualism and corporate authority that the first notable Adams, John, initially made his mark. But neither he nor his eldest son, John Quincy, proclaimed any textbook ideology except freedom in its broadest sense. Both lived and practiced their dogma rather than merely orating about it; practiced it in years of honorable public service. But what they practiced was the purest, noblest form of true democracy.

Not until the fifth trans-Atlantic generation of Adamses did the family produce an individual, John, of outstanding importance: author, statesman, and political leader. He graduated from Harvard, the local college, and became a conventional school teacher. He confessed in his own diaries to an immense desire to write, and then shifted from education to law as a profession.

During the mid-eighteenth century (as ever since), lawyers had risen in eminence, importance, and versatility in the social, business and political worlds. Even so, rather suddenly, the 1750s disclosed new paths to power, usefulness, and influence for members of the bar. And it was as a constitutional lawyer that John influenced the profoundly important events that turned the British colonies in North America, south of the present Canadian border, into an independent nation.

It is really quite astonishing, if one looks back to 1756 when John gave up his job as a school teacher in order to study law, to see the comparative scale of importance between Boston, center of Adams's activities, which was just a sprawling village of only about 15,000 people, and London, its great opponent, which boasted a population of 1.5 million. But a moment of immense historical import was invisibly shaping up, and the modest novice attorney was well suited to his forthcoming career as revolutionary, diplomat, politician, and statesman.

He was not remarkable looking. Today he would be judged short and stodgy in appearance. Nor did he evince any of the qualities of popular appeal that marked his second cousin, the flamboyant orator Sam Adams. He was often intense and outspoken, sometimes impetuous, but always thoughtful, patriotic, independent-minded, and unflinchingly courageous. His character was not without blemishes. He was modest enough in truth to note in his own diary that he was "puffy, vain, conceited." Yet he was strangely given to quarrels with great contemporaries like Washington, Jefferson,

Franklin, and he unabashedly manifested petty streaks of envy and jealousy during his subsequent career.

As a young man, despite the profound earnestness of his character, he considered himself a bit of a gallant. However, any such playfulness seems to have vanished after he married, in 1764, the illustrious, well-connected Abigail Smith, who was to become the most cultivated, strong-minded wife of any United States president, at least before Eleanor Roosevelt.

In 1765, the year after John and Abigail's wedding, Britain's parliament enacted the Stamp Act to tax the commercially developing colonies. This provoked mass violence, which, to the intense distaste of John Adams, was fanned by his kinsman Sam's propaganda. John preferred the calm but more effective recourse to legal action. At the end of the critical year, he delivered a speech before the colony's governor and council pronouncing the act invalid because Massachusetts, possessing no representative in London's Parliament, had not assented to the decree.

The next ten years were of vital importance. In 1768 John Adams moved from Braintree to Boston itself. It was becoming increasingly manifest to this overseas "British subject" that a government without the power to levy taxes was no government, and there could be no rightful taxation if those affected were not represented and allowed to express their views. The only alternative to a lack of such representation was independence. He arrived at this conclusion with icy logic.

In 1770 British troops were landed around Boston to tranquilize that restless area. Adams acknowledged the likelihood that this move would inevitably be bound to lead to a physical showdown. The popular resentment against legislation imposed without representation by the citizenry legislated against mounted steadily and perceptibly. John Adams became an intellectual leader of this ever more significant current of thought.

On March 5, 1770, a fight, dubbed the "Boston Massacre," broke out between a small crowd and a handful of British soldiers. Four of the former were killed. An English captain and seven other ranks were arrested and charged with murder. Adams and Josiah Quincy accepted the unpopular task of defending the redcoats, recognizing this as their duty. The captain was acquitted together with the majority of soldiers. Two of the latter were found guilty of manslaughter, branded in the hand, and then released.

It is a tribute not only to Adams but to the inherent good judgment of the Bostonians that, despite the inflamed state of opinion, his upright conduct was approved by a heavy majority vote electing him to the Massachusetts House of Representatives. That body named him and Sam

Adams as part of its delegation to a Continental Congress in Philadelphia from all the American colonies of Britain. He remained a member of that body, the country's protonational administration, from 1774 until late 1777.

In June 1775, consciously working toward unity and independence from London, he delivered a eulogy on George Washington and seconded Washington's nomination as a commander in chief of the army of independence. With the Virginian's unanimous election, North and South were *de facto* cemented together in a common cause.

The idea of liberty was starting to advance. On June 7, 1776, Adams seconded Richard Henry Lee's sonorous resolution that "these colonies are, and of a right ought to be, free and independent states." The next day he was named together with Jefferson, Franklin, Sherman, and Livingston to a committee to formulate a Declaration of Independence. This was principally drafted by Jefferson, who wrote it, and Adams who played an outstanding part in the debate over its adoption.

The legislative role of John Adams was primordial. In a debate on foreign affairs he cautioned: "We should separate ourselves as much as possible and as long as possible from all European politics and wars." He dominated the committee assigned to establish an American navy, and he is even today considered its real father.

Adams had by then earned a position of a sort extraordinarily rare in American politics. He was regarded as an honorable, fearless, trusted leader despite personal prejudices that he took no care to hide. By far the worst of these was an undisguised jealousy of the prestige and position of Washington as the revolutionary nation's number one citizen, a prestige based upon the general's own great reputation and also upon, to a large degree, Adams's own recognition of this fact and his insistence upon its cardinal importance to the fledgling cause. Jealousy of Washington became, as James Truslow Adams was to write so much later, "the greatest blot upon his own career."

The biographer-historian described this unpleasant trait of John Adams, the statesman, as "compacted part of envy and part of disdain," the kind of warped relationship that "the thinker has for the man of action and the intellectual for the practical." It is sad, for those who would romanticize or sentimentalize their own past history, but it became widely known that Adams belonged to the anti-Washington faction, in some respects despising the father of his country, whose reputation he himself had done so much to manufacture and often to acclaim.

In 1778 Congress recalled Silas Deane from his diplomatic mission to France and named Adams instead. This was not an assignment coveted by Adams who was well aware that the three colonial commissioners in Paris—

Deane, Benjamin Franklin, and Arthur Lee—had been quarreling, and that he was simply being substituted for one of the disputing parties. Nevertheless, Adams dutifully accepted the task and set sail, taking along with him his ten-year-old son, John Quincy.

After his arrival, Adams soon made plain again this peculiar streak of envy he seemed to cherish for outstanding associates, in this case the sly, demure, intelligent, lively philosopher Franklin, who had made a great name both for himself and his cause at the court of King Louis XVI, above all with the principal minister, the Comte de Vergennes. He confided to his other associate, Lee, that while Franklin might be "a great satirist and a great politician," it was dubious that he was "a great philosopher, a great moralist and a great statesman."

Indeed, it is always possible that Adams's personal view was more correct than that which was then and subsequently maintained in Paris. Yet there is no doubt it discloses a nasty twist in the honorable Adams character.

In 1779 Adams returned to Boston after Franklin was appointed sole American agent. With wearily cynical humor, the latter had suggested the former should remain in Paris and have a good time at public expense, which must have irked the prim Bostonian. But Congress soon realized it would be useful to have in France its own man solely bearing authority to negotiate with England treaties of peace and of commerce, when such agreements became possible. Adams was selected for the job and, on September 27, 1779, named as minister plenipotentiary for this single purpose.

The time, however, was not yet ripe. London did not consider conditions appropriate, and Paris suspected Adams correctly of not being maneuverable and also of being overly suspicious of Vergennes. The result of the consequent stalemate was that the young American government was induced to appoint Franklin, Jefferson, John Jay, and Henry Laurens to cooperate with Adams. Jefferson never participated and Laurens played a minimal role.

Adams did not like the French, whose finesse had so successfully won over Franklin (and vice versa), and he resented the effort of Vergennes to gain information concerning his own secret instructions from the Congress in Philadelphia. He himself was determined to take a line on American fisheries claims and extended boundaries that opposed French wishes, but he was too clever to hint this to Paris.

However, his venomous dislike for the British forced restraint on his mistrust of the French. And, after all, Franklin was the accredited American minister to Louis XVI's government; Adams's assignment was simply to open negotiations with England when that became possible.

Despite this restricted position, Adams undiplomatically wrote a long letter directly to Vergennes urging much greater French naval aid to the Americans and also demanding that the French minister should endorse his own mission to the British. Vergennes, accustomed to dealing with Franklin, answered negatively and with evident contempt.

At this point, Adams made an unpardonable mistake. He did everything within his power—unsuccessfully—to, in effect, supplant Franklin as minister to France because he felt the amiable philosopher was doing his job incompetently. All he managed by this awkward and inexcusable maneuver was to further anger Vergennes and to start a needless and unhappy personal quarrel with Franklin. Adams was never a smooth, unruffled, conciliatory diplomat, but this was beyond any doubt his worst mistake.

Curiously enough, Congress chose that moment to assign two additional negotiating tasks to Adams: one as minister to Holland, and the other to arrange for a series of loans. He was entirely successful in gaining Dutch recognition of American independence and also brought about a much needed set of financial borrowings. In 1785 his diplomatic career was crowned by formal appointment as the first United States minister to the British Court of St. James's, after heading the brilliant American team that negotiated the victorious peace treaty of Paris ending the War of Independence.

His diplomatic task in London was testing and a personal trial. The British were scarcely cordial to a rebel—above all one who had succeeded—and Adams found none of the friendly cooperation he had occasionally imagined possible between the two ex-enemies. His wife, Abigail, acutely resented the cold treatment they received.

When he first presented his credentials, in 1785, to King George III, the most personalized enemy of Americans until the German Kaiser Wilhelm II came along in 1917, the British sovereign hinted he knew Adams had little confidence in France's government. Adams acknowledged this was true but then bluntly added: "I must avow to Your Majesty that I have no attachment but to my own country." The sovereign was certainly unaccustomed to such outspoken frankness from diplomats presenting their letters of credence.

While in London he published a book many Americans wrongly claimed favored wealth and aristocracy; this harmed him. In 1788 he resigned and sailed for home. He had been the first of three successive generations of Adamses who acted as minister to England during moments of exceptional strain between the two peoples, a bitter joke by fate at the expense of this "most English" of American families.

At the end of the year the new republic of the United States of America elected its first president, who was sworn in early in 1789. The then Republican Party (in modern terms, equivalent to today's Democrats) nominated Thomas Jefferson and Aaron Burr for the number one and number two positions on the ballot, president and vice president. In those early days, the man with the second-largest vote among all those listed automatically became vice president, making it quite easy to have a chief executive of one party assisted by an emergency replacement from the other. Everyone assumed that George Washington, whose strong character and honorable personality had led the ragged revolutionary forces to victory, would be chosen to head the state. So the vote was really for a vice president.

The Federalist Party nominated Adams, ignoring Washington's brilliant young aide, Alexander Hamilton, and the suavely eminent John Jay. Both were considered too unpopular among the voting public, the first because of his taut financial policy, the second because of a disliked treaty he had negotiated with England. But Hamilton remained the strongest political figure in the Federalist Party, a maker of presidents if not a potential president himself. And unfortunately for Adams, he and Hamilton were outright enemies, a fact that affected their own careers as well as the course of the nation.

There was little doubt that Adams, with his long record of integrity, patriotism, and public service, was entitled to lead the Federalists, however much Hamilton detested him. He knew Adams was not malleable and wished personally to remain the power behind the party throne. After the electoral votes were counted, it was found that Washington had received all sixty-nine, becoming the new nation's first chief of state, but none of the other nominees had received a majority for the second position; Adams, leading all other contenders with thirty-four, thus became vice president. Hamilton's vindictive interference had produced this unsatisfactory minority solution.

However, Adams (who respected Washington as a commanding general but not as a political leader) dutifully carried out his two terms as vice president through 1796, exerting a more powerful influence on Senate votes, as presiding officer, than any of his successors in that office.

It became known in 1796 that Washington would not under any conditions agree to stand for a third term. The Federalists therefore again nominated Adams, along with General Charles Cotesworth Pinckney, and the Republicans proposed a ticket of Jefferson and Aaron Burr. Adams defeated Jefferson by seventy-one to sixty-eight, thus producing a Federalist president and a Republican vice president.

The young U.S. government had not yet developed many of its current traditions, and the custom of completely changing official advisers when a new president was installed did not apply. Adams therefore retained Washington's entire cabinet. This meant that some of its leading members believed their prior loyalty was owed to Hamilton, their party boss, and not to President Adams. That unfortunate fact exacerbated the sore already existing between the two Federalists, impinging upon the dignity and judgment of both. Hamilton sought to apply executive rule behind the scenes as party chief and to diminish the real power of the president.

Almost from the moment of the national government's creation and until the end of the Napoleonic wars, including America's own second conflict with Britain, the War of 1812, U.S. foreign and domestic politics were dominated by relationships with England and France. The Federalists, who favored strong government, became increasingly friendly to the British monarchy.

The Republicans, emotionally favoring the French Revolution more than they understood it intellectually, were pro-France. In this difficult situation, Adams showed himself commendably impartial. He sympathized with neither of the two great powers but saw correctly that there was no benefit to the United States in tolerating the insults of one more than the other.

This was the situation vis-à-vis France, which had just refused to accept General Pinckney as American envoy and which had instituted even more repressive decrees with regard to U.S. commerce than the common enemy, England. Talleyrand, architect of French policy, in addition refused to receive any American mission unless sizable bribes were first paid to individual French officials and America increased a promised loan to Paris. When some members of Congress learned of the bribe proposal, Adams allowed publication of official reports on the matter, substituting the initials X, Y, and Z for the names of the key French agents involved, resulting in the documents henceforth being known as the "X.Y.Z." letters. They caused a scandalous uproar in the United States.

The Federalist Party began to urge war with France, a move desired by Hamilton, who thought he could use the occasion to conquer the southwest "Louisiana Territory." This was a huge tract, held at that time by France and previously by Spain.

Adams was determined to avoid such a conflict if this could be done with honor. Talleyrand sent word via Holland that Paris would accept a minister to negotiate terms for ending differences between the two countries. The Federalist president accepted this gesture, to the anger of the Hamilton Jingo faction, and extended the olive branch of peace.

In 1800 Hamilton published an excoriating attack on Adams as unfit "for the station of Chief Magistrate," but wound up his criticisms in a peculiar way by announcing he would vote for his reelection anyway. The Adams cause was badly damaged with predictable results. At last, the Republican, Thomas Jefferson, was elected president, primarily because the leader of Adams's own party had pronounced him not competent to lead the nation.

The long career in public service of the versatile, if occasionally jealous and vindictive, Bostonian was over. His final act before retirement was singularly important: he appointed John Marshall as chief justice of the Supreme Court.

Adams had thus played a vital role in preparing the Declaration of Independence, in helping to secure George Washington's position as military commander, in assisting the formulation of the new country's foreign policy, in creating its navy, in setting out the lines for avoidance of entanglements in European wars (soon to be temporarily put aside under a successor, James Madison, when the 1812 conflict erupted), and in naming the great jurist Marshall, who established the basis of fundamental American law.

The seat of government was shifted from Philadelphia to the newly built town of Washington at the very end of his term. On November 1, 1800, Adams became the first tenant of the White House. But very soon thereafter, he rode out of the capital and thus refused to meet the successor he detested, the handsome, red-haired Tom Jefferson. Following years of public service and diplomatic travel abroad, he retired at last to his farm in Quincy, Massachusetts.

Adams summed up his career accordingly: "In every considerable transaction of my public life I have invariably acted according to my best judgment, and I can look up to God for the sincerity of my intentions." Even Jefferson, his old rival and political opponent, called him "Disinterested as the Being who made him." The only truly negative action of Adams's administration was the passage of the Alien and Sedition Acts, which brought discredit to the Federalists and widened the gulf in that party between Adams and Hamilton. This factor combined with Jefferson's personal popularity to put an end to Adams's long and varied career.

The ex-president preferred the rural life of Quincy, where he was not well liked, to the growing town of Boston. He felt hurt and resentful because of his enforced retirement from public life amid unflattering comparisons with George Washington, his predecessor. And the blemish in his character, which had so long indicated envy of and resentment for the first president, was inflamed when John Quincy Adams, his son, named his own son George Washington Adams. The poor grandson ended up by committing suicide.

In 1812 the second president admitted that the eleven years he had already spent in Quincy surrounded by children and grandchildren had been most comfortable and he had "never enjoyed so much any equal period." Moreover, he began that very year, which saw the outbreak of another conflict with England, by writing a letter to President Jefferson renewing their erstwhile but long-lapsed friendship.

These resumed cordial relations must have brought much satisfaction to the two old leaders who, by extraordinary coincidence, died the same day, July 4, 1826, fiftieth anniversary of their Declaration of Independence. Adams's last recorded words were: "Thomas Jefferson survives." However, with amazing simultaneity, Jefferson died at almost that precise moment. The two remaining signers of the Declaration vanished together.

As James Truslow Adams wrote of America's leading family:

> There has always been in the Adamses a strong tendency toward dramatizing themselves and making themselves imaginatively play the leading roles in whatever situation they may be found. In indulging in this they exaggerate the elements in every such situation, intensifying in their own minds the odds against which they have had to struggle.
>
> A competitor is not merely a competitor; he is a malignant enemy, come from the Devil to destroy the noblest work of God. Circumstances that may oppose their plans are not accidents; they are damnable efforts on the part of society to thwart an Adams.
>
> It is not pleasant to dwell upon this aspect of the family mentality, but it is necessary to understand it, for it has been as continuous a trait as has the great intellectual ability displayed by every generation beginning with John, and in its way, of almost as great an influence upon the family's history. It is a trait that is characteristic of the early New England divines, who felt that any opposition to their own ideas or wishes were assaults of the Devil upon the Kingdom of God.

This is an astute observation and makes for interesting speculation upon the longevity in some families of a particular genetical strain. One can see it displayed on occasion in the life of John Quincy Adams, just as it marred his father's career from time to time, both in personal and political relationships.

John Quincy was born July 11, 1767, a few months before the family moved to Boston and settled in Brattle Square in what became locally known as the "White House." Clearly thanks to his mother's well-honed features, he was a far better-looking boy than his father, and physical distinction became as much a family trait as intellectual ability.

In 1778 he accompanied John on the latter's first mission to Paris and like his father kept a detailed record of his experiences, although he was only ten years old when he began this diary. With remarkable maturity, he described how their frigate captured one British ship and was chased by another. In 1797 John Quincy married Louisa Johnson, daughter of an American father and English mother, who had been brought up in France and was much admired for her beauty.

Just before his marriage, John Quincy was named American minister to Portugal. He accepted the post with some embarrassment because his father had already won the 1796 election and was president-elect of the United States. But his assignment was changed to that of the more important post of minister to Prussia after Washington, in his last presidential days, wrote the incoming second chief of state to voice a *"strong hope* that you will not withhold merited promotion from Mr. John [Quincy] Adams because he is your son. . . . I give it as my decided opinion that Mr. Adams is the most valuable public character we have abroad, and that there remains no doubt in my mind that he will prove himself to be the ablest of all our diplomatic corps." On the basis of Washington's admiring opinion, President Adams wrote his son that he should feel no lack of impropriety in accepting the mission.

There is no doubt that John Quincy already had much experience and a distinguished record. He studied in Holland after his first arrival in Europe and then, in 1781, when but fourteen years old, was sent to Russia, where he remained for a year as secretary to the American minister, Francis Dana. As a brilliant boy, he was already starting to develop an austere, cool, diffident manner. He already spoke French and Dutch and, while in St. Petersburg, studied German, Latin, and Greek.

After his tour in Russia, he returned to the Dutch city of Leyden to resume his studies there, stopping in Stockholm en route and announcing after six weeks there that he liked Sweden better than any European country he had visited. In 1785, remarkably educated and widely traveled, he was offered the post of secretary to his father, whom he had served in Paris and who was by then the first American minister to London.

Instead, the youngster made up his mind to return alone to the United States, graduate from Harvard, and then prepare himself for the bar. He wrote in his journal: "I had rather continue some time longer in obscurity and make some provision for fortune before I sally out in quest of fame or public honors." This sage and prudent decision showed that John Quincy was already aware of the need for him to pursue a personal policy free from the influence of any party of special faction.

On his twenty-seventh birthday he was named as American minister resident at the Hague, journeying via London to carry confidential dispatches to John Jay, by then minister to Britain. In Holland once again, this time on a significant diplomatic mission, he studied Italian and read continually in four languages. Three years later he married his charming bride, whom he took on to Berlin with him when he was ultimately sent to Prussia.

However, he became increasingly eager to return to America, homesick, eager to strike out on a new career, removed from diplomacy, and embarrassed by the fact that he had been appointed to Berlin by his father who would be succeeded in the White House by Jefferson, at that time regarded with extreme dislike by the Adamses, especially by the loyal and devoted Abigail.

In 1803 the thirty-six-year-old John Quincy was elected to the U.S. Senate, where he was soon to prove himself perhaps the most intelligent of all the Adamses. In Washington, where his social, intellectual, and worldly gifts were less appreciated than in other cities, he was soon made aware of the considerable enmity for his father, which persisted, and the deep, bitter factionalism within the Federalist party. It was quipped that "the Republicans [under Jefferson] trampled upon the Federalists and the Federalists trampled upon John Quincy Adams."

Thus caught up in political quarrels not of his own making, John Quincy added to the unpopularity he had inherited from his father by displaying an unconciliatory rigidity in personal relationships and a blatant political independence, stressing his refusal to sacrifice his concepts of integrity to party interests. At the end of his first senatorial year he wrote: "The country is so totally given up to the spirit of the party that not to follow blindfold the one or the other [Federalist or Republican] is an inexpiable offence." The Massachusetts senator's position became more and more balanced between the Federalists and the Anti-Federalists. And when he introduced resolutions supporting Jefferson's Non-Importation Act of 1806, defending the rights and honor of America, this view made his breach with the New England Federalists open and incapable of being healed.

In 1807, when he again backed Jefferson's policy, Federalist anger with him became unlimited. The Federalist legislature of his home state opposed the president's trade embargo and improperly elected a senatorial successor to John Quincy Adams nine months before his legal term had ended. He resigned.

He wrote: "On most of the great national questions now under discussion, my sense of duty leads me to support the anti-Federalist Administration and I find myself of course in opposition to the Federalists in general. . . . As my term of service nears its close, I am constantly approaching to the certainty of being restored to the situation of a private citizen."

Both by his actions and by the notations he entered in his diary, we know that John Quincy was ambitious to hold high office. However, it was clear that he would never do anything to obtain such a position. When Madison was elected president, he offered John Quincy the post of minister to Russia and Adams accepted. But the Senate, dominated by his enemies, voted that such a mission was not required. Later in the year, Madison repeated the offer, and this time the Senate changed its mind, confirming Adams in the post.

The former senator was a highly cultivated man of the world, and he made no secret of his attraction for Europe. However, he regretted having to leave behind his elderly parents and the two of his children still remaining at school in Boston. But with a return to diplomacy, he felt he could indulge his craving for culture, what he personally described as "an eager relish for the pursuits of literature and . . . a taste for the fine arts."

Both John Quincy and his wife spoke excellent French, even today a rare American achievement. French was the lingua franca of the Russian court and society. The American minister was thus easily able to converse with Czar Alexander, whom he met frequently at both official and social occasions. Alexander, who was engaged in war with Napoleonic France, offered to mediate the conflict that had broken out between America and England (the War of 1812), but London spurned the offer.

Subsequently, Britain expressed willingness for direct negotiations, and the United States delegated John Quincy and three commissioners to seek a treaty of peace. This was agreed upon in the lowlands city of Ghent in a negotiation of which the Marquess of Wellesley [later Duke of Wellington] said in the House of Lords that it demonstrated the Americans displayed "a most astonishing superiority over the British."

Adams left Ghent for Paris in January 1815 in the wake of peace. It had been thirty years since he was last in the City of Light, and he settled down with his wife to enjoy himself. He was treated with respect and friendship, and Washington's old friend Lafayette even came to the capital from his country home to see him.

However, very soon John Quincy was appointed U.S. minister to London and crossed the channel with his wife, renting as headquarters a distant house—eight miles from Hyde Park corner—to save money. In 1817 he returned to Washington when President James Monroe named him secretary of state.

The main problem inherited by the great new secretary was the question of Florida. This was combined with the definition of Louisiana's western boundary and Spain's patent inability to put down freebooters from Amelia Island and Galveston. These complex matters were intermixed with the United States' effort to adhere to a neutral position in the various wars between Spain and her Latin American colonies, actions that stimulated threats by other European nations to intervene.

The tense situation worsened when General Andrew Jackson marched into Spanish Florida, seized it, captured two Englishmen in the process, and executed them for instigating Indian hostilities. Thus, Washington for a time seemed on the verge of simultaneous wars with Madrid and London. Fortunately, the policy of Britain's foreign secretary, Lord Castlereagh, basically sought friendship with America and conflict was avoided.

President Monroe and his whole cabinet except for Adams opted for openly disavowing Jackson. Finally, on February 22, 1819, the secretary of state signed a treaty with the Spanish minister to Washington ceding Florida to the U.S. and arranging a precise western boundary for Louisiana. This steady, unemotional diplomacy achieved by Adams alone was a significant personal triumph.

During Monroe's second term in the White House, the greatest success of the secretary of state was his formulation of what came to be known as the Monroe Doctrine—for the president, rather than the Adams Doctrine, after the man who envisioned it—and its requirement as a touchstone for American foreign policy. The purpose of the doctrine was to warn off European nations seeking to establish or expand lodgments in the western hemisphere.

There had already been difficulties with Russia over North America's Pacific coast. Adams called in Tuyl, the Czar's minister, and warned that the United States "would contest the right of Russia to any territorial establishment on the American continent, and . . . would distinctly assume the principle that the American continents were no longer subjects for any new European colonial establishments."

He won Monroe over to this line, and the president's message in 1823 declared that Washington would oppose colonization in this hemisphere and regard "any attempt on their [the Europeans'] part to extend their system to any portion of this hemisphere" as dangerous to U.S. safety and to peace. The doctrine has hitherto had a profound impact upon American diplomacy and strategy, although its validity is being brought increasingly into doubt.

So impressive had his record as number one cabinet member been that there was much reason to anticipate Adams would succeed Monroe as chief of state when the latter's second term ended in 1824. However, the jealousy of political rivals and the vindictiveness of personal enemies spawned a succession of virulent, often scurrilous attacks on his appearance, his honor, and his pride.

John Quincy wrote ruefully but philosophically in his diary:

> To suffer without feeling is not in human nature; and when I consider that to me alone, of all the candidates before the nation, failure of success would be equivalent to a vote of censure by the nation upon my past service, I cannot dissemble to myself that I have more at stake upon the result than any other individual in the Union. Yet a man qualified for the elective Chief Magistracy of ten millions of people should be a man proof alike to prosperous and adverse fortune.

The results of electoral vote-counting were delayed, although Andrew Jackson clearly had more votes than Adams. Jackson supporters planted a fake news story in the press saying that Henry Clay, whose backing was crucial, would throw his influence behind any candidate who would agree to make him secretary of state. Clay was the obvious candidate for that post in any case.

The electoral contest was settled by the House of Representatives. Adams was elected. Clay was soon named to the State Department, and roars of a slanderous nature were heard throughout the country from Jacksonians. Adams remained aloof. He did nothing to help his own cause or reputation. He simply wrote an immediate report to his aged, tottering father who replied:

> My dear son—I have received your letter of the 9th. Never did I feel so much solemnity as upon this occasion. The multitude of my thoughts, and the intensity of my feelings are too much for a mind like mine, in its ninetieth year. May the blessing of God Almighty continue to protect you to the end of your life, as it has hitherto protected you in so remarkable a manner from your cradle.

On the date of his inauguration, March 4, 1825, John Quincy wrote in his journal: "After two successive sleepless nights, I entered upon this day with a supplication to Heaven, first, for my country; secondly, for myself and for those connected with my good name and fortunes, that the last results of its events may be auspicious and blessed."

It was immediately obvious that the headstrong and popular Jackson would be a strong candidate in the 1828 elections, and he began his fight for the presidency as soon as Adams entered the White House. The old political party leaderships were disintegrating as newcomers jockeyed for power. It soon became clear that in this competitive flux the ultimate fate of John Quincy's administration would be negative. Adams would promise nothing as a reward for political support. The Jacksonians promised the moon.

Adams proclaimed in his inaugural address:

> While foreign nations, less blessed with that freedom which is power than ourselves, are advancing with gigantic strides in the career of public improvement, are we to slumber in indolence or fold up our arms and proclaim to the world that we are *palsied by the will of our constituents*? . . . Moral, political, and intellectual improvement are duties assigned by the Author of our Existence to social, no less than to individual man.

Herein is the kernel of American democratic ideology.

Despite the lavish Jacksonian offers of widespread patronage if their champion defeated Adams, the latter removed only twelve office-holders in four years—each with just reason. He was subjected to endless libelous attacks. Even his vice president, John C. Calhoun, opposed him by refusing, as presiding officer of the Senate, to rule attacks upon the president as out of order.

It soon became apparent that, together with his own father, Washington's successor, John Quincy Adams would be the only other single-term chief of state of the first six elected. One might call this an indifference to political skill or, more justly, a testimonial to the moral honor and independence of the only father-son team to lead our country. The 1828 election was dirty and partisan on both sides; and Jackson won easily. Primitive populist democracy reigned.

The Jackson Administration contained many members, starting with the president himself, who at one or another time had been indebted to Adams for his services or help. But now, with the exception of Martin Van Buren, none even paid the departing leader the customary ceremonial visit. Adams noted: "After fourteen years of incessant and unremitted employment I have passed to a life of total leisure, and from living in a constant crowd to a life of almost total solitude."

Rather to his and the national astonishment, however, his native district around Quincy asked if he would serve as candidate for the House of Representatives. He agreed but said he would not solicit votes. Nevertheless, he won a smashing victory and courageously returned to Washington, where for so long he had been a national and international star, to serve as a plain Congressman, beginning again "like a boy," as Clay said sympathetically. This modest step symbolized his commitment to the three interdependent legs upon which the tripod of American democracy rested.

As a humble Congressman, Adams continued to try to improve the condition of his countrymen through the development of natural resources, a policy he had insisted upon while president. He also sought to minimize political patronage and encourage able, honest men to seek careers in the civil service.

Unfortunately, the new mood of cynical, self-seeking ambition that Jackson had discerned and successfully employed in rising to power, prevailed in the nation and its legislature. Nevertheless, the congressman from Quincy maintained his courage and his dream of moral integrity, stimulated in addition by the crisis over slavery, which he foresaw and which he feared might shred the Union. As a fierce old champion of the good, he made more enemies but also earned widespread admiration. He fought stubbornly against the "gag" rule enacted by a heavy majority in the House, which sought to limit debates on the slave issue.

In a dramatic speech, he opposed seizure of Texas and thereafter noted that prevention of slavery's extension "is a cause upon which I am entering at the last stage of life, and with the certainty that I cannot advance in it far; my career must close, leaving the cause at its threshold."

Despite the increasing weight of age, Adams took heart in the constancy of his Massachusetts supporters and persisted in attacks on the unconstitutional "gag." Finally, when he was almost eighty, the House rescinded the closure restriction in December 1845. That day his diary terminated: "Blessed, forever blessed, be the name of God."

The following year he had a stroke. Notwithstanding, after a partial recovery, he resumed his congressional seat. The entire House rose to honor the venerable patriot, who had by that time opposed almost every member on one or another occasion. Adams was never strong enough to speak again in the chamber. On February 21, 1848, he attempted suddenly to rise from his seat but toppled forward in a coma. The final words he was able to utter were: "Thank the officers of the House. This is the last of earth! I am content!"

Once again the nation, although its psychological and political moods had greatly altered, witnessed the greatness of an indomitable Adams. The father, John, is generally held to be the outstanding member of this distinguished clan. Which of the two was the better president is hard to say. Neither could be termed popular; both were indomitable. John was on the whole better suited to the popular mood of his period at the helm.

Be that as it may—there can be no doubt of the total absence of pliancy in John Quincy's presidential record—I can think of no American whose life as a public servant has surpassed that of the younger Adams. He was exceedingly cultivated, well read, educated to an unusual degree, far traveled, discreet, careful, a splendid diplomat despite his tendency toward rigidity, a fine negotiator, and a remarkable linguist. It is almost unquestionable that he was the best secretary of state the United States ever had. He was also an uncompromising political champion of the antislavery cause in Congress.

His outstanding role in conceiving the Monroe Doctrine, stimulated by his then unique perception of a Russian threat to North America, is probably more acutely pertinent today than at any time since 1823.

Certain marked traits were obvious defects in the unusually noble characters shared by the only father and son to gain the White House. Neither courted popularity; each accepted office but didn't seek it.

Both were subject to the jealousy of their rivals and vindictiveness toward many who disgreed with them. Both were unusually intelligent, simultaneously ambitious and modest, and thought more of serving their country than anything else.

It is impossible to say how many of these characteristics, marking both men, were inherited by the son from the father or were acquired in boyhood by John Quincy from the example of John. John perhaps achieved more in his life because of the vital and critical situation in which he found himself as revolution burst into flame around him.

John Quincy, a remarkable diplomat and statesman perhaps more brilliant and surely more cultivated than his learned father, was even more endowed with enemies. Yet he had vast influence and, like his father, always thought first of his nation, then himself.

Neither father nor son was popular. Both were indomitable—and great; the most splendidly democratic congeners America has yet produced.

X

A Family Enterprise: Jawaharlal Nehru and Indira Gandhi

Motilal Nehru, father of India's first prime minister and grandfather of India's first woman prime minister, was an interesting, dominating, self-willed man. He came of Kashmiri Brahmin descent, perhaps the highest layer of the highest caste in India's complicated class society, which Nehru and his daughter, Mrs. Gandhi, tried gradually to eliminate. But it is a difficult task to alter a complex ancient set of intricate social and religious distinctions.

The only successful effort in this respect has been that of Islam. When India's Moslem conquerors produced the great Moghul Empire, imposing their concepts upon the sub-continent, they eliminated caste differences for all the millions they could convert. The multi-caste heritage stems from the multi-god concept of Hinduism, not the monotheistic concepts of Mohammed.

I gathered from personal conversations with both that Motilal Nehru had less influence on his son than on his granddaughter. As one close friend of Motilal said of him and his famous son: "Motilal sat still and expected the world to come to him. Jawaharlal was always running about going to see people himself."

Like his descendents, Motilal was handsome. He was born a refugee from the 1857 Indian Mutiny (against Britain). The stricken family had already fled from Delhi to Agra, seat of the magnificent Taj Mahal. There they were accepted by both Hindus and Moslems because their Kashmiri family could trace its ancestry back to Islamic-sponsored Hindu Brahmin Pandits (learned teachers).

Mrs. Gandhi, as Prime Minister, inferred to me in 1969 that she had been even more influenced by her grandfather than by her father: "He

[Motilal] started with very little; it was the kind of story you Americans like. Our family has had many ups and downs and also we have always had a very close-knit family system in which a young man may have to support everyone.

"My grandfather started poor but he was a very good lawyer and became rich. He saw to it that even all his nephews were educated in Europe. And although we had a disciplined upbringing, he was fond of the good life. He got on very well with the British, but he was always keenly conscious of India's situation and he fought hard for greater rights.

"He joined the Congress party [essentially the creation of Mohandas Gandhi] early when it was a small middle-class party, and saw Gandhi make it into a mass movement. This was partly through the influence of my grandfather as well as Gandhi. He gave up everything and joined."

Motilal, as was traditional in India, was most ambitious for his son, Jawaharlal. He was determined to win the boy entrance to Harrow, the famous English public school which was attended by Winston Churchill. From there Jawaharlal went to Cambridge.

Many of young Nehru's most intimate friends in England were Moslems, including the brother of Khan Abdul Ghaffar Khan who, under the inspiration of Mahatma Gandhi, was to become known as the Frontier Gandhi and suffer long imprisonment in Pakistan.

Analyzing himself later Jawaharlal saw this period of his life as nebulous: at Cambridge he had drifted on a vague desire to enjoy a pleasing life.

He recalled that religion had no appeal for him, he disliked its repression. "I was superficial and did not go deep into anything. And so the aesthetic side of life appealed to me, and the idea of going through life worthily, not indulging it in a vulgar way but still making the most of it and living a full and many-sided life attracted me."

At the same time "risk and adventure" fascinated him. Like his father he was a "bit of a gambler at first with money and then for higher stakes, with the bigger issues of life."

Nehru's father knew through his own experience that there were various types of British, including the racist snobs and the honorable meritocracy and also that all people must be evaluated according to their merit. His thought was to live by this standard.

From his youth Motilal had espoused the cause of Indian nationalism and rejected the taboos of old-fashioned Hinduism as they applied to Brahmins. He saw to it that caste restrictions and privileges were never observed in his own household. But he used the increasing profits of his own admired legal talents to comfort with luxuries the loneliness of his distant son in England. He also advised his boy to be sure to wield a cricket bat with skill if he wished to be admired by his English schoolmates.

Motilal was, moreover, tolerant of the boy's intellectual growing pains. Young Jawaharlal was swept up by the scientific mysticism then becoming a notable international influence under the sponsorship of Mrs. Annie Besant. He announced to his father that he wished to become a member of her Theosophical Society.

Motilal simply laughed, causing the boy to feel his father lacked "spirituality," but he did not prevent him from carrying out his wish. It was not long before Jawaharlal, lacking the essential Hindu piousness, dropped theosophy while retaining a personal affection for Mrs. Besant.

Much insight into the complex character of Nehru is given in an article by a certain "Chanakya" that appeared in 1937 published by a Calcutta review. Later Nehru acknowledged that he had written the piece himself for his own amusement and sent it to a lady friend. The latter passed it on to someone else, who published it.

"Chanakya" was, in fact, the name of a counselor of the great Indian Emperior Chandragupta who had talked with Alexander the Great. The piece exposed many aspects both of Nehru the complicated introvert and Nehru the charming extrovert. In it, he admitted that within him lay the makings of a dictator. A curious little vanity, that piece; it exposed sentiments and egocentric traits more than policy ideas. But he pointed out to me that in a decade at the forefront of Indian politics these character weaknesses had not manifested themselves in actions.

The best analysis I have heard of Nehru came from the most astute and possibly the least known United States ambassador to New Delhi, the career diplomat and brilliant public servant, Loy Henderson. Henderson was the first American envoy to the newly independent Indian republic after partition and British withdrawal. On April 22, 1950, I lunched with him and asked him for his personal summation, above all with respect to Nehru's anti-American bias, which had already manifested itself. Henderson said:

> Nehru went down very well with the American people but not very well with the U.S. government during his trip to the New World. He was too vague and theoretical in his talks with Washington officials. He is a curious, vain and petulant man with certain great qualities.
>
> For example, he had a way of thinking out loud in a direct and honest manner which he can do to one person or to a large

crowd and in either case with an astonishing effect of winning support. He also always had a direct mass appeal to the broad masses in India and deliberately cultivated the thinking aloud method which fascinates them.

Nehru, however, has certain inner secrets. He is strongly anti-American. This stems from several things. His governess when he was a boy came from the British middle classes and regularly hammered into his head the concept that Americans were vulgar, second-rate people. This, as his sister has confided, had an effect. Whenever an American was invited to the house, the governess would alert the children and then comment on the visitor's manners afterward in a critical way.

Secondly, Nehru is by nature a tremendous introvert and automatically resents the normal extrovert manner of Americans. Furthermore, he tends to look down upon them as cheap and non-intellectual. Nehru has been bitterly disturbed by American race attitudes and this has led to a strong and perhaps subconscious reaction of pride. All this was reinforced in one way or another by his education at Harrow.

Nehru is by conviction a Socialist. He used to be a Marxist but now tends more toward the British form; Harold Laski had a very strong influence upon him. Nehru does not like the autocratic system of Russia but probably in his heart of hearts he is less anti-Russian than he is anti-American.

He is a man of great knowledge and also one who enjoys life. He is more fond of the company of women than of men, probably because he was brought up by and with women. He had a tremendous friendship with Lady Mountbatten [wife of the last British Viceroy], which may even have been more than that.

Nehru himself admitted to me later that he was "a little timid where sex was concerned."

Henderson's analysis continued:

Nehru is passionately loyal to his friends. Although his wife was from Kashmir and his own ancestors came from there, the primary reason for his personal interest in Kashmir is that he is a devoted personal friend of Sheikh Abdullah, whom he appointed prime minister of Kashmir.

In personal conversations Nehru always criticizes the United

States and never Russia, but privately he says that if India could not be neutral in another world war she would be on the side of Western democracy. Nehru opposes Communist tactics in India but he does not criticize communism in the broad sense, whereas he frequently criticizes the United States in public.

He assails America for colonialism, racial discrimination and unequal distribution of resources. He says America has not yet recognized that European colonialism, no matter what its form, is only the domination of colored people by the West. Nehru is obviously a complex personality with great and petty qualities.

Henderson had two other comments on the fascinating character of Nehru. The first was that Nehru was essentially a feminine personality. Secondly, Nehru was very vain. For example, he was bald and therefore almost always wore a hat.

There seems little question that Nehru did have a personal streak of anti-Americanism, even though he admired and/or liked many Americans. In 1955, Donald Kennedy, the U.S. chargé d'affaires told me in Delhi that our collective embassy analysis was that Nehru's undoubted prejudice stemmed from four sources: Racism—a resentment of American attitudes about white "superiority"; imperialism—the white man stuck with his fellows, and we had supported the French in Indochina; forthrightness—Americans tended to be too blunt and outspoken; and "uncouthness"—Nehru's feeling was that most Americans were simply "uncouth."

Our ways irritated him: private investment, advertising, pushiness. And the close advisers around Nehru shared this view and nourished his bias. Not that we ourselves weren't stupid about our expressed attitudes.

At a dinner given for Nehru by a group of bankers, during his official visit to the United States in 1949, the host boasted that so many billion dollars were represented by the people gathered about the table. Nehru shuddered.

At a White House dinner he sat on President Truman's right: Justice Vinson on Truman's left. Most of the meal was taken up in debate between Truman and Vinson on the relative merits of Maryland (Vinson's state) and Missouri (Truman's state) Bourbon whiskey.

If Henderson's analysis of the psychological influence of Nehru's English governess on the children was sound (and I'm sure it was), one can easily see that these irritant seeds fell on receptive soil.

I had my first extensive wide-ranging talk with Pandit Nehru on April 26, 1950. He received me in his private residence in New Delhi, a large comfortable building which used to be the home of the commander-in-chief of the Indian Army during the British raj. We sat in a living room on the second floor in comfortable armchairs. Orange juice and cigarettes were served. I noted then:

> Nehru was wearing his usual jodhpurs and long coat of linen, but he did not have on his customary Congress cap. His bald head gives him a different appearance from when I saw him last at a reception with his cap on. He was fairly friendly in contrast to my curt first meeting when he was irked about some dispatches I had written from Pakistan.
>
> He had a curious way of speaking. It is indecisive and indirect. You ask him a question and he begins to answer it by talking continually in his famous "thinking aloud" method; but just when he seems to have reached the climax he stops.
>
> I started off by asking what he thought should be American policy in Asia and he replied with the following oblique answer:
>
> "Our general approach to all these problems is governed by certain idealistic factors. Essentially it is one of having enough troubles to face at home, without taking up burdens elsewhere. Also it is the realistic approach of not saying something you cannot do.
>
> "By force of circumstances the United States has an economic responsibility to face. I can only tell you rather generally how we for our part try to act wherever possible. We think that generally speaking the problems of Asia cannot be solved by military means. However, they might be affected by military measures.
>
> It is obvious that the people of Asia are in a state of acute mental change. They are more politically conscious because of the changeover from the period of colonial rule. Their first national reaction is to expect a betterment of their economic conditions. Primary problems of these undeveloped areas are things dealing with the essentials of life. Other matters are relatively theoretical.
>
> Another fundamental urge is what might be called the nationalist urge. This, after the colonial stage, is strong. Moreover, people incline toward any policy or proposition that tends to realize or improve their condition—whether it does or not is

another matter. [I quote Nehru directly and as a result this sounds confused.]

"Where the nationalist urge and the economic urge join, that produces a powerful movement. Where they tend to split up, there is weakness. It should be our purpose, therefore, to help and encourage the nationalist urge, plus giving it the economic content of future betterment.

"The strongest 'anti' feeling in these countries is the relic of colonial days and it is against any retention of colonial forms of control. These are the basic factors out of which we feel policy should grow."

Since Nehru had not answered my question on what American policy should be, I repeated it. He replied:

"It means encouraging national elements as such and helping them in so far as possible toward economic advance. These elements are split up. If sufficient incentive is given to national feeling plus economic advance, that would attract many people.

"I should imagine most intelligent people don't regard the Untied States as a colonial power. But I suppose there are plenty of people who have rather vague and undefined suspicions, mainly because the United States is a very powerful country economically and in other ways. Take the relationship of England and India today; there is not a ghost of a chance of their imposing any policy on us. I am not in the slightest degree afraid of such. But past suspicions remain"

I asked him about Russia and he replied, "There has been in India an impression on the one hand that in the past, chiefly in central Asia, the Soviet Union was a liberalizing force that raised the tone. Partly that was because of the frightfully backward conditions prevailing which gave a relative feeling of appreciation for cultural advances in that area.

"There were many people here who admired the cultural achievements of the Soviet Union but who do not like at all the tendency towards the suppression of individual freedom which apparently is growing more and more into what might be called a nationalist expansionist policy rather than the old style concepts of communism. This has created an adverse reaction among many people in India including some who were previously struck by cultural advances of Russia."

I asked him if Asia felt squeezed between the blocs of the United States and Russia. He said: "It is very difficult to distinguish between pure black and pure white. Maybe in a moment of crisis one would have to choose. That depends on the nature of the crisis. Naturally every country thinks in terms of its own survival and self-interest. Talk of crisis and another war is a council of despair. The prospect of a new war is too terrible to contemplate. Whatever other consequences there might be it would represent the degradation of the world. So one tries to avoid decisions in terms of a crisis, to the utmost.

"Obviously at the present moment our contacts, economic and otherwise, are far more with what might be called the Western countries than with others. They are our trade and support.

"To a good extent our political ideas and constitution have been derived from the West. To some extent also certain political ideas have been influenced by Socialist trends." But Nehru made it clear by implication that he did not mean "Stalinist." He said, "Our constitution may be considered as a kind of epitome of what we have been thinking. Our whole concept has been one of political democracy, but it has been influenced more and more by ideas of economic democracy."

On the subject of Pakistan, Nehru said the two countries were so close in terms of geography and tradition that he thought they should draw together even more closely than two friendly countries like the United States and Canada. Partition had cut up a living entity—economic, psychological and cultural. Thousands of people on both sides were related to each other. The quarrel had the bitterness of a family quarrel but ultimately there must be developed common policies for economic, defense, transport, communications and irrigation affairs.

I inquired what he thought of the chances of Titoism in China. He gave me his usual indirect answer: "Countries like China and India, not only by reason of their size, but also by reason of the essential national characteristics which are deeply imbedded, can hardly be expected to function on behalf of someone else. They may be affected by outside forces but they are bound to find some kind of level in keeping with the national genius. In the long run this is bound to happen." Nehru said he was certain China could not grant prior allegiance to another country—meaning Russia.

He added: The Soviet Union "more and more" is following a "nationalist expansionist policy rather than the old-style concepts of communism." He said the problems of Asia "cannot be solved by military means."

Of Soviet ideology he observed: "Marxism is an analysis of history. The present-day Communists have changed this about a lot. Therefore I take what helps me from Marxism and discard the rest."

He added: "The people of Asia are in a state of acute mental change. They are more politically conscious than ever before as a result of the change-over from the period of colonial rule. Their first reaction is to expect a betterment of their economic condition. I refer to things dealing with the primary essentials of life."

That October in Washington, Dean Rusk, then in charge of Eastern affairs at the State Department, said Nehru, unfortunately, was doing what we did for twenty years: lecturing us upon our faults without participating in world affairs on a responsible basis, just the way we used to traditionally lecture the British on their administration in India and Ireland. Rusk said we must make Indians aware of what we think of them and not just continue to worry about what they think of us.

On October 24, 1951, the first United Nations Secretary-General, Trygve Lie, told me he thought the Kashmir dispute the most dangerous quarrel then going on—outside of Korea. Nehru had admitted to him in the past that his policy was to do nothing about settling the Kashmir question because he was convinced Pakistan cannot survive as an independent state and will some day have to come "crawling back" to India.

In New Delhi, November 21, 1952, Ambassador Chester Bowles (who apparently got on well with Nehru), read me a letter he had recently sent to Secretary of State Acheson requesting the formulation of a long-range policy for India. The letter said:

We are not facing up to the fundamental crises in Asia. A free India is vital to world peace and to our own security. We must build a program to meet the requirements of the situation. The choice in India is between the present democratic government and communism. There is no other organized force. It would be a catastrophe if the present government fails. One-sixth of the world's population lives here. In the last war India provided an army of three million.

A Communist India would help communism to dominate southeast Asia. India has rich mineral resources and a strategically important location. It defends South Asia. In Communist hands it would block the Suez Canal route to the East. India's loss to the West would cause Moscow's prestige to soar. Millions around the world would join the Communist bandwagon. Europe's confidence in us would be deflated and Africa would blow up. The prospect of a free world would be jeopardized.

What are the chances of India remaining free? Paul Hoffman said that India in 1952 is like China in 1946. This is too simple. There are certain favorable factors. India has a good civil service. Most of its leaders have a western tradition and are non-Communists. They have an Anglo-Saxon respect for the law. The Army is free from politics. Nehru has vast prestige. The five-year plan is a good program for growth. During the last seven years the Untied States has been improving its Asian relationships.

But there are also negative factors. There is considerable graft among the minor politicians. The Communists use this politically. The older leaders are tired. Some of the younger leaders have drifted toward communism. When Nehru dies, the Congress party will splinter. Nehru is the only cohesive force. He cannot push through reform because of the complicated situation. There is a great need for land reform and the servicing of the debts of the poor, and the Communists stress these facts.

The Indian educational system turns out streams of cynical youths. The caste system causes frustrations. There is a psychopathic fear of colonialism and racism. Furthermore, the Chinese have sold themselves well here. India needs United States aid to accomplish its five-year plan. This should come on the scale of aid to Greece. It would take less than $1 billion to get the five-year plan through. There is a need for village and land reform before communism goes into the villages. And communism *is* moving in. The youth must be given a sense of participation in progress. But the Congress party is too far removed from the people.

The Chinese have given their people a sense of participation. For example, they build their own schools, physically speaking.

We don't understand the appeal of communism out here. At the lower levels the Communists do a good job of what passes for democratic participation. The people ask, "What shall we do?" For those with their own political ideas, and therefore opposi- tional forces, there is the whip. But most people want only to build a better ditch. *Their* opinion is asked in terms of how can a better ditch be dug. But their opinion is asked for the first time. The Indian universities are turning out Communists.

Bowles said Nehru used to be very violently against French colonialism. Now his attitude had grown somewhat softer. In fact, he would have probably been disturbed if the French got out of French Indochina. Nevertheless Nehru was more anxious about nineteenth-century (British) colonialism than twentieth-century (Soviet) colonialism.

Nehru saw new trends in our policy; an ascendance of Republican belligerency. He thought the outgoing Democratic administration had been influenced by the recent elections. Nehru recognized that China was as hard to deal with as Russia. He admitted that it would take much longer before China broke loose from Russia than he had originally calculated.

According to Bowles:

India, it may be seen, is being stirred up with a great stick. All types of traditional systems are undergoing change: the caste system; the educational system; the old relationship between the landowner and the tenant. A Pandora's box is being opened and nobody knows what will fly out. For example, as the illiterates are being educated, they learn to read Communist propaganda which unfortunately is better than ours. Nobody can foresee if and when a period of violence will ensue. In the United States when we had 15,000,000 out of work just after the depression began, there was no violence; but by 1936 when the workers had food in their stomachs the sit-down strikes started.

Old structures are cracking up in India. The minds and the hearts of the population must be filled as well as their stomachs. Obviously the first stage in this great social development will create immense new problems. We must do more than help the Indian people fill their stomachs, we must also influence their minds.

India is not a "Socialist" state. Her leaders do not think socialism will work. Thus, for example, India has guaranteed that three new refineries we are helping to open up here will not be nationalized for at least twenty-five years. But although they are skeptical about socialism, the Indians don't like British scarcity capitalism. We Americans would like to introduce our own incentive system and high wages rather than the restrictive British system of capitalism.

That evening I saw Nehru in his residence. We sat in a relatively small study decorated with carved ivory. The two of us were perched upon a comfortable stuffed sofa. Nehru was so delicate and graceful that he made one feel awkward. He was dressed in a long russet-brown Indian jacket and white leggings. He seemed relaxed and affable. Coffee was served and we smoked occasional cigarettes.

But although he was cordial in his curiously diffident way, what he had to say was not of penetrating interest. Furthermore, I had a constant awareness of his mental arrogance and assumed contempt for the intellectual capacities of Americans. Time and again I asked him questions concerning ideologies, Marxism, and so on, and he gave me rather childish and, I thought, contemptuous—certainly unsatisfactory—replies.

I noted:

> He is a confused man who is unquestionably enveloped in a cloud of his own egotism, which is obviously kept charged by admirers. That he is sincere, intelligent and potentially dynamic is beyond a doubt. Nevertheless, I had the feeling that he is groping his way through many difficult problems without a very clear idea of where he was going and without any preconceived plan, either moral, political or economic.

In addition, I received the impression that he was so tied up in the weary process of day-to-day administration that he no longer had a chance to feed a mind which requires the stimulation of continual new intellectual intake.

We started off with a discussion of Marxism. He said that when he had read Marx and other books by Soviet leaders, he had been very impressed; "but it was not the dogma I adopted." He continued:

"Marxism is an analysis of history. The present-day Communists have changed this about a lot. Therefore I take what helps me from Marxism and discard the rest. Socialism as such is

naturally making its way in the world through economic doctrines. Progressively in each country there is more and more
social control by the state—even in the United States.

"Thus in India there is a definite tendency for the state to
assume increasing control. But this is limited by a paucity of
financial resources and of available administrative personnel. The
state needs to control the key strategic vital sectors such as
transportation. Thus the railways are owned by the state. Motor
transport is largely state-owned. Air India is one-half state owned
although privately operated."

This was a rather vague definition—if such it may be called—of
socialism, and I remarked as much to Nehru. I asked him if he felt himself
socialistically inclined, and whether he considered having the Congress
party adhere to the Second (Socialist) International. I pointed out that
Marshal Tito had just told me he was contemplating having his People's
Front join it.

Nehru answered that the Second International was merely a trade union
organization. (Of course, he was wrong there, but I didn't want to get into
a debate with him.) He said, "Our trade unions might some day join it, but
the question has never come up."

I asked if India thought of signing any strictly defensive alliances with
any powers or joining a mutual defense coalition of a regional nature. He
answered, "No alliance is contemplated. After all, what is a strictly defensive
alliance? A defensive alliance automatically becomes a military alliance and
the purpose of a military alliance is to deal with preparations for war. We are
obviously interested in what happens along the regions near our borders;
thus, for example, we are interested in what happens in Burma or Pakistan,
but we are not resolved on any concrete policy of what to do."

I asked Nehru if he could explain to me in his own words just what it
was that held India together as a state against the various centrifugal forces
operating in this newly independent country. He replied:

"In one word, it is a certain nationalistic sentiment. This goes deeply
into the past. Throughout history you will find that, politically, India was
often divided but it remained more or less a unit. The same ideas coursed
through India, the same background of culture. The people never attached
too much importance to politics. That was for the kings and emperors. Now
to this matrix of a common past two or three germs of politics have been
grafted. I must say that one of the politically unifying forces was the British
occupation."

What did he think of the possibility, in long-range terms, of India federating in some fashion with Pakistan and perhaps Burma? I pointed out that, after all, they shared the same common "matrix" of the subcontinent's cultural past. He answered:

Yes, that common matrix of culture is also applicable to Pakistan. We share the same community of history despite present differences on a purely political level. When Pakistanis and Indians meet—aside from politics—they do not meet as nationals from two different countries. They have the same background and speak the same languages. We are often misled by publicity given to extremist opinions in both Pakistan and India. But the masses of the people do not feel this.

I do hope that India and Pakistan will cooperate in a very large measure. They should not lose their common tradition. They cannot reverse history. They must increase the area of mutual cooperation. Groups of Pakistanis come here—refugees from the Punjab. They are not bitter. They weep together with their old friends and discuss old memories.

In the modern world unless we destroy each other by war, there must inevitably be larger spheres of cooperation; regional cooperation and ultimately world cooperation. India, Pakistan, and Burma ultimately should cooperate in that way. Perhaps they might form some kind of superfederation but always keeping their identities. However, these things must develop automatically—not artificially.

India is a big country. It is frightfully difficult to define its idea and conceptions in a single phrase. But generally speaking, out approach to problems—economic, political and so on—is pragmatic, not dogmatic. Our new five-year plan will soon be out—in a month or so. It may well be varied considerably from the original project as it is carried out. There are many uncertain factors.

We based our five-year plan upon what I might call present advantage. The choice is between present advantage or future development. The Russians, in their five-year plans, have chosen the latter. But to do this requires an authoritarian government. We also want to plan for the future but our first requirement is to plan for the present and this makes for a sort of juggling act. We must deal with a heavily populated country. There is not enough land to go around as there is in Russia.

This, as Nehru indicated, was the reason that India was not planning for heavy investment in capital industry to anything like the degree of Marxist five-year planners such as in Russia and the satellites. Nehru meant that India must satisfy popular requirements for such things as consumer goods and keep the people happy. It was not a monolithic state that could order its helots around as does the Soviet dictatorship.

Later, after an inconclusive conversation held standing up, Nehru guided me to the door and shook hands in a rather nervous, diffident way. Going down the stairs, as I passed through one of the salons, I noticed a curious melange of signed photos inscribed to Nehru. Standing on a table side by side were the pictures of the prime minister of Afghanistan, President Truman, and Haile Selassie of Ethiopia. Truman was in the middle—whatever that signified.

Nehru, during the agitated days when India was about to be partitioned, was held in jail along with his father as Earl Mountbatten, the last British viceroy, drove along deserted Delhi streets that had changed a great deal since the Pandit's uncertain Cambridge days.

Gandhi had decided that Jawaharlal was to be his heir, and that his impulsiveness could be restrained. Just before Nehru took over the presidency of the Congress party, Gandhi's faith in him underwent a searing test. Nehru was called upon to take part in a huge demonstration staged as a "reception." He had become the "Jewel of India" to the mass of people, the "embodiment of sacrifice."

He traveled third-class on trains, rode to villages in bullock carts, often walked vast distances to reach a meeting. He was so persuasive through his thoughts and actions that he had long since induced his Cambridge Moslem friend, Syed Mahmud, to abandon comfort and devote himself to Congress. He had talked him into traveling without his servant.

Jawaharlal was certain that Hindu-Moslem collaboration within Congress and without was the kernel of Indian unity that they envisaged as a secular state. He made no pretense then, or later, of concealing his scorn for Mohammed Ali Jinnah, the proponent of a separate Islamic Pakistan. Isolating himself, Jinnah slowly developed his two-nation theory—that Moslems formed one nation in India and Hindus another.

Krishna Menon, the leftist Hindu, maintained: "The only man to lead India into the modern world is Jawaharlal Nehru. Gandhi can't do this. Nehru has a modern, scientific mind." Menon dedicated himself to this man rather than to Gandhi.

After his years in jail, Nehru was publicly cherished. But his social and international ideas were little understood by the Congress hierarchy. With many admirers, he still lacked disciples. He found one in Menon. Nehru wrote begging Gandhi to help some of Hitler's Jewish victims find a new home in India. The Mahatma's reply was: "I boycott foreign goods not foreign ability."

Panditji, as he was more and more called, assessed Churchill, whom he would ultimately meet: "For all his courage and great qualities of leadership, he represents the nineteenth-century, conservative imperialist England, and seems incapable of understanding the new world with its complex problems, much less the future which is taking shape."

Nevertheless Churchill, surprisingly, had sent word through a mutual friend wishing Nehru well on a journey to China. His last word on Nehru would be that he was "fearless and without rancor."

The British had intercepted and arrested Nehru long before partition. He was put on trial in November 3, 1940, in the prison of Gorakhpur, where he made one of the great statements of his life. His culminating words were: "I saw the name of this appeasement and how the lamps of liberty were put out [by war].

"I am convinced that the large majority of people in England are weary of Empire and hunger for peace.

"But we have to deal, not with them, but with their government. . . . With that we have nothing in common." He said that he had been tried and convicted seven times. An eighth or ninth term made little difference to him. After his defense of humanity, he was sentenced to four years rigorous imprisonment. Even Churchill was said to have been shocked, and it is said Nehru came to the point where he could say it was "better to die than to live a miserable, hopeless life. Out of death, life is born afresh . . ."

At first, nobody knew where Nehru and his comrades had been taken. For two years they were never to see a single Indian except each other.

Nehru, closed away from the world in Ahmednagar Fort, needed some creative outlet. In April 1944, he wrote his third and last book, *Discovery of India*.

It was natural that Panditji, with a policy of his own, had no desire that American influence should replace British. Naturally, the United States aimed to hitch the coming independent India to "the West." But the aim

would be foiled. Nehru's primary concern was the concept of One World.

In Delhi, Nehru was handed power by the British and sworn in as Prime Minister. He began to govern India at midnight on August 14, 1947, saying: "Long years ago we made a tryst with destiny, and now the time comes when we shall redeem our pledge, not wholly or in full measure, but very substantially. . . . A moment comes but rarely in history, when we step out from the old to the new, when an age ends, and when the soul of a nation long suppressed, finds utterance."

Prime Minister Nehru's faith in the United Nations could not reconcile itself, after Pakistani troops entered Kashmir, to the idea of an Indian army sweeping them back. Either as his own decision, or together with Lord Mountbatten, he insisted the case of Pakistani aggression be taken to the U.N., where it remained unsolved for the rest of his life.

Shortly thereafter, the world reeled in shock at the assassination of Mahatma Gandhi, shot because he had violated Hindu prejudice in asserting the brotherhood of Moslems, Parsees, Hindus, Sikhs, Christians, and Jews within India.

The policy of nonalignment was evolved by Nehru and Menon in stages, the first being that of the rather nebulous Third Force. "Nonalignment" subsequently emerged, the designation being devised by Krishna Menon.

Nehru explained in 1954, when nonalignment became a cornerstone of Panchsheel—coexistence—that his foreign policy was "not born out of sharp intellect, but is the direct result of the freedom movement." It was a means of achieving economic assistance from the two Power Blocs.

Nehru's first statement as Member for External Affairs in an Interim Government had said: "In the sphere of foreign affairs India will follow an independent policy, keeping away from power politics of groupings aligned one against the other." The mode was to serve as a bridge between the two power groups in the hope that hostility between them would diminish and disappear.

Though he rejected all religions, at heart Nehru came nearer to being an unorthodox Buddhist than anything else. Whatever he derived from his extensive study of Buddhism appears to have been applied to relations between nations in the preamble to the Panchsheel agreement. Five principles were laid out—among them, mutual noninterference in each other's internal affairs, equality, and lasting peaceful coexistence.

To draw China into the community of nations was a cornerstone of Nehru's foreign policy. He always insisted that "whether we like that shape and form or not" of the Marxist China which had emerged victorious, "we

have to recognize that a great nation has been reborn and is conscious of her new strength."

Between mid-summer 1954 and April 1955, when the Bandung Conference opened in Indochina, Nehru stood out as a unique negotiator. In October 1955, he accepted Prime Minister Chou En-lai's invitation to Peking. He returned deeply impressed by China's economic progress. At a press conference on his return, Nehru said: "I did not go either to be preached to, either to give guarantees or to demand them, but rather to understand, to be impressed and to impress in a friendly way."

Yet his prejudices appeared increasingly. Nehru said he recognized the right of any country to enter into military alliances for its own protection, but NATO appeared to have been molded into a "protector of colonialism" especially in Morocco, Tunisia, and Algeria.

Nehru's anti-colonialism was only directed against the West, never against the Soviet Union. He used the same kind of double-think as Secretary of State Foster Dulles when he argued that India couldn't be more "helpful" on Israel because he didn't dare to inflame India's Moslem minority of 40,000,000.

In February 1957, when my wife and I were passing through India, Nehru very kindly asked us for lunch, a long meal, two and a half hours sitting under a peach tree with drifting pink blossoms. Marina approached the prospect rather warily, having conceived an innate dislike and mistrust for this famous man (whom she had never met) because of his policy statements. But in about thirty seconds our charming host, handsome, courteous, and sensitive, had her eating out of his hand.

Nehru was wearing a white Gandhi cap which he later took off, exposing a sudden bald head much paler than his sunburned face. Also white, tight pants and a buttoned, homespun jacket. A rose was inserted in the second buttonhole.

He had returned and was going off again on his electoral campaign. Indian elections were very different from those in the United States, where radio and television had assumed such importance. Direct contact with the masses, public appearances, and speeches were the thing in India. Nehru professed astonishment at the interest and patience of people who came out in the thousands, waited for hours in the hot sun, and then listened with great attention. I asked if he tried to discuss local issues, he said no; he didn't even know them. He left that to others. He talked about broad things: "Even international affairs, sometimes." The women were amazingly interested in politics. Congress had a set rule to encourage them: to have 15 percent of the candidates women.

I asked what in his opinion was holding India together. He said:

Culturally we are remarkably united. In a sense it is like the old idea of Christendom in Europe—but even more intense. Political divisions didn't upset the idea of a common culture here. Our chief places of pilgrimage are widely separated—south, east and west; there were constant streams of pilgrims coming and going to them from all over India.

Another factor that was very important in the past is Sanskrit. This language has not been spoken since the days of Buddha—2,500 years ago. But it is still the language of the learned.

And then, the modern theme of unity was, strangely enough, brought about by Britain. The British enforced their unity. And our opposition to their rule was a unifying factor. The Congress party started seventy-one years ago as a small movement, but it was always aimed at all India. Today we are politically and intellectually united against an external danger. But when we get complacent internally then we fall out.

When we had finished our enjoyable lunch, Nehru suggested we come and look at his pet pandas. He led the way to a large wire cage under a tree. I noticed he put on a pair of white cotton gloves before opening the cage to try to induce his pets to eat. They ignored his persuasion.

"I can't get them to mate either," he remarked in mock disgust. Again he tried to persuade, first one panda and then the other to eat. But neither responded. I watched his face set in stubborn lines as his pets thwarted him. He was determined to bend the white-faced, cuddlesome pandas to his will. When they continued to refuse to oblige him, his lower lip pouted. He had to give up. He pulled off his gloves, and I noticed his hands. They were not elegant hands to match the rest of his physiognomy, but capable hands which could have belonged to a man accustomed to manual work.

He had been to Washington and I asked him his impressions of Eisenhower. These were interesting:

I was greatly impressed by the President. He is a big man and very frank. That is a great thing. But I don't understand from a practical point of view what your military policies can lead to. I am not suggesting that a country should be weak. But all that talk of strength and problems. Keeping a country strong is all right;

but nevertheless one shouldn't speak of this strength too much. It is not secret that you are strong. And the Soviet Union is always talking about its strength also—even in a threatening way.

I mentioned all this to President Eisenhower—with some hesitation. I told him you were giving help to other nations which was a very good thing. But so much of it was in the form of military aid; and that doesn't really help any country. Giving this aid to some countries merely helps strengthen the feudal and reactionary elements in them and then you become associated with that in their public opinion. President Eisenhower admitted as much to me, and he said it was indeed a problem.

I remarked to the Prime Minister that in one of our previous talks I had asked on which side India would be in case of war. He had replied reluctantly that in the end it would be with the West because of a common political tradition and a dependence on maritime commerce. He commented querulously:

Did I say that? Really? Well, most of our economic contacts are certainly with the West—our intellectual contacts also. And the mere fact of English being used and known here as a language and in our periodicals and books is important. Furthermore, of course, there is the bond of our governmental and parliamentary systems.

But in the event of a war—I just don't know. We would certainly try and keep out of it. And what developments would lead into—I don't know. Geographically we are favorably situated. We are outside the normal way of war.

Motilal Nehru had said of his son: "He is a jewel of a man and a perfect gentleman. He trusts everybody for he thinks others are like himself. Remember, people will take undue advantage of him. He will be duped and deceived often." After a pause, he concluded: "But he is not to blame. He has led a sheltered life and not seen the seamy side of it."

This was scarcely an accurate assessment. Of course, the seamier realities of Panditji's life came after his father's death, although the two had actually served simultaneous jail terms under the British. The great strains, such as the Kashmir crisis, threats of war with Pakistan (which never broke out while Nehru was alive), the mass religious fratricide of partition and the actual war with China, all occurred later; also personal losses such as the death of his dear friend, Lady Mountbatten.

In the last months of Nehru's life, it would frequently be said that he began to lose his control over Congress sometime in 1955. It was said that by compromising on the issue of reorganizing state boundaries according to language, he unwittingly opened the door to endless linguistic friction.

In 1955 an announcement came that evoked a great deal of discussion and speculation: Mrs. Indira Gandhi was named to join the Congress Working Committee and, therefore, become one of the country's policy makers.

Mrs. Gandhi was an outstanding personality: attractive, intelligent, ambitious, tough. Yet when asked, Nehru said it was very unlikely that his daughter would succeed him. He had certainly not been grooming her to do so.

Nobody equaled Indira Gandhi in knowledge of what it meant in terms of responsibility and problems to accept the leadership of India. From 1947 onward, many of the most difficult tasks were assigned to her, or she voluntarily took them up. Less of a natural optimist than her father, possessed of a severely critical mind, Indira Gandhi herself had been conscious for a number of years as to where the internal power lay and where her own destiny might lead.

Mahatma Gandhi, like Mao Tse-tung of China, had devised the method and led the Indian revolution for independence. Her father, Panditji, had guided and organized it like Chou En-lai to the north. It was up to her to shape its strength and maturity.

Nehru had been particularly close during his life to his father, to his lovely wife, Kamala, who died of tuberculosis in 1936, to Gandhi, to Krishna Menon, and to the beautiful, stimulating Edwina Mountbatten. And of course to his daughter, Indira.

Jawaharlal was both delicate and strong, as one could judge from his relatively frail body, well-cut features, and powerful hands. He survived well, living to the age of seventy-five. Ten of those years had been spent in prison. Prison was the only place where he did any writing. To my taste, his writing was undistinguished and not to be compared with his personality, character, conversation, and oratory.

Philosophically, he was a tolerant man, especially for one gifted with the talent of leading millions of people in crises. He used to say: "We must always remember that every Indian to whatever religion he might belong is a brother and must be treated as such. . . . Long ago the Buddha taught us this lesson. From the day of Ashoka, 2,300 years ago, this aspect of our thought has been repeatedly declared and practiced. In our own day Mahatma Gandhi laid great stress on it and indeed lost his life because he laid great stress on communal good will and harmony."

In 1965 he wrote the president of the Indian Buddhist Society: "I do not participate in functions for the propagation of any religion." A year later he wrote again that "I do not believe in what might be called institutional religion."

From this it might appear that he was relatively more Buddhist than Hindu, the creed of his parents. But that is an unfair deduction. He was simply tolerant of the spiritual beliefs of others. . . . On his bedside table the day of his death (May 27, 1964), there was found a verse in his own handwriting that he had copied from the American poet Robert Frost:

> *The woods are lovely, dark and deep*
> *But I have promises to keep*
> *And miles to go before I sleep,*
> *And miles to go before I sleep.*

In his will he requested: "A small handful of my ashes should be thrown into the Ganga [Ganges]. . . . My desire to have a handful of ashes thrown into the Ganga at Allahabad has no religious significance so far as I am concerned. I have no religious sentiments in the matter. I have been attached to the Ganga and the Jumna rivers in Allahabad ever since my childhood and as I have grown older this attachment has also grown."

Indira Gandhi, Nehru's only child, was the next great figure to rise in the Indian firmament, after inconclusive rivalries between less visionary and more politically obsessed traditional leaders. Indira was undoubtedly a tough, resolute, wily chief of government who knew a great deal about politics before she assumed her present role and was also thoroughly educated. She had the additional advantage of her family's good looks, with dark, aquiline features, mobile mouth, expressive eyes, and the Indian woman's inborn gift of seemingly quite unconsciously knowing how to twitch a sari at the shoulder in a fetching and becoming manner.

She was undoubtedly a determined and ambitious woman; ambitious for herself, her country, her special ideas of the world including an increasingly important India, and a strong affection for her somewhat tactless and unscrupulous politician son, Sanjay.

This combination of qualities made for a very complex and interesting personality. She was resourceful and flexible, having recovered from a severe political defeat in defense of Sanjay. Some people at the time compared this with Nixon's disaster of 1974. But she was completely restored, never losing her poise and regaining her full power. I found her very "human," enjoyable to talk with and with at least as much charm as her legendary father. One reason I suspect that she seemed closer, in conversations, to her grandfather, Motilal, was that Jawaharlal always made a point of the fact that he was not grooming his daughter to succeed him or to take high office.

She was a small woman with dark brown eyes and hair that was black before it grayed. Despite her powers of decision and crispness, on occasion, she was distinctly feminine.

I once remarked to her that there must be both advantages and disadvantages to being a woman chief of government. She said: "I don't think it really makes any difference. Obviously every person has some advantages and some disadvantages on a job like this. For India you can have pluses and minuses in terms of the region you come from or the caste to which your family belongs. Some people say that a woman hasn't as much stamina as a man. Of course, I can't tell, never having been a man. But I certainly have more physical stamina than anyone else around here."

I observed that, in any case, a woman prime minister might benefit because men were more polite to her. "Certainly not," said she with only half a smile. "They surely are no more polite. Don't think that."

I said her father's ideology had been described frequently as Fabian socialism although I personally thought that a rather fuzzy label. How would she describe her own ideology? She answered:

> I don't think I can be said to have any ideology at all in this vague sense. After all, I have to face specific problems and specific situations. You just have to find the best way of doing things as they arise. Sometimes you just have to compromise with what you would prefer. For example, we didn't want to import food. But we had to; it was a matter of life and death.
>
> Our party wants to use the tool of socialism to raise living standards, but this obviously isn't necessarily the socialism of other countries. Our methods must be fitted to the minds and the backgrounds of our people.
>
> Essentially, there are no two ways open to us. Ours is such a large mass. so poor and so backward economically that you can't afford to just let things take their course. The people won't wait

that long. The state must take things upon itself. It would just create more problems were we to leave everything to private enterprise. Private enterprise always seeks to make a profit and you can't have a profit in all the aspects of the problems facing us, above all with the enormous need for social justice and for welfare. We must be pragmatic.

It's hard to say just what our ideology is. We use the word socialism as the nearest thing. But there is no particular prophet of our socialism. We are seeking a new and middle path. We believe in a mixed economy.

Apropos of ideological trends, I asked her what writers or persons had had the greatest influence in shaping her ideology and personality. She replied:

I suppose the influences were mostly Indian. I was a very voracious reader and when I was a child I simply devoured books. I could name Tagore as one influence, but I know Americans would never have heard of the others. My father, of course, exerted an influence, but my mother quite as much.

And you must remember that my childhood was right in the middle of our freedom struggle. Therefore, I was impressed at the time by any stories having to do with freedom anywhere. As a small girl I was told about Joan of Arc, about Garibaldi in Italy, and about many others.

I got the impression from these remarks and from a later aside on her grandfather that she wasn't quite as influenced by her father as many people make out. She wanted to stand on her own feet, to be accepted by and as herself.

I said her father had once suggested to me that the next generation of India's political leadership would suffer the disadvantage of not having been heroes of the revolution and the freedom struggle. She commented:

"This is no longer the case. For our younger generation, the years of the freedom struggle no longer have any meaning. They don't harp on it. It's not that they are bored; they simply accept the fact that freedom is here."

I asked if her late husband's family had any connection with Mahatma Gandhi. She said: "My husband's family was Parsee, originally from Persia. There was no relationship with the Hindu Gandhis. And the voters aren't in the least concerned with the fact that I'm Nehru's daughter. After all, I established my own political life. I entered the working committee of the Congress party in 1955 and I had been working at the village level long before. I became president of the party in 1959. And don't forget, my husband was very well known at the village level before his death."

I asked whether the essential policy of nonalignment was practical any more in a world where "imperialism" and "colonialism" no longer played a prominent role. She answered that nonalignment remained valid. There was nothing "dogmatic" about it.

> It just means that we do not wish to belong to any alliance or political bloc. In fact, nonalignment is very valid as a concept now because more and more countries are subscribing to it.
>
> The world was very sharply divided between Eastern and Western blocs, involved in a cold war, when we started this policy. Only later a period began in which the outlines of this cleavage were more blurred. The cold war is still on in a way but many people are crossing the barriers of alignment into each other's camp—on such matters as trade, culture, and other relations. They work more and more with the people of the other bloc than their own. Therefore it is really the concept of alignment that has changed, not the concept of nonalignment.
>
> India never wanted to be part of a special bloc for two obvious reasons. First of all, there is our geographical position, our neighbors. And then, if you are aligned, you irritate those who are not in the same bloc. Certainly that's not worthwhile.

I observed that some people thought that India—and her government—were overdependent on Russia because it was so heavily the source of the country's military equipment nowadays. She said: "That's the argument of the Swatantra and the San Sangh [the extreme right-wing parties]. But, in fact, we don't wish to be dependent on any country or any group. We are now seeking, and will always seek, more diversification in the sources of material and to get things where we can. We want to stand on our own feet and we try our hardest to be self-sufficient. And remember this—just because we get equipment from a country doesn't mean we'll do what they want. We won't do what anyone wants simply because we get hardware there."

I asked if ideology represented any barrier between India and the

United States. "Not for us," she said. "What does come up is this sort of thing. When we learned that the CIA was indirectly financing institutions that were helping us there was a wave of anger at getting any such help. That's upsetting. But we have no ideological divisions; I have none and I hope the majority of us don't.

"Some people in the United States say that we are too close to Russia and that we vote too often on the Soviet side in the U.N. But this really isn't so; it is only true on such issues as those involving colonialism and racism, and here it is not a question of us following the Russians but a question of the Russians taking the stand that happens to agree with ours. The Russians have simply shown a greater understanding of the needs and mentality of newly freed peoples. And when you are so close to pre-independence times and attitudes as we still are, you remember these things very well. You are a little touchy on some of these matters. It takes time to adjust and to get used to being a country."

I asked how she felt about the "Brezhnev doctrine," under which Moscow claimed the right to interfere in other "socialist" lands. She said: "We stand firmly for the right of all other states to independence. Each country must be free. The only thing in the U.N., during the debate on Czechoslovakia, was that we didn't want to 'condemn' Russia because we had never used the word 'condemn' before. But we made every point stressed in the U.N. debate right here in our own parliament, and before these points were made in U.N. I wish to be very clear about that."

Once I asked Mrs. Gandhi if she would agree to tell me a bit about her private life. She nodded amiably and said that, while she didn't have much spare time, "I try to squeeze private things in when I can. Of course, I have no rigid schedule, but I like to see my family when I can. Normally I take my meals with my family. And if I have a moment, I like to go to exhibitions—sculpture, painting, manuscripts, tapestries, all kinds of things—on Sundays. I like music but that I hear mostly at home. I rather like classical music—Bach, but also folk music, also Indian music.

"I do my reading mostly while traveling or on weekends. On the whole I prefer reading something that retains my interest. You know, with detective stories I either guess who did it or I look at the end to see. So that doesn't really do."

I asked if she actually enjoyed being prime minister. She smiled and said: "You know, I had a very strict training. My grandfather, who died when I was thirteen, brought us up in a most Spartan way. There wasn't even any heating for us young people during the winter in Allahabad where we lived. My grandfather told us: 'You can never do anything well unless you enjoy it. If you think a job is boring or a drudgery you will never succeed in it.' I guess that is your answer."

Indira, who was called "Indu" (the moon) by her father, traveled a good deal for an Indian youngster, visiting Italy and attending the International School in Geneva. As her family became increasingly engaged in politics, she is said to have dreamed at times of becoming her country's Joan of Arc. When she finally married—to the Parsee Feroze Gandhi—Mahatma Gandhi, no relative of the bridegroom, stood with the family.

As India gained its independence and Nehru was chosen prime minister, he asked Indira to become his hostess. She had already been drawn into the political world, having spent a year in prison as a rebel against British rule, and now she was to learn both more about politics and something about the international diplomatic world. Inevitably, Peroze receded into the background to lead a more separate life. Despite periods of conflict, the marriage did not break up.

For all Indira's seemingly retiring quality, she had an imperious temper. She was a boiling cauldron, with a deceptively calm surface.

The one person who believed Indu could transcend the insecurities of her youth was her father. He relied on her even if, in the end, she was no longer a mirror reflecting himself. What he did not grasp, apparently, was the burden of isolation he was willing upon her. She was not akin to her aunts, who enjoyed the fruits of power. Yet she would, without lifting her little finger, be reckoned the most powerful woman in all India, where many powerful women were emerging.

During her year in prison she had looked after a woman prisoner's child to steady herself. As Maria Seton wrote: "Complex facets of her personality emerged: one, intimate, leisurely and provocatively intelligent with the strongest inclination for the company of creative people; the other side, business-like, cool in appraisal, and with a swift withdrawal to irritability, when interrupted by a member of the staff about some formal arrangement to be made."

When the 1958 Congress party session took place, no candidate for the Congress presidency for 1959 presented himself. Both Mrs. Annie Besant and Mrs. Sarojini Naidu had been presidents of Congress before Independence. There was no bar to a woman holding the office. Mrs. Gandhi's name was put forward.

The moment she became Congress president both the sophisticates and opponents of her father became convinced that the Prime Minister had schemed his daughter's election and had been grooming her to become his successor. She strongly denied this.

Later when she reached the acme of power as chief of government, she was asked whether the office had been "thrust upon her." She replied: "It can't be thrust upon me if I do not want it."

In her father's postscript to his letters to her, he had said, "Personal misfortune is of little account in this world of sorrow and strife, which demands from us all our strength in the struggles that convulse it." He had recounted the history of humanity, its failures and its triumphs with the accent on revolutions. In his letter for her thirteenth birthday he wrote: "You are fortunate, I have said, in being a witness to this great struggle for freedom that is going on in this country."

Jawaharlal Nehru said of his daughter when she was elected Congress president: "It goes without saying that I have great affection for her. I have known her closely and it is possible my assessment suffers from imbalance. But I have great regard for her qualities and temperament, her energy and her integrity. I do not know what she has inherited from me. I am inclined to think she has derived these qualities from her mother."

Thus, of the three great revolutions that have taken place during the twentieth century, only India's has been largely a dynastic, family affair— and that only by chance. Lenin's Soviet revolution saw its progenitor succeeded by a man who was not only unrelated but of a different race (not Slavic but Georgian) and one of whom he disapproved, Iosif Stalin. Mao's successor in reality was Chou En-lai, a man much more like Nehru, worldly and intellectual. Chou ran the show because Mao was virtually in his dotage during his last years. The competition for power since the deaths of both Mao and Chou has probably not yet run its course but there is nothing remotely dynastic about it.

The hereditary vigor of independent India's first family is fascinating. Grandfather Motilal, originally a rich and somewhat snobbish Brahmin bourgeois, gave up all for Gandhi's revolution, went to prison for it, and was chosen president of the Congress party. His son Jawarhalal was an unusually cultivated, stylish man who hid his great strength and energy behind a silken exterior. And his daughter, Indira, had equal charm and culture, enough strength to lead and fight two wars and to stage a wholly unexpected come-back from the ashes of internal political dispute. The leadership strain runs strong.

It is sad that the daughter was murdered by Sikh fanatics. Indira's indicated successor, Sanjay, her older son, died young. His younger brother Rajiv started off well. It is too soon to forecast the result.

XI

The Drunken Cobbler and His Son: Vissarion Djugashvili and Iosif Stalin

The fact that Stalin's father beat him constantly and cruelly when he was a little boy certainly had a profound effect on the youngster's subsequent life and, therefore, upon the history of Russia and the world. Being beaten was both painful and humiliating, as Stalin discovered, and he relished subjecting his opponents to this double punishment.

"Beat, beat and once again, beat," he commanded the prosecutor of the "Doctors' Plot" in which confessions were thus extorted from Jewish physicians falsely accused of planning or attempting to murder Soviet leaders. Constant and undeserved, dreadful beating in his youth had given the heartless dictator a very special reverence for this form of brutality, partly because of his own victimization and partly because Vissarion Djugashvili, the father, had similarly tortured Iosif's mother, whom the boy clearly loved and also respected.

It is paradoxical but obvious that Djugashvili, the good-for-nothing and virtually illiterate cobbler in Gori, a small town of the Czarist Russian province of Georgia, should, thanks to his cruel treatment of a runtlike son who was to become the twentieth century's greatest despot, have had a profound influence on world destinies.

Georgia is not and was not then the least bit Slavic, much as Stalin himself hated to admit this. He was a non-Slav who became a pan-Slav. Much of his early life was indeed paradoxical and produced unanticipated results. Subconsciously or consciously he applied on an unimaginably vast scale the lessons he drew from his early unhappy provincial experience.

His only education was at a parochial school run by the Orthodox Church in Gori and at a Tiflis religious seminary that accented Christian theology and supposedly prepared the majority of its graduates for the Orthodox priesthood.

Yet, for as long as this world survives, Iosif Vissarionovitch Djugashvili, who chose the alias of Stalin (Russian for "steel") by which he is known, will be an object of keen attention. Dozens of studies, memoirs, and analyses of Stalin have already been published in every major language. The great majority of these are exceedingly hostile and unfavorable, with the exception of what has been written in the Soviet Union itself by self-seeking Communists or what has been written there with the tight disciplinary approval of an all-extensive censorship. Some of Stalin's and Stalinism's enemies managed as "dissidents" to prepare manuscripts of a more objective nature that have been smuggled and published abroad. Other students of Marxist-socialism have passed through pro-Stalin periods of obsession and escaped these to recount their former belief in "The God That Failed."

There are a few odd originals in the collection of authors so far extant on Stalin. First is his only daughter Svetlana Alliluyeva, whose *Twenty Letters to a Friend* and *Only One Year* (the first written in Russian and smuggled abroad; the second written abroad) are in many ways contradictory in their impact on a reader, the *Letters* being far warmer and affectionate in their attitude to her father than the second, perhaps more mature and experienced volume.

Another original is *Conversations with Stalin* by the redoubtable Jugoslav, Milovan Djilas, who became an ardent Communist in his youth, was imprisoned by his country's royal regime, then was named general in the ranks of Marshal Tito's Communist army fighting the Axis occupation forces, rose to the top in the Tito hierarchy, and, as the Partisans' best Russian speaker (with others), represented it in all conversations with Stalin. He stood firmly by Tito when the latter broke with Stalin and his allies in 1948, and subsequently broke with Tito himself, became a liberal-social-democrat, and was returned to jail for two more long terms—this time sent by his comrades.

To show how powerful and complex a personality Stalin was, I shall quote from a few of those who had a chance to know him personally, even a little. In 1983 Djilas made two devastating remarks in conversations with me: "Stalin was a liar, but he believed his lies; he was a demagogue who believed his own demagogy." A few days later (we were on a fishing trip in Serbia and had ample time to talk), he made the extraordinary observation that "Stalin was the worst killer in all history. Even Genghis Khan never killed any Mongolians, but Stalin killed his own Soviet people, his own Slavs. He was worse than Hitler. Hitler exterminated the Jews, but he treated them as a people having two loyalties and therefore not being totally German. Stalin simply exterminated anybody he felt like getting out of the way." To me this was somewhat of a non sequitur. Hitler killed many non-Jews, including Catholics, Protestants, Communists. Stalin killed many Jews—and was getting ready to increase the number when he died.

In the French edition of *Conversations*, Djilas writes: "Stalin is a vampire who still influences and will continue to influence the world for a long time. Nobody wishes to be his inheritor, but many derive their strength from him. . . . Khrushchev renounced him, but that didn't prevent him from admiring him. The present Soviet leaders don't admire him, but they are warmed by the same sun."

"I admit he continues to haunt me," he added in conversation. Djilas, in *Conversations*, cites Trotsky as calling Stalin "the most eminent mediocrity of our party," which isn't that far off from Lenin's opinion. As he lay dying, the founder of Bolshevism dictated a letter to his wife in which he said, "Stalin is too brutal" to succeed as boss and should, as Djilas interprets it, be bypassed for someone more loyal, more polite, more patient.

Djilas, an exceptionally courageous fighting man, and one capable of being pretty tough to prisoners, wrote that Stalin knew he was one of the cruelest and most despotic personages of history, but it didn't bother him so long as he applied history's verdicts. "Despite his mass murders, his conscience was never troubled."

There is no doubt Stalin's views were cynically realistic. Djilas quotes him accordingly: "This war doesn't resemble those of the past. Whoever occupies a territory imposes his own social system. . . . The whole world imposes its system as far as its army can advance."

On February 10, 1948, Djilas headed a group of Jugoslav Communist leaders who, together with Bulgarians, visited Moscow. They discovered Stalin was getting ready to put an end to the Greek civil war in which that country's Communists, aided and armed by Communist Albania, Jugoslavia (it was just before the break with that land), and Bulgaria, were trying to oust the royal government and take over.

Stalin asked Kardelj, Tito's vice premier, what he thought the chances of success were. Kardelj answered he thought good—"if foreign intervention doesn't increase and political errors aren't made." Stalin interjected: "If! If! No, they have no prospect of success at all. What do you think, that Great Britain and the United States—the United States, most powerful nation in the world—will permit you to break their line of communication in the Mediterranean Sea? Nonsense. And we have no navy. The uprising in

Greece must be stopped, and as quickly as possible." (It may be added that Moscow gave no direct aid to the Greek rebels at any time; only its own satellites did.)

Stalin was frightened about possible adverse consequences arising for the U.S.S.R. and for world communism from the Greek civil war, and every known discussion he had on the subject stressed Soviet naval weakness and Anglo-American naval strength. In 1944 Churchill and Stalin had an argument about Bulgaria when they bilaterally divided up the Balkans in a terse, checked-off working paper.

When Churchill kept on emphasizing what jackals the Bulgarians had been during World War II, Stalin said it was improper to base foreign policy upon "motives of revenge." What should it be based on? Churchill asked. Stalin: "Upon the calculations of forces." In the days before Admiral Gorshkov had built a mighty blue-water fleet for the Soviets, and when America had overwhelming nuclear superiority, the balance of forces in the eastern Mediterranean was strongly against Russia. Stalin knew it and acknowledged it.

Churchill was more interested in individual human beings than in ideology. On July 10, 1956, during a day I spent with the old man at his Kentish home in Chartwell, he told me: "I think Stalin was a great man; above all, compared to Khrushchev and Bulganin [who had by then come to power], Stalin never broke his word. We saved Greece that way." (He was referring to the restoration of independence to Greece when the Germans fled northward). "When we went in, in 1944, Stalin didn't interfere. You Americans didn't help, you know."

What most people say of Stalin is that he was a brutal, murderous despot, but they disagree on whether he accomplished much or helped his nation or its people. De Gaulle called him "this great czar . . . with the shadowy charm. Stalin was a great man. He did something. He was a brutal man but he created a modern state."

André Malraux thought Stalin had been a devil, "but a great devil." Djilas liked Churchill as a "romantic," yet he acknowledged that Stalin, despite his brutality, was "the greatest man" he ever met. Djilas said: "Stalin had complete control of himself. He knew how to use power. And he had great charm when he wanted to use it, horrible as he was. He was brilliant but he killed as many men as Hitler. Hitler also was brilliant; but mad and a fanatic. Stalin was cold and clear."

In Communist China everyone seemed to forget that during the last days of Mao Tse-tung and Chou En-lai, when concentration was only on being anti-Russian, Peiping even thought Stalin good compared with his successors. In 1973 Chang Chi-cheng, a Shanghai ideologue, assured me: "We still think of Stalin as a great Marxist." But the Soviet ambassador sneeringly told me: "The Chinese still listed Stalin with Marx, Engels, and Lenin only because he was admired for liquidating the kulaks and for building Soviet industry and military strength."

In November 1956 my wife and I attended Governor Averell Harriman's small birthday party in Albany, N.Y. He told me Stalin was "the most powerful and visibly self-confident man" he had ever met. He also said the Russian had a "genuine liking" for both Roosevelt and Churchill (which I doubt).

This may have been true (although at best dubious), but as I came to know more about Stalin I learned that a "genuine liking" could be flicked away like an irritating eyelash when such a change suited Stalin's fancied convenience. It is like Churchill's recollection: "He never broke his word." How about the very opening day of the Yalta Conference in February 1945 when Stalin totally called off his Berlin offensive and moved toward the Balkans instead, without even hinting at such a climactic move to his Big Three partners?

Stalin could be—and often was—a master of deceit; a man without adjectives: plain, simple, abrupt. Djilas thought him "perhaps greater than Lenin." He added: "His basic work, the *Foundations of Leninism*, published in 1924 from a series of speeches just after Lenin's life ended, is as important as Marx's *Communist Manifesto*. Today [and he said this long after Stalin's death and disgrace] Stalin is underestimated as a theoretician. But after Marx, theory was no longer important; only practice."

Arvo Tuominen, last survivor of the Presidium of Lenin's Comintern, said, "Stalin in the name of the Central Committee of the Communist party had practiced the most brutal violation of the socialist law, torture and violence that led, as we have seen, to the slandering and self-accusation of innocent people."

Andrei Sakharov, the eminent nuclear scientist and Soviet dissident, estimates that "no less than fifteen to twenty million Soviet citizens" were destroyed in Stalin's prison camps. Yet, as Tuominen stresses in his *The Bells of the Kremlin:* "Stalin used many highly effective forms of propaganda but the most effective may have been the invitation of foreign delegations and tourists to the Soviet Union and their entertainment there," a propaganda device used with "unique skill."

How long a jump is it from the wide-eyed Lady Astors and Bernard Shaws to the peaceniks and Greens being used differently but with equal effect these days?

Once I remarked to President de Gaulle that, like Macchiavelli, Stalin had named fear as the principal force motivating man. De Gaulle commented: "One must draw a distinction between the individual and the collective masses. For the individual, it is ambition and a taste for adventure. I think the real motivation, the primordial motivating force of the individual, is ambition; for the masses it is fear. There Stalin was right. And this applies to the masses of all countries."

Opinions of Stalin, both Russian and foreign, Communist and anti-Communist varied immensely. But few of them, favorable or unfavorable, failed to discern his greatness.

Malraux met Stalin only once—at Maxim Gorki's house. Stalin told him he adored Shakespeare and never missed a performance. His other hobby was the dance—watching other people dance (people like Khrushchev, as the latter acknowledged in his famous debunking speech of 1956). Stalin told Malraux that the way he destroyed Trotsky was by making him write. Odd?

On rare occasions Stalin made evident pro-American gestures. When Harriman called on him at night to inform him of Roosevelt's death in 1945, Stalin acknowledged to him that Russia and America must now cooperate strongly. Three days later former U.S. Secretary of War, Patrick Hurley, on a mission as special American envoy in China, passed through Moscow after a London visit on his way to try and bring Mao Tse-tung and Chiang Kai-shek together.

Hurley told me (following a two-hour midnight conversation in the Kremlin): "I said I thought freedom was a logical necessary development of history and that any progressive country would face that fact. Stalin disagreed; he laughed. I continued that, after all, Stalin could only judge by Russia and the Russians. Stalin laughed again." Hurley curiously maintained that he had far less difficulty selling the idea of a free and united China to Stalin than to Churchill. "I had no trouble with Stalin," he boasted. "He played ball." Anyone who trusted Stalin more than Churchill should have had his head examined. Hurley ought to have known Stalin was then backing Chiang against Mao, as proven in Yalta. (Harriman cabled Washington asking that Hurley be warned not to believe everything Stalin said.)

Stalin sometimes could not conceal his contempt for the ignorance or inefficiency of foreigners. He told U.S. Ambassador Chip Bohlen that he had been in Germany around 1907 and a secret German Communist Party meeting was convened. The German comrades queued for subway tickets in orderly, tedious fashion—and never showed up.

Louis Joxe, French ambassador to the Soviets in the 1950s, explained to Stalin that the Atlantic Pact was a purely defensive peaceful alliance without any aggressive intentions. Stalin laughed and turned to Andrei Vyshinsky, who was there, saying: "If that is the case, why don't we join, Vyshinsky?"

Joxe must have found the old tyrant in an exceptional mood. When he expressed polite pleasure at being received, Stalin replied like some old Mongol khan: "In this country even the shepherds are well treated." Referring to the change of name for the East Prussian city of Königsberg (absorbed by Russia) to Kalinin, Stalin remarked at the incongruity: "Kalinin—and a king." Kalinin was an unimpressive Russian Communist chosen for the unimportant job of president, a purely ceremonial function. *König* means "king" in German.

Stalin treated his European satellites to all kinds of cock-and-bull stories. When Edvard Beneš, Czechoslovakia's prewar president, visited him in 1945 as the war was ending, Stalin assured him earnestly there was "absolutely no thought of setting up any sort of puppet German government (like the then Hungarian one). That only came by armed coup in 1948.

The little Transcaucasian town of Gori situated in the valley of the Liakhvi River in the former kingdom and the present Soviet republic of Georgia (conquered by pre-Bolshevik czars), is famous for but one thing: Gori was the birthplace of Iosif Vissarionovitch Stalin, originally Iosif Djugashvili. Iosif grew up in an impoverished, rickety, rented hut in what is today almost the middle of a square but was then on the outskirts of Gori. To honor Stalin, the shack he once called home has been lavishly encased in marble, much as if Abe Lincoln's original log cabin had been placed within an alabaster palace.

The town also contains a Stalin museum. Its principal interest to the contemporary visitor is found in a heavy-lidded, sensual death mask and in pictures adorning the wall, including one of little Iosif Djugashvili dressed as a choirboy.

As a youngster Iosif, like his no-good father, was scrawny, small, clever, and obviously tough. He learned the art of survival the hard way. Vulgarity, obscenity, and brutal fights were not unusual in the shoemaker's rude household. Although his mother loved him, she also beat him; his father reacted by beating her. The boy then sought to defend her and once threw a knife at the savage little cobbler. Vissarion took out after him hollering, but neighbors hid the recalcitrant son.

Iosif was the only one of four children to survive. His parents, descended from serfs, were exceedingly poor. They lived in a neighborhood locally called the "Russian Quarter" because of nearby czarist military barracks. At the time of Iosif's birth, Gori contained less than 9,000 inhabitants.

As a youngster he was called "Soso," which is the usual Georgian nickname for Iosif. Before his marriage, his father, Vissarion, had moved to Tiflis (now Tbilisi) where he found a job in a leather factory. When a man named Baramov started a shoe repair shop in Gori, Vissarion returned to his birthplace. There he met and eventually married a much younger woman named Ekaterina Geladze.

Their house—in fact but a hut—was comprised of two tiny rooms used for sleeping, eating, and working. The cooking was done in a low cellar with a fireplace.

Vissarion was thin and wiry, with black hair, beard, and mustache. He was a heavy drinker, gruff, and with a quick, sharp temper. He seems to have beaten both his wife and his son frequently.

Little Soso was intelligent, bright, energetic, and good at games. He had an ear for music, and his high-pitched voice sang in the Gori church choir. He was very small in size, but strong, muscular, and basically healthy. His face was freckled, his nose prominent, and his eyes dark and glittering.

Iosif Iremashvili, who knew Soso as a boy, recalled him as unemotional and never seen to cry. "As a child and youth he was a good friend so long as one submitted to his imperious will," he added.

Both parents were Georgian and not averse to violence. It is odd that, despite this background and the fact that he spoke Russian poorly with a marked Georgian accent, Iosif always preferred things Slavic and Russian to any Georgian connection. However, today, dead, he is regarded as a great hero in Georgia and condemned by most Russians.

His father's greatest achievement, before he finally was knifed to death in a drunken bar fight, was to get a job as a cobbler in the local shoe factory. His mother was more ambitious. She desperately, if unsuccessfuly, sought to guide her boy into the venerated priesthood, thus improving the sordid existence lived both by her son and herself. She was genuinely religious and, still young when her husband was cut down, worked feverishly to support and educate her boy.

Stalin's daughter, Svetlana, indicates he held his mother in devoted esteem all his life. He described her as intelligent, if uneducated. She would smack him when he misbehaved just as she smote his father when be became obnoxiously drunk.

Iosif was a hard-boiled, tricky village kid who had more than his share of rows with friends. The only hint of intellectual talent he gave at the seminary was in arithmetic and mathematics. He also liked to sketch crude little drawings which fostered a later habit of doodling. It is said he remembered some smattering of seminary Greek almost until his death. Whether this was the archaic spoken version of Orthodox prayers is hard to know.

There is no doubt that his mother sought to spark any latent signs of ambition in the boy so that he might climb life's ladder. But, although theological education was the only formal learning he ever encountered, the church quite obviously had no appeal for him. At seventeen, he encountered and joined a Social Democratic group and began agitating among Georgian workers. In 1902 he was jailed for organizing demonstrations in the Black Sea port of Batum, and the following year he was exiled to eastern Siberia. That was the start of his *real* schooling.

Yet Ekaterina still dreamed religion would triumph. When he called on her in 1936, shortly before her death, she murmured to him—the tyrant of all the Russians: "What a pity you never became a priest." Djilas recalls that Stalin told him she once visited him at the Kremlin and wasn't very impressed; only regretted that he had chosen the wrong career.

Had Stalin tended even slightly toward psychological complexes, his might well have been an Oedipal relationship such as Alexander the Great certainly had with his mother.

The extremely scholarly Robert Tucker quotes the future dictator's boyhood friend accordingly: "Iremashvili tells of brutal blows inflicted upon the boy by the frequently drunk Vissarion, and of the gradual growth of an aversion in Soso for his father. . . . He also developed the vindictiveness that would characterize him in later life, and became a rebel against paternal authority in all guises."

There is no doubt his intellectual determination grew under his mother's urging. He graduated first in his class at the Gori parochial school, and the Tiflis seminary admitted him on a full free scholarship. But he was poor material; he had ceased believing in God at the age of thirteen, apparently after becoming acquainted with Darwinism.

While still a student, he learned Russian well (it had recently replaced Georgian and become mandatory for schools). However, he read widely among Georgian writers, and in one story about the famous tribal imam Shamyl he came across a literary figure named Koba, a fighter and avenger, and used the name as one of his early aliases to throw the police off his track.

Iosif turned increasingly against the Tiflis seminary, which he saw as "Jesuitical" and "in the pursuit of bad ends," as he told Emil Ludwig, the German author. His hostility engendered the spirit of revolt which had been simmering since the earliest days of his paternal disputes. He even slackened his interest in study—except for logic and secular history: better preparation for a revolutionist than for a cleric. He forsook his liking for games and read, read, read.

It was while he was in his first prison camp that he chose his Russian pseudonym—*Stalin*. It also started him on the road to Marxism. He ultimately wound up a Bolshevik follower of Lenin instead of becoming, like most other Georgian Marxists, a Menshevik. His ultimate dream was to be another Lenin, one of history's "heroes."

As Khrushchev was later to depict him in his famous speech to the Twentieth Congress of the Soviet party, Stalin was by nature intolerant of criticism and dissent, was prepared to see any person he considered an "enemy" die or suffer, was deeply distrustful and suspicious, thirsted for glory, suspected plots all around him. It is noteworthy that none of these traits necessarily conflict with the first law of the Russian czar: "The Emperor of All the Russians is an autocratic and unlimited monarch. God himself commands that his supreme power be obeyed out of conscience as well as fear." Stalin believed in limitless autocracy—under him; in absolute obedience; in fear. He clearly did not believe in God.

As an obscure worker in the Transcaucasus, Stalin started to revere Lenin as a Social Democratic leader—a definition no Social Democrat would today accept. He was especially impressed by Lenin's views on the doctrine of leadership in his pamphlet, "What Is to Be Done?" It is strange to think of the physically and mentally unappealing Stalin, notable only for his ruthless will and courage, as so attracted by what he considered Lenin's charismatic and messianic qualities.

He was drawn by the magnetism of Lenin's remarkable personality and clear-cut, uncompromising views. Stalin acknowledged: "I was captivated by the irresistible force of his logic." And he was fascinated that Lenin considered that a revolution in Russia would be but the first of a series of European socialist revolutions.

As he read increasingly from the underground revolutionary pamphlets being circulated in Russia, and talked with revolutionists both inside and outside concentration camps, he became experienced in all the conspiratorial techniques of the time: robbing banks to obtain funds for arms and propaganda; how to hide, change aliases, establish hidden contacts; the art of escaping the most arduous confinement; how to write for and edit insurrectional papers like *Pravda*. He was named to his party's central committee and fought both the White Russian czarists and the Polish army during the civil war that followed the downfall of Nicholas II—and then the liberal Kerensky.

At the outset of the revolution, Stalin's reputation was not outstanding. He was known as "touchy" and quick to hit anyone for uttering even innocuous remarks. He joined various underground study circles in which it became evident that he was intolerant toward those who disagreed with him and that he craved personal authority. He spread his reading to include Western literature and even wrote some unimpressive poems in Georgian, influenced by the language's famous classic, Rustaveli's *The Knight in the Panther's Skin*. Marshal Voroshilov later recalled that Stalin had a good memory for quotations.

His revolutionary activities steadily increased. Between 1902 and 1913 he was arrested eight times, exiled seven times, and escaped from exile six times. The February Revolution of 1917 freed him the seventh time—from a remote icebox in the far north. Escapes from internal exile were not infrequent in those days—before Stalin's own regime.

In his subsequent travels around Transcaucasia, he became wholeheartedly Leninist and also an ardent expert at "expropriations"—bank robberies to raise party funds. He was sent abroad on brief trips to attend party congresses in Stockholm, Berlin, London, Cracow, and Vienna—the first such major travel prior to his Big Three meeting in 1943 at Teheran with Roosevelt and Churchill.

In 1902 he married Ekaterina Svanidze, whose brother had been a fellow student at the Tiflis Seminary. In 1908 Ekaterina produced Stalin's eldest child, a son named Yakov, who later died in a Nazi prison Camp. Ekaterina died in 1910.

Iremashvili, who attended the funeral, said Stalin pointed to the coffin saying: "This creature softened my heart of stone; she died and with her died my last warm feelings for people." He placed his right hand on his chest and added: "It is all so desolate here inside, so inexpressibly empty." Yakov was brought up by his mother's sisters.

Following this personal tragedy, which clearly annealed a heart already turned to iron, Koba—as he was increasingly known in the underground—began to enjoy in the Transcaucasus the reputation of being a second Lenin, "the best authority on Marxism." He was vividly attracted by the original Marxist dogma that a hostile proletariat and bourgeoisie were locked in deadly combat. He insisted that Russia was "one and indivisible."

Stalin's initial personal contact with Lenin was by letter smuggled from Siberian exile in 1903. He saw Lenin for the first time in 1905 at the Tammerfors conference in Finland and was greatly impressed. He soon began to try and emulate him, to identify with him, but this proved difficult. Lenin came from the minor bureaucratic nobility, was well educated, and gave the impression of being a more intellectual, more normal, and more human personality. Nevertheless, Stalin unhesitatingly aped Lenin's mannerisms and repeated his thoughts.

Neither Stalin nor the Social Democratic element with which he had first associated were successful among Georgian revolutionaries. Stalin blamed Georgia for this, not himself. From then on he stressed more and more the "Russian" element in his spoken and written communications, and in what was to become "Soviet" history. He strongly attacked the "Jewish faction" as against the "true Russian faction" and proposed a pogrom in the party—something he personally supervised some years later.

Thus, paradoxically, Djugashvili, representing the oppressed Georgian subject people, joined the Russian "nation" via Bolshevism. He tended increasingly to condemn Georgian nationalism—a fact seemingly ignored or forgotten by today's Georgians. As Lenin's commissar for nationality affairs, he sneered at the "little piece of Soviet territory called Georgia." As for his anti-Semitism—it became obsessive, even within his own family circle and among his friends, as Svetlana, his daughter, strongly brings out.

During the Bolshevik Revolution which overthrew Kerensky's short-lived liberal interim government, Stalin spent an increasing amount of time with the Alliluyevas, a Marxist intellectual family that lived on the Gulf of Finland. Stalin eventually married Nadezhda ("Nadya"), daughter of the household, a charming, humane girl who became Svetlana's mother. Theirs did not prove to be a happy marriage, and in the end she died violently—almost certainly of suicide, although some of Stalin's enemies rumored that he had murdered her himself.

When the Bolsheviks, guided by Lenin's magnificent organizational plans, finally seized power, the first functioning Politburo was created to govern Russia under Lenin, as chairman of the council, and Stalin was charged primarily with nationality affairs. Even before that, during the peak of the hodgepodge fighting, he was named director of food supplies in southern Russia and head of the war council of the north Caucasus military district. At Trotsky's "categorical" insistence, Stalin was recalled from the Tsaritsyn (later Stalingrad, then Volgograd) Front, where things were going badly. Yet he remained Lenin's deputy on the Revolutionary War Council and was elected to the All-Russian Central Executive Committee.

Stalin saw Trotsky as an intruder trying to break up his own special relationship with Lenin—and he always took pains to emphasize that the brilliant chief of the Red Army was a Jew. But Stalin won little military acclaim in the civil war, while Trotsky climbed upward. Stalin concentrated on continually amassing political influence in the Soviet regime itself. His war work, put succinctly, was his own political self-aggrandizement. He ended up with far more power than glory, despite the fact that he was an indifferent organizer and never cut out to be an administrator.

What he did understand as well as any man who ever lived was how to dispose of his enemies. Trotsky claimed Stalin said: "The supreme delight is to mark one's enemy, prepare everything, to avenge oneself thoroughly and then go to sleep."

Stalin prepared a long time and assiduously to inherit the leadership of Russia's single party as it became increasingly evident that the ailing Lenin was doomed to an early death. He had already carefully read Macchiavelli's *The Prince* in his final period of Siberian exile, terminated by the Kerensky Revolution. In that book he studied the Italian's classic advice for the power-seeker.

Once free, he carefully and shrewdly made his way up through the Orgbureau and gained a seat on the center of Communist bureaucracy, the Secretariat. When Lenin and Trotsky came to an ideological and method-ological clash in that committee, he avoided opting openly and totally for either. It was at the Tenth Party Congress, where this occurred, that Trotsky, who had earned acclaim through his inspiring oratory and his military novelties, first suffered a serious political setback. Numbers of his supporters lost their seats on the Central Committee to avowed Stalinists. This was the first intraparty purge of Soviet history. Stalin didn't revise the existing machinery that had been set up—but took it over and used it to his advantage.

During these maneuverings, his young wife, Nadya Alliluyeva, was an important asset. She was given a variety of secret assignments by Lenin and certainly knew many of the supreme leader's innermost thoughts, which, presumably, she shared (to a degree at least) with her dominating and, when he wished to be, charming husband.

Her background was quite different from the brutal, rough-edged, frequently violent Stalin. Although they were awarded an apartment in the vast Kremlin complex in 1919, she saw to it that they also took over a country house, and there the family lived and Nadya built up a domestic staff to help care for and educate her son, Vasily (who died a drunkard), and daughter, Svetlana (who, for many years, lived abroad as a voluntary emigre).

Stalin seemed to enjoy this life—in which he rarely partook because of party and state assignments—and he increasingly built up his "Russianness" at the expense of his Georgian heritage. Already in 1922 he was identifying himself as "a Muscovite" and commonly using phrases like "we Russian Bolsheviks."

After Lenin died and Stalin finally outmaneuvered his rivals and took control, he saw to it that each Central Committee secretary employed numerous assistants, and among them he placed persons he considered loyal to himself. They kept him informed of all state or party intrigues even before they had hatched. At a dinner of principal Soviet dignitaries in 1926, he said, in a discussion of "collective leadership": "Don't forget we are living in Russia, the land of the czars. The Russian people like to have one man standing at the head of the state."

There is scarcely a literate human being today who does not know the major events of Stalin's career as Soviet leader. They marked Russia and the whole world for years to come. They are marking them today. No one will ever be able to calculate the lives lost through Stalin's maneuvers or by his command. Millions of Soviet citizens died in horrendous concentration camps. Tens of millions died during his elimination of the kulaks (small farmers) to enforced collectivization. Tens of millions died in his ill-prepared, ill-disposed armies until by his own sheer stubbornness and strategic talent, the skill of his generals, Allied help, and the immense bravery of his troops, the tide of war turned from disaster to victory.

The "cult of personality" which saw all these appalling disasters (and I have referred only to the slaughter and destruction of the Russians, not their enemies) truly began with the elaborately arranged propaganda accompanying Stalin's fiftieth birthday celebration in 1929. It kept mounting until Khrushchev cut his image down, three years after his death, at the Twentieth Party Congress in 1956.

In terms of international propaganda and politics, the personality cult was a markedly zigzag affair. Prior to his nonaggression pact with Hitler in 1939, all the right-wingers of the world were violently anti-Stalin, as symbol and boss of communism, while leftists hated Hitler and Mussolini so much that many became at least lukewarm Stalinists. Both factions, right and left, tended to split up into segments or modified their opinions from 1939 until 1941, when Hitler invaded the Soviet Union and came within an ace of smashing it.

Stalin, the boss (or *khozyain*, as the Russians put it), was held responsible for all the accomplishments and failures of that melodramatic period and above all for the limitless cruelty which devastated small farmers; created needless famines; wiped out or transported whole peoples such as the Crimean Tatars and the Chechen-Ingush; ruthlessly shot innocent and harmless individuals as "Trotskyites," "Fascists," "Titoists," "spies"; constructed and populated enormous new concentration camps, especially in the

Asian provinces and the far north; and scared everybody, including many officials who participated in these savageries, quite out of their wits.

Most analysts agree with his daughter, Svetlana, that Stalin's evil genius was the secret police boss Lavrenti Beria, a toadlike Georgian who somehow wriggled himself into Stalin's total confidence. Beria was evil incarnate, a sadist, sex maniac, alcoholic, and ruthless liar with ambitions and a lust for power that vastly exceeded even his wicked abilities. But as the worst of the "Chekist" leaders (so-called after Cheka, the abbreviation for the first "counterrevolutionary" police created by the Bolsheviks in 1917), he came to symbolize the very worst and most bestial deviltries of the regime, even among its supporters. When Stalin died in 1953, Beria hoped to gain supreme power; instead, he was shot in a cellar at the command of the army and, once his demise was announced, with the support of the masses.

I was an exceedingly naive young man of twenty-eight when I first visited Russia in 1941, a few days after Hitler had launched his blitzkrieg against the tyrant who had been his ally since August 1939. I started from Ankara, Turkey, which was then filled with correspondents trying to get to Moscow: men and women of right, left, and center opinions, and representing all sorts of organizations. I worked for *The New York Times* and had habitually written of Stalin as "Hitler's partner in depredation," thus avoiding the label of outright "enemy" or "ally." But I was the only one of the lot granted a visa. The Soviets desperately wanted a *Times* man there.

My first glimpse of Stalin—one which was repeated endlessly—came in the form of long, rectangular posters depicting him in color, a stern yet benevolent-looking tall man in a long army greatcoat down to his ankles and a marshal's military insignia. It was only much later, when I saw him close up in the flesh, that I realized his stature was diminutive, his face was pockmarked (as a result of smallpox), and his eyes were gleaming and evidently shifty. My entry trip—which was by train—took over a week, so I had time to study that widespread poster frequently. It resembled the original, as I was to discover, as accurately as the *khozyain* himself resembled Sir Galahad.

The best view I ever had of Stalin was from a press box to the right of the seats in the Kremlin hall where the Soviet Presidium met. Stalin was wearing a fawn-colored uniform with the decoration of Hero of Soviet Labor. I was about twenty feet away and at the same level. One could see his facial skin blemishes and the streaks of gray in his full head of hair. His mouth was disguised by a slightly drooping mustache; it was impossible to mask his eyes, but his face was bland and self-satisfied. He seemed to be scribbling on a small pad: undoubtedly the doodles, or what psychologists call "automatic writing," for which he was known. These included wolves, nooses, lopsided hearts, girls, castles, geometric designs, and meaningless squiggles, according to persons who saw them close up in conferences. I could make out nothing except that he had strong, square hands with manicured fingernails.

When he arose with the other delegates to applaud—the subject generally being himself—I noted his small stature and was surprised to learn later that he was even more diminutive than he appeared—he was just under five feet five—being given to wearing a form of elevator shoes. Quite some contrast to the huge poster figure whose features so frequently accompanied me on the bumpy railway tracks north from the Caucasus.

I have said earlier that perhaps Stalin was the most successful statesman of his time, but I do not wish that to be taken as fulsome praise. He extended the country's frontiers to include almost all the areas at one or another time ruled by the czar—save for Finland, eastern Turkey, and bits of Iran and China. Far more important, he took a ramshackle impoverished land torn by two world wars, revolution, civil war, and famine, and turned it into one of the two superpowers of the latter twentieth century, militarily perhaps supreme, technically in the foremost rank, with the first earth-girdler, the mightiest missile force, and a navy that became number one, quantitatively at least, after ending the war with only two capital ships, a battleship loaned for the duration by Britain, and a heavy cruiser borrowed from the United States.

Soviet scientists, artists, technicians, and athletes are of the first rank, although some, like Andrei Sakharov and Alexander Solzhenitsyn have benefited less than somewhat from their eminence. The economy and agriculture are still a scrambled mess, but, seeing what the dictatorship has managed to accomplish in other fields, I see no reason to assume it will not master these problems.

Popularity and trust are two things it seems unlikely that any Bolshevik regime will ever manage to instill in the patient, intelligent, brave, and durable Russian people, who make up the large chunk of the Soviet Union's multinational population. In fact, the permanent theme song of the great Slavic matrix is, has been, and perhaps will always be that expressed by Nikolai Alexeivitch Nekrassov in his well-known poem: "Who Can Be Happy and Free in Russia?"

The inferential, deep-rooted psychological problem represented by this question and the lack of any kind of faith—save for a primitive belief in "Russianness" that marked the tenets of the Orthodox Church when it was the official religion—which attended even the least competent czars, and features Moscow's interpretation of world Communist parties as its own private tool, is the astonishing absence of faith in humanity and human beings as such that one encounters in the U.S.S.R. Svetlana Stalin herself told George Kennan and Chip Bohlen in the United States that she was staying at Beria's house on the June night in 1941 when Germany attacked Russia and Stalin telephoned her and ordered her home. Grumpily he asked: "Why at such a moment were you staying with a man I can't trust?" This very question implicitly contains its own answer. During the Great Terror of the 1930s, thousands and thousands of Soviet citizens, including many who thought of themselves as loyal party members, were condemned as overt or covert enemies of the people so that Djugashvili, the little Georgian conspirator, could prove to himself and to the world that he was really Stalin, the man of steel, the great boss of Russia.

Stalin had odd habits and few diversions. He rose very late in the day and worked very late at night, completely discomforting the lives of those who had to deal with him regularly. Djilas thought he drank only a little wine but ate enormously for a small man. Others have noted that he drank heavily on occasion and sometimes he even mixed red wine in the same glass as vodka. He liked well-cooked Caucasian and Russian food, but was essentially a man of far simpler tastes than, for example, Brezhnev. His vanity took absurd forms; like jockeying for a position a step higher than others when photographs were being taken. He was a bad public speaker, whose voice didn't carry, who found it difficult to express himself except from a prepared text, and who, although he deliberately played down his Caucasian origin, talked with a strong Georgian accent.

He was enormously ambitious, wholly pitiless, and had been so since youth. In 1918, during the civil war, he ordered a Caucasus official: "With respect to the Daghestani and other bands who are obstructing the movement of trains from the North Caucasus, you must be absolutely ruthless. A number of their villages should be set on fire and burned to the ground, to teach them not to make raids on trains."

Lenin, his one acknowledged hero (save, perhaps, Peter the Great), produced more than one memorandum urging Stalin's removal from the job of general secretary in order to reduce the danger of internal conflicts at high party levels. Lenin wrote: "Stalin is too coarse and this fault, though quite tolerable in relations among us Communists, becomes intolerable in the office of General Secretary. Therefore I suggest to the comrades that they think of a way of transferring Stalin from this position and assigning another man to it who differs from Comrade Stalin in only one superiority: more tolerant, more loyal, more polite and more considerate of his comrades, less capricious, and so on."

No liberal himself and tough as leather on his opponents, Lenin preferred not to insult them or injure their self-respect. Stalin, on the other hand, simply sought to break them to his will like unruly horses or to roughly cast them aside. He wished to humiliate and degrade people, and when one realizes that this tendency had become bluntly visible five years before Lenin's death, one better understands the famous "testament" Lenin dictated to Krupskaya, his wife, recommending that the party should avoid Stalin's leadership. And this might well have happened had Stalin been less cunning and forceful. Apart from Lenin himself, Trotsky, Zinoviev, Kamenev, Bukharin, and Rykov were far better liked in the party.

But Stalin played a cunning game. First of all he detected in his fellow Georgian, the unspeakable Beria, a "good Chekist" who had learned enough to present Stalin as a self-effacing disciple of Lenin with an unassuming exterior and a simple style of dress. At a stormy Politburo session in 1926, Trotsky pierced these pretenses and proclaimed: "The first secretary poses his candidature to the post of gravedigger of the revolution," words Stalin would never forget. Stalin ruthlessly hunted Trotsky out of the country and finally had him murdered in Mexico.

Stalin was a hardy little man who, despite the sufferings of his various imprisonments and physical beatings, was fiercely courageous. He impressed his nation and the world by remaining in Moscow while it was almost entirely surrounded by the Nazi Wehrmacht in 1941 (although it was known to but a handful of people that secret, protected headquarters had been prepared for him in Kuibyshev on the Volga, where the rest of the government and diplomats were evacuated by train).

Arvo Tuominen, last survivor of Lenin's Comintern, made this rather paradoxical observation: "I attended many affairs at the Kremlin, even rowdy ones, but I never noticed any signs of vainglory in Stalin, not even when he was under the influence of alcohol; he merely became more garrulous than usual, his voice grew slightly louder and he laughed more readily."

Tuominen, however, reports a Christmas party at the Kremlin where: "As soon as we were seated, Stalin to our surprise clinked his glass for silence, rose and spoke ceremoniously in this manner: 'Comrades! I want to propose a toast to our patriarch, life and sun, liberator of nations, architect of socialism, omniscient genius [he rattled off all the appelations applied to him in those days] and great leader of peoples, Iosif Vissarionovich Stalin. And I hope this is the first and last speech made to that genius this evening.' " The adjectives and phrases selected made many of the guests regard each other briefly askance or peer into their plates.

According to Tuominen, Stalin designated a committee to write his biography, but the first draft failed to satisfy the subject because he felt it was insufficiently laudatory. He therefore added the following phrase: "Despite the fact that Stalin fulfilled his task as the leader of the people and the party with consummate skill and enjoyed the unreserved support of the Soviet people, Stalin never allowed the slightest vanity, conceit, or tinge of self-praise to impair his work."

Karel Radek, the brilliant editor and writer, was a fine source for jokes against Stalin, although, until he was purged in 1937, he was a good party member. He apparently originated the following: Stalin calls in Radek and berates him for derogatory jokes when, after all, he is the adored leader of 200 million Russians. Radek supposedly replies: "That is a joke I didn't originate."

In two separate books, Svetlana Alliluyeva, the dictator's daughter, showed both love and hate for her detestable father. In *Twenty Letters to a Friend*, she wrote: "I loved my father more tenderly than I ever had before. . . . Yet even the grandchildren who never saw him loved him—and love him still."

She remembered all kinds of tender, paternal traits in this monster. He "always had a fire in the winter." He had "a good collection of Russian, Georgian and Ukrainian folk songs." He was pleasant to servants: "courteous, unassuming and direct with those who waited on him." She added: "My father never cared about possessions. He led a puritanical life and the things that belonged to him said very little about him. He lived in one room [on the ground floor], in fact, and made it do for everything. He slept on the sofa made up at night as a bed and had telephones on the table beside it. . . . The garden, the flowers and the woods that surrounded the dacha [the vacation house near Sochi, where Stalin moved from the Kremlin after Nadya Alliluyeva's suicide] were my father's hobby and relaxation." He had an "enduring love of nature and the soil."

She speculates on the effect of her mother's suicide and wonders: "Was it that her suicide broke his spirit and made him lose faith in all his own friends? And even had she summoned up strength to leave my father, whom she loved, her fate would have been even worse, because he would surely have taken his revenge."

Svetlana sounds like an emotional, tender, and very confused woman.

Though she had several good things to say about her father in her first book, *Twenty Letters*, she more warmly admired her cultivated, educated mother, who filled the house with air and gaiety, while her father was "just the father of a family," not a "god" or a "cult." In those days, they lived in a sunny country house at Zubalovo, outside Moscow where Stalin went daily to work. But there was also an apartment in the Kremlin, where a German-Latvian ran the household on the ration cards customary to upper Soviet bureaucrats.

Svetlana wrote that her home was like that of other people. Stalin went hawk-shooting with a double-barreled rifle or stalked hares at night from a car. He bowled and played billiards. He liked walking in the woods, and often carried his little daughter in his arms and called her pet names. Her nurse would tell her: "Bring papa some violets.'

In fact, it was a peculiar and far from tranquil family. After he had driven his wife to suicide at only thirty-one, Stalin had a picture of her in a shawl enlarged and hung in all rooms of his Kremlin apartment. Yet, before her death, he kept quarreling with her. At a spat during a banquet celebrating an anniversary of the October Revolution, he ordered her: "Hey, you. Have a drink!" Svetlana says she shouted: "Don't you dare 'hey' me," and ran from the table. That night she reportedly shot herself with a German officer's pistol. Infuriated by a letter she left reproaching him, he neither attended the funeral nor ever visited her grave.

During the ensuing decade he made quite a fuss over Svetlana, although he had little use for his sons, Yakov and Vasily. He talked with Svetlana and Vasily at home and signed their regular school exercise books. Stalin was strict with Nadya's son, Vasily, but couldn't bear his eldest, Ekaterina's boy, Yakov, whom he considered too Georgian for his increasingly assimilated Russian tastes.

He played the affectionate "Little Papa" with Svetlana, to whom he addressed numerous letters: "To my housekeeper, Setanka," "Hello, Setanka!" or "I give my little sparrow a big hug." He occasionally soothed his children by singing in a tuneful, high-pitched voice, but it was always in Russian. Vasily complained to his sister: "You know, Papa used to be a Georgian once."

While Nadya was still alive, the family often spent summer vacations in a dacha near Sochi and the fish hatchery on the Mitchesta River. But after her suicide, state bureaucrats under Beria took charge of the household staff and reported to their boss on who was being received, what was being said. Stalin became increasingly remote from his children and instructed a Chekist "guardian" named Vlasik on how they should be brought up.

He insisted that Svetlana learn English. He scolded Vasily for his bad marks until the latter turned to the military as a career, studied at the artillery school, and then went to the aviation institute.

According to his daughter, Stalin's increasing submission to Beria started in 1938. She claims that he was "more treacherous, more practiced in perfidy and cunning, more insolent and single-minded than my father. In a word, he was a stronger character. My father had his weaker sides." (This seems hard to believe.)

Before that, Svetlana recalls, Stalin would kiss her goodnight and showed the traditional Georgian tenderness toward his children. He took them to special movie showings in the Kremlin, frequently double bills, and then saw to it they arrived at school on time. He often sent baskets of fruit to Svetlana, signed: "From Setanka-Housekeeper's wretched secretary, the poor peasant, Stalin."

She writes of those days, just as the war was starting: "I shall never forget his affection, his love and tenderness to me as a child. He was rarely as tender to anyone as he was to me. At one time he must have loved my mother very much. And he also loved and respected his mother.

"He must have inherited his character from her, too, for there was nothing rough or harsh or fanatical about him. [Compare these words with Lenin's famous testament on Stalin.] He wasn't brilliant, but he was simple, unassuming, hard-working and capable. He had a quiet charm."

These words are so totally different from those written by others on Stalin, even if the writers obviously didn't know him as well as his daughter, that they flabbergast. And they are just as dumbfounding as many other things Svetlana wrote of her father after she had decided to run away to India, to America, to England.

In *Only One Year*, Svetlana writes: "Knowing my father well, I could now perceive the origin of his anti-Semitism. Undoubtedly it had stemmed from the years of struggle for power with Trotsky and his followers, gradually transforming itself from political hatred to a racial aversion for all Jews bar none." This seems rather oversimplified.

During the winter of 1942–43 Svetlana met and fell in love with Alexei Yakovlevich Kapler, a Jew. She writes: "Because of him my relationship with my father was ruined and was never the same." Kapler was arrested and flung into Lubyanka, Moscow's most dreadful prison. He was charged with contact with foreigners. Having known several foreign correspondents stationed in the U.S.S.R., he did not deny this.

On March 3, 1943, Stalin strode into his daughter's room and demanded all letters Kapler had written her. He seized these to read personally.

Svetlana was still a teenage schoolgirl, and when she returned from her classes was ordered to go to the dining room, where her father was awaiting her. He was furiously tearing up Alexei's letters and photographs and tossing them into the trash basket, muttering: "He can't even write decent Russian." Kapler was sent to a northern concentration camp for five years' heavy labor.

Svetlana continues: "In the spring of 1944 I got married. My first husband, Grigory Morozov, was a student at the Institute of International Relations. I had known him from our schooldays together. He was Jewish and my father didn't like it. However, not wanting to go too far again he somehow accepted the marriage."

Stalin proved as obdurately hard-hearted to the daughter he had loved as a child as he was accustomed to being to others. She and Morozov were given a flat outside the Kremlin on condition that Grigory set no foot there. Stalin never even laid eyes on him. Svetlana then produced her first child, a boy named Iosif. After three years the marriage ended, for personal reasons, and Stalin eased his harshness to the extent of displaying some affection for his grandson. In 1947 he invited Svetlana to Sochi and later sent a note concluding: "I send you a kiss. Your Stalin. Oct. 11th, 1947."

Two years later Svetlana again married, this time to Yuri Andreycvitch Zhdanov, of whose father her own was a friend. After an illness and one more baby, the marriage to Yuri also collapsed. In 1948 Stalin invited Svetlana, little Iosif, and Yakov's girl, Gulia, his eldest grandchild, to visit him in the south. On December 21, 1952, Svetlana saw her father on his seventy-third birthday—the last time before she was summoned to his deathbed outside Moscow the following year.

That was a cruel, bitter event for a sensitive and emotional young woman. All Stalin's last cronies were gathered together: Beria, Malenkov, Bulganin, Mikoyan. The dictator's son, Vasily, by then a hopelessly alcoholic air force general, sprawled there drinking and abusing the doctors.

Svetlana is by far the more interesting source on Stalin's personality and habits. Fear, cruelty, unreality, bullying, strangely sudden appearances and disappearances dotted her entire life until she resolved to take the ashes of her third husband, an Indian, to his homeland and from there finally made her way with great resolve to the West. With her, she brought the manuscript of her *Twenty Letters*, which was written in a village outside Moscow during 1963. By then, she had legally changed her name from "Stalina" to "Alliluyeva," after the mother she adored, because "I could no longer tolerate the name of Stalin."

It is difficult to assess Stalin as a human being. Tuominen said,

"Outward modesty was his masquerade costume" and "Stalin undeniably was a highly gifted and above all a highly energetic man." He had a slight acquaintance with languages, including Georgian and the Latin and Greek he studied in school. Svetlana says he didn't eat or drink much, but some other writers speak of him in his cups and Djilas was astounded by how much so small a man could eat. He liked getting others drunk (as do so many Russians) and he adored practical jokes.

As a youth he was fond of fishing and hunting and he liked dogs. He was remarkably strong for so small a man, but as he grew old his blood pressure suffered, he became sclerotic, and the elbow he had injured in childhood bothered him increasingly.

He could turn on personal charm effectively but had a hot temper which flared up. On more than one occasion he struck his children. He was more easily fooled than he thought. A great fan of motion pictures, he believed what he saw in Soviet films portraying collective farms with tables groaning under loads of geese and turkeys. He did not travel through the countryside or investigate rural conditions himself.

In terms of foreign policy, he made an incredible error. He had considered his 1939 pact with Hitler a triumph because it would turn the Germans and French against each other and he could pick up the pieces after their war. But Hitler fooled him. Stalin paid no attention to detailed warnings from British and other intelligence services saying the Nazis were planning a huge and imminent Blitzkrieg. What is more, he came within an ace of losing.

Stalin was essentially a crafty political manipulator and no philosopher. Despite his parochial schooling, he had no feeling for religion, prayers, or the nonmaterial. Realism, mankind's struggles, not ideals, were his topics of interest. He had a generally low opinion of humanity's good points.

His formal education was very limited, but he acquired considerable technical knowledge. He also seems to have had a natural genius for military strategy and normally knew when to act on intuition. He was fascinated by and knowledgeable in the essentials and importance of different weapons. But he was ignorant and dogmatic on history, sociology, philosophy.

In most respects he was personally a simple man. He couldn't count money or evaluate it except in old, prerevolutionary terms. If he gave a present, he had no clue to its real value. He never spent any money, and let his salary accumulate in desk drawers. All his needs—houses, servants, food, clothing—were paid for by a special division of the secret police with its own accountancy.

The only real luxury he fancied was good Georgian wine (despite his preference for Russia and things Russian). He kept a wide selection of bottles at hand.

He was a callously cruel man but in an almost indifferent way. He seemed to forget that close friends or relatives he had murdered ever existed. One of his most virulent strains of evil was the militant anti-Semitism he encouraged ideologically, especially after World War II. He not only endorsed this credo but propagated it as much as he could. This was not difficult in the Soviet Union, which had old Russian roots for this evil ailment.

In a great many respects Stalin was an odd man, a mechanical man. There was neither peace nor happiness hidden away inside him. In *Only One Year* Svetlana summed up her father:

> Under no circumstances could one call him a neurotic: rather, powerful, self-control was part of his nature. He was neither hot-tempered, nor open-hearted, nor emotional, nor sentimental; in other words he lacked all that was characteristic of a typically Georgian temperament. Georgians are impulsive, kind, easily shedding tears when moved by compassion or happiness or when enraptured by beauty. Aesthetic feelings, music, poetry, plastic art, play a great role in their lives.
>
> But not my father. In him everything was the other way round, and cold calculation, dissimulation, a sober, cynical realism became stronger in him with the years. . . .
>
> I loved and respected him—until I grew up.

It is possible that in a sense there was an element of a Freudian Oedipus complex in Stalin, despite his metallic soul, although this kind of speculation can easily be misconceived by the amateur. As a girl, Svetlana recalls, "I loved him tenderly, as he loved me. He used to say I was like his mother. That touched him, I think." In her *Twenty Letters* she writes:

> My grandmother had principles of her own. They were the principles of one who was old and God-fearing, who'd lived a life that was upright and hard, full of dignity and honor. Changing her life in any way whatever was the furthest thing from her mind. She passed on all her stubbornness and firmness, her puritanical standards, her unbending, masculine character and

her high requirements for herself to my father. He was much more like her than like his father.

In *Only One Year* Svetlana continues:

> Any tenderness and love remembered from his childhood days was personified in his mother. But he was so removed from her, both geographically and in spirit, that he knew not how to make his feelings felt by her as something real; they simply never reached her, getting lost in those vast distances between them. . . .
>
> Everyone to whom he had ever been attached, for whom he had ever felt any affection had been connected in his consciousness with his mother. His first wife bore her name—Catherine [Ekaterina]. This quiet, pretty girl had pleased the mother and at the mother's insistence the marriage had been solemnized in church.

Stalin said his mother was an intelligent woman. He was thinking of the quality of her mind and not her education, since she was hardly able to write her own name. Svetlana writes: "Sometimes he'd tell us how she used to spank him when he was little and how she used to hit his father when he drank too much. Apparently she had a strict, decisive character. My father was delighted by that. . . . She was about eighty when she died in 1936. My father was deeply upset and spoke about her for years afterwards."

Apart from his mother and from his second wife, Nadya Alliluyeva, Stalin's relations with the rest of the family varied between disagreeable and uninteresting. His father was a ratty, nasty little man who could have been invented by a Russian Charles Dickens.

Yakov, the dictator's eldest son (by his first wife), sounds like an unfortunate if pleasant mediocrity. He spoke with a thick Georgian accent that irked his father, and when he unsuccessfully attempted suicide, Stalin mocked: "Ha! He couldn't even shoot straight." Yakov went to Leningrad to live with his step-relatives, the Alliluyevas, until, during the war, he was taken prisoner by the Germans and killed. There is one story that he deliberately died by flinging himself into an electrified barbed wire fence. But I have also been told the Nazis offered to exchange him for Field Marshal Paulus, the captured commander of the vast Axis army at Stalingrad; his heartless father, however, dismissed the suggestion in a curt rage. Svetlana's womanly warmth and charm emerge in her writings, but she appears more agreeable than remarkable.

By far the most horrible—worse than his grandfather and instinctually perhaps even worse than his father—was Vasily, the great air force general. Vasily was obviously a bum and a bully from the start. He started in aviation. At just twenty, in 1941, he began the war as a captain. He finished it at twenty-four as a lieutenant-general. In 1947 he was transferred from East Germany to Moscow and made air commander of the capital's military district. Yet everyone knew he was an incompetent alcoholic who could no longer fly a plane.

With Stalin's approval, he was given a vital command and then seized a dacha, unlawfully, filling it with loot stolen from Europe. His father's toadies passed up the word that he was very capable, but it soon became widely known that the thirty-year-old general had been destroyed by vodka, and he was dismissed.

On April 28, 1953, he was arrested for carousing with foreigners and eventually sent to a military hospital. He remained there more than six years. Khrushchev, then boss, summoned him. Vasily was given an apartment and a dacha; his general's rank and pension were restored; and he was reinstated in the Communist Party. However, after being again imprisoned, he was released to a hospital with a liver ailment and died March 19, 1962, ruined by alcohol at forty-one. He had led a useless life. As Svetlana was to write: "I do not like vodka, with its concomitant slice of herring, because my brother drank too much of it and ended up a hopeless alcoholic."

The fact that both Vissarion and his son Iosif were unquestionably brave was not a rare virtue in the domain of the czars, where courage was needed simply to survive. The other traits Stalin inherited from his parent or the latter's actions had far more psychological importance to his development and therefore to world history.

Having suffered in his boyhood, he later used the power he gained to make others suffer likewise. His minions followed instructions and applied torture in the name of dogma, but with a sadistic twist like Torquemada's inquisitorial brutes in Renaissance Spain.

The warped application of Stalinist sternness had deep psychological origins. Robert Tucker concludes: "Since all people in authority over others owing to power or seniority seemed to be like his father, there soon rose in him a vengeful feeling against all people standing above him. From childhood on the realization of his thoughts of revenge became the aim to which everything was subordinated."

Vissarion objected to Ekaterina's efforts to educate the boy. He wished to pull him out of parochial school and train him as a shoemaker. Stalin quit school on his own—and as Tucker recounts: "The parent with whom he identified positively was his mother. . . . It is evident that he formed a strong mother attachment which greatly influenced the development of his personality. The nature of the influence is suggested by Freud's remark that 'a man who has been the indisputable favorite of his mother keeps for life the feeling of a conqueror, that confidence of success that often induces real success.' "

Had history of contemporary Russia been written with a Freudian twist rather than a Marxist rigidity, we might well have come up with those grandly simplified assumptions: just as Alexander the Great's personality, molded by mother-adoration, had been in a position to use his father's military machine and strategic dreams to launch his own huge conquests, Stalin's personality, profoundly touched by an Oedipal relationship, was perfectly attuned to the modification of Lenin's visionary methods and an impressive thrust for world power.

Part Four

MYTHMAKERS

XII

Camelot: Joseph and John Fitzgerald Kennedy

John F. Kennedy, one of the most qualified American presidents when he assumed that office, actually received it almost by right of heritage in a republic that thoroughly discourages such pseudo-monarchical procedure. His father was not chief of state, nor was he himself an eldest son. Moreover, the people of the United States, by specified traditions laid down in the nation's earliest days, have dutifully elected their leader every four years by popular suffrage, which eventually became universal.

But Joseph P. Kennedy, Sr., who fathered nine legitimate children, including four sons, was a Celtic clan chief in spirit. What he clearly could not obtain for himself, he decided to pass on to his first boy, Joe, Jr.—and that was the key to the White House. But young Joe, a courageous, spirited youth who had yet to display any particular wisdom or political talent, was cut down cruelly during the war when the bomber he was flying exploded under German antiaircraft fire. Joe, Sr., then turned to his second son, Jack. With jovial cynicism, the millionaire father told friends: "We'll sell him like soap flakes." He did—and the nation rapidly discovered the young man was an eminently salable character.

It is only fair to any reader of these pages that I should declare my own personal bias early in this account. I heartily disliked Joe, Sr., and never knew young Joe. I much liked and admired Jack, but disliked and mistrusted Bobby, the third to die tragically before he had made his true mark on history. As for Teddy, the Benjamin, it is needless to recount a viewpoint; he has yet to be embraced by destiny.

The tragedy of the Kennedys is that fate arranged for a blemished father and a brave brother to fall by history's wayside before the faltering torch of political fame was seized by ambitious young Jack only, all too soon, to be extinguished in his blood. President Kennedy was an intelligent, attractive political leader on the road that might well have led to statesmanship. But the Washington world he engendered, the atmospherics of his administration, contained too much of Father Joe, the tribal leader, to depict the myth it sought to make reality.

Joseph P. Kennedy, head of the family that had immigrated two generations earlier, developed a passion for and talent in politics which so many compatriots from Ireland showed once they had grown new roots on the Atlantic's western shores.

I once asked Larry O'Brien, President Kennedy's election expert, why he thought the Irish, who showed little political skill in their Emerald Isle, managed to develop it so remarkably once they transferred to North America. "That's obvious," he said. "America is the land of immigrants. But after the original Anglo-Saxon colonial settlement, we were the first minority to arrive speaking English. Like all minorities, we cared for each other, we were bound together by mutual ties of family and friendship, but when we got here we were able to express ourselves in the majority's native tongue."

Jack Kennedy could boast descent from politicians on both sides. His mother's father was John F. ("Honey Fitz") Fitzgerald, a popular mayor of Boston and controller of a significant bloc of Massachusetts votes. His own father, Joe, had made himself a passionate politician in his quest for power and prestige to offset what he considered the disadvantages of being a Roman Catholic Irish-American in a country where the White Anglo-Saxon Protestant held significant advantages in social, political, commercial, and financial affairs.

Joe's father, Patrick J., entered the liquor trade, started a profitable saloon, and branched out into Democratic party politics just as the Irish minority was beginning to assert control over Boston voters. As a result of Patrick's prosperity, Joe was educated at the nation's most prestigious public school, Boston Latin, and went on to Harvard, its most prestigious university. There he was bruised by snobbery. It kept him from admission to social clubs he wished to join and conceivably hampered his ambitions to be thought a fine athlete.

In response to such slights, Joe decided to seek money and power. He recognized that the rich could buy their way upward in the layered American society and that money was the key to power. During his life, he showed great talent in amassing a fortune in Wall Street banking, movies, real estate, and liquor marketing. He virtually cornered the American outlet for Scotch whiskey by getting James Roosevelt as his partner in "Somerset Importers," when F.D.R., James's father, was president. Kennedy moved in to acquire U.S. monopolies as soon as he learned through Washington connections that prohibition was doomed.

Joe was an unabashed social climber ever since Harvard. He keenly resented exclusion from high society and relished a sardonic satisfaction as, later on, leaders of the exclusive WASP element began to kowtow to his growing fortune. What he had personally resented in the smug Boston Brahmin attitude toward Irish-Catholics he personally repeated vis-à-vis American Jews; J. P. Kennedy turned openly anti-semitic, and was later quoted favorably in this respect in Nazi diplomatic dispatches.

I came to know Joe when he worked in Washington for Roosevelt as chairman of the Securities and Exchange Commission and the U.S. Maritime Commission. Also, later, in London as American Ambassador, where he was favorably regarded by Prime Minister Neville Chamberlain's appeasement clique. The better I knew Kennedy, the more I disliked him, despite the fact that he initially treated me with the amiable jollity he reserved for newspapermen expected to do his bidding.

Knowing I was acquainted with Roosevelt's new envoy, a widely circulated American magazine asked me to write a piece on him for a generous sum. I called on the Ambassador. He promised to help in all respects. He introduced me to two principal members of his personal public relations unit, Harvey Klemmer, formerly of the U.S. Maritime Commission, and the well-connected Harold Hinton, formerly of the The New York Times in Washington. Kennedy made himself available for as many conversations as I wished. He only requested the privilege of seeing my completed article ("to avoid errors").

He told me: "I don't expect to live out the ordinary span of life. I've been living too hard. Therefore, after this job, I want to quit public life. I know I'll die young" [which he didn't]. I want to establish my older sons firmly enough so they can look after the younger children."

Joe always protested to all but intimates that he had no interest in the Presidency himself. This was baloney. He played all kinds of games, courted all sorts of factional spokesmen, in search of support for just such a crown. He did not fail for a lack of trying but for mistakes he made.

I inquired among well-placed Washington friends and then noted in my diary: "Kennedy says he has received approaches suggesting he run for the presidency. Claims he will not run because he loves his family too much. His present job is bad enough for the children without absolutely ruining them."

An influential member of Roosevelt's government establishment wrote an analysis for me authorizing publication if I did not mention his name:

As for Joe Kennedy, you probably know all about him because of his gift for charming newspapermen into writing reams as are usually reserved for occupants of the White House or the electric chair. So far, he has evinced no public aspiration for either. However, he has received a great number of letters from Americans announcing they will vote for him if he runs for the presidency in 1940. He has also been sounded out by certain political sources. He told a friend of mine he wouldn't dream of taking such a job because it would be too tough on his family. He told me:

"I'm not a good candidate. I'm no good at getting out and asking the public to vote for me. So far, I've managed to keep hold of my personal independence and I've never given the presidency a serious thought. I will go back to business when I finish here (London). The last time I went back to public office (as chairman of the Maritime Commission) I didn't go back for glory."

Here is what a friend of his says, a fellow who knows him well and who, in addition, is an extremely influential person in Washington: "Joe is intensely interested in public affairs but equally interested in his own power, position, and promotion. Generally speaking, he likes to do a spectacular job and move on as he did with the SEC and, less successfully, with the Maritime Commission. I think he had his eye on a Cabinet post in Commerce or, preferably, in the Treasury.

"Neither seemed to be available when he was receptive. Then his mind turned to an ambassadorship. He probably sensed the possibility of war and increasing importance and popular interest in foreign developments. The social prestige of the position probably weighed significantly with him. I think he did feel that the position would mean a great deal to his wife and children. Joe seldom plans to stay in any position long. But I don't know that he has set any time limit [on London]. That might depend upon his being asked to take up an equal or higher post here [Washington].

"From his early experience as a speculator, Joe has learned that it is a good thing to get out as well as sell out when your stock is riding high. Joe has been written about as a possible candidate in 1940; Joe is too smart to get out on a limb. Yet he is smart enough to seize an opportunity if it comes his way. I am by no means trying to run him down. But I think one must make an emotional rather than an intellectual analysis of Joe. And a psychoanalysis of the greatest of men is likely to find explanation in the simplest emotional forces."

Kennedy feels this analysis is unfounded in many respects. "I never thought about an ambassadorship," he says, "and this offer came as a complete surprise. I was offered the Secretaryship of Commerce but I didn't want it. The only reason I went back to Washington was to tackle the dirty job of starting off the Maritime Commission and we feel that our report on the situation was a good start. When I'm through with this post, I'm through with public life. I've been working hard and I want to get my sons off right in the world."

Joe Kennedy is known as a loyal Roosevelt man and he is personally fond of the President. However, he criticizes some of the chief executive's left-wing advisers and certain policies, particularly in the realm of taxes. In England, he has occasionally ventured blunt remarks. He told a group of Oxford students that, if United States bonds went down another 10 percent, every insurance company and bank in the country would go bust.

When I wrote my article in 1938, Kennedy was still popular in England and Chamberlain's friend. The charm and liveliness of an ambassadorial family with nine children captured the English imagination. Only after disaster struck in 1940, with the fall of France and the naming of Churchill's war cabinet, did the British intelligence services report to the new prime minister that their taps of Kennedy's personal and official communications had showed him much more appeasement-minded than Chamberlain. The Churchill government quietly clamped down. Kennedy, who had figured as a social lion (a role he relished), was suddenly isolated; hostesses abruptly ceased inviting him. His sources of official information withered.

But none of this had yet happened when I finished my work. I showed the piece to the ambassador as I had promised. He was furious with what he read. I refused to change it despite his blandishments and threats. He then said: "You know, that magazine's publisher is my close friend. I'll see to it your piece is never printed."

I stood by my statements and mailed the manuscript home. Weeks later, when I was in Prague, Czechoslovakia's capital, the proofs were forwarded.

The piece had been so altered it seemed as if the ambassador himself had written it. All reference to his political views or aspirations was gone. I wired my editor; no luck, so much time had elapsed that the article was already in print.

I first met Joe's second son, John Fitzgerald, in Belgrade during the summer of 1939. He had come from London on a trip to familiarize himself with eastern Europe while still a Harvard undergraduate. The American minister to Jugoslavia, to whose care Ambassador Kennedy had confided Jack, asked me if I'd look after him because I knew Belgrade well and was much nearer his age.

He was a nice, friendly, inquiring kid, skinny, intelligent, and eager. After a couple of evenings together, he somewhat timidly asked whether I'd mind if he called me "Cy." Little did I suspect I was getting on cozy terms with a future president.

Thus, just before the outbreak of World War II, I had the fortune to wind up an acquaintanceship with Joseph P. Kennedy and to begin one with his second son, both significant figures in mid-twentieth-century America. Fortunately, the latter was more significant. Jack was a man of quality, even though the legend he bequeathed was more mythical than real.

The father's cardinal rule in bringing up his clan of nine children was: "The important thing is to win; don't come in second or third—that doesn't count; but win, win, win." Joe's example served as a symbol of success in all but national politics. Roosevelt used him (and his money), but dumped him before he became too much of an embarrassment.

He had already made a fortune and succeeded triumphantly in his social climbing. In America, money is far from being the root of all evil.

The clan chief taught Jack, his most brilliant pupil, that money could purchase talent. Arthur Krock, the journalist, helped to expand the youth's Harvard thesis on Britain's faulty policy before the war into a well-edited book called *While England Slept*. This succeeded handsomely, assisted by lavish ambassadorial spending on promotion and advertising. Later Jack was to gain a Pulitzer prize of questionable merit (because the work was so substantially ghost-written by his aide, Ted Sorensen) for another volume entitled *Profiles in Courage*.

He also earned a reputation as a splendid and effective orator, although his speeches were also carefully ghosted. George Ball, an intelligent and liberal Democrat who supported Stevenson but served Kennedy's administration faithfully as under secretary of state and ambassador to the United Nations, wrote in his memoirs:

If it is now part of the mythology that he was a gifted speaker, that is only by contrast to those whom we have since endured. He spoke with a peculiar Bostonian cadence, letting his voice fall just when it should have risen to gain maximum effect. An attractive figure on the platform, easy in manner, armed with eloquently phrased speeches interlarded with questions and poetry, he projected charm but little passion. Though audiences liked him and found him disarming, they were rarely roused as Roosevelt, for example, had roused them. . . . He could not impose his own personality on the events of the day as I had seen Roosevelt do three decades earlier.

Young Jack was helped along by his durable bravery in his successful pursuit of the prize glimpsed by his determined father. This was not simply the bravery he displayed as an impressive war hero; more difficult to maintain was the enduring courage of one who suffered excruciating pains from a desperately bad back, further inflamed by athletic and war injuries, and by Addison's disease and other achingly disquieting maladies. (Addison's disease is an adrenal disorder which causes weakness, loss of weight, and subjects a victim to easy infection.)

An ordinary man under no pressures would have spent at least half his time on crutches. Young Kennedy used them sparingly. He drove himself to lead a more-than-normal life interlarded with sports (at which he had some talent), and the steadiest flow of ladies since Warren G. Harding's day passed through the White House. Jack's, however, were more attractive. Nevertheless, a few who slipped in had unsavory contacts with shady characters or criminals, including a mafia boss.

He brought with him to the nation's highest office some heavy baggage passed on by his father's prejudices: a brooding concern about gold reserves and a connection with Joe McCarthy, whom he had befriended when in the Senate. Joe, Sr., liked this uncouth rabble-rouser, and Bobby worked for him until he cast off that besmudged totem to wrap himself in the liberal shroud of Adlai Stevenson. Jack explained he found it difficult to berate McCarthy while his brother worked for him.

Yet John F. Kennedy was not wholly swaddled by his father's prejudices. He had a quick intelligence and could speed-read 1,200 words a minute. He was a pragmatist and avoided Joe's rabid isolationism, as indeed he had done since his Harvard days. There was nothing pro-Nazi or anti-Semitic in his makeup. Also he clearly held the English in great esteem, which his father only pretended to do early during his London mission. As Ball was to write: "The father's noxious views had not infected the son."

It is difficult for outsiders to appreciate the force of Joseph P. Kennedy: bitter, ambitious, charming, ruthless, and disappointed. As head of the family, he was tyrannical. During August 1962 I spent a few days with Jackie; her sister and brother-in-law, the Radziwills; and Italian friends at Ravello, Italy. I was struck one day, while Jackie and I passed hours stretched out chatting on the deck of a handsome yacht, to hear her refer to her father-in-law, whenever she mentioned him, as "Mr. Kennedy." She spoke of the president and the attorney general of the United States as "Jack" and "Bobby."

There is no doubt that Joseph P. had a profound influence on each of his children. Yet a friend of Jack said: "When he spoke I could hear his mother's voice. She's the one who put the family spirit in them." Rose spent much time mothering her brood, reading, shopping, sightseeing, and seeing to their religious life. The father was tough and blunt, intent on climbing psychological ladders, principally his own; apart from winning a game, he had no interest in it or the rules of fair play.

At first Joe's crude charm worked well in Chamberlain's England. His anti-Semitism and isolationism hurt him minimally; the fact that he made a hole-in-one in a round of golf helped greatly. Yet Harold Ickes, Roosevelt's curmudgeonly interior secretary, wrote: "At a time when we should be sending the best we have to Great Britain we have not done so. We have sent a rich man, untrained in diplomacy, unlearned in history and politics, who is a great publicity-seeker and who is apparently ambitious to be the first Catholic President of the United States." Joe is quoted as having told Harvey Klemmer: "Roosevelt and the kikes are taking us into war."

When Churchill finally took office in 1940, he sent William Stephenson to establish headquarters in New York for Britain's secret intelligence service. Stephenson reported on Kennedy's pessimistic views concerning Britain's chance of staving off defeat. Kennedy was in close contact with the America First Committee and congressional isolationists, just as he later cottoned to Senator McCarthy. "I always liked him," he said of the evil, alcoholic legislator. "He was a pleasant fellow."

Churchill's arrival at the top was bad news for Ambassador Kennedy. Not only did this spell eventual defeat for Hitler, although the envoy was telling Roosevelt: "Only a miracle can save the British Expeditionary Force [at Dunkirk] from being wiped out, or, as I said yesterday, surrender." It put a finis to Joe, Sr.'s inclinations to personal power, anti-Semitism, and isolationism in world affairs. (He even blamed Roosevelt for the death of his eldest son. Truman later quoted Joe Kennedy as referring to: "That crippled son of a bitch that killed my son Joe.")

Fed by Stephenson and astute British snooping, the Foreign Office opened a file on the American envoy called "Kennedyana." Among entries included was this: "Mr. Kennedy is a very foul specimen of double crosser and defeatist. He thinks of nothing but his own pocket. I hope that this war will at least see the elimination of this type." The foreign secretary, Lord Halifax, initialed this opinion.

On January 15, 1960, I noted in my diary:

> Yesterday, I saw Randolph Churchill twice—for lunch and again in the evening. He had the following story about Joe Kennedy, Jack's father—and he swears he can confirm its truth:
>
> In 1933, Jimmy Roosevelt came over to London just before the inauguration of President Roosevelt, together with his friend Joe Kennedy (who paid for the expedition). Randolph took them to his father's for lunch, little knowing what the purpose was. He soon found out. They explained that Kennedy had gotten in touch with all the biggest whiskey distillers, told them he had given $50,000 to Roosevelt's campaign (before the convention), and was in the middle of things. He could assure them Prohibition would shortly end and he wished to line up contracts to represent the best firms. He got a fistful.
>
> The next time Randolph laid eyes on Kennedy was after he came over as ambassador in 1936, to represent Roosevelt at the Court of St. James's. Word was passed around (before his arrival) to be nice; consequently the establishment went to work. He was invited to house parties, dinners, golf and shooting by dukes and earls.
>
> However, war came, and it soon became apparent that Kennedy thought England was dilapidated and done for; he indicated a private personal preference for the Germans. This became known and the government quietly told the establishment it was no longer necessary to be nice. Suddenly Kennedy found himself isolated and alone.
>
> In 1940, Clare Luce came over to stay with him. The Luces were busily organizing a campaign to prevent Roosevelt from getting a third term. They secretly arranged with Kennedy, who

had been telling people that he didn't think much of Roosevelt, for Kennedy to fly over to the United States and, in a surprise move, come out in public opposition to a third term.

Kennedy flew home as planned. A delegation of Luce's henchmen was waiting at the airport, but they could not find their man. They were supposed to whisk him up to the Luces, but Kennedy had disappeared. The next thing heard of him was when he emerged from the White House at the end of that same day and made a statement to the press endorsing Roosevelt's candidacy.

What had happened? The British were very anxious to get rid of Kennedy and to get Roosevelt back as President. Therefore, their Secret Service, which had been tapping Kennedy's wires and found out he was not only anti-British but also certain they were going to lose the war, consulted Churchill on what to do. Brendan Bracken amassed a sheaf of tapped conversations of Kennedy's in which he expressed critical opinions of Roosevelt. These were given to Harry Hopkins, who was outraged, and showed them to Roosevelt, who was infuriated.

The British knew about the Luce plot. So they tipped off Hopkins, who arranged to have a jeep waiting on the airfield when Kennedy's plane came in. In the jeep was a representative of the White House and Kennedy's wife, Rose, a very devout Roman Catholic. Kennedy was disembarked before the plane reached the regular ramp and was whisked to the White House where, in addition to Roosevelt and Hopkins, Jimmy Byrnes was waiting. Byrnes was an example of the former Catholic who had left the church and, as a consequence, had had his political career wrecked because he had lost the Catholic vote and had never gained the anti-Catholic vote. Mrs. Kennedy pointed out to her husband that if he got into trouble with the Roosevelt machine, he would be finished in politics, because the Catholics would turn against him. He cracked, and backed Roosevelt.

This episode more than anything else put a period to Joe Sr.'s presidential ambitions. Then, when Joe Jr., the crown prince, was killed in 1944, the succession passed to Jack. The father once observed of Jack and Bobby, next in line: "Bobby is more direct than Jack. Jack has always been one to persuade people what to do. . . . Bobby resembles me much more than any of the other children."

Bobby was a skillful dissembler. From his original political role as McCarthy's right hand (a position his father approved and his brother Jack accepted), Bobby was able to give the impression of moving leftward and became an idol of the Democratic liberals. Thanks to Joe, Sr., who felt that when things became difficult Jack, as president, would need a wholly trustworthy aide beside him, Bobby was named attorney general.

Young Jack, who had been a sick child, emerged as the family's greatest hero. Bobby wrote of him later: "At least one-half of the days that he spent on this earth were days of intense physical pain." By sheer determination he persuaded the navy to accept him, and he had a heroic career (while his father was earning money running a shipyard).

Service in the U.S. Navy was more difficult for young Kennedy than for other men. He was not well, although his strong character refused to admit this. However, he was a good swimmer, knew small vessels well, and was therefore suitable for command of a fast motor torpedo boat, P.T. 109.

P.T. 109, on service in the Solomon Islands, was rammed in the early morning of August 2, 1943, by a Japanese destroyer. Jack behaved with calm courage and resolution, leading and saving his crew, summoning help successfully. Alvin Cluster, U.S.N., who commanded two P.T. squadrons in the Solomons, said afterward: "He was a good naval officer, a good navigator, an excellent leader, a good boat-handler. According to an official rule out there, if your boat got sunk, back you went to the States. When his P.T. 109 was sunk in August 1943, he insisted on staying out there, even though some of his crew got transferred. For my money a more courageous guy never lived."

On his twenty-seventh birthday Jack was decorated for "extremely heroic conduct." He was then in Chelsea Naval Hospital for an operation on his lower back for a chronic malady that had been aggravated by the pounding of patrol boat hulls. He also had malaria. The effort of surgeons to correct the spinal disk problem from which he suffered was a failure. Jack commented: "I think the doc should have read just one more book before picking up the saw." Thereafter he had a hole in his back with a metal plate visibly attached to his spine. The wound never healed and was exceedingly painful.

Kennedy did not permit this physical disability to inhibit a political career upon which he had resolved after his elder brother was killed. Joe Sr. urged this upon him, and the candidate had ample financial support. He ran for Congress in East Boston in 1946, winning the election after a vigorous campaign. He was easily reelected in 1948 and 1950, and decided to run for the Senate in 1952 against Republican Henry Cabot Lodge, Jr., the very symbol of all his father detested and envied. Jack managed to win in a year when Eisenhower led the Republican Party to national victory.

During his first year in the Senate he married Jacqueline Lee Bouvier, but allowed neither family life nor recurrent illness to restrain his activity. He did not distinguish himself by being the only Democrat who failed either to vote or pair against the malevolent McCarthy, for whom Bobby had become chief counsel. He also did not hide his poor opinion of General Marshall, accused by the senator of "losing" China.

During his Senate term, Kennedy warned against the John Foster Dulles policy of depending on the threat of nuclear retaliation against guerrillas, with special reference to Southeast Asia. This is of particular interest because, as president, Jack was the first U.S. chief executive to dispatch American ground forces to Vietnam, seeming to forget his own senatorial warning against "the wrong kind of aid which would alienate the people of great sections of the world who might feel that the remedy was worse than the disease." He also correctly predicted that "no amount of American military assistance in Indochina can conquer an enemy of the people which has the sympathy and covert support of the people."

With Eisenhower retiring as leader of the Republicans, Kennedy decided to go for the presidency in 1960, beginning his campaign very early. He won reelection to his Senate seat by a huge margin in 1958 and worked hard from there on. Joe, Sr., had already admitted to an interviewer: "I got Jack into politics. I was the one. I told him Joe was dead and that it was therefore his responsibility to run for Congress. He didn't want it. He felt he didn't have the ability. But I told him he had to." Jack confirmed this, telling a journalist: "I was drafted. My father wanted his eldest son in politics. Wanted isn't the right word. He demanded it. You know my father."

On November 8, 1960, he was elected president by the narrowest of margins. John Kenneth Galbraith, the witty economist, one of several intellectuals who had shifted from Stevenson to the Kennedy bandwagon, said what his new flag bearer wished was "a government of the rich by the clever for the poor."

Right away, Kennedy set about revising several U.S. policies. For national defense, he reverted to theories already suggested by Generals Maxwell Taylor and James Gavin, who, because their ideas had been rejected, had resigned from the army. Substantially, what they demanded was a build-up of conventional armed forces in order to offer some other option than immediate nuclear warfare.

The first big problem faced by Kennedy was Cuba. He had inherited from Eisenhower's administration a plan devised by the C.I.A. to invade the island with a small army of anti-Castro emigrés trained in Central America. The expedition, launched in April 1961, was a mess: no security, indecision in operations, bad planning. The attacking force was totally destroyed and the United States blamed.

United States officials were caught lying in public. Kennedy assumed responsibility for all that went wrong. This was true in the sense that he had accepted C.I.A. estimates and then failed to make up his mind on giving the invaders air support. Eisenhower privately called the humiliation a "profile in timidity and indecision," contrasted with the "courage" of which Kennedy had written. Dean Acheson sardonically commented: "It was not necessary to call in Price, Waterhouse to discover that 1,500 Cubans weren't as good as 25,000 Cubans."

The Bay of Pigs tragedy had a considerable effect on Kennedy's future foreign policy. He told Arthur Schlesinger: "If it hadn't been for Cuba, we might be about to intervene in Laos in early May," so he thanked God for being spared by a Cuban failure from an even more disastrous Asian commitment.

His first year at the helm, 1961, was fortunate for me as a journalist who lived abroad because events permitted me to see more of the new president than at any earlier time. That spring, on Kennedy's first official overseas excursion, he met de Gaulle in Paris and Khrushchev in Vienna. Prior to his visit to de Gaulle, Schlesinger and Tom Finletter visited me on Kennedy's behalf to ask for a memorandum on de Gaulle, whom I knew better than did other Americans at the time. I recommended: "When the serious exchanges begin, we should follow the formula: 'first things last.' In other words, I think a more favorable atmosphere could be created were the President to seize the earliest possible opportunity to steer the conversations to subjects where there is inherent agreement between Washington and Paris."

On June 2, after the talks had ended, Kennedy received me in his French state apartment for a good talk, which I recounted in my diary immediately afterward. I quote in part from my record:

> This afternoon, I had a forty-minute chat with the President in his apartment at the Quai d'Orsay. He was friendly and informal. Nobody else was present. Right at the start he said: "Please protect me on this. Don't indicate in any way that you have seen me and don't tell anybody."
>
> He said the paper I had sent him was "invaluable" and very

useful. I had suggested that the best strategy would be to discuss first things last. I asked Kennedy if this was what he had done and he smiled and said yes. They began with Berlin and then moved on to Asia, Africa, Latin America, etc., before hitting the more direct problems. He said Berlin was easy because we knew in advance we agreed.

I asked if we were now prepared to treat France, in terms of consultation both inside and outside the NATO area, on a basis of complete parity with the way we treat England? Without any hesitation he replied: "There is no doubt of this. We will improve the consultation procedure in every respect."

He added: "We consult in such an intimate way with England because the English are easy to consult with. We have a kind of community point of view. But now we are going to try to improve our own procedures of consultation with France, which is involved in so many regions with us and where we are interested, such as Africa and Laos."

Kennedy said that despite de Gaulle's austere public manner he had been very "warm during our conversations. . . . "When I was leaving, he said, 'I have more confidence in your country now.' "

Kennedy returned to de Gaulle's suspicions of the U.S.A. and said: "You were quite right [in the paper I had sent him]. His anti-American feeling and suspicions go way back and are very deep-rooted. I think it is tremendously important for a man with my responsibility to know something about the people I have to deal with. That helps me make up my mind when the moment for decision comes."

In Vienna, Kennedy was disheartened by the toughness and willingness to compromise displayed by the bearlike Khrushchev. The president told me later: "One always has a tendency to think that reason will prevail in personal conversation, but now I have been able to judge him. Now I know that there is *no* further need for talking. The only reason to meet again would be to make the final arrangements in any previously prepared settlement."

Later in 1961 Khrushchev gave me his own views in Moscow. He recalled:

President Kennedy said to me: "Our forces are equal. We have the ability to destroy each other." I agree with this, although privately I contest his analysis, as I feel we are stronger. But certainly we should not start a war to find out who is right. That would be savagery.

He added:

> Nevertheless, my impression after our Vienna meeting was that Mr. Kennedy understands the need to improve relations between our countries. But evidently he is meeting with difficulties. The advantages Eisenhower had over Kennedy were that he was an older man, a hero of World War II, a man who commanded great respect in the U.S., and therefore if he said the U.S.A. should not go to war, no one would dare accuse him of being afraid. . . .
>
> President Kennedy is in a different position. Politically, he has a much broader outlook. When I talked with him in Vienna, I found him a worthy partner. He himself conducted the talks without depending on Rusk the way Eisenhower always depended on Dulles. At Geneva, in 1955, Eisenhower always waited for Dulles to scribble something on a piece of paper telling him what to do before he said anything. Kennedy formulates his own ideas. That is his superiority to Eisenhower. I had a feeling he understood things better.
>
> But he is not a lawyer; he is a president. Franklin Roosevelt would have agreed to our solution in Kennedy's place. He would have said it is foolish to fight over this. Many people would have opposed Roosevelt, but the population would have supported him. Kennedy is too young. He lacks authority and prestige to settle this issue correctly. But he doesn't want to fight. Only an idiot wants war. If Kennedy appealed to the people—if he voiced his real inner thoughts and stated that there was no use fighting over Berlin—the situation would be settled quickly. All this talk of our desire to seize West Berlin is an invention. Why? If Kennedy does the logical thing, the opposition will raise its voice and accuse him of youth, cowardice, and a lack of statesmanship. He is afraid of that. Eisenhower could have said this and no one could have accused him of being young, inexperienced, or afraid.
>
> If you are personally in a position to meet Kennedy, I would not be loath to establishing some sort of contacts with him to find a means, without damaging the prestige of the U.S., to reach a

settlement. But on the basis of a peace treaty and a free Berlin. And through such informal contacts, the president might say what is on his mind in ways of solving the problem—if he agrees on the principle of a peace treaty and a free city of West Berlin. Otherwise there is no use in contacts. If he does wish to make such contacts, he can express his own opinions on the various forms and stages of a settlement and how to prepare public opinion so as not to endanger Kennedy's prestige and that of the U.S.

I was struck by Khrushchev's continual use of the word "prestige." He said: "We must mutually take into account each other's prestige. You went ahead and signed the Japanese treaty and now you want to prevent us from signing a German treaty. We cannot tolerate that; we have rights of our own."

From Paris I sent his message off by diplomatic courier. I then went to the United States and was received by Kennedy in Washington. I noted:

He brought up Khrushchev's message. It was hard to figure just what it signified. I thought the only way to interpret it was in terms of Aesopian language; one must stress the point of *prestige*. But whenever the word "Kennedy" was used, the word "Khrushchev" must be substituted and wherever the word "Rusk" was used the word "Gromyko" must be substituted. I told him that to me the message made no sense unless one used such an interpretation. . . . Khrushchev wanted private, nondiplomatic channels to Kennedy. Kennedy said Khrushchev suddenly had been "much softer" in his approach to Berlin. He had noticed a distinct change. At Vienna Khrushchev . . . had shown no realization of the fact that American prestige was involved. *Now* he does and his attitude is less rigid!

It is noteworthy that Khrushchev sent a K.G.B. agent named Georgi Bolshakov to Washington as his special contact with Kennedy outside diplomatic channels. Many negotiations during the 1962 Cuban crisis took place via Bolshakov, for Khrushchev, and via Attorney General Robert Kennedy, for the U.S. president.

Kennedy found himself forced by realities to devote more and more attention to Berlin and to nuclear arms. The former German capital was the touchstone of war versus peace and a terribly sensitive spot in the Western alliance, since war meant wholesale nuclear destruction. The apparently separate issues of Cuba and Berlin both involved the sudden establishment of Soviet missile equality with the United States, because in both cases medium range rockets would supplement intercontinental rockets already in place; and because Washington feared Moscow might grab all Berlin while our attention was diverted to the Caribbean.

Kennedy's most dramatic public gesture stressing American determination to keep West Berlin free came June 26, 1963. The president, who flew to that city for the purpose, said in a speech that came after the 1961 moment of showdown and which was probably the most intemperate of his career: "Two thousand years ago the proudest boast was *civis Romanus sum.*' Today, in the world of freedom, the proudest boast is *Ich bin ein Berliner.* There are some who say that communism is the wave of the future. Let them come to Berlin. All free men, wherever they may live, are citizens of Berlin, and, therefore, as a free man, I take pride in the words *'Ich bin ein Berliner.'* "

But Berlin was preceded and succeeded by Cuba as a Kennedy administration crisis point: first, the Bay of Pigs in 1961; then, missile sites in 1962. Just as Cuba—through the Bay of Pigs invasion—had been the first major foreign problem to hit Kennedy's administration, Cuba was the last flamboyant crisis to feature his final weeks in the White House. The outstanding diplomatic myth of his brief term was of that great "victory" over Moscow. Indeed, a victory for common sense was registered; but the formula for settlement was at best a standoff.

Marina and I flew to the United States as the prospect of a Cuban nuclear holocaust was terrifying the world. We spent our first night in Cambridge, Massachusetts. Sir Isaiah Berlin, the brilliant, Russian-born English polymath, came for a drink. He had just been to Washington and seen Kennedy.

He had found him "still psychologically dominated by his father and his father's record as ambassador during the period of British appeasement. Jack's early book, *While England Slept*, inferentially seemed to excuse his father's record by pointing out that a state must move early to confront an aggressor, or otherwise it cannot really fight. Berlin said the president was surrounded by "a group of activists who are very stimulating but who are not long-range thinkers." He wondered if "deep in the president's mind he may not have a presentiment that he may not live a long time and that he must make his mark in history quickly." This is a remarkable case of parapsychological analysis.

Anyone who reads this book is already familiar with the grim tale of the 1962 missile crisis, and is undoubtedly aware of the tapestry of lies unfolded by Soviet officials, the careful reconnaissance of Cuban missile silos by American aircraft, plus the invaluable espionage reports from Moscow of Colonel Oleg Penkovskiy, the C.I.A.'s well-placed agent who supplemented all information obtained by mechanical devices. Penkovskiy was later executed.

The U.S. president behaved with commendable caution as it became clear that Khrushchev was preparing to menace us by a deadly nuclear missile force positioned in Cuba. Had the Soviets succeeded in their venturesome double-cross efforts, they would have advanced their position in a nuclear parity contest by nearly ten years. By October 15, 1962, the U.S. government was in possession of hard evidence that launching sites for Soviet MRBM's had been established at San Cristobal and intermediate IRBM's at Guanajay and Remedios. The IRBM's had double the MRBM range and could strike targets at 2,000 miles.

There were increasing suspicions that Khrushchev would use the tension to move on Berlin. But the Russians, after insistently denying missiles were in Cuba, subsequently accepted an exchange: they would be withdrawn if the United States withdrew Jupiter missiles from its NATO ally Turkey. This was complicated because America only owned the atomic warheads; Turkey owned the missiles. The Turks and General Lauris Norstad, U.S. commander of NATO, strongly opposed their removal.

Subsequently, Anatoly Dobrynin, who represented Moscow as its able ambassador in Washington during the crisis, told me: "Robert Kennedy came to see me fifteen times. The last time he handed me a letter. It said: 'You take your missiles out of Cuba and we will take our missiles out of Turkey.' It was signed 'John F. Kennedy.' " Whether Bolshakov figured vitally in these exchanges isn't known to me. Kennedy aides have contended ever since that there was no *quid pro quo* under pressure. They pointed out that the Jupiters were obsolete (although they'd been emplaced in Turkey since Kennedy's inauguration), and, according to Bobby Kennedy, the president had already ordered their removal.

Dobrynin told me he had suggested to Bobby that the U.S.S.R. felt just as menaced by U.S. missiles in Turkey, on its frontier, as the United States did by Soviet missiles in Cuba. Bobby immediately grasped the point that Moscow wanted an exchange. He said he would ask the president. There was no document, according to Dobrynin; merely a gentlemen's agreement. Kennedy obliquely promised Khrushchev to act as agreed in Turkey only on condition that the Jupiter withdrawal would not appear to be part of the Cuban settlement.

The Soviet missiles left Cuba promptly and the Jupiters left Turkey in

April 1963 (five months later). The C.I.A. meanwhile began plotting to murder Castro under the guidance of a top official, Desmond Fitzgerald, and a Cuban renegade named Roland Cubela, codenamed AM/LASH by American intelligence, who knew Castro well. The United States had sworn not to invade Cuba, and Russia promised not to use it as a base. Nevertheless, in 1970 Moscow began to construct a submarine and possibly land-sited missile facility at the port of Cienfuegos. Cuba now houses a Soviet garrison.

Marina and I dined at the White House on Friday, November 9, 1962. The others present were: the Kennedys, Joe and Susan-Mary Alsop, Isaiah and Aline Berlin, Arthur and Marian Schlesinger, S. N. Behrman, the playwright, and the president's pretty, young, blond friend Mrs. Meyer. Kennedy looked well, calm, and relaxed, and sat around chatting until 11:00 P.M. He wanted to talk only about politics or foreign policy.

He said all missiles would be out of Cuba by the coming Monday (November 12): "I am astonished at how fast they've been able to get them out." But Kennedy said he did not think the Russians had had an advance emergency plan for speedy evacuation in case of necessity. They had merely been able to improvise brilliantly. He thought the Russians, once they saw how determined we were, were afraid we might capture some of their missiles. The real alternative to a naval quarantine would have been a conventional assault on Cuba, not an air attack.

He could not understand why Khrushchev went into Cuba. If he had thought America wasn't going to fight in the heart of an area of vital national interest, he surely must have assumed we weren't going to fight in Berlin. Therefore, "Why didn't he go straight for Berlin?"

Several times Kennedy talked about his "terrible responsibility" in terms of making war or peace. "I know the figures," he said. "One-hundred million Europeans would be dead in a day—and eighty million here. A war can destroy humanity." He complained: "Europe wants a free ride in its defense." What he meant was that the NATO allies weren't doing enough to build Western defense and were counting too much on our protection. The Cuban crisis showed that large conventional forces were needed. "We would have had to go into Cuba with conventional forces had we attacked. The Europeans wanted our atomic umbrella. They wouldn't build up the necessary conventional forces."

Kennedy warned it was always easy for the United States to make a deal on Berlin and avoid war. The Europeans should realize this and do more about arming themselves instead of relying on us. We couldn't go on forever carrying the burden largely alone. He betrayed a considerable distaste for and suspicion of the Germans.

The following week (November 20, 1962) I had an extensive conversation with the president in his White House office. I noted: "He was calm, collected, and I am always struck by his remarkable memory. My fundamental impression was that despite apparent victory in Cuba, he was by no means overoptimistic."

I inquired if we had any way today of checking as to whether the Russians had left any nuclear warheads in Cuba. "No," he said flatly. "There is not any way, but I certainly assume they won't do so." I asked: "You mean they wouldn't leave such toys in the hands of such screwballs?" "That's right," he said.

Had we any intention of offering new inducements to our NATO allies to provide more conventional divisions? He shrugged his shoulders and said: "What more can we do? Sooner or later they will have to produce more conventional forces or otherwise there will be no sense to NATO."

He said Khrushchev had backed down "a little bit," but the crisis wasn't over, and "also look at China." The world was still filled with trouble and "the human race remains in peril." He thought "Europe should realize the advantage of adequate conventional defense, which would give us a chance in case of trouble to have time to pause and negotiate."

Had he been scared by the immensity of the task and its responsibility at the start? He said with a grin: "No, not scared. At the beginning, you are protected by the value of your own ignorance. But I can do the job much better now, and I could have done this much better earlier if I had had experience. Let me show you what I mean. After Cuba—the Bay of Pigs—we began to talk about maybe going into Laos. But all the generals and other people disagreed about this, and you don't know whom to believe and whom to disbelieve. It is a very hard thing at first. Another problem that kept arising was Southeast Asia." He was thoroughly briefed on the tragic French effort to reconquer Indochina and had long ago concluded: "to pour money, material, and men into the jungles of Indochina without at least a remote prospect of victory would be dangerously futile and self-destructive."

As part of his broad retreat from Eisenhower-Dulles policies he realized were outmoded, Kennedy stressed the need to develop antiguerrilla units and techniques. He created an organization known as "Jungle Jim," which became the pioneer of U.S. counterinsurgency strategy, and a special group was designated to operate in specific areas such as Laos. At the same time, the new president withdrew from the tough line assumed by the Republicans and worked in Laos for a neutralist government backed by popular support but not penetrated by communism, a concept about as realistic, given the circumstances, as organizing the penguin population of Antarctica. In South

Vietnam, the C.I.A. was encouraged in its efforts to organize Montagnard tribesmen to oppose North Vietnamese communist aggression just as Meo tribesmen were similarly organized in Laos.

Everything seemed to be conspiring to prevent the entry into Southeast Asia of American combat troops. President Ngo Dinh Diem of the Saigon government didn't want to see that happen; he feared the United States might willy-nilly take over not only his war but his country. Nevertheless, the Americans were so enthusiastic in their determination to prevent Hanoi from taking over the south through the Vietcong, that by the end of 1962 there were 11,000 U.S. troops in that country under what was called a "Military Assistance and Advisory Group." Shortly before Kennedy's death, the Joint Chiefs of Staff requested an increase to 17,000 in American strength and the president approved. The cards were dealt for the American disaster in Indochina. Vietnam was, in truth, Kennedy's war, not Lyndon Johnson's.

Although the Joint Chiefs of Staff produced a plan to withdraw American advisers between 1963 and 1965, there is no confirmation that the president supported this. He told Senator Mike Mansfield: "If I tried to pull out completely now from Vietnam, we would have another Joe McCarthy red scare on our hands, but I can do it after I'm reelected. So we had better make damned sure that I am reelected." Kennedy dispatched his old Massachusetts political rival, the Republican Henry Cabot Lodge, Jr., to Saigon, partially because he spoke good French (*lingua franca* of the country) and partly to assign a portion of the blame, if things went wrong, to an opposition standard bearer. Thus Lodge came to share in the responsibility for Diem's assassination in Saigon, three weeks before that of the American president.

Kennedy's last days were tinged with sadness. In December 1961 his father, of whom he was truly fond, had suffered a bad stroke, from which he never recovered. The son told me old Joe would never again be able to speak, although his mind was all right and he managed to communicate some ideas. The president observed: "It is better to go fast." He said with tears in his eyes: "He's the one who made all this possible; and look at him now."

In August his prematurely-born infant son, Patrick (not yet two days old), died of a membrane disease. This deeply affected both Jack and Jackie. Their marriage had not been going particularly well. Jack, like his formally devout father, was an enthusiastic and successful womanizer, the most proficient of all our presidents in this sport. This fact undoubtedly did not overwhelm Jackie with joy. It might well have encouraged her prodigious zeal for spending gobs of money, especially on clothes, which clearly displeased Jack. His father actually offered a millon-dollar gift to ease the financial burden on the president's family budget. Although Jackie welcomed the position of first lady in many respects, relishing the injection of cultural American influences into the White House, Jack's disregard of fidelity and her own flamboyant extravagance combined with the normal cooling off of ardor to threaten their ties.

In 1963, after the death of little Patrick, she accepted an invitation (transmitted from Athens via her sister, Lee Radziwill) to take a cruise aboard the yacht of Aristotle Onassis, the immensely rich shipping tycoon. Thus, at the end of a tragic period in terms of their family life, Jackie flew off to Greece for a fortnight's excursion into pleasure, leaving behind her two children as well as the president.

Onassis was not a felicitous choice of host. The United States government had been attempting to sue him for fraud in connection with the use of surplus American ships without paying taxes. Ultimately he paid a fine of $7 million to avoid facing a court trial. To compound the undiplomatic aspect of her journey, she stayed in Athens at the house of another shipowner, named Nomikos, who owned at least one vessel engaged in trade with Cuba. Jackie was invited to lunch at the royal palace but declined because she disliked the queen. The American ambassador persuaded her to accept another invitation—to tea—but she wrecked this because she asked permission to bring Lee and her husband, Prince Stanislas Radziwill. The queen heartily disliked Radziwill.

Jackie was back at her White House duties in November, in time to accompany Jack on his climactic trip to Texas, during which her radiant smile before the assassination and her dignity afterward won the hearts of the American people. On November 22, 1963, they arrived in Dallas. As the entire world knows, the president was shot to death by an American sniper, who had lived in Russia and who was himself slain by a deranged Dallas nightclub operator named Jack Ruby. Five years later, Bobby Kennedy was also assassinated.

There is an element of classical Greek tragedy in the end of the four oldest men of the Kennedy clan. Old Joe, who clearly had coveted the U.S. presidency himself, was forced by his own errors in judgment and the crudity of his undisguised aspirations, to sit back like some thwarted Celtic chieftain and bequeath to his sons a position he did not possess but to which he aspired.

When young Joe, the apple of his eye and spiritual heir, was killed in action on a dangerous mission against the Germans in a war to which the father was certainly opposed, Joe, Sr., accepted his deep personal loss with bitter gallantry and handed the "succession" torch to his second son, the remarkable Jack.

And when, after his fantastic triumph, that successful choice was extinguished by a mysterious murderer, the torch was handed on to Bobby, the third son, the one who most resembled his father in character and lack of scruples. Bobby too, already climbing the ladder of ambition, was slain, by a strangely unconnected Arab. Old Joe, the tragic founder of this extraordinary political generation of the Kennedy clan, outlived all three of his eldest sons and was condemned by the gods to suffer in silence as his latterday dreams were extinguished.

Charles de Gaulle, much interested in President Kennedy after his Paris visit in 1961, told me on December 12, 1963, following attendance at the young American's funeral, how he thought history would regard him. He recalled that Sophocles wrote twenty-five centuries ago that none could describe the day that passed until the sun had set. I said to de Gaulle: "Alas, the sun has now set on President Kennedy; how will history view him?"

The general replied:

> I cannot really say. He was very likable and he certainly had great value. He wanted to solve problems, but, unfortunately, he lacked the necessary time. He wanted to solve enormous problems: the race problem in your country, the problem of the dollar, the underdeveloped lands, Latin America, Europe, disarmament. These were and are enormous problems and they require a great amount of time. History will probably say of Kennedy that he was a man of great ability who lacked the time to prove himself.

Kennedy, the romantically inclined young president, had aspired to becoming an American Churchill. Above all he sought to establish his fame on foreign testing grounds. But his first Cuban adventure was disastrous; his second was a dismal *quid pro quo* deal.

Although Kennedy had properly identified the importance of guerrilla warfare and the difficulty of opposing it with normal means, he started to introduce mass U.S. forces into Vietnam (which Eisenhower had avoided) and began the American march to Indochinese military disaster. He allowed the Soviet lead in nuclear missiles to continue to build up and failed to match Moscow's construction of a huge blue water fleet.

During the season of "Camelot," glamor overshadowed quality: ghost-written prose replaced long-range analysis. Kennedy enchanted a generation of youngsters inspired by his elegantly articulated visions of effective democratic leadership. This was the generation that eventually discovered their murdered totem had been an orphan of failure, in terms of accomplishment, and but an interim president.

Following the 1962 missile crisis and Kennedy's 1963 assassination, we watched development of a worrisome aftermath: reduction of U.S. influence in Turkey after the Jupiter missiles left; installation at Cienfuegos, Cuba, of a heavily armed Soviet naval base; dispatch of Cuban soldiers all over the earth to fight against U.S. interests; disastrous failure of American policy in Vietnam; frightening growth of a Soviet strength in missiles and naval power; and defeat in our most disastrous, if never declared, foreign war.

Slowly America's friends abroad came to realize these sad truths. The dean of ambassadors on the NATO council, Belgium's André de Staercke, said regretfully: "I fear the New Frontier is the last border. Perhaps Europe underestimated Eisenhower *a posteriori* and overestimated Kennedy *a priori.*" George Ball, a loyal Democrat who served Kennedy, described him as "the pragmatist *par excellence*. . . . When one tried to point out the long-range implications of a current program, Kennedy would often say politely but impatiently: 'Let's not worry about five years from now.' "

Harvard's president, Derek Bok, told me: "The cult of pesonality has declined substantially. This is evident in the later view of President Kennedy." Senator William Fulbright observed: "Kennedy . . . his brother and intimate friends . . . made decisions without consulting the State Department and Congress." Senator Mansfield added: "President Kennedy's administration pushed down the morale of the Foreign Service by tending to ignore the secretary of state in favor of Bobby Kennedy and [Defense Secretary] McNamara, and also tending to ignore many of the career diplomats."

André Malraux observed astutely: "Kennedy was like a young boxer. He was nothing but reflexes—jabs and reactions." When Henry Kissinger was quietly dispatched by Kennedy to see Konrad Adenauer in Bonn, the president instructed him: "I want you to find out what's gone wrong with our German policy." "That will be easier," Kissinger said, "if you tell me one small thing: What is our German policy?"

After Watergate there was a new public fascination with wiretapping and spying. Kissinger said later that Kennedy had had eighty people bugged and that his wiretapping had been aimed "especially against newspapermen."

His tragic term failed, as de Gaulle observed, to endure long enough for anyone to assess the chances of his aims. The actual achievements do not add up to much.

*   *   *

President John F. Kennedy was the brilliant creation of a grasping, dynamic father who sought to install in power a son who would imitate his own egocentric image. Happily, in this he largely failed; for Jack, although like his father in several ways, had far finer qualities and sensitivities.

Both were vigorous, ambitious, exceedingly competent, and gifted with a talent for public relations. Both were philanderers, though none who was not a member of their families would have cared had not the son conducted the amorous campaigns, begun in Harvard, from the hallowed recesses of the White House.

Old Joe was disturbingly arrogant as well as untrustworthy, qualities I never detected in his famous boy (despite Adlai Stevenson's objection to his crude, rough tongue). Jack was surely far more patriotically inclined than his father and more attuned to the sentiments of his generation. He was immensely brave, both in warfare and in dominating painful afflictions. Yet he wavered on the evils of McCarthyism. Old Joe sat out the war as a shipyard supervisor, but sought manfully, if unsuccessfully, to overcome ghastly illness. Jack escaped the vulgarity of his father and brothers.

Jack came to the White House with limited political or executive experience. He was self-conscious about this lack, and it surely led him to falter dangerously and to equivocate on decisive issues in Cuba and Vietnam.

Both father and son were wedded to remarkable women—and were faithless to them. Each suffered tragedies: Joe lost three sons and a daughter to violence; Jack lost two baby children. Joe worshiped money, the key to success. He boasted when he financed Jack's 1946 congressional campaign: "With what I'm spending, I could elect my chauffeur." Joe used the idea of his ultimate death as a prod to his ambition, seeking early success. Jack told friends: "You've got to live every day like it's your last day."

The president was aware of the ambassador's weaknesses, but also of his own intimate consanguinity. And when I asked him who in his lifetime had most influenced him, he replied without hesitation: "I suppose you could say my father—and the atmosphere he created around all of us as we were growing up." This credo, in summation, meant there is no substitute for winning, by whatever means: climb, and get to the top.

Thus, "Camelot," a lovely myth; the final curtain of the last production. Its conclusion: John F. Kennedy, a delightful president, was not overwhelmed by the job; neither did he overwhelm it. Pushed to power by his father, in a way he was destroyed by his own success.

XIII

Protecting the Princess: Henri and Charles de Gaulle

Charles André Joseph Marie de Gaulle inherited from his father his appearance, his name and ancestry (the name, originally Flemish, implies no nobiliary particule or aristocratic title; the Flemish *de* means "the"), plus the enduring vision of France as the princess in a fairy tale. Opposed during his lifetime by extreme rightists and extreme leftists, he was often denigrated as a "man of the day before yesterday and the day after tomorrow." Few people dare denigrate him today, nearly a quarter century after his death.

He left behind him an enduring legend of grandeur, and he revived the spiritual vigor of the French soul after it had been sullied by defeat and widespread collaboration with the Nazi occupiers. De Gaulle produced greatness in adversity. The name of the myth he created is "France."

I once asked him who, living or dead, had most influenced his long and eventful life. Without hesitation he replied—and in this order—"My father and Marshal Pétain." His father was a "professor" of philosophy and literature at a Jesuit "collège," which, in fact, means a teacher at a Catholic seminary. But his career and reputation were far more significant than that modest description implies.

Henri de Gaulle was an exceedingly cultivated and highly regarded man of no little intellectual distinction. He was sufficiently known in cultured circles so that Henri Bergson, the most respected philosopher of his day, a Nobel laureate renowned for his theory of intuition as the means of apprehending the true nature of things, was a close acquaintance.

Henri de Gaulle's family disapproved of the French Revolution of 1789 and remained loyal to the monarchy and the Catholic Church. Henri himself, although a legitimist, was not active in the monarchist movement.

As a boy, his son Charles adored playing with lead soldiers (like Churchill), and it soon became understood he would seek a military career. This determination was reinforced when the boy read Rostand's *L'Aiglon*, about Napoleon's unhappy son. He was also influenced in many ways by the right-wing chauvinist Charles Maurras and his "Action Française" movement. He developed an anti-British bias when his father rigorously condemned Britain for its aggressor role in the Boer War. However, Henri became a supporter of Dreyfus after that famous case developed.

Charles studied at a Jesuit school in Paris where his father taught until the Jesuits were expelled from France in 1905. He finished his civilian education in another Jesuit school in Belgium and then entered St. Cyr as a military cadet in 1909. Looking back in his *Mémoires*, Charles recalled his father as "thoughtful," "traditional," "cultured," "imbued with a feeling of France's dignity." He added: "He discovered history for me."

As for Philippe Pétain, he commanded Charles de Gaulle's first regiment, the Thirty-third Infantry, and served as the young officer's initial patron. The marshal even agreed to serve as godfather of Philippe de Gaulle, Charles's son, who was named after Pétain. For his part, years later, de Gaulle, who had been sentenced to death *in absentia* by the Vichy government, over which Pétain presided, and whose provisional government after the war in turn sentenced the erect but senile marshal to military degradation and death, subsequently changed to life imprisonment, was hoping to have the old man released during the summer of 1951 when he died, the center of a controversy that has not abated.

De Gaulle respected Pétain's upright personal character and independence of spirit, insisting on his own views of tactics and strategy, despite the opinions of those who commanded him in World War I. Those opinions, of course, differed strikingly from the theories elaborated by the younger officer who was to emerge as France's savior in a subsequent war.

Pétain had taken de Gaulle under his wing after World War I. He encouraged him and named him to his own staff, following de Gaulle's wartime imprisonment by the Germans and after his distinguished service in Poland as a volunteer against the Russian Red Army. While under Pétain's wing, de Gaulle first evolved his unorthodox military views. These conflicted with the French command's Maginot Line complex but were devoured with fascinated approval by Germany's future Blitzkrieg strategists.

His father's precedence on the list of those who influenced him clearly derived, in addition to affection, from the parent's devoted patriotism, his extensive knowledge of French history and culture, and his conservative appreciation of excellence and the old-fashioned virtues. Although the son always addressed the father in letters as *"Mon cher Papa,"* signing his name with "respectful affection," he also always addressed him with the formal plural *"vous"* as was the custom of the time, not the informal singular *"tu."*

It is clear that Henri de Gaulle, like the son in whom he imbued the idea, also tended "to imagine France, like the princess in the fairy tales or the Madonna in the frescoes, as dedicated to an exalted and exceptional destiny." It was through his father's influence that Charles de Gaulle initially concluded that "France is not really herself unless she is in the front rank," that "France cannot be France without greatness."

This was the intuitive side of Bergson's teaching; and as the philosopher urged, it had to be supplemented by action. Such action was the essence of de Gaulle's career. To achieve his goal he was always on guard against what he discerned as "the natural propensity of the French to yield to foreigners and become divided," as in World War II.

On rare occasions someone arrives on the historical horizon who can make something out of nothing. Such a man was Charles de Gaulle. From the first, he knew he was capable of great achievement and prepared for a summons to demonstrate this talent. He somehow suspected it would be his role to act as savior for his country's honor. He was not a man with evident human warmth, but he proved equally able to muster individual and passionate emotions to awaken his people as, for example, both President Roosevelt and Winston Churchill did theirs.

His was an apparently cool and distant personality. One of his military instructors said of him as a young man: "He always behaved like a king in exile." Later it was quipped that he adored France but disliked the French.

The only single human for whom he is known to have shown exceptional visible tenderness was his retarded daughter, Anne. He had a special heartbreaking bond with the little girl. Had he, like Churchill, been a man capable of tears, he would have manifested them for Anne; but he was not a sentimentalist. Nevertheless, when she finally died in 1948 after a tragic little life, aged twenty, and was laid to rest in the tiny village graveyard of Colombey-les-deux-Églises, where the de Gaulles made their home, the general grasped his wife's hand by the graveside as the last shovelful of earth covered the coffin and, turning slowly away, said to Madame de Gaulle: "Come, now she is like the others."

He also—and of course this is in no sense comparable—liked dogs. For years he had a large Alsatian who would come into his bedroom each night as he and his wife retired. *"Ah, non, Charles,"* Madame de Gaulle would say. *"Pas cette nuit."* *"Mais non, chèrie,"* came the deep-voiced reply. Then, as the lights were extinguished, the faithful animal jumped on the bed to sleep at the general's feet.

Once, driving back from Germany to Paris with my beagle, Christopher, I stopped at Colombey, now a national monument, and the two of us scrambled around the hill behind de Gaulle's large and somber mansion. Nobody objected, and I am sure the general would have approved as the little fellow sniffed and scurried about this hallowed ground.

Also, although I was unable to explain this to my companion or to his kinsman and predecessor, Benjamin, I hope they were delighted that the man assigned by the State Department in Washington to read, analyze, and interpret my columns on the general was named Biegle, pronounced "Beagle." I met him long after de Gaulle had left this life and the diplomat's assignment had changed.

André Malraux, ministerial colleague and friend of the general (and, I am proud to say, myself), had a strange theory that mankind could be divided into two basic groups: those who loved dogs and wood, and those who preferred cats and iron. He classified himself among the latter, although I have often seen my dogs go wild with delight greeting him. He placed de Gaulle in the former group, not only because of his Alsatian but also because the general spent so much of his retirement sitting among the trees of his Colombey retreat and watching the foresters hewing and sawing as he pondered. The primordial subject he contemplated, I venture, was France, the fairy princess, a princess he had reawakened like Sleeping Beauty.

At the time of de Gaulle's birth in 1890, Pétain was a little known young officer, Professor Henri de Gaulle was a little known monarchist and rather right-wing Catholic teacher, and Bergson was a youthful aspirant philosopher hoping shortly to teach at Paris's famous École Normale Supérieure.

From his father, Charles learned history, patriotism, and a moral code of honor as well as his concept of *grandeur* as essential to France. Had his father possessed a similar literary talent (Charles was possibly the best French prose writer of this century), he too might have penned these words: "The emotional side of me tends to imagine France . . . as dedicated to an exalted and exceptional destiny."

Charles—one of five children—was reared in a devout, conservative, and highly patriotic atmosphere, strongly influenced by the classics: fifth-century B.C. Greek, early Roman, seventeenth-century French. A close adviser later was to describe his formation as "primarily Greek—but in a Roman envelope." When he was a prisoner of war in the German officers' reprisal camp of Ingolstadt, de Gaulle did an immense amount of studious reading and kept notes on what struck him, including this quote from Virgil: "Roman, do not forget to lead the people with authority."

Once, the general told me he especially admired Corneille, Racine, and Bossuet, all of whom possessed "grandeur." *"Ça c'est toujours mon goût."* And, he added: "Shakespeare. What grandeur. What power." He also liked Rostand and was called "Cyrano" by schoolmates because of his prominent nose.

He admired Bergson greatly. "I have always admired *les gens efficaces* (effective people). Like our history. Clovis. Charlemagne. Joan of Arc. Charles VII. Henri IV. The real statesmen, the people who accomplished something."

Once, when I brought up the subject of Bergson whose theories were to have a profound influence on de Gaulle's actions, he said:

> I was much influenced by Bergson, particularly because he made me understand the philosophy of action.
>
> Bergson explains the role of intelligence and analysis. He saw how necessary it is to analyse questions in search of the truth. But intellect alone cannot act. The intelligent man does not automatically become the man of action. Instinct is also important—instinct plus impulse. But impulse is also not sufficient as a basis for action. The two, intellect and impulse, must go together.
>
> Bergson showed me that action comes from the combination, the combined application of intellect and instinct, working together. All my life I have been aware of this essentially important explanation. Pure intellect cannot by itself produce action, and impulse can produce folly if it alone serves as a guide, whether in politics or in military affairs.
>
> The two must be linked, and this is Bergson's theory of intuition. The great men have both intellect and impulse. The brain serves as a brake upon pure emotional impulse; but also there must be such impulse and the capability for action in order not to be paralyzed by the brake of the brain. I remember this from Bergson, who has led me in this field during my entire life.
>
> But surely you will agree with me that philosophy has never changed anyone. Men are still what they are. Philosophy helps them to express themselves better and to understand each other better, but no man has ever been created a philosopher.

De Gaulle actually boasted to me (in 1957) that he had already twice staged *"coups d'état"*—declaring himself the chief of French resistence in 1940, and the "establishment" of his own "government" in Paris in 1944. He was thus prepared, when circumstances were ripe, to stage a third—which he, of course, did with clever obliqueness, in 1958. Moreover, de Gaulle was always, throughout his life, accused of having an authoritarian manner, although he was certainly no dictator.

He reproached the French general staff of 1914 "for not being Bergsonian enough" (a rare complaint in an officer's mess: one is more customarily used to thinking of the intellectual salon influence of Bergson on Marcel Proust). De Gaulle, politically and philosophically, seemed to most people more a conservative, Jansenist, family man whose cultural ideas were mostly those of his father as shown by his preference for conventional painting, music, and literature, with heavy emphasis on the great *French* creative artists. He had a special fondness for the Romantic composers, who reacted to the Napoleonic wars. "I crave music," he told me.

Athough he was a military officer—the usual profession, besides the clergy, open to a moneyless young conservative in the France of his youth—he always insisted that the military be subject to civilian control and also that "the army in France has never been a political force." He argued that the French Army did not stage successful coups itself; it merely followed a leader. "Even Bonaparte, when he made his coup, made it himself because the country wanted a *coup d'état*." But in 1958, guided by the Bergsonian mixture of intuition and decision, de Gaulle knew well how to use the army for political purposes, while keeping it subject to the state. He returned to power on the backs of insurgent generals whom he later crushed.

He liked his advance to be disguised by indirection: the old Descartes formula, *Larvatus prodeo* ("Masked, follow"). And once restored to authority, he behaved as a benevolent despot, governing firmly by indirection but summoning public support for questioned policies by means of brilliant oratory and use of television. After one of his remarkable discourses, a friend of mine on the Central Committee of the French Communist Party (which hated de Gaulle) said to me: "Nobody in France has made a speech like that since Louis XIV."

I was asked, as I have written earlier, to prepare a secret memorandum on de Gaulle for President Kennedy's 1961 Paris visit. In this I wrote: "I am impressed by de Gaulle as a powerful personality and as a major and fascinating historical figure. But he is largely black and white by coloration. Many of his conceptions are, I believe, either false, outdated or premature."

He believed as much as Hitler (in his evil way) in the leadership principle and that France could only achieve its destiny by disaster and chaos mastered by a dominant individual Frenchman with the ability to discern what was needed and how to achieve it. "We must have some chaos first," he told me prior to his own return in 1958. "Blood? There is always a little blood. *Hélas, que faire?*" And in the army de Gaulle preached: "The will of the leader is the center . . . from which everything branches."

All this reflects how much de Gaulle was influenced by the stew of a conservative, patriotic, intellectual bourgeois mixture, represented by his father, and by the need to recognize how to act and what to do, advocated by Henri de Gaulle's acquaintance, Bergson.

Charles de Gaulle, an immensely tall (six feet four) haughty-looking Frenchman with elongated features, disdainful of his colleagues and endowed with what André Malraux called "geological courage" (he was wholly without fear), had a splendid record in World War I, being wounded three times and finally being taken prisoner while unconscious from a wound. But he was unpopular with many of his fellows. At the superior staff college, he had already earned the reputation of haughtiness.

During World War I de Gaulle served under the renowned Pétain who, he wrote: "taught the art and meaning of command." He was awarded the Legion of Honor and was also decorated for bravery with a lavish citation. Subsequently, he volunteered to help the Poles as a major in their war against the Soviets and received their highest award for courage, *Virtuti Militari.*

He had learned from Pétain the value of independent thought despite the opinion of superior officers (Pétain believed in heavy artillery bombardment, not simple mass infantry attacks like the World War I general staff). De Gaulle evolved his own idea of a professional army limited in size, magnificently trained, and equipped with large, independent formations of tanks. There, he and Pétain parted company. However, he remained Pétain's admirer.

But then a publisher asked de Gaulle for a book, and he provided one based on historical studies of the French soldier he had made while serving in 1925 on Pétain's staff. He wrote the marshal asking permission to use this material. Pétain demurred unless de Gaulle made clear in a dedication that his superior had been the stimulator of the work. De Gaulle refused, and the two men broke—for good. In 1932 the two great influences departed from his life: Henri de Gaulle, his father, died; and Philippe Pétain brought on a split through the folly of his arrogant vanity.

Yet Pétain was respected by his maverick colt until the end, as shown in de Gaulle's statement about the marshal's influence upon him. Militarily, while his strategic theories had diverged from those of Pétain, just as the latter's had broken with the French staff of World War I, he always agreed with the marshal on the philosophy of an economy of means or, as Napoleon's Marshal Auguste Marmont said: One does not go to war to get killed; one goes to conquer the enemy." And just before retiring from the army in 1931, Pétain forgot his rancor sufficiently to transfer de Gaulle from a station in the Levant to the secretariat of the Superior War Council.

World War II was disastrous for de Gaulle in a variety of personal ways. He saw his beloved country crushed primarily because its strategists had ignored the theories of armored conflict he had evolved and which were well known to and ardently studied by Heinz Guderian and Erwin Rommel, Hitler's greatest experts in tank warfare.

And within no time he found himself in London, cut off from his homeland and family by the Nazi victory following the Dunkirk evacuation to England. After Poland's defeat in 1939, he had told a group of British M.P.s: "Gentlemen, this war is lost, so we must prepare for and win another war: with machines."

On June 7, 1940, right after Dunkirk, Prime Minister Paul Reynaud, who had come earlier to support de Gaulle, dispatched him to England as a young undersecretary of defense with the military rank of brigadier general. He was assigned to ask Churchill to reequip French troops brought across the channel and then repatriate them. On June 15, after Reynaud and his last-gasp government had retreated to Bordeaux, he sent de Gaulle back to London to ask for British ships and planes to shift the French leadership to North Africa.

Churchill's response was to suggest an idea elaborated by de Gaulle and Jean Monnet for a British-French union. France's leaders spurned it. Reynaud's cabinet ousted him, called back Pétain from Madrid, where he was ambassador, and surrendered.

On June 18 de Gaulle, in London, called upon all Frenchmen to continue resisting the occupiers and, in what he later called his first *"coup d'état,"* constituted himself as the leader of a free French movement. It is from this moment on that "the General," as he was soon widely known, began his life as a significant historical figure.

The story of de Gaulle's stiff-necked leadership of what was, at first, so insignificant a force that it gained no diplomatic recognition is well-known to contemporary readers and does not bear retelling. Although both Churchill and Anthony Eden admired and respected the general, they resented his overbearing manner and his lack of discretion. Such resentment was repaid with Free French bitterness at the British naval shelling of France's still-neutral naval squadron in Algeria and subsequently by the rebuff administered to de Gaulle (who was present at a second sea battle) through his unlucky flotilla at Dakar, Senegal.

By 1942 de Gaulle had so enraged the Americans, at war with the Axis since Pearl Harbor, that they would have nothing to do with him. President Roosevelt wrote Churchill: "When we go into France we are going to have to consider it as a military occupation," not, by implication, as a liberation. He described de Gaulle as being the "victim of a Messiah complex."

The general had managed to have his family evacuated to England. He was personally always grateful for the hospitality and support of a large number of Britons, despite his quarrels with their leadership. And, although many of these disputes were merited—like the failure to tell de Gaulle of the North African invasion and then the Normandy landings until the very last instant, because of lax Gaullist security—he was unjust in his attitude.

Churchill was to stand up for him manfully at the Yalta conference and later. But de Gaulle was always at his strongest and bitterest when he was in a weak position, although few of those he had to deal with realized this or appreciated the psychological reasons.

Once he had managed to touch the soil of France, a few days after the first Anglo-American formations scrambled ashore, de Gaulle brushed aside the puzzled English-speaking administrative officials named by Washington, and designated his own, patriotic (meaning Gaullist) prefects. He obtained Eisenhower's pledge that Paris would be liberated by the Free French armored division of General Leclerc, and then staged his second *"coup de'état"* by announcing in the capital's town hall: "The Republic has never ceased to exist. Vichy [Pétain's collaborationist régime] was always null and void. . . . I myself am president of the government of the Republic. Why should I go out and proclaim it?"

By making himself a persistent, single-minded nuisance and by reminding the world of France's past and present existence, de Gaulle succeeded in winning Churchill's staunch support for a truly important French role in future Europe. Otherwise, the British prime minister could see nothing to counterbalance a resurgent Germany in the West. The Americans were reminded that although they had been the arsenal of democracy in the Second World War, France had been an arsenal for U.S. troops in the First—and had also bled a great deal more.

It is on the postwar actions of France and the subtle policies and stratagems of de Gaulle that I propose to concentrate. From the San Francisco meeting where the United Nations was formed and where France played its part, gaining an eventual permanent seat on the Security Council, the French began the march toward their present position.

France is not a superpower; there are but two. But today it is one of the recognized nuclear-military powers. France is a strong figure in the European Community, whose Common Agricultural Policy, designed to suit the French farm vote, serves as a basis for one of the community's main economic commitments. It is a major diplomatic influence on all inhabited continents, save Australia, and has reestablished a cultural and educational position on the level to which the French have been accustomed for generations.

Whether he or she has been, is, or will be a Gaullist (the general's own analysis applied this formulation), de Gaulle's vision for a French citizen has materialized to a degree far beyond the conception of most French people two generations ago. De Gaulle, who considered himself France's caretaker when he didn't confound himself with France itself, always had his keen intellect simultaneously focused on three periods at once—the present, the immediate future, the long-term future—while talking poetically about another period, the past.

He was the opposite of that elegant Socialist premier Léon Blum, of whom it was said: "He knew where he was going but did not know how to get there." The general always knew how to get there—even if, on occasion, it took a long time—but not (as with Algeria) necessarily where he was going. In Algeria, he wanted simply the best deal possible for Paris.

For the immediate present, the first tasks were to reestablish stability, economic productivity, and international recognition for France. He managed this, including the ultimate extrication of Paris from all but vestigial colonial positions, by the device of twice resigning his post as chief of state, despite the fact that his enemies called him a "dictator." Dictators don't resign; they are pushed or they are murdered.

For the short-term future, he insisted on playing off one country against another, on using France's gradually increasing importance for its nuisance value. He recognized early that the United States (even more than Britain) opposed the idea of admitting France to a three-power NATO "security council," since this might offend the Germans and Italians.

So he developed France's own nuclear force, despite U.S. efforts to discourage such moves by refusing all help, although it had already given a great deal to Britain. De Gaulle realized that possession of such a small but extremely efficient force would assure French qualifications as a permanent U.N. Council member and would also make France militarily stronger than West Germany while maintaining a smaller, and above all less costly, armed establishment.

The general saw from the start that, while it was highly unlikely such a "force de dissuasion" would ever be used against an enemy, such as Russia, it could be used diplomatically against allied nations. It contained the threat of selling warheads or techniques to Third World countries bent on conquering their neighbors despite Anglo-American pleas that they calm down.

The very long-term Gaullist vision of France is not yet clear—to me, at any rate. But the general certainly had a striking perception of the dramatic and symbolic role he could carve out for himself in history as it will be remembered a century hence. When he wrote his *Mémoires* (in his own handwriting—and no ghosts allowed), he would invariably copy out the original, sloppily corrected version with his pen to prepare a neat and impressive "original manuscript for history" (as did Dumas *Père*, who thrived on ghosts).

He disliked the press, knowing its greed for unintended impressions, although, as one of his closest collaborators noted, he was once a journalist himself (writing newspaper articles on military and political affairs for various Parisian journals). He was determined to dramatize his exceedingly dramatic personality.

He personally thought, as he confided to me, that after the victorious struggle to refurbish the worn French soul, almost destroyed by war, his greatest achievements had been to give his country a new constitutional stability and to push it from its traditional agrarian base into a modern industrial and technological society. He commented:

> Until now industrialization has not been France's avocation, but from now on it must increasingly be so. This is quite evident because this is an industrial epoch. We have done much, we have advanced perceptibly, but not by any means enough, and we must proceed in this direction and accomplish such a change in depth.
>
> France's population and above all France's youth are most interested and preoccupied with this question. The youth especially insists upon this movement. But it will not be excessive; France will not exceed in this direction. France is a country with social and economic traditions and traits that never tend to excess. Furthermore, we lack many raw materials. And our population is not too dense. As a consequence, there is no pressure urging toward excessive industrialization. We are fortunate in this respect.

The essence of the general's foreign policy, as it developed together with French recovery, was the concept of total independence from any other national system or ideology, a concept that appeals to many Cartesian French minds not particularly given to compromise. He explained his view to me accordingly:

> We are not anti-American. But you must remember that you are a big people, a colossal power. You have a huge industry, a gigantic economy and military force which give you enormous political strength, the greatest in the world. Inevitably a country like France, wanting its own independence, doesn't want to be dominated, led by, or integrated into your system. But this does not make us hostile to you; not at all. We are simply taking precautions to avoid being absorbed because you are so especially powerful.
>
> Perforce a country like France must be on the alert to preserve its own personality. But the same thing is true vis-à-vis the Soviets. Without the United States—or with a less mighty United States—we would have to be very much on the alert against the Soviets. Indeed, we are on the alert vis-à-vis the Soviets, and we do not wish to be absorbed by them. We are for an equilibrium. We are obliged to be for an equilibrium by the simple geographical and political facts. We oppose any hegemony, either American or Russian. But this does not prevent friendship.

The last time I visited the Elysée Palace to see the general was February 14, 1969, two months before he retired. He resigned April 28. He said that because there was a new U.S. administration (Nixon's) it would be easier to improve Franco-American relationships. He continued:

> For us the principal question between our countries was NATO. Now that is all over. It is no longer a subject for discussion as far as we are concerned. There is no NATO for us French [meaning, no alliance *Organization*], so there is no reason to have a problem on this with Washington. Then there was Vietnam. But President Johnson started negotiations while he was still in office. The negotiations are bound to go on for a very long time. That is inevitable. But it has started and, in the end, it will lead to peace.
>
> There is no reason for major differences between us now. Our problems are on the road to regulation. Of course, there is the question of the Middle East. We have not been in accord with

you on this since 1967 [the Six-day War]. But you should remember that this is merely a reverse of the previous situation.

"With the Fourth Republic, there was also disagreement. You were against France and Israel in 1956, at the time of the Suez invasion, for reasons that are just the contrary of our differences now. Now the United States is with Israel, which wishes to take the Suez Canal. The United States has changed its policy—and so has France. In 1956 the Fourth Republic backed Israel. But the Fifth Republic doesn't want Israel to exaggerate.

And there is another aspect to the whole problem—namely relationships with Russia. Little by little, you are becoming more like us in your view of this problem. Like us, you don't want to have them submerge Europe. But you are beginning to see that it is useful to develop practical contacts such as those we started. You will follow the same path that we have been following because it is the practical approach. . . . After all, nobody thinks the Russians will move West any more, do they? . . .

And you should remember that we have old reasons for being friends of Russia. For us, in Europe, this Russian friendship has always been necessary as a counterweight to Germany. Constantly in history, we have sought to be on good terms with Russia, with the czars, with the Soviets, as a counterweight to Germany. We have been old friends with America and old allies of Russia. And the Franco-Russian feeling is a natural event. Today we have no reason to renounce friendship with the United States. Neither, especially now that Germany is reemerging, have we any reason to break off with Russia. . . .

France is as it is and the French are as they are. If the French don't think of France, it disappears. But you cannot think of France if you lose a sense of independence. The friendship of the United States requires no American hegemony. The same is true with Russia. It is for that reason that the Communists have never succeeded here: for national reasons, not for social reasons.

Germany's history is not the same as that of France. The Germans are readier to accept a United States hegemony—and anyway they can't avoid it. As for Britain, Britain has renounced its independence. It has sold it off for advantages of all sorts. And Italy counts for little. It knows less than one century as a united, independent country.

The general thought American troops should remain stationed in Europe "until there is a real East-West *détente*. . . . The fact that you have troops in Germany now doesn't irritate us; so have we." De Gaulle foresaw that if Germany ever became militarily strong and "a danger" (above all "in a nuclear sense"), "then we would have an alliance" again with Russia. "Neither of us can accept a dangerous Germany."

He predicted—more than a decade before the event: "If Israel were to attack Lebanon, we would not let it fall. We would take action." De Gaulle liked to imagine alternative policies for the unforeseeable future, devised to face potential situations. Thus, he always contemplated the ultimate role of China, which he foresaw as a huge superpower in a few decades. In the 1950s, when he was an exile prior to his 1958 coup and return to power, he was visited by Sergei Vinogradov, the Soviet ambassador. "I know why you have come," said the general. "You do?" said Vinogradov, puzzled. "Why?" "Because you are afraid of China," answered de Gaulle.

A man of impeccable manners, except when he wished to be rude, of unflinching courage, which never permitted him to duck a bombardment or a hail of bullets, who was an exquisite master of his beloved French language, both as an orator and as a writer, he created a historical image of an individual who could only be French and was modeled on no identifiable predecessor. He used unusual and strange words like "*quarteron*" and "*chie-en-lit*" to express his moods, but, like those of James Joyce in English, these were real if rare words, not invented like Lewis Carroll's.

As he sought grandeur for France, he sought glory for himself. And, as the German Rainer Maria Rilke wrote, "*La gloire est la somme des malentendus qui se forment autour d'un nom.*" The misunderstandings that whirled about de Gaulle's name during his lifetime (and still today) are manifold. Whatever the truth, his existence marked France forever. His ablation from French policy-making changed his motherland's destiny as much as his intrusion, I believe; but this must yet be proven by events.

De Gaulle made it clear that he felt superior to all Frenchmen (except possibly his culture minister, André Malraux, who was a good enough writer *not* to be a member of the French Academy) and most foreigners (save for chiefs of state or government). His views about humanity were often sardonic. When one of the English aides of General Billotte, de Gaulle's wartime chief of staff, was caught sleeping with an M.P.'s wife, the general ordered his staff chief to discharge the aide. "Why? He's a nice fellow and does his job." "Obviously he's a fool. He shouldn't have been stupid enough to be caught in bed. Fire him."

Incidentally, one aspect of de Gaulle unknown to the public was his own love life. On the whole, most restrained for a Frenchman, when he sought to play the gallant in his youth, it was, according to a man he knew for years, "in the heavy cavalry fashion." During the war, a general under whom de Gaulle had served as a junior in the Levant, before the conflict, escaped to Algiers, then under Gaullist control. He was accompanied by his wife, who had once briefly been de Gaulle's mistress. De Gaulle politely asked the couple to dine the night of their arrival, and then dispatched the pair to Beirut the very next day.

He had many rows with Roosevelt, who disliked and mistrusted him in an exaggerated way, largely because F.D.R.'s "man in Vichy," Admiral William Leahy, in whom the president had great faith, was close to Pétain. Yet de Gaulle respected Roosevelt, admired his political sense, and later studied his personal propaganda techniques.

Incidentally, F.D.R. sneered that the general considered himself another Joan of Arc, while Churchill complained that the heaviest cross he bore was that of Lorraine, symbol of the Gaullist movement.

However, Eisenhower, who had plenty of troubles with de Gaulle, told me he understood and sympathized with the general. He acknowledged that Roosevelt had mistreated de Gaulle, hadn't understood his pride or his determination "to represent the noble things in France." Adenauer said he thought de Gaulle's twelve-year exile from politics at his home in Colombey-les-deux-Églises had "done him immense good and now he is the ablest statesman in the West."

De Gaulle often showed a strangely paradoxical way of speaking on delicate subjects, although he normally had an almost sensual desire to articulate and hear well-phrased sentences. I once asked him what France thought of the United States, and he replied: "There is no hate for America in France. But the French people don't like the American people. The United States is our friend and will remain so; but the American people are not regarded sympathetically. The United States will remain our friend in moments of great danger."

I am not sure what he meant here by the distinction between the people and state. Personally, I have met with nothing but friendship during the more than forty years I have been based in France. But the general undoubtedly resented the fact that the United States (not France) had become the greatest power in the West. He also suspected a kind of invisible

Anglo-American conspiracy to keep France from recovering its prestige. He even thought President Truman had labored to create a "third force" in France to prevent his own return to power after he first resigned in 1946. (I am not sure de Gaulle was wrong about this.)

Although he wished to make friends with West Germany—he had a particularly close relationship with Adenauer—and favored tying the Federal Republic firmly to the Occidental camp, he also wanted to give France a military advantage—despite the larger number of German divisions—through a rapidly growing, small, French nuclear deterrent (this was called by the entire world, de Gaulle himself excepted, the *force de frappe*).

De Gaulle professed himself as favoring the Common Market, although he didn't show any public enthusiasm for it and although he opposed British membership, claiming that Britain wasn't really part of "Europe" but was an offshore island tied to the United States. As late as December 1966 he told me: "I don't think Britain can qualify to come into the market." And he had no use at all for the United Nations, which he sometimes referred to as "a gimmick" and also an "augmented Babel." He had no strong feeling about whether Communist China should be admitted to the United Nations (before France recognized Peking) because "this would merely add another hostile voice to insult the West."

The methodology of de Gaulle's foreign policy was intellectually and philosophically based upon a cynical but possibly very sound realpolitik: (1) France must remain among the forefront of nations; (2) relations between states, whether allied or not, are based only on power and guile (the first of which he sought, the second of which he amply possessed); (3) ideologies are of relatively small importance; the only true forces confronting each other in the international arena were the individual nations. When the astute Maurice Couve de Murville spoke of "states that are friends of France" at a cabinet meeting, the general interrupted: "The minister of foreign affairs [should know] that a State worthy of the name has no friends."

Personally I think the general regarded himself as the benevolent custodian of democracy in France, although his adversaries called him authoritarian. While he displayed contempt for French Communists as "foreign agents," he privately showed more dislike for the extreme right than for the noncommunist left. An aspect of his personal impact on foreign affairs was evident in the French game played with the Soviet Union. Whenever there was a French election, de Gaulle went out of his way to visit Moscow or to invite some Soviet dignitary to Paris, thus outflanking the French Communist Party in public opinion. Yet he was far from pro-Soviet, only seeking when possible to make use of the Kremlin for his own purposes, a very venturesome and dangerous gamble.

He occasionally referred to "Europe" as extending from "the Atlantic to the Urals." When it was pointed out to him that much more of the Soviet land area lay east of the Urals than west of the range, he told me:

> I recognize that this phrase irritates the Russians, but that is their affair, not mine. The real Russia stops at the Urals.
>
> All the rest—Turkistan, Siberia, parts of Mongolia—these are all colonies, colonies colonized by the Russians. And probably, almost surely, they will become a part of China. China has seven hundred milion people [this was 1965]. It is not a great power today, but in twenty years it will be a great power and in fifty years it will be an enormous power.
>
> The Russians know this well—and so do the Chinese. This is the inner basis of their quarrel. Of course, being Communists, they always put everything on an ideological basis. But the truth is the opposition between Russia and China has national origins.

With respect to the Communist giants, André Malraux told me that, regardless of what he said for political effect at given moments, de Gaulle had no intention of shifting France's alliances or making any deal with Moscow because "he is not an idiot."

Of France's traditional enemy, Germany, de Gaulle said to me in December 1966: "Don't forget, German unity is never *necessary*." He stressed the last word. He added that France, which had withdrawn from NATO's military command and expelled NATO's political and military headquarters, would nevertheless "remain in the alliance. We will not denounce the treaty."

I wrote a note to myself about this particular conversation: "I confess when summing up that, all in all, despite his tantalizing maneuvers with the various Communist nations, he strikes me as very much a man of the West, suspicious of the Communists and perhaps a bit inclined to look down on them, and wedded to Richelieu's old basic rule of French foreign policy: "Keep Germany divided; also, beware of the English.' "

The one essential change in de Gaulle's policy—and that of subsequent governments—resulted from the spurning by Washington and London of the general's idea, proposed in 1958 in letters to President Eisenhower and Prime Minister Harold Macmillan, of a three-power NATO directorate to decide on policy in critical areas outside the area defined as within the North Atlantic Treaty but nevertheless of vital concern to the West.

I have no doubt that the 1962 Cuban crisis—during which de Gaulle staunchly and faithfully supported the United States against Soviet threats—stimulated the consequent loosening of French bonds with NATO. De Gaulle immediately saw there was a danger that members of the alliance, including France, could be drawn into wars in Africa, Asia, and Latin America if they remained full, "integrated" members of an organization clearly dominated by the United States. When Eisenhower and Macmillan turned down his directorate idea, thus giving France no voice in decisions involving non-NATO areas, he resolved to extricate himself from too close an automatic bond, while reserving all French rights to NATO protection in case of a Soviet attack in Europe.

This reaction had undoubtedly begun simmering in de Gaulle's brain after he found his allies unwilling even to pretend France was a leading power. He was not reassured as a privileged ally, although he gained great prestige from the U.S. administration by saying to Dean Acheson, President Kennedy's special envoy sent to show him the U-2 reconnaissance pictures of Soviet missiles: "Why bother? I don't need to see them. If you and the president tell me this is so, that is enough for France."

Thereafter de Gaulle basked for a time in a position of special honor, but concluded the Americans would not risk the worst to protect their own security. He wondered if they would do so for each of their allies. The question boiled down to: will Washington trade Boston for Hamburg, or Chicago for Lyon? And to his skeptical mind, the answer was negative.

He assured me: "There are only three real powers in the West today [inferentially excluding West Germany]; each has a certain amount of atomic force. These three powers are charged with the defense and security of the West; one must work through them." He hinted very plainly that if this view were not heeded by America and Britain, France's support for NATO would be reduced.

What he said as early as January 20, 1962 (before the Cuban crisis but after his Eisenhower-Macmillan letters), was: "If our wish in this matter is not granted, we will no longer support the *Organization*." He didn't refer to the actual pact. He would take the "O" out of NATO, as far as France was concerned. He did. "We will only be an ally—and fully independent."

He also said he was certain the United States would never offer France aid in developing its nuclear weapons—nor would he do so were he in Washington's position. And he was pleased. France could go its own way and benefit industrially from its own scientific fallout. "We really would not save very much money if such aid were offered—even unconditionally."

De Gaulle believed in détente, but far from blindly. He said:

> After Truman said no to MacArthur's proposal in Korea to attack China, major war was excluded. The English want business with Russia. The French want an arrangement in Indochina. The United States wants export markets. These are the imponderables that make for a modus vivendi. This is not entente or détente; it is armed peace.
>
> Communism is finished. They have lost faith in themselves. They still, of course, call themselves Communists, but it is no longer the same thing. The bureaucracy in the Russian administration is made up of Communists; but they have no faith in their movement. They saw that they could not conquer Poland. They saw that they could not conquer Hungary—morally, I mean. Therefore they realize that they have lost their dynamism. They can no longer dream of conquering Italy. They cannot even hold what they have.

These analyses, uttered a generation ago, may have vanished during the present age of brand new weaponry and enormous Soviet naval power. But certainly some of de Gaulle's views are still logical. He said: "There *can* someday be a real cooperation between Russia and the West. And, indeed, there must be; otherwise there must be war. You cannot have a cold war for an indefinite period." He added: "I suppose that some day, in the vague future, we can imagine concord among the white people."

I have always been perplexed by the racism implied in these and similar phrases the general used in conversations with me. After all, some of his earliest political supporters, when he led a tiny movement in Britain, were African chiefs of state, such as the Ivory Coast's Houphouet-Boigny and Senegal's Léopold Senghor. And he brought peace to Algeria and the withdrawal of a large and bitter white colonial minority to France. Moreover, it was de Gaulle who abruptly switched French policy from strong support of Israel (including help on its atomic weapons projects) to vigorous backing of the Arabs.

He was a practictioner of realpolitik, moved by neither emotion nor sentiment. He saw that the Arabs were far more numerous and, thanks to their oil, far richer than the Jews of Israel. Yet he remarked sardonically to me:

Who are the Arabs? The Arabs are a people who, since the days of Mohammed, have never constituted a state successfully. Mohammed made a state because of Islam. After him there has been nothing but anarchy. Have you ever seen a dam built by the Arabs? Nowhere. It doesn't exist; it has never been seen anywhere. It has been like that for centuries.

The Arabs say that they invented algebra and built huge mosques. But this was entirely the job of Christian slaves they captured [a strange distortion of fact]. It was not the Arabs themselves. We French tried to do much for them. And the Russians before us tried. But they can't do anything alone."

This is a weird hodgepodge of wisdom, absurdity, and misstatement. No wonder de Gaulle, during his lifetime, was regarded in strikingly different ways by those who supported him, opposed him, or were disappointed by him. However, even when Israel was furious at the way he changed what had been a most favorable French policy, David Ben Gurion, the founding father, remained true to him and even insisted on going to his funeral.

In France, the extreme Right called him a Communist and the extreme Left called him a dictator. He disdainfully played both extremes off against each other. He was seen as ruthless by those he smashed, guileful by those he deceived, and disloyal by those who expected a reward for their fidelity.

He is the one statesman with whom I have talked who could easily and accurately quote Sophocles or Goethe or Charles Péguy during the course of a routine chat. However, his views of mankind as a whole were uncomplimentary.

There were few people he considered outstanding. These included Stalin, Churchill, and Roosevelt, but not Eisenhower, although he liked him. "Stalin," he said, "was certainly a big man. Of course he tried to be affable and almost charming. But even that was merely an exterior. And sometimes he didn't show that at all. He was a tyrant, a real czar. He controlled everything. He had absolute authority and absolute confidence. He did everything himself. Yes, there is no doubt he was a great man."

But, he added: "Giants can do nothing now. Churchill and Roosevelt are dead. Stalin died—too late." He thought the vanishing of giants from the political scene indicated a genuine relaxation in the world situation because it was only during times of crisis that nations "throw up giants. They don't come in normal times." A glance at today's political horizon, following this theory, would imply that these times are more "normal" than we suspect.

Returning to his favorite scene—the abnormal world of giants—he noted: "Stalin . . . did something. He was a brutal man, but he created a modern state. Churchill was a great man, although, as you know so well, I had many differences with him. And Roosevelt led the United States into war and through the war on to victory. He was a man of quality." He assessed Khrushchev after his visit to Paris: "Sophocles said that one must wait until the evening to see how splendid the day was; that one cannot judge life until death. To be a great man one must realize something. One must achieve something definite." Khrushchev was then still very much alive.

The policy of the U.S. government was consistent in its dislike of de Gaulle—from Roosevelt, during the war, until Kennedy, who broke the ice with his 1961 Paris visit and who had what was especially in the general's eyes a great asset: a charming wife who spoke fluent French.

In 1960, while Eisenhower was still president, the French security services became convinced that America was backing, in the words of his former prime minister and eventual successor, Georges Pompidou, "a very serious plot" to oust de Gaulle. The ex-premier told me he had persuasive information that this scheme aimed at replacing the general as president with Antoine Pinay, a former prime minister who was backed by Georges Bidault, another ex-premier who had split with the general over the Algerian question.

Pompidou said that Alain de Sérigny, an Algerian-French editor and political leader (who conspired with Roosevelt's chief agent in North Africa, Bob Murphy, to help neutralize opposition to the 1942 landings in North Africa), was playing a major role in the conspiracy backed with American money and political leaders. I told this to our ambassador, Amory Houghton, who blanched. "My God," he said to me, "I had a perfectly innocuous letter from Sérigny and replied just two days ago." "Well, there's some more evidence for them," I said mischievously. "Their spooks certainly read it."

Houghton frantically begged me to arrange a very private lunch with Pompidou and to act as interpreter (neither man spoke the other's language); the ambassador didn't even trust anyone on his own staff. I did the job. It was a bland, friendly lunch, and Pompidou seemed to believe all Houghton's assurances. At least the plot never occurred.

There is no doubt the French remained suspicious of America. Kissinger's first book, which said no country could afford to start a nuclear war except in defense of its own particular territory, simply added to de Gaulle's suspicion about American unwillingness in a test to risk trading New York or Washington for Paris.

More than once de Gaulle told me he didn't think "any real entente is possible between the East and West as things are." However, he added:

> But I think for a certain time each can co-exist with the other and trade with the other. Neither Russia nor the United States wants to make war now. As a result, the cold war has become insupportable. It costs too much. It weighs on the budget, business, and the spirit.
>
> A cold war cannot be continued if nobody wants it to lead to a hot war. There must be a modus vivendi even if nothing is signed. It will provide for more exchanges—tourists, students, athletes, and goods; and it can last a long time, A modus vivendi: this is not an entente; it is aimed at peace.

Shortly before he resigned as president for the second time and retired to Colombey, I asked de Gaulle if the tremendous spectacle of Winston Churchill's funeral, which he had of course attended, had incited him to make similar plans for himself. Churchill had prescribed every detail of his final ceremony.

"No," the general answered. "It is indeed important and I have thought about it a good deal. But my funeral will be the opposite of Churchill's. There will be no spectacle. There will be no spectacle for de Gaulle," he concluded lugubriously. This, as he no doubt foresaw, could not be and was not the case. There was a simple interment in Colombey but a magnificent commemoration in Notre Dame Cathedral, and almost every important leader in the world fought for a place in the audience's serried ranks.

De Gaulle's death changed the French political picture. He had been losing authority, and it was evident there would be no chance of his influencing the policies of France by threatening to come back. He was an old man, with bad eyes and prostate trouble, and he knew it.

As his successor, Georges Pompidou, told me December 1, 1970: "The national symbol of the general now that he is dead removes from the adversaries of Gaullism a personal element. There is that much less of a difference, a division, between pro- and anti-Gaullists who used to think in terms of personality. And all French citizens acknowledge the greatness of de Gaulle as a figure today." He said that "Gaullism without de Gaulle" was in no sense changed by the general's death because the continuity that had been established after de Gaulle left the Elysée would simply continue.

The device de Gaulle had used as an excuse to explain his second voluntary retirement was a referendum he convoked, as provided for in his Fifth Republic constitution—a needless referendum which he was certain he would lose, given the changed political climate brought about by the violent uprisings provoked in 1968. These had been touched off by French students backed by trade union support and infiltrated by jobless military mercenaries and die-hard members of the Secret Army Organization.

The latter was a clandestine armed soldiers' movement, led by three insurgent generals, which sought to keep Algeria a French colony when it became clear de Gaulle was secretly negotiating a settlement based on Algerian independence. It had sworn to assassinate the general, trying many times and missing by a fraction of an inch at a Paris suburb called Petit Clamart.

When, in 1969, the general finally retired for the second time as chief of state, he was seventy-nine. Yet, despite his famous statement that "old age is a shipwreck" (first uttered, I believe, by Chateaubriand, but immortalized by the general), he appeared surprisingly fit; his eyes were piercing, shrewd, if optically weak.

I saw him ten weeks before he resigned. He took off his glasses and peered at me. I knew he could barely see a thing, but his personality bored right into me. He talked with immense assurance.

He recalled that he had always warned the Americans they could not succeed in Indochina. The ground there was rotten. (*Le terre est pourri.*) It was impossible. "We in France know. We failed and you will fail." He also thought it would be far easier for the United States to leave Vietnam than it had been for France, with its hundreds of thousands of French-Algerian settlers, most of whose families had been there for decades, to leave Algeria.

I asked him to analyze his own public life. He said: "Because of events, I started from a very, very low beginning. It was a terrible situation, a desperate situation from which I began. This was not true for the others. It is not true at all for Roosevelt. Churchill was in a dangerous situation, but not a desperate one. The same may be said for Stalin. But my beginning was desperate."

I told him Stalin thought the principal force motivating men was fear. Others cited religion, family. What did he think was the primary influence? Without a moment's hesitation he answered: "One must draw a distinction between the individual and the collective masses. For the individual it is ambition and a taste for adventure. I think the real motivation, the primordial motivating force for the individual is ambition, but for the masses it is fear. There Stalin was right. And this applies to the masses in all countries."

De Gaulle had only a rather short time left to live in final retirement at his beloved home of La Boissiére amid the gloomy Merovingian woods. It was a vast house with a cluttered entry, a large salon furnished in the traditional French bourgeois manner—a mixture extending from Louis XV to Napoleon III and the English styles, real or false, dotted with accumulations of wedding gifts, garrison life, and functional souvenirs.

The family clustered generally in the dining room or a small salon next to it, where everybody gathered after meals. Finally, after playing with his grandchildren, whom he adored, the general in the summertime would retire alone to the tower he had ordered constructed years earlier to add dignity to the mansion, looking down on the trees he loved, the carpenters who fascinated him, and the playing children and dogs who were the special passion of his old age for, as he told Malraux, "they are not afraid of me." De Gaulle himself was afraid of no one, of nothing. He died painlessly, peacefully, after winning a game of solitaire, November 9, 1970. He had proven himself an effective man, *efficace* in resurrecting his fairy princess, France.

Professor Henri de Gaulle, the general's father, was not a well-known man, but he did his country an immense service, which, as a patriot, he would have wished: he served as the conduit for a remarkable son, supervised his upbringing and early education, and handed on to him the aspiration to behave grandly in order to achieve grandeur for his country. Once, the general said to me:

> My father was a great influence on my formation. He was a modest professor but a very eminent man, very cultivated and a gentleman, very balanced and reasonable, very, very patriotic. His influence on my formation was capital.
>
> Then, also, there was Pétain; Pétain also had a great influence on my formation when I knew him as a young officer. I learned much from his method and manner of command when I was a lieutenant and he was my colonel. His influence was great, but when he ceased to be the same man it ended, of course. Events separated us and turned us against each other. But he ended by moving toward me. Did you know that he sent someone to me, Admiral [Paul] Auphan, when I came to Paris in 1944?

Auphan brought me a message from Pétain saying: 'You must take over, you must lead France,' but, of course, that was too late, alas, and you know how things ended."

In 1908 young de Gaulle had written a poem under the anagrammatic *nom de plume* he used for such efforts, Charles de Lugale, in which he said: "When I must die I would like it to be on a field of battle. . . . I would like it to be evening. The dying day gives to him who leaves a less burdensome sorrow. . . ." But, more than sixty years later when his time came, it was alone, in encroaching dusk, in a house filled with his family and amid peaceful thoughts removed from the thunder of war and any "burdensome sorrow," in the late afternoon of a well-spent life.

At the moment the general slumped over his card table, he had outlived his intellectual monarchist father by almost four decades (he had died May 3, 1932, before his son's career really began to unfold) and his revered and hated patron, Pétain, by twenty-nine years. On November 10, 1970, when news of the general's decease was broadcast, I reread the summation of his life he himself once made for me:

> Success contains within it the germs of failure and the reverse is also true. Certainly France suffered a terrible failure as a nation in 1940. It was catastrophic. But what occurred in 1940 merely reflected what had really happened inside France.
>
> And now France has been notably reestablished both in its own eyes and in the eyes of the world. How far that will continue into the future of course we cannot foresee. But the comparison between France in 1940 and France today is very evident, very striking. That was a success for France, and I think I have participated in this success, but no one can foresee where it will all lead.

As a youth he had said: "If I were not an officer, I would go into politics." The man who thought he had awakened the sleeping princess of the fairy tale believed his legend and hoped it would endure.

XIV

The Monument:
Lord Randolph and
Winston S. Churchill

On November 30, 1874, Winston Leonard Spencer Churchill was born prematurely at Blenheim Palace, Oxfordshire, the most magnificent Briton since the myth-swaddled figure of Alfred the Great, Anglo-Saxon King of Wessex, or, if you prefer, William Shakespeare. The baby was directly descended from the first Duke of Marlborough, the renowned seventeenth-century general who never lost a battle, through his father, Lord Randolph Churchill.

His mother was a beautiful American heiress, Jeanette, daughter of a business tycoon and part owner of *The New York Times*, Leonard W. Jerome.

Lord Randolph had a reputation for brilliance and was described as the most outstanding of his line since the victor of Blenheim. Yet he died of tertiary syphilis at the age of forty-six, after a promising but unsuccessful career. One unverifiable tale had it that he was infected after practical-joking friends drugged him and left him in the arms of a loathsome, haggish whore.

Winston's mother, who became famous for her numerous love affairs after doctors forbade her husband to have physical contact with her, seemed utterly indifferent to her son. Only when, as a young cavalry officer, he began to make an initial reputation did she start to show interest in him. To be fair, she displayed no such dislike for her boy as did her husband.

Absence of filial interest was commonplace among Victorian parents. This was probably because so many mothers were separated from their offspring at boarding schools while their fathers were off painting the world map imperial pink.

During Winston's childhood and youth, Lady Randolph was astoundingly neglectful and spent much of her time on frivolous affairs. A gossip journal dubbed her "Lady Jane Snatcher" with a penchant for "husband-hunting and fiancé-fishing." Yet later, Winston remembered her as a "fairy princess," de Gaulle's very phrase for an idealized concept of his motherland, France.

Young Winston's affections perforce concentrated on his doting nanny, Mrs. Everest, whom he called "Woom" or "Woomany," and whom he adored until the day she died. Woom had instilled in him, as was often the case with nannies for aristocratic Victorian and Edwardian families, the middle-class virtues of courage, honesty, patriotism, modesty, and honor, which were not always encouraged by the example of their parents.

Winston allegedly told Frank Harris, the snobbish literary agent who edited the *Fortnightly Review* and hung around London's late-nineteenth-century intellectual and social circles, that he disliked his father, adding: "He treated me as if I had been a fool, barked at me whenever I questioned him. I owe everything to my mother; to my father nothing." Actually, the boy had an astonishingly generous nature and showed little evidence of paternal dislike. Indeed, he worked extremely hard in preparing a two-volume biography of Lord Randolph which displayed no bitterness; quite the opposite.

However, he allowed the loneliness of his boyhood to escape into other writings, remarking, for example, that "famous men are usually the product of an unhappy childhood." His generous soul was later able to respond with increasing affection to his glamorous mother, once she made an effort on his behalf. Nevertheless, until the end, he did not muster more emotion than regret at his desire for mutual affection with his father, which the latter never requited.

Lord Randolph didn't even heed his son's craving for love when he was away at preparatory boarding school. He met an acquaintance in Brighton, a short walk from the pining boy, isolated during a holiday period, and Winston wrote him: "I cannot think why you did not come to see me while you were in Brighton. I was very disappointed, but I suppose you were too busy."

After physicians became aware that Lord Randolph was suffering from a frightful venereal disease, he went to Ireland to serve as secretary to his father, who had been named lord lieutenant. Jenny, whose lusts were not to be inhibited by her husband's enforced chastity, fell in love with a wealthy Anglo-Irish officer. He fathered her second son and served as godfather; in Dublin, the boy was christened John Strange Spencer Churchill, after both his real and his adopted parent. Lord Randolph accepted Jack as if he were of his own proud blood, which was not the case—fortunately, since the bastard was thereby freed of infection. Jack was regarded by Winston as a full, true brother, and genuine fraternal affection always existed between them.

Lord Randolph seems to have maintained that he had been "perfectly cured" of his diabolical malady, but his doctors were horrified at this misplaced optimism. By 1881, when Winston was only seven and his father thirty-two, Lord Randolph suffered an initial attack of paralysis, ushering in the final, tertiary phase of his illness.

The aristocratic Tory's doom was now apparent to most of his friends and colleagues, causing sympathy and regret. Gladstone, the outstanding British statesman of the time, called him the "greatest Conservative since Pitt." Many of his fellow members in the House of Commons (as a junior peer he was ineligible for the Lords) admired his intense, vehement manner of speaking. However, the sickness worsened despite periods of remission; Winston and Jack, who saw him so little, were unaware of the terrible disintegration taking place. Indeed, when Winston first became an M.P. in 1900, he vowed to pursue the aims and vindicate the memory of his father, who had died five years earlier.

It is interesting to speculate on how Frued might have gauged the possible Oedipean influences on Winston Churchill of his unusual relationships with a hostile father and distant mother during the especially sensitive period of his extreme youth. It is certainly improbable that the doughty Englishman would ever have been a helpful subject on a psychoanalyst's couch. Robert Rhodes James, in his book on Churchill between 1900 and 1939, does, however, make a noteworthy speculation in comparing the subject's youthful personality with the psychiatric analyses of Freud's former pupil Carl Gustav Jung. Jung founded the theory of analytic psychology— which bore unconscious parallels to the Bergsonian theory of intuition that so influenced Charles de Gaulle.

"Wherever intuition predominates," wrote Jung, "a particular and unmistakable psychology presents itself. . . . The intuitive is never to be found among the generally recognized reality values, but is always present where possibilities exist. He has a keen nose for things in the bud pregnant with future promise." Jung stressed that the extroverted intuitive's "capacity to inspire his fellow men with courage, or to kindle enthusiasm for something new is unrivaled."

Robert James concludes: "The essential similarities between Jung's portrait of the extroverted intuitive and Winston Churchill are so striking that they merit at least a digression and not least because Jung points out that an individual of this type is 'not infrequently put down as a ruthless and immoral adventurer' which the great Englishman certainly was not."

Nor was his subconscious ever to be laid bare to an analyst's probing. Lady Asquith, daughter of a famous prime minister, said of Churchill: "His world was built and fashioned in heroic lines. He spoke its language." And, as was the case with Jung's extroverted intuitive, this heroic type could indeed be ruthless, although one might never for an instant see Winston tinged with immorality. His ruthlessness was devoted to victory, no matter what the cost, over his country's enemy. It was obdurate and inspirational; it was unyielding. When President Roosevelt sent Sumner Welles to Europe in 1940 to seek a basis for ending World War II, Welles asked Churchill to outline possible minimum terms. That doughty warrior said: "Well we might commence with Hitler's scalp."

Victory had by all odds the first priority in Churchill's mind; the second priority was preservation of the British empire. As he confessed in analyzing his youth (in *My Early Life: A Roving Commission*): "I was a child of the Victorian era . . . when the realization of the greatness of our Empire and of our duty to preserve it was ever growing stronger." This thought would have been instilled in him as much by Mrs. Everest as by his schoolmasters and male relatives. As for his mother, he always associated her with Ireland, where as a small boy he recalled "a radiant being possessed of limitless riches and power. . . . She shone for me like the Evening Star. I loved her dearly— but at a distance. My nurse was my confidante. . . . It was to her I poured out my many troubles, both now and in my schooldays." After her death, he wrote: "She had been my dearest and most intimate friend during the whole of the twenty years I had lived."

Winston was virtually condemned by economic circumstances to seek a career in the armed forces where, even so, an officer had considerable expenses and required an income of his own. When this impelling reason was added to his early fascination with lead soldiers (for which he had a passion, ignored by his parents, and would marshal them in legions), he aimed at a Sandhurst education from his boyhood and wrote: "For years I thought my father with his experience and flair had discerned in me the qualities of military genius. But I was told later that he had only come to the conclusion that I was not clever enough to go to the Bar. However that may be, the toy soldiers turned the current of my life. Henceforward all my education was directed into passing into Sandhurst."

Winston was an unusual boy both mentally and physically. He did not excel as a pupil, nor did his astonishing memory, elegant style of writing, and abundant oratorical gifts have much chance to display themselves in school-days at Harrow and cadet days at Sandhurst. He was a small, puny lad of less than average height and weight; yet he showed himself a fine horseman, a champion fencer, and an excellent swimmer; his courage was always impressive. But, despite the confidence he gained and his basically cheerful nature, he was always haunted by the same sadness:

> I would far rather have been apprenticed as a bricklayer's mate, or helped my father dress the front windows of a grocer's shop. It would have been real; it would have been natural; it would have taught me more; and I should have done it much better. Also I should have got to know my father, which would have been a joy to me. . . . A boy would like to follow his father in pursuit of food or prey.

The young aspirant general unfortunately seems to have felt he was doomed to a thwarted career by the period in which his life had to be lived. He later confided:

> If it had only been 100 years earlier what splendid times we should have had: Fancy being nineteen in 1793 with more than twenty years of war against Napoleon in front of one! However, all that was finished. The British Army had never fired on white troops since the Crimea, and now that the world was growing so sensible and pacific—and so democratic too—the great days were over. Luckily, however, there were still savages and barbarous peoples. . . . Some of these might, if they were well disposed, 'put up a show' some day.

Lord Randolph was not impressed by the lad's early musings. Besides, he didn't think much of a cavalry career, fancying instead a smart and famous infantry regiment if his backward boy was forced to wear a uniform. But he soon accustomed himself to the fact that the career of a cavalry officer was socially acceptable. Indeed, he occasionally took Winston, already an excellent rider, to stay with his racing friends. Yet this did nothing to improve ties between father and son.

The latter wrote:

> If ever I began to show the slightest idea of comradeship, he was immediately offended; and when once I suggested I might help his private secretary to write some of his letters, he froze me into stone . . . Just as friendly relations were ripening into an Entente, and an alliance or at least a military agreement seemed to my mind not beyond the bounds of reasonable endeavor, he

vanished forever. . . . More than ever do I regret that we did not live long enough in company to know each other.

My father died on January 24th [1895] in the early morning. . . . All my dreams of comradeship with him, of entering Parliament at his side and in his support, were ended. There remained for me only to pursue his aims and vindicate his memory.

The young man's subsequent recollections were that his mother, who was only nineteen years his elder (like Alexander and his mother), "soon became an ardent ally, furthering my plans and guarding my interests with all her influence and boundless energy. She was still at forty young, beautiful and fascinating. We worked together on even terms, more like brother and sister than mother and son. At least so it seemed to me."

If one allows a loose interpretation of the word "soon," there is no doubt the account rings true. Winston required aid to further his fortunes in India and subsequent battlefields, he sought help in obtaining books and her wiles in garnering promotions; she proved increasingly effective. Quite obviously, such desires proved appealing to her own ambitious personality, as did his unabashed and frequently mentioned quest for fame that would accelerate the triumphant career he intended.

He was accepted as a junior officer in the Fourth Hussars, a splendid horse regiment. In 1896 the Hussars sailed for India with their silver plate, their officers' mess traditions, which Winston was able to help support (thanks to a contribution from Jenny), and their mounts, including five good ponies which the young subaltern had acquired in order to pursue his new passion, polo.

He immensely fancied cavalry life. However, at the same time, he resolved to educate himself above the mediocre level he had so far acquired and wrote his mother frequently to ask for books, which she helpfully provided. Having heard that Lord Randolph delighted in that great historian, he decided to begin with Gibbon. Both he and the world benefited immensely from that decision. He recounts: "I was immediately dominated both by the story and the style. . . . I read for four or five hours every day."

It was while he was serving on India's famous northwest frontier that he first exchanged shots in anger, explored the Himalayan foothills and saw the vicious *mahseer* fish rolling in the blue-green streams below the Malakand Pass to Swat, Gilgit, and Chitral. He also engaged in the sideline of war correspondence permitted to talented officers with useful contacts. The first of his many books, *The Story of the Malakand Field Force,* based on newspaper dispatches, was delivered at this time.

As a young Hussar in India, Churchill developed his talents at polo—which were considerable because of his courage—his skill as a horseman, and his enthusiasm. After injuring an arm, he insisted on continuing to play, strapping the damaged limb to his chest. He also, to use his ponderously humorous words, "acquired an entirely new faculty":

> Until this time I had never been able to drink whiskey. I disliked the flavor intensely. I could not understand how so many of my brother officers were so often calling for a whiskey and soda. I liked wine, both red and white, and especially champagne, and on very special occasions I could even drink a small glass of brandy. But this smoky-tasting whiskey I had never been able to face. I now found myself in heat which, though I stood it personally fairly well, was terrific, and with absolutely nothing to drink, apart from tea, except either tepid water or tepid water with lime-juice or tepid water with whiskey.
>
> Faced with these alternatives I grasped the larger hope. I was sustained in these affairs by my high morale. Wishing to fit myself for active service conditions I overcame the ordinary weaknesses of the flesh. By the end of those five days I had completely overcome my repugnance of the taste of whiskey.
>
> Nor was this a momentary acquirement. On the contrary the ground I gained in those days I have firmly entrenched and held throughout my whole life. Once one got the knack of it, the very repulsion from the flavor developed an attraction of its own; and to this day, although I have always practiced true temperance I have never shrunk when occasion warranted it from the main basic standing refreshment of the white officer in the East. . . .

Thanks particularly to his mother, who by then was engaging with whole heart in the conspiracy to push him up the ladder, the young Hussar had himself transferred to Lord Horatio Kitchener's army in the Sudan, assigned by the righteous Victorian imperialists to avenge the death of their favorite general, "Chinese" Gordon. In this role, Winston managed to participate and also to share as a journalist in the Battle of Omdurman against the fearless Islamic dervishes of the Mahdi, a Sudanese religious fanatic. This was the last military encounter in which the famous centuries-old British infantry square formation was used and also history's last great cavalry charge.

Churchill, in the language of his time which was equally enjoyed by his mother and by Woom, found "this was only a sporting element in a splendid game. . . . I commend such moments." He wrote of this notable encounter:

> Ancient and modern confronted one another. The weapons, the methods and the fanaticism of the Middle Ages were brought by an extraordinary anachronism into dire collision with the organisation and inventions of the nineteenth century. The result was not surprising. As the successors of the Saracens descended the long smooth slopes which led to the river and their enemy, they encountered rifle fire. After an enormous carnage, certainly exceeding 20,000 men who strewed the ground in heaps and swathes like snowdrifts, the whole mass of the Dervishes dissolved into fragments and into particles and streamed away into the fantastic mirages of the desert.

To encompass this event within the same lifetime that experienced the explosion of the first atom bomb, the moon landing, and the creation of Britain's own nuclear weapons force, is the best possible confirmation that history itself is in the process of exploding. The dervishes reminded the incurably romantic young Churchill of the Norman and English armies "in the Bayeux tapestries" celebrating William of Normandy's eleventh-century conquest, England's last.

Churchill had by then proven to his own secret satisfaction and to the admiration of his colleagues that despite a round-face, pudgy, and deceptively babylike appearance, his courage was boundless, aggressive, and unquenchable. This was a source of much satisfaction; on this courage and the vital energy and ambition that accompanied it, he catapulted to public fame, as he had always intended, first by instinct, then consciously.

He managed not only to be captured but then to escape from the dreary fate of prisoner of war, during the conflict of the British with the stern Afrikaner Boers' General "Slim Jannie" Smuts, subsequently the South African prime minister and British ally in World War II, who became a true friend and often-heeded advisor of Churchill.

He had already spent a short time with the Spanish forces fighting a Cuban insurrection before his regiment was shipped to India. The combined impact of his dispatches from the Caribbean, his accounts of Indian northwest frontier skirmishes, his flamboyant report of the Battle of Omdurman, and the widely heralded tale of his escape from the South African Boers, had catapulted him to an eminence of fame and popular attention. Alice Roosevelt Longworth, Teddy's daughter, told me his activities in Cuba also touched off a quiet grudge feud with the American politician Theodore Roosevelt, whose Rough Riders, on the side of the rebel nationalist forces, launched him to the White House; but Winston's visit to the Spanish army was nonpolitical. He was merely in search of battle.

In 1899 Churchill resigned his commission and successfully, on a second try, contested a parliamentary seat as Conservative member for Oldham. From that moment he became an enthusiastic supporter of the House of Commons, although his allegiance to the Tory leadership was far from steadfast. He was already a well-known figure in London society, first as a bachelor hero, later as the promising husband of the lovely, warm, intelligent Clementine Hozier, with whom he shared his long, exciting life.

The energetic young hero was an enthusiastic extrovert and took well to social life. In his account of that period, Churchill wrote: "I gave myself to the amusements of the London Season. In those days English Society still existed in its old form. It was a brilliant and powerful body, with standards of conduct and methods of enforcing them now altogether forgotten. In a very large degree everyone knew everyone else and who they were."

During his first years as a politician, before he wedded, he learned without embarrassment of his mother's energetic love life. She was known to have been the mistress of most of the leaders of the English international set, from the Prince of Wales (later Edward VII) down and including rich or politically well-known Americans and other foreigners. Her best-known long-term lover was the Austro-Hungarian Count Kinsky, who had taken Winston and Jack to the circus when they were boys, and whom Jennie hoped to marry when Lord Randolph died. She was disappointed; Kinsky's family had seen to it that he safely found a bride acceptable to the Habsburg court of Vienna.

Winston demonstrated from the start that he had a political knack. He rallied support under his father's slogan, which stressed "Tory democracy." While inferentially supporting the British class system, he argued: "The best class and the lowest class . . . come together naturally. They like and esteem each other." Despite the implied snobbery of his views, such an attitude is by no means always a political handicap in England. Moreover, in later times of crisis he showed particular appeal to the poor and underprivileged. And he wholly disproved his father's prediction for him: "You will become a mere social wastrel."

As a parliamentarian, Winston developed into an increasingly fine orator and also honed his talent for sensing the interests and desires of Britain's electorate. Like Demosthenes, he mastered a youthful speech impediment. He displayed a remarkable gift for that mixture of orotund phrases, withering sarcasm, and sentimental magnetism which seems to feature in successful English political speaking.

Winston shifted to the Liberal Party in 1904, and a year later obtained his first ministerial post as undersecretary of state for the colonies. He did not rejoin the Tories until 1924, then again rebelled a decade later, staying with the Liberals until World War II broke out. During his first period of Liberalism he evolved his pat theory: "Socialism exalts the rule; Liberalism exalts the man. Socialism attacks capital; Liberalism attacks monopoly."

His responsibilities broadened with time. He was appointed president of the Board of Trade, and then became home secretary in 1911. In that position, he proved himself to be a resolute strikebreaker in the name of law and order, a reputation that did not help politically with the masses. Herbert Asquith, the Liberal prime minister, transferred him to the Admiralty in 1911. He enthusiastically went to work preparing the Royal Navy for instant readiness in case the gathering war clouds he discerned should unloose their torrents. When this did occur in the summer of 1914, the fleet was ready for general mobilization. However, early successes were overshadowed by the unhappy Dardanelles expedition, which Churchill favored against influential opposition.

In 1915 he resigned. In the flexible British system of his day, he was sent on active service to France as a lieutenant colonel of the Sixth Royal Scots Fusiliers, an infantry regiment. The following year, after the furor over the Dardanelles fiasco subsided, Lloyd George named the efficient and hard-driving Churchill minister of munitions in a coalition cabinet. In that post, he foresaw the practicality of a marriage between the recently developed gasoline combustion engine and protective armor, thus stimulating production of the tank, a weapon he had already envisioned while at the Admiralty. Tanks became a decisive factor in both world wars.

By 1922, after playing a role in sponsoring intervention on behalf of the anti-Bolshevik forces in Russia, aiding the Poles, arranging a Middle East settlement that foresaw a role for Jewish Zionists, preserving peace between the new Irish Free State and Protestant Ulster, and checking expansion of the Turkish nationalist revolution, Churchill lost his parliamentary seat. He retired perforce from politics.

He had shown himself to the English people as generous, compassionate, courageous, and determined; intelligent and eager to understand; manly, flamboyant, durable, and wholly unable to contemplate the very idea of fear.

He was also a clever politician with riveting oratorical talent and a shrewd sensitivity to the times. And he governed his life by the motto he devised for a monument to the dead in France: "In war, Resolution. In defeat, Defiance. In victory, Magnanimity. In peace, Goodwill."

During the 1920s, Churchill found an outlet for his furious energies in painting; with more talent than the ordinary amateur; in writing, with an ornate but telling style, producing a six-volume war history called *The World Crisis;* and in moving into a new family seat, Chartwell, his manor in Kent, which he purchased with the profits of that work.

In essence, this remained his position until the outbreak of World War II: a respected and much heeded voice offstage; a painter of probably sufficient caliber to be admitted to the Royal Academy (not an overwhelmingly impressive distinction), an author with a flair and a gift (like that of Alexander Dumas) for organizing teams of researchers and assistants to improve his productivity. His position, without a global conflagration, remained similar to that of Charles de Gaulle, who would have gone through life to be remembered as an intellectual French officer and patriot with a precise and beautifully developed literary style. How many champions, for lack of fortuitous opportunity, has history lost?

Churchill pursued his retirement with customarily energetic fury. He added to *World Crisis*, wrote two autobiographical volumes and a four-volume study of his great ancestor, the invincible first Duke of Marlborough. He painted, traveled, lectured, drew ever-closer to his children, became an enthusiastic amateur farmer (this included building a handsome brick wall and filling a fish pond with golden carp which, to his delight, recognized his footfalls when he came to feed them). The only shadow of those days (and it was immense and lowering) was that of Adolf Hitler.

During the Stanley Baldwin government, and even more during that of Neville Chamberlain, Churchill sought to muster support for and to exert influence on a British policy favoring a rearmament program, especially in the air. But he met with slight success. Few persons of importance on the British power scene agreed with the rambunctious, aging hero, whose reputation for early achievement had been tarnished by sponsorship of the unsuccessful Dardanelles campaign, inability to retain parliamentary importance, and failure even to rally public opinion behind King Edward VIII in the famous abdication crisis.

And, behind the scenes, where major British policy decisions are often formulated, Churchill found he could muster insufficient support to offset the so-called "Cliveden Set." This informal group comprised influential political, journalistic, and social figures prepared to endorse appeasement.

It was not until Chamberlain was impelled down the road to war by his supine naiveté at Munich, his embarrassing failures from 1938 on, and his final decision to back Polish independence, that Hitler was able to ram the violent conflict he desired down England's throat. Ultimately this brought about Churchill's political resurrection and splendid final triumph. On September 3, 1939, Chamberlain unhappily was forced to honor his pledge to support Poland against invasion.

Chamberlain clung to power thanks to the lassitude of Parliament until the so-called "phony war" ended with the Nazi attacks, in spring 1940, on the lowlands and then Denmark and Norway.

Churchill, in a Tory national cabinet and back at the Admiralty, had sought immediately to use his fleets for offensive purposes. His return to the bridge sparked a signal throughout the Royal Navy; "Winston is back." He helped provoke the Norway campaign which sought to block Sweden's iron ore shipments to Germany. The Nazis promptly responded.

The following month, May 1940, Hitler invaded the Low Countries. Chamberlain dismally resigned, hoping Lord Halifax would succeed him. That gloomy, elongated peer declined the responsibility. Churchill, the hope of infuriated public opinion, took over as prime minister of a coalition government including Conservative, Labor, and Liberal ministers.

Churchill's dauntless flame aroused the dispirited English people the way a musical genius like Toscanini could electrify a somnolent orchestra. He conceived his own basic policy principles: Hitler's Germany was the enemy; nothing should deflect Britain from bringing about its defeat. Anyone willing to share the burden, even a Communist, could be regarded as an acceptable ally; American support was indispensable and everything must be done to bring it into the conflict as an active partner.

Yet he perspicaciously saw that the catastrophic bloodshed of World War I must be avoided by revising strategy; otherwise an anemic Britain could not manage its widespread empire, on which the national prestige and economy was based. The war, he recognized, must be truly total and unhampered by orthodox economic traditions, inherited conventions, class privileges, or military etiquette.

The prime minister should delegate as much power as possible while retaining ultimate authority in all fields. This would enable him to goad the complete war-making machine whenever and wherever it faltered. He should particularly prod the armed services chiefs but never oppose their collective judgment. And he must always regard the House of Commons as the fundamental instrument of national power, the source of his own personal strength.

Almost on the heels of his rise to authority, Churchill was faced with the greatest tests of his leadership talents: the evacuation of Dunkirk, the surrender of France, Britain's attacks on the French fleet at Oran and Dakar, the careful husbanding of the brilliantly organized but numerically sparse Royal Air Force to safeguard its island fortress in the Battle of Britain. To achieve all these goals, which he did, Churchill declaimed some of his most magnificent speeches. He brought home to all Britons who heard him the realization that "[we must] therefore brace ourselves to our duties, and so bear ourselves that, if the British Empire and its Commonwealth last for a thousand years, men will say, 'This was their finest hour.' "

However, despite Churchill's careful husbanding of available resources in men, matériel, and money, within a decade the empire had vanished, save for a few isolated pinpoints like Hong Kong, Gibraltar, and the Falkland Islands.

As his country's democratic champion, Churchill showed extraordinary ability to bring out the nation's best characteristics: resolution, dogged courage, a gift for improvisation, well camouflaged and imaginative intelligence, audacity (especially on the sea and in the air), and cheerful good humor in adversity. He personally pushed for further development and effective usage of his brainchild, the tank; he sponsored another old creature of his imagination, the production of landing craft that could deposit armored vehicles ashore; he urged scientists and inventors to produce ballistic rockets; he was responsible for various devices to confuse enemy radar vision, and for the artificial harbors and "Pluto" (pipeline under the ocean) that facilitated and fueled the mechanized Normandy invasion.

Churchill was acutely aware of the implications both to victory and to the survival of a *Great* Britain that the rush of scientific advances had intruded into policy-making calculations. His physician, Lord Moran, noted later in his well-written memoir: "Winston is a proud man, and it hurts him to think how vulnerable, in the atomic age, a small, densely populated island like Britain has become." Once Churchill remarked unhappily to Moran: "I wish flying had never been invented. The world has shrunk since the Wrights got into the air; it was an evil hour for poor England."

The year 1940 provided the condition most suited to his impestuous nature. He himself wrote in *My Early Life* that "I have always urged fighting wars and other contentions with might and main till overwhelming victory, and then offering the hand of friendship to the vanquished; thus, I have always been against pacifists during the quarrel, and against Jingoes at its close." He once told Averell Harriman: "The finest way to die is in the excitement of fighting the enemy."

Winston Churchill was sixty-five when he became prime minister to fight the toughest battle of his combative life. Every literate person knows the rest. It was of course England's most famous victory. Inspired and led by their rotund and aged warrior chief, the indomitable British alone demonstrated to the world, and above all to Adolf Hitler, that they were resolved to defend their little island of democracy against the entire world, if need be, and to their last drop of blood.

At that time virtually all Eurasia was assembled against them, under German guidance or occupation. From pro-Axis Spain at the Straits of Gibraltar up to occupied Norway's Arctic circle, the Atlantic fringe of western Europe was held by a powerful assemblage of predominantly German forces. Italy, with its important fleet and colonial possessions in Libya and the Dodecanese Islands, supported the Nazi war machine in the strategically crucial Mediterranean. This help was magnified soon after that machine overran Jugoslavia and courageous Greece, which had been successfully repelling an Italian invasion.

To the east lay the endless Soviet Union. Since the Hitler-Stalin deal of 1939 partitioning Poland and recognizing certain "spheres of interest" between the Baltic and the Sea of Marmora, Stalin had been a virtual ally of the Fuehrer, giving him logistical, economic, political, and propaganda support against the capitalist West. Japan, although congenitally inimical to Russia, had signed a "Pact of Steel" with Moscow's cobelligerent, Berlin. And under Japan's military control, much of China lay supine and perforce neutralized.

Against this mass stood tiny Britain, strong solely in its own heart. Its only friends were the mighty but unprepared United States and the brave Greeks. Had Churchill not come to the fore as Britain's relentless and unwavering leader, keeping it in the fight long enough for Hitler to recoil from the Royal Navy and the Royal Air Force to strike eastward at Stalin's immense realm, the ending might have been otherwise.

It was Churchill's "come and get us" challenge to Hitler that wrecked the Fuehrer's great plan to conquer the world: first Europe, then the Soviet Union, and then, by one or another means, the United States. Throughout this tremendous test, Churchill's resolve and inherent bravery were strengthened by the confidence the half-American prime minister reposed in sustaining help from the United States.

Finally, he was always certain that the British Empire with its widespread resources would follow blindly along the road to liberty. The only trouble with this portion of his vision was that the British Empire no longer effectively existed.

The Commonwealth had diluted it in 1931 through the Statute of Westminster. This set up a seven-nation organization of independent countries, under London's titular leadership, comprising the English-speaking, white-dominated erstwhile colonies and dominions. Of these, the United Kingdom and India contributed by far the largest armed contingents between September 3, 1939 and August 14, 1945—World War II. Yet it is significant that India would be partitioned and granted its complete independence within two years of military triumph.

Gradually, almost all the imperial structure disintegrated save for ties, not mandatorily binding, with white dominions like Australia and a handful of tiny colonial outposts which seem inevitably doomed to sever British connections. It is significant that the United Kingdom can no longer count on automatic aid in any military confrontation from some dominions unless they are bound to London by separate alliances such as NATO.

I haven't the slightest doubt that Churchill and a very large segment of the English population subconsciously assumed that if the war was won, their Empire, in one or another form, would continue as an effective military, political, economic, and commercial assemblage. Such an outcome would assure British continuation as a great world power in a sense now applied only to the United States and the Soviet Union.

Thoughtful and skeptical Labor Party leaders and intellectuals were seen as overly pessimistic or eccentric by a majority weaned on Rudyard Kipling.

No antidictatorial Westerner could fail to be heartened by the Union Jack even at a moment of Britain's lowest ebb. One could sit on the terrace of Shepheards' Hotel in Cairo, sipping a Suffering Bastard (an excellent drink invented by that hostelry's bartender), and look down at the sidewalks of strolling passers-by ambling toward the opera house where Verdi's *Aïda* was first produced while subconsciously encouraging one's own latent optimism. The onlooker saw, mixed with the battledress or summer shorts of English troops on leave from the nearby desert, Australians and New Zealanders with broad-brimmed, tilted hats; huge South Africans; sturdy Canadians, Gaullist Free French, identifiable by their insignia and strutting walk regardless of their local military tailors; Greeks from the "Sacred Company" (*Ieros Lochos*) comprising young men who had escaped from their occupied land to fight again or from foreign Hellenic settlements; determined Poles with hard lines on their faces from suffering in battles and Soviet prison camps; handfuls of Jugoslavs; and Indians from a large subcontinent of Punjabis, Mahrattas, Sikhs, and Gurkhas shipped westward to fight under British commanders in Africa and Europe.

At El Alamein, one of the global conflict's turning points, a French unit fought heroically at Bir Hakeim and kept Rommel from turning the British line. The Greeks captured Rimini in Italy. The Poles under General Anders, all of whose considerable force had been extracted from Soviet camps to freedom and to a Russo-German war which, for them, could never know victory, took the long-contested mountain salient of Cassino.

This imperial illusion of an enormous amalgam of peoples from each of the six inhabited continents joined in a single fight against Britain's enemies continued into 1946, when a splendidly impressive Victory parade was staged in London. One could sense the spectacle of *imperial* triumph.

The brilliant Professor Harold Laski told me in 1945 how Churchill, at the Yalta Conference, when the subject of trusteeships arose, had said: "I did not come here to see the fumbling fingers of fifteen nations prying into the British heritage." Nevertheless, despite the prime minister's cautious strategy of seeking total victory while conserving the lives of Britain's young men, the empire was fast disintegrating. As for Britain's vibrant economy, built upon imperial preference, imperial trade, imperial finance? Keynes called it "a financial Dunkirk."

When Nazi bombers flew over Churchill's prime ministerial country residence, Chequers, he jibed to his aide: "I bet you a monkey to a mousetrap they don't hit the house." On his first trip to Moscow in 1942, the Soviet dignitaries who greeted him at the airport dressed in impressive uniforms were horrified to see descending, instead of the handsome, hawk-featured, militaristic aristocrat they expected, a roly-poly little man (wearing his famous rumpled "siren suit"—a battle dress cut of dark blue flannel with a zipper down the front—and, in the words of Anastas Mikoyan, the Politburo veteran, "looking like a mechanic").

The Englishman's attitude toward Soviet Russia was clear. He had vigorously opposed Bolshevism from the start and helped sponsor intervention against it by troops from the victorious Allied armies of World War I. He abhorred Stalin for his brutal purges, his mass inhumanity, and his cynical pact with Hitler.

But as Sir Stafford Cripps recalled later, at the time Hitler launched his attack against the Soviets, Churchill read to him and U.S. envoy John Winant the draft of his sentimental speech about the suffering Russian people. "Tears," said the thin-blooded, unemotional Cripps, "were streaming down his face." He added: "Winston is politically bad about Russia but sentimentally excellent."

When criticized for his total switch in apparent views on Stalin, Churchill grunted: "If Hitler invaded Hell, I think I would find a kind word to say about the Devil in the House of Commons." Nevertheless, he wrote General Eisenhower, during the war's final spring: "I deem it highly important that we should shake hands with the Russians as far to the east as possible."

Two months later he warned President Truman against "bringing Soviet power into the heart of Western Europe and the descent of an iron curtain between us and everything to the eastward." After the war he told me: "Russia fears our friendship more than our enmity. The Soviet dictatorship could not stand free intercourse with the West. We must make Moscow fear our enmity more than our friendship."

Churchill realized even during the war, although he did not openly admit it, that Britain's role as a superpower was doomed, that it would have to rely on intimate links with the United States, and that both France and partitioned Germany would have to be rebuilt to stave off Soviet expansionism from the east. Yet he dreamed of clinging to an empire.

Despite his unshakable resolution, Churchill was not an optimist by nature. Eisenhower told me that in the spring of 1944, when the Allied invasion of Europe was being planned, the general said he planned to be on Germany's western border by Christmas. "Entirely out of the question," Churchill commented. At the final briefing held for "Overlord," the actual amphibious landing, Ike said Churchill advised those present, including King George VI, that his attitude was "hardening" toward the negative on its chances.

"That was a hell of a way to inspire faith in my officers," was General Ike's sardonic comment. Winston presumably took refuge behind his private theory: "If a military man explains something to you and you don't understand, it is he who is stupid, not you." He didn't think generals were as important as they themselves thought, saying of Britain's great commander: "Montgomery was indispensable to the world for two weeks. The trouble is that this experience made him think he was indispensable forever."

Churchill was a true democrat. He relished power bestowed by the people, but at the same time adored the system, as represented in England by the House of Commons. He assiduously studied its arcane and often eccentric traditions. Moreover, he kept his finger on the pulse of changing British public opinion in order to fight his electoral battles. He often said of himself, when he had become a grandiose monument to Britain's courage and erstwhile power: "I am a child of the House of Commons."

I had the moving experience of accompanying Churchill (together with his son, Randolph) on his very last campaign tour, in May 1955, to help the

Conservative candidate in Chigwell, Essex. It was fascinating to see the old man (more than eighty), with his pot belly and encumbered movements, with his strong jaw, set smile, and returning resonance in his voice, seeking to serve his party through the candidacy of another, not especially distinguished man. Having carefully re-read the veteran's speeches from his first by-election campaign, in 1899, in this last contest on someone else's behalf I was struck by the similiarity of their themes and language.

He peered over his archaic half-moon spectacles, alternately grumpy (with the world) and pleased (with himself), determined, smiling, sentimental. He played with his heavy Edwardian gold watch and chain and shook his head in denial when he was introduced as "the greatest Englishman of all time."

"Winston," as everyone always called him, had been a mugwump (party-switcher) all his political life but had seen, at the time of his final campaign, that the Liberals, whose candidates he favored when he was not a Conservative, had been displaced by the Labor Party. So he said: "There is no chance of making liberalism a party issue at this election. These famous doctrines have been removed from party controversy."

He spoke with relish of "Tory democracy" as if he had just conceived the phrase, although it had been invented in Victorian days by his father. Then he rubbed his rotund stomach, regarding it with pleasure as he added: "We have a higher standard of living than ever before. We are eating more. And that is very important." He believed, quite rightly, that this old political saw could be even more effective when uttered by a plump, sagging octogenarian than by a lean young hero. He was certainly correct.

The power he sought and exercised, from his first days during World War I through those months when the global cause of freedom teetered at the end of his cigar tip, was never allowed to lie in desuetude. Nevertheless he took pains not to transcend the restraints imposed upon him by England's unwritten constitution. But power, democratic power, was his. After he had met with Marshal Tito, a mutual friend asked the latter what he learned from Churchill. "*Vlast, vlast, vlast*," said the Jugoslav. Power, power, power.

Winston withdrew from politics on April 5, 1955, after quipping: "I must retire soon. Anthony [Eden] won't live forever." Following the old man's final retirement, his son, Randolph, told me his father was "grumpy. He can't relax. He's used to power and misses it."

Physically, Churchill was remarkable. At no time did he appear strong or rugged, although this he certainly was, despite serial strokes and heart attacks during his final years. A small man, originally frail in appearance, he was astonishingly vital, with an enthusiasm for sports and games. At various